Many people see American cities as a radical departure in the history of town planning because of their planned nature based on the geometrical division of the land. However, other cities of the world also began as planned towns with geometric layouts so American cities are not unique. Why did the regular grid come to so pervasively characterize American urbanism? Are American cities really so different?

The Syntax of City Space: American Urban Grids by Mark David Major with Foreword by Ruth Conroy Dalton (co-editor of *Take One Building*) answers these questions and much more by exploring the urban morphology of American cities. It argues American cities do represent a radical departure in the history of town planning while, simultaneously, still being subject to the same processes linking the street network and function found in other types of cities around the world. A historical preference for regularity in town planning had a profound influence on American urbanism, which endures to this day.

The Syntax of City Space

American Urban Grids

Mark David Major

Foreword by Ruth Conroy Dalton

NEW YORK AND LONDON

First published 2018
by Routledge
711 Third Avenue, New York, NY 10017

and
by Routledge
2 Park Square, Milton Park, Abingdon, Oxon, OX14 4RN

Routledge is an imprint of the Taylor & Francis Group, an informa business

© 2018 Taylor & Francis

The right of Mark David Major to be identified as author of this work has been asserted by him in accordance with sections 77 and 78 of the Copyright, Designs and Patents Act 1988.

All rights reserved. No part of this book may be reprinted or reproduced or utilized in any form or by any electronic, mechanical, or other means, now known or hereafter invented, including photocopying and recording, or in any information storage or retrieval system, without permission in writing from the publishers. Printed in Canada.

Trademark notice: Product or corporate names may be trademarks or registered trademarks, and are used only for identification and explanation without intent to infringe.

British Library Cataloguing-in-Publication Data
A catalogue record for this book is available from the British Library

Library of Congress Cataloging-in-Publication Data
Names: Major, Mark, author. | Dalton, Ruth Conroy, writer of foreword.Title: The syntax of city space : American urban grids / Mark David Major; foreword by Ruth Conroy Dalton. Description: New York : Routledge, 2017. | Includes bibliographical references and index.Identifiers: LCCN 2017025847| ISBN 9781138301566 (hardback) | ISBN 9781138301573 (pbk.)Subjects: LCSH: Grid plans (City planning)--United States. | Cities and towns--United States. Classification: LCC NA9105 .M345 2017 | DDC 720.973--dc23LC record available at https://lccn.loc.gov/2017025847

ISBN: 978-1-138-30156-6 (hbk)
ISBN: 978-1-138-30157-3 (pbk)
ISBN: 978-0-203-73243-4 (ebk)

Typeset in Minion Pro/Myriad Pro
by Carousel Productions

Publisher's Note: This book has been prepared from camera-ready copy provided by the author.

About the Front Cover
Based on a photograph by Matthew S. Simpson, 2008.

For more information about the author, visit www.outlaw-urbanist.com or www.markdmajor.com.

Table of Contents

	Foreword by Ruth Conroy Dalton	viii
	Preface by Mark David Major	xii
Introduction	The American Urban Object	2
PART I	FORMAL COMPOSITION	
1	The Regular Grid as Historical Object	20
2	The Regular Grid as Historical Subject	36
3	The Essential Right Angle	50
4	The Regular Grid in America	66
PART II	FORM AND SPACE	
5	The Spatial Logic of American Cities	82
6	The Grid as Generator	106
PART III	SPATIAL CONFIGURATION	
7	Order and Structure in the Regular Grid	128
8	Complexity and Pattern in the City	154
9	Learning from the Grid	176
Conclusion	The Tapestry Being Woven	198
Acknowledgments		214
Bibliography		218
Illustration Credits		230
Index		236
About the Author		244

"Cities happen to be problems in organized complexity."
Jane Jacobs, The Death and Life of Great American Cities

*"Man walks in a straight line because he has a goal and knows where he is going;
he has made up his mind to reach some particular place and he goes straight to it."*
Le Corbusier, The City of To-morrow

Foreword by Ruth Conroy Dalton

Never has there been a better time for a new book about the American city. We have only recently passed the point at which more people around the world live in cities than in the rural hinterlands. At the same time, we are being told that the city itself is on the cusp of a revolution via new technologies. Discussions of a New Urban Crisis, smart cities, responsive and resilient cities, technology-enabled cities, Big Data cities, or (fill in an appropriate new 'buzz word' here) cities abound. These are cities in which the citizen is ever more engaged, enabled, and, perhaps, even liberated via technology. This is a future in which citizens are able to instantly interact with other citizens via numerous electronic devices while the devices themselves communicate with yet more devices. This all occurs against the ever-present and technologically enabled background of the city which, in turn, tracks or senses its citizens to respond instantly to their every whim. This future vision and its brusque rate of change can feel bewildering – a leap into an unknown future. If you do not feel mildly terrified about this, then you might not have given it enough thought.

Nonetheless, isn't this what America has always been about; a brave leap into the unknown? *The Syntax of City Space: American Urban Grids* takes us on a journey right back to the origins of cities in America such as New Haven, Philadelphia, and Savannah. It is clear (especially once you have read the book) that this period in history was yet another in which America was undergoing a rate of rapid change and frenetic urbanization quite unlike anything else hitherto known in the world. Major demonstrates in this book that while the thrall of the new can entice, what lurks beneath are a few immutable spatial laws. And so, at this current time of techno-revolution, we can take reassurance from the main message of this book. While the onslaught of new technologies and their concomitant social issues can seem relentless, beneath the surface – rather like some large, betentacled behemoth of a sea creature lurking in the deep, still waters of urban planning – the constancy of space and spatial laws abide. The simple message of this book is that the American urban grid is both new and different yet, at the same time, possesses familiar underlying mechanisms – namely, the social logic of space – which prevail. But this reassurance in the face of change is not the only purpose of the book. A far more prosaic purpose was to conduct a comprehensive survey of America cities using objective, rigorous, quantitative descriptions "of the thing itself" as Major so succinctly phrases it. Why? So we can better understand the American city in all of its myriad complexity. To achieve this, Major begins the book by reviewing the history of regular grid planning in the world. And so we arrive, perhaps a little belatedly in this foreword, at the American urban grid!

I have only had the pleasure of living in one American city, but what a city! Atlanta, Georgia. This is the city that still lays claim to the dubious accolade of having the longest average, daily automotive commute in the United States. When I first arrived in Atlanta, I remember taking a walk on foot (!) in order to try to find the nearest grocery store; a typical quest for any newly arrived citizen. Prior to my arrival, I had diligently identified on the map where I thought this store should be located and which, according to my naïve European perspective, should have been a mere 15-minute walk away, i.e. about a mile. My walk began in Downtown Atlanta adjacent to Woodruff Park, an area known as Five Points, the widely accepted geographic center of Atlanta. It felt suitably downtown-ish containing an impressive number of respectable, Southern banking-type buildings, hulking stolidly around Woodruff Park in an easy camaraderie. As I walked away from the center, it astonished me how suddenly the character of the neighborhood changed. As if by magic, I had crossed some imperceptible threshold, some invisible line, and I was clearly in the wrong neighborhood. In reality, this represented the difference between just one urban block and the next. And yet, in other terms, I had found myself to be an entire world away from where I had begun my journey. All I really knew, and what every instinct was telling me, was that I should probably not be walking through that particular neighborhood. In European cities, this simply does not happen. And yet, in the American gridded city, this is surely an experience that every reader of this book will be familiar with. So much for the supposed equivalency and democratization of space.

In Orwell's dystopian satire, *Animal Farm*, he coined the now famous maxim, "All animals are equal, but some animals are more equal than others." I believe that this can be cheekily paraphrased and applied to the American city, "All spaces/streets/blocks are equal, but some spaces/streets/blocks are more equal than others." In this book, Major suggests that, "the typical view of American urban space… is intimately tied to the egalitarian nature of American self-identity." And yet he then gleefully goes on to demonstrate the inherent spatial discrimination and lack of democracy in the American urban grid. If there is one 'take home message' in this book, it is the fact that space is not merely some passive background to urban life. It has agency and a tangible effect on the social life of the city-dweller and this is as true of American cities and the idealized urban grid as it is of anywhere else in the world.

I first met Mark David Major 22 years ago when he was the Course Director of the Masters course in Advanced Architectural Studies at University College London. 'Advanced Architectural Studies' was a deliberately vague and all-encompassing title for a Master's course. For those in the know, it was nothing less than the essential training ground for anyone interested in space syntax; a family of theories, techniques, and methods for the quantitative analysis of spatial systems. There was something rather special and exhilarating about space syntax in London during this period of time. If this foreword seems to be focusing on the theme of times of transition, then this period in London during the 1990s was certainly one of them. The reason is that space syntax was rapidly becoming mainstream. Common, household-named architects such as Norman Foster, Richard Rogers, and Zaha M. Hadid were utilizing space syntax analysis in design work. Space syntax was being employed as indisputable evidence in public hearings and planning appeals throughout the United Kingdom. It was no longer niche but in the process of evolving into the conventional and commonplace. Major was there at the very epicenter of this intellectual and professional explosion. Key to this development was the first Space Syntax Symposium, which was organized by Major and took place in 1997. I also happen to be one of the select few who attended this first symposium as well as one of the even more select few who attended the last one as well. It has now grown into a fully-fledged international conference, celebrating its 10th biennial occurrence in London in 2015. Over the years, Space Syntax Symposia have attracted a huge following with hundreds of papers submitted to each event from all around the world. I will repeat myself here: Major was there at the beginning of all of this. He was one of the first of the new/next/second generation – a blossoming generation – of space syntax researchers and practitioners standing on the shoulders of Bill Hillier, Julienne Hanson, and Alan Penn.

The Syntax of City Space: American Urban Grids is great for three reasons. First, and most seriously, because the book presents the most complete, systematic spatial analysis of a large database of both historic and contemporary American cities. Second, this book is sorely needed because American cities have been woefully underrepresented in the corpus of space syntax writings while, at the same time, American urban design professionals have been equally – and also woefully – uninformed about space syntax. I hope that this book will go some way in redressing this balance. Finally, this book is great because Major can actually write! This is not a comment often made about academic books. Major has a gift for rendering a topic that can be, on occasion, somewhat inscrutable into a text that is conversely easily accessible.

This is a scholarly yet gracious book: a hard balancing act to achieve. Major achieves this balance magnificently.

Professor Ruth Conroy Dalton is an architect, academic, and author.

She is an alumna of University College London, where she received her doctorate. As a licensed architect, Ruth has worked for Foster and Partners and Sheppard Robson Corgan Architects on projects in France, Spain, and England. She has taught at the Architectural Association and Bartlett School of Architecture and Planning in London and the Georgia Institute of Technology in Atlanta, Georgia. Ruth is the Professor of Building Usability and Visualization at Northumbria University and co-editor of *Take One Building: Interdisciplinary Research Perspectives of the Seattle Central Library*.

Preface by Mark David Major

Space syntax can be daunting for the uninitiated. If it is any consolation, it is equally daunting for the most experienced and talented of space syntax practitioners or researchers, too. It is not because the ideas of space syntax are difficult. Quite the opposite; most are simple. The simplest being people tend to gather in a circle to interact and walk in a straight line to go somewhere.

In the late 1990s, a client was interviewing a distinguished architectural firm for an urban redevelopment project with an estimated cost of nearly $1 billion. Space syntax consultants were members of their project team. The client asked the project leader, "Space syntax? Don't they only tell you the obvious?" This person thoughtfully paused for a few moments before replying, "Yes, but it's only obvious to us after they say it." This exchange is telling. Space syntax challenges our assumptions about the built environment; some taught, learnt, and held for a long time, especially over the last century or so.

In some ways, space syntax has been a victim of its own success. Its premise proved so simple and powerful that it led to an explosion of new methodological ideas and theoretical possibilities for researching the built environment. Like any scientific research program, it takes time to conjecture, hypothesize, measure, observe, test, and refine its ideas, methods, and terminologies, and then disseminate to a larger audience. Along the way, researchers developed a proverbial cornucopia of measures for the space syntax toolkit. Over time, many proved valuable and some esoteric while others were tested and eventually discarded. It takes years, even decades, for this scientific process to work itself out. In the meantime, the sheer quantity of available information about space syntax has a tendency to overwhelm people. It leaves them unsure about how best to proceed in the absence of a 'sink or swim' dive into a literature growing at an almost exponential rate over the last four decades.

This is only the beginning.

Practitioners and researchers develop innovative ways to interrogate space syntax models for detecting 'deep structures' in spatial networks of the built environment. This is a matter of explaining technique, not necessarily measurement. A wide range of disciplines interested in some aspect of the built environment utilize space syntax. Because of this, space syntax people often have to tailor their explanations for the background of a particular audience, i.e. academic, professional, language, education, and so on. Sometimes, particular audiences possess quite different backgrounds and/or agendas, i.e. cost, profit, regulatory, style, method, academic 'silos,' professional 'turf wars,' and so on. Finally, space syntax practitioners and researchers are people, too. Some explain space syntax better than others. Others get 'lost in the weeds' and lose sight of the story they were trying to tell. It is human nature.

Given these circumstances, it is easy to feel overwhelmed whether you know a great deal about space syntax or nothing at all. Do not be discouraged. This book is a good place to start. It attempts to disseminate the basics of space syntax to a larger audience with a particular interest in American urbanism. In doing so, it runs the risk of lacking the terminological precision expected and/or demanded by some in the space syntax community. It is an acceptable risk given the widespread exportation of American design and planning principles around the world during the post-war period and the potential importance of space syntax for the future of our built environments and cities.

Dr. Mark David Major, AICP, CNU-A

The Syntax of City Space

American Urban Grids

Mark David Major

INTRODUCTION
The American Urban Object

"The street is a spatial entity and not the residue between buildings."
- Anonymous

Urban theorists often describe cities based on characteristics of their physical form. These descriptions are usually expressed in terms of a dichotomy where meaning emerges from contrasting cities as organic or regular, unplanned or planned, natural or artificial, generated or imposed, and so on (Gallion and Eisner, 1963; Alexander, 1965; Moholy-Nagy, 1968; Kostof, 1991; Batty and Longley, 1994). Kostof (1991) suggests this dichotomy is "the most persistent, and crudest, analysis of urban form" whereby the first stresses process over time in terms of "unplanned evolution" or "instinctive growth" and the second stresses the conscious act of design in a "centrally planned scheme" (43). Such descriptions have proven useful for a basic understanding of cities across different cultures, geographical regions, and time. The usefulness of descriptions such as 'organic' or 'regular' lies precisely in the fact that they are theory-loaded terms. They seemingly convey a lot of information in an easy-to-grasp manner. It can be said 'seemingly' because they are such theory-loaded terms that it can often lead to confusion, which makes their descriptive value sometimes "more a hindrance than an aid" (ibid). For example, 'regular' seems to be an explicit description of both the physical form and process that gave rise to that composition. However, the term 'organic' seems to only pertain to process. According to Batty and Longley (1994), organic cities "grow naturally from a myriad of individual decisions at a much smaller scale than those which lead to planned growth. Planned cities or their parts are usually more monumental, more focused, and more regular, reflecting the will of one upon many, or, at best, reflecting the will of the majority through their elected representatives" (8).

The term 'deformed' is sometimes used to describe the physical form of organic cities but, more often than not, it is tacitly understood as a given about such cities. Describing the physical form of cities as 'deformed' or 'regular' is also theory-loaded because it implicitly characterizes them in geometrical terms. The premise is an incidence or deficiency of a readily apparent geometric logic in the physical arrangement of streets and blocks in plan, i.e. the composition. For example, the composition of Greek, Roman, and American settlements tends to possess such geometries so they are regular grids. On the surface, the layouts of European or Middle Eastern 'organic' settlements lack such geometries so they are deformed grids (Karimi, 1997 and 1998; Hillier, 1999a and 2009b). This explicit and implicit description of form and process in cities is the foundation of the dichotomy since most cities are easily classified as having attributes in common with or different from others based on the degree to which they can be characterized as organic or regular. There have been frequent attempts to develop a more precise terminology, usually in better uniting or divorcing form and process as aspects of the description (Moholy-Nagy, 1968; Kostof, 1991). Such attempts tend to only lead to a plenitude of jargon that confuses as much as it clarifies in urban studies (Marshall, 2005).

The far-reaching effects of urban space having such characteristics may be in giving shape to the material world in which we live, work, and play. Hillier and Hanson (1984) argue in *The Social Logic of Space* that the physical arrangement of space "has a direct relation – rather than a merely symbolic one – to social life, since it provides the material preconditions for patterns of movement, encounter and avoidance which are the material realization – sometimes the generator – of social relations" (ix). In everyday practice, this can become complicated because of the tendency to view and design space in discrete terms, independent of its larger geographical, topographical, and/or urban context. In doing so, we often minimize, misunderstand, or even ignore the importance of design in establishing the material preconditions for our everyday use of urban space. Marshall (2005) defines this anomaly as the difference between *composition* and *configuration* to distinguish between how we view the city (composition) and how it actually works (configuration). Implicit in his distinction is the difference between a static and dynamic view of the urban environment whereby composition is an easy-to-grasp, understand-all-at-once type of descriptive shorthand and configuration is a more complex description of relations between elements with the potential to affect urban functions. In making this distinction, Marshall (2005) explicitly seeks to separate form and process so our descriptions can provide a better understanding of the relation, if any, between these two essential components of the urban object. His goal is to avoid the theoretical dead-ends to which we are inevitably led when the differences between composition and configuration are misunderstood.

This is particularly relevant for the study of American urban space. The widespread use of the regular grid in the United States has led some to view American urban space as a neutral background against which social relations are played out. The geometric logic of physical arrangement in the American city, i.e. its composition, somehow establishes a form of egalitarian or democratic space, whereby a societal belief in the ideal that all people are equal, deserving of equal rights and opportunities, becomes embedded or reflected within the construction of space itself; in effect, neutralizing space as a factor in social relations. Copjec (1991) describes this as the democracy of the grid. The premise of this view is all locations in American urban space are equal because the metric characteristics of street length and width, block size, and subdivision of blocks into lots of equal size tend to be consistent to all other streets, blocks, and lots similarly arranged in the layout. The historical use of regular grids in the settlements and colonies of the city-state of Athens during the Greek Classical Period, the Roman Republic, and later the Roman Empire – commonly perceived as the political predecessors of American democracy and power – seems to tacitly confirm this hypothesis.

This view of American urban space is largely consistent with the prevailing paradigm view of cities in the disciplines of architecture, planning, and related social sciences during the 20th century. This paradigm conceptualizes space as "being without social content and society without spatial content," where social relations are independent of – and unaffected by – the physical arrangement of space, and urban space is merely the residue left over between buildings (Hillier and Hanson, 1984; x). Hillier and Hanson (1984) collectively describe this as an "a-spatial domain of society" (ibid). Kostof (1991) traces the origin of this approach to 16th century Italian philosopher Giovanni Botero. Botero wrote, "the city is… an assembly of people, a congregation drawn together to the end they may thereby the better live at their ease in wealth and plenty… and the greatness of the city is said to be, not the largeness of the site or the circuit of walls, but the multitude and number of inhabitants and their power" (Botero quoted in Kostof, 1991; 227). This paradigm is an explicit rejection of the idea that "the organization of space (is) not only a social product but simultaneously rebound(s) back to shape social relations" (Soja, 1989; 57). The typical view of American urban space appears to arrive at the same conclusion by means of an entirely different logic, which is intimately tied to the egalitarian nature of American self-identity. In this case, the effects of space *are* generative and related to social relations but physical arrangement in the American city somehow neutralizes these effects because streets, blocks, and lots share some characteristic of 'sameness.' Urban space is only important in how the regular grid renders it into a neutral background to social relations and, thus, irrelevant to urban studies of the American city.

In terms of designing the city, this view of American urban space became so prevalent during the 20th century that the planning profession in the United States became a social science only marginally concerned about the physical design of settlements; the act of design being conceded to architects and engineers (Boyer, 1983). Architects understood the purely semantic artistry of architectural and urban design whereas engineers understood the mechanical requirements of site design. The planning profession focused its efforts on trying to understand the relationship between socioeconomic and political factors in cities to better formulate public policy and, by implication, participate in the planning of society itself. Urban space was merely the blank canvas onto which these societal complexities were painted. According to Boyer (1983), the results for the American city were both profound and disastrous since this paradigm went to its logical conclusion. A constricted set of parameters defined the role of architects and planners, which still largely characterizes both professions today. In architecture, there was an almost zealous regard for the formal articulation of the architectural object. Since the architectural object is devoid of social content, the only limit to exploration of its composition was purely technical in nature. Planners abandoned the act of physical design and administrative planning emerged in its place. Planners became preoccupied with the administration of public policy and finances since effective intervention in the city could only occur at this more 'social' level. While architects submerged themselves in form, planners submerged themselves in paper, and the gulf left between the two disciplines was seemingly vast and unbridgeable. "Since architects and planners had given up trying to understand the structure and morphology of urban form and the overlaying historical and interpretative elements, they thus (inserted) new functional components randomly into the existing urban fabric" (Boyer, 1983; 287).

It was only with the advent of the New Urbanism and Geographical Information Systems (GIS) that the planning profession in the United States slowly began to return to its origins as the art and science for the physical design of settlements. New Urbanism emerged in the late 1970s and early 1980s seeking to qualitatively re-exert the importance of architectural and urban design in creating the material preconditions for social relations (Katz, 1993; Talen, 1999; Duany et al., 2000). GIS software emerged in the 1990s seeking to quantitatively map complex socioeconomic and political data onto representations of settlements and regions (**Figure 0.1**).

Progress in refuting the view of American urban space as a neutral background to social relations since then has been slow but gradual. However, a cursory review of the latest architecture/planning literature and research in the United States reveals a tendency to still undervalue what Hillier and Hanson (1984) describe as the social logic of space and the spatial logic of society. The role of design in giving shape to the physical preconditions for encounter, interaction, and avoidance – the material realization of social relations – is still often poorly understood. Examining the role that urban space might play in generating social relations is only perfunctory at best. The design principles of New Urbanism are often applied in the vertical construction of buildings while – simultaneously and paradoxically – streets disconnect from the surrounding urban context in the horizontal dimension of the site, rendering it into a pseudo-suburban development in practice even though it bears the visual appearance of a traditional neighborhood. In part, many of these New Urbanism developments do also possess characteristics of a traditional neighborhood in the horizontal dimension, whereby the layout internally maximizes intra-connectivity, i.e. street connections within the project boundary, even as it minimizes inter-connectivity, i.e. street connections to the external context (**Figure 0.2**).

On the other hand, the use of GIS often fosters the illusion of accounting for urban space as a factor in social relations because planning research presents socioeconomic and political data in map form. However, the mapping of this data only allows for the possibly of discerning spatial arrangement as a factor in geographical distributions – usually at a very gross level – so analysis of socioeconomic and political factors becomes effectively prioritized in the research. Batty refers to this as "the geography of locations not relations... the geography of place in

Figure 0.1 – *(left) Seaside, Florida is the earliest, most renowned example of New Urbanism designed by Andres Duany and Elizabeth Plater-Zyberk (Photo: Alex MacLean/Landslides); and, (right) GIS 'racial dot map' in metropolitan Chicago, Illinois based on 2010 U.S. census where blue represents White, green represents Black, red represents Asian, orange represents Hispanic, and brown represents Other; each dot is representative of 1 person.*

an absolute sense, represented by points, lines and polygons which enable attributes to be associated with these geometrical objects, attributes which are largely unordered. This happens because the representational basis of GIS largely avoids even the most rudimentary distortions of… space as reflected, for example, in the notion of the network" (Batty quoted in Hillier, 2005b; 7).[1] In this way, the prevailing paradigm of urban studies during the 20th century as a social science independent of physical design is insidiously re-exerted. Physical design remains misunderstood at best, or purposefully marginalized at worse. This is quite common in American urban theory whereby the end-result confirms the preconceived assumptions of the theorist. This greatly complicates the study of American urban space because the evaluation of competing – and often conflicting – theories becomes an exercise in conceptual ground clearing whereby we have to understand *a priori* baggage the theorist brings along with them as much as the theory itself.

GIS is a powerful tool for representing data in spatial form but it is not a theory of urban space. Nor does GIS even offer an objective description of urban space itself. It can be a useful method for discerning a spatial distribution to socioeconomic and political variables. It may even be possible that some of these distributions can be explained based purely on these factors, i.e. unrelated to the generative or contributory effects of urban space. However, it is extremely difficult to discount urban space as a factor in such distributions without a quantitative description of the thing itself. In *The Death and Life of Great American Cities*, Jane Jacobs argues "cities happen to be problems in organized complexity" (1961; 453). If she is correct, then a comprehensive investigation into American urban space founded on, first, qualitative survey of the literature and historical town plans and, second, quantitative analysis of some historical and contemporary American cities using an objective description of space should prove useful in advancing our knowledge.

This is the methodological approach of the book. The objective description used is space syntax. Over time, space syntax has proven useful for drawing conclusions about the "social logic of space" in cities (Hillier and Hanson, 1984). Space syntax – developed by Hillier, Hanson, and Penn as well as many others – provides a measurable description of space, which can account for the factor of physical arrangement in giving shape to – and being shaped by – social relations in settlements. The principles of space syntax are relatively simple. First, space is a material in that its

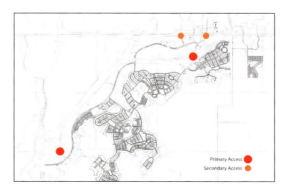 

Figure 0.2 – *(left) Plan showing the layout and access points; and, (right) satellite view from 8 km of Celebration, Florida. These indicate there are only four road connections to the urban context, i.e., two primary access points via a perimeter road to surrounding highways to the west/northwest and two secondary ones at street level to the extreme north of a highway.*

What is space syntax?

Space syntax is a research program.

The built environment is both a product of society and an influence on society. Space syntax aims to investigate and understand this relationship. It has developed a set of techniques for the simple representation of architectural and urban space. These representations are most usually plan-based on objective, easily understood constraints of the built environment for the most generic of human uses such as movement, occupation, and visibility. It has developed tools for modeling these representations in large spatial layouts, be it a building or city. At the most basic level, these representations will directly relate via *connection*. If you can move or see from one location, space, or street to another without accessing an intermediary one, they are connected. These days, most people create and process space syntax models in the computer. Some space syntax models of cities, metropolitan areas, and/or regions can include tens of thousands of locations, spaces, and/or streets.

Space syntax has developed mathematical measures for quantifying architectural and urban layouts as a network of spaces based on their topological characteristics, commonly referred to as *configuration*. Topology is the mathematical study of the geometrical properties of arrangement and spatial relations of constituent parts derived from set theory. Its importance seems obvious for buildings and cities in the real world. Architecture, urban design and planning professionals are preoccupied with space, dimension, and transformation of the built environment in design and policy actions. Space syntax has gathered a large body of evidence and developed theories about how the spatial and social interact. Crucially, it offers a means to test these theories in evidence-based design practice by identifying and evaluating *ex ante* (before the fact) implications of design and *ex post facto* (after the fact) use of built environments in the real world.

Space syntax is all of this… and much more.

The earliest origins of space syntax began with a 1973 article, "The man-environment paradigm and its paradoxes" by Bill Hillier and Adrian Leaman of University College London (UCL), published in *Architectural Design*. However, most people mark the beginning of space syntax with publication of *The Social Logic of Space* by Bill Hillier and Julienne Hanson in 1984. It explained the theoretical and methodological basis (in exhaustive mathematical detail in some passages) for a new way of describing and analyzing spatial layouts in buildings and towns developed during the late 1970s and early 1980s by Hillier, Hanson, John

Figure A.1 – *King's Cross, London Masterplan by Foster & Partners, 1988 (Photo: Richard Davies).*

Peponis, and several others at UCL. The Unit for Architectural Studies (UAS) at UCL began promoting real world applications of space syntax in design practice. Paul Coates, Stefan Czapski, and later Nick "Sheep" Dalton shepherded the dawn of space syntax in professional practice by writing and upgrading successive generations of its earliest Mac-based software packages. In 1987, UAS consulted on the King's Cross, London Masterplan. This 'brownfield' redevelopment represented the first successful use of space syntax in professional practice (see **Figure A.1**). It was innovative for its day, marrying the signature Late Modernism building designs of Foster & Partners with a street layout that we would commonly describe today as traditional urbanism.

In the early 1990s, UAS was renamed the Space Syntax Laboratory (aka Space Syntax Limited). They served as design consultants for some of the highest profile projects in Europe at the time, including the London Millennium Footbridge, Tate Gallery Millbank (now Tate Britain) Redevelopment in London, Nottingham University Jubilee Campus Masterplan, and the Linz Solar City, Austria Masterplan (see **Figure A.2**).

In the two decades since the first international symposium held in London in 1997, space syntax has evolved its multi-platform software packages. They are now used in more than 50 countries around the world with well-established research centers at UCL, Georgia Tech in Atlanta, and several universities in Brazil. Researchers use space syntax across a wide range of fields from archaeology and architecture to economics and sociology to any field where you can attach 'urban' as an adjective, e.g. ecology, history, geography, and so on. Consultants use space syntax in the design of buildings, neighborhoods, and settlements for dozens of multi-million dollar projects, generating tens of millions of dollars in additional profits and/or revenue for the private and public sector, respectively.

Today, the most expansive use of space syntax occurs in Europe, South America, and China.

Figure A.2 – *(left) London Millennium Bridge by Foster & Partners, Arup Group, and Sir Anthony Caro, 1999; (right) Linz Solar City, Austria by Foster & Partners, Richard Rogers Partnership, Renzo Piano Building Workshop, and Thomas Herzog Architects, 1999 (Photo: Luftbild Pertlwieser/PTU).*

attributes are describable in terms other than style or construction. Second, the arrangement of space has a logic that follows general laws, which we can analyze in terms of the 'topological' relation of constituent parts using graph theory. Topology is the study of geometric properties and spatial relations unaffected by the continuous change of shape or sizes of the individual elements ('continuous change' being a key characteristic of cities). Third, the logic of built space is social in nature.[2] Space syntax is based on examining the configuration of the urban object, that is the interrelation of constituent parts and the collective effects in giving rise and shape to – and being shaped by – the urban whole (Hillier, 2002 and 2003). If we really want to understand cities, then "we must learn to see them as things made of space" in strongly relational systems (Hillier, 1996b; 335). Hillier and others argue configuration is the key to how "space both acquires social meaning and has social consequences" (Hillier and Vaughan, 2007; 3).

A series of inserts or 'asides' in each chapter but one discusses the ideas, principles, and issues of space syntax. These asides (such as the previous two pages) represent bite size morsels, designed to ease readers into the world of space syntax without overwhelming them with the details. They run concurrently with the main story of this book, which is about American urban space. The asides provide useful information for a better understanding of that story.

Space syntax and the American city
American cities have been a subject of sporadic curiosity in space syntax over the last three decades. Since the publication of Hillier and Hanson's *The Social Logic of Space* in 1984, there are still only a handful of notable studies about American cities using space syntax relative to the number of studies in other parts of the world, especially Europe (Major, 2015a and c).

Most tend to focus on what Hillier (1989) describes as Type 1 laws governing the generation of the urban object though some make a conjectural leap into discussions of – or attempt to quantify – Type 2 laws governing the effects of spatial form on urban function. A few even try to discuss Type 3 laws governing the way the urban object influences society in generating a distinctive spatial culture (Hillier, 1989). At the same time, other cities of the world have been a frequent subject of intense focus for space syntax. Findings about many of those cities are broad and substantial while those for American cities remain sparse and suggestive. Twelve major American cities have been the subject of some of these studies including: Atlanta (Peponis et al., 1989a-b; Allen et al., 2001; Jiang and Peponis, 2005 and 2009; Peponis et al., 2007b; Haynie et al., 2009), Baltimore (Shah, 1996b), Boston (Raford, 2004), Chicago (Tremonto, 1993), Detroit (Psarra et al., 2013; Wineman et al., 2014), Las Vegas (Major, 1997a), New Orleans (Bone, 1996), New York (Fortes de Sousa, 1985; Stonor, 1991; Al Sayed et al., 2009), Oakland (Raford, 2003), Portland, Oregon (Howsley, 2003), St. Louis (Major, 1993), and Washington, D.C. (Fortes de Sousa, 1985) (**Figure 0.3**).

In the main, the purpose has been to test out whether space syntax provides a realistic picture of any particular American city on the ground. Because of this, some focus on the design and/or growth of the urban grid over time, or analyze particular design approaches such as New Urbanism and other alternative transportation modes (Fortes de Sousa, 1985; Shah, 1996a; Bone, 1996; Allen et al., 2001; Kim, 2007; Al Sayed et al., 2009; Haynie et al., 2009). Some seek to test out the proposition that space syntax can successfully predict movement flows using data compiled from observed levels of movement in an American city (Peponis et al., 1989a-b; Stonor, 1991; Raford, 2004; Raford and Hillier, 2005). Finally, others use space syntax to speculate about the potential effects of spatial configuration on areas and neighborhoods experiencing significant socioeconomic malaise (Major, 1993; Tremonto, 1993; Psarra et al., 2013), middle class gentrification (Howsley, 2003), or pedestrian risk (Raford, 2003).

Most of the findings run the gambit for several different reasons (**Table 0.1**). In some, the prevailing urban studies paradigm since the early 20th century – viewing space as a neutral background to social relations – takes hold in the research and leads to an implicit default to a-spatial reasoning when satisfactory research results are not immediately forthcoming. In others, technological and methodological limitations at the time played a role in constraining research results about American cities. Meanwhile, Hillier has been consistent about embedding American cities in the same theoretical framework as other cities, usually as 'and this includes American orthogonal grid cities' asides within larger arguments about urban form in general (Hillier, 1996b, 2002 and 2005b; Hillier et al., 2010). To date, Psarra et al.'s (2013) analysis of

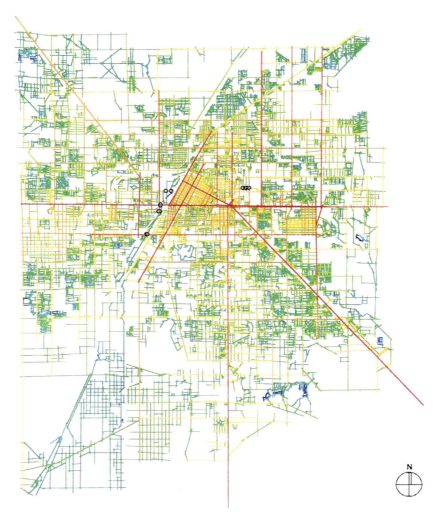

Figure 0.3 – *Major's (1997a) space syntax model of Las Vegas, Nevada showing the pattern of accessibility in the urban spatial network; colored in a range from red (most integrated or shallow) through orange, yellow, green to blue and purple (most segregated or deep) (Scale=1:300,000).*

the Detroit street network and its socioeconomic dimensions, specifically industrial land uses, from 1796 to the present day probably represents the most successful application of space syntax to an individual American city. Their study also focuses on a specific problem, i.e. the relationship, if any, between spatial configuration and socioeconomic malaise in Detroit. It provides compelling evidence implicating regulatory restrictions on riverfront development as a generative factor for the initial flight of industrial land uses and jobs (specifically, the automobile industry) to the city's periphery; a cycle that continues to this day (Psarra et al., 2013). However, their conclusions are modest; perhaps too much so. Only two studies ever attempted a comprehensive approach to surveying the spatial configuration of contemporary American

Year	Author	Venue	City/Focus	Conclusions
1985	Fortes de Sousa	MSc Thesis	Manhattan and Washington, D.C.	Inconclusive
1989a	Peponis et al.	Ekistics	Atlanta	Inconclusive
1989b	Peponis et al.	Geoforum	Atlanta/Peachtree Center	Inconclusive
1991	Stonor	MSc Thesis	Manhattan	Suggestive but inconclusive
1993	Major	MSc Thesis	St. Louis/East St. Louis	Suggestive but inconclusive
1993	Tremonto	MSc Thesis	Chicago/Cabrini Green	Suggestive but inconclusive
1996a	Shah	MSc Case Study	Multiple Historical Town Plans	Inconclusive
1996	Bone	MSc Thesis	New Orleans	Suggestive
1996b	Shah	MSc Thesis	Baltimore	Suggestive
1997a	Major	Space Syntax Symposia	Multiple Cities	Suggestive
1997b	Major	Space Syntax Symposia	Multiple Cities	Suggestive but inconclusive
2001	Allen et al.	Georgia Tech Report	Suburb of Atlanta	Suggestive
2003	Howsley	Space Syntax Symposia	Portland	Inconclusive
2003	Radford	Space Syntax Symposia	Oakland	Inconclusive
2004	Radford	MSc Thesis	Boston	Suggestive but inconclusive
2007	Kim	Space Syntax Symposia	Atlanta/New Urbanism	Suggestive
2007b	Peponis et al.	Space Syntax Symposia	Atlanta	Suggestive
2007a	Peponis et al.	Space Syntax Symposia	Multiple Cities	Suggestive
2007	Jiang and Peponis	Space Syntax Symposia	Atlanta	Suggestive
2009	Al Sayed et al.	Space Syntax Symposia	Manhattan and Barcelona	Inconclusive
2009	Haynie et al.	Space Syntax Symposia	Atlanta	Inconclusive
2009	Jiang and Peponis	Space Syntax Symposia	Atlanta	Inconclusive
2009	Ozbil et al.	Space Syntax Symposia	Atanta, Chicago and Dallas Rail Ridership	Suggestive
2009	Scoppa et al.	Space Syntax Symposia	Atlanta	Inconclusive
2011	Ozbil et al,	Urban Design International	Atlanta/Pedestrian Movement and Land Use	Strongly suggestive
2012	Zook et al.	Environment and Behavior	Atlanta	Suggestive
2013	Psarra et al.	Urban Design International	Detroit	Strongly suggestive
2014	Wineman et al.	JPER	Detroit	Suggestive

Table 0.1 – *Summary of notable studies of American cities using space syntax, 1984–2014.*

cities (Major, 1997a-b and Peponis et al., 2007a). The first had tentative findings about striking metric and configurational differences in American urban layouts while still being subject to the same spatial laws found in European ones (Major, 1997a-b). However, it suffered from methodological inconsistencies that were later rectified (Major, 2015a and c). When doing so, it was found these striking differences were real, fundamentally related to block sizes and street lengths, in giving shape to the massive scale of American cities in the horizontal dimension (Major, 2015c). The second focused on testing then-new space syntax measures without establishing a baseline of how long-established topological measures were systemically realized or related across multiple American cities (Peponis et al., 2007a). One purpose of this book is to address this problem by conducting a comprehensive survey of American urban space based on quantitative description of the thing itself in order to better understand their 'organized complexities.' In particular, we want to understand: how and why did the regular grid come to so pervasively characterize the American urban landscape? In doing so, the book answers a supplementary question to the first. Is the spatial pattern underlying the readily apparent geometric order of American cities really so different? In doing so, we are seeking to:

- Establish a broader perspective about American urban space

- Develop a cohesive theoretical model for the design and growth of American settlements

- Provide a basis for more effective design intervention in the American urban object itself

- Introduce possibly fruitful avenues for future research on American cities.

The principles of space syntax provide the heuristic foundation for a qualitative survey of the literature and historical record. The topological measures of space syntax provide an analytic foundation for the quantitative survey of contemporary American cities as well as representative examples from the historical record. In taking the space syntax approach, this book principally focuses on widespread use of the regular grid in American cities as pertaining to Hillier's Type 1 laws governing the generation of the urban object itself. The book implicitly accepts as a given that space syntax can tell us something useful about American urban space, including Type 2 laws governing the effects of spatial form on urban function and Type 3 laws about the way the urban object influences society in generating a distinctive spatial culture, both of which are discussed throughout the book.

In the past, there has been a great deal written about regular grids, in general, and American cities, in particular. There are many ideas stretching across a number of fields including archaeology, architecture, history, human ecology, geography, philosophy, sociology, and urban planning. Many of these ideas may be right. Some are certainly wrong. However, no one has ever filtered through these ideas, and the theoretic assumptions underlying them, to produce a comprehensive and cohesive story about the urban morphology of American cities founded on objective description and quantitative analysis of the thing itself, i.e. the American urban object. In addition to several new, original findings about American urban form, many applicable to the study of cities elsewhere in the world, a distinctive and significant objective of the book is to lift the 'theoretical fog' permeating around American cities over the last century to better tell the real story of American urbanism.

The order of things

Of course, there are non-physical factors affecting the composition of American settlements and serving to structure urban space in terms of its configuration, which we will discuss throughout the book (Hillier and Hanson, 1984; Marshall, 2005). However, we rely on the principles and representational techniques of space syntax – as well as Marshall's (2005) distinction between composition and configuration – as a basis to better classify and analyze the American urban grid in qualitative and quantitative terms. The book is composed of three sections. The first section, **Formal Composition**, focuses on historical and theoretical review of the regular grid. The middle section, **Form and Space**, serves as a fulcrum, which transitions the book from review to analysis. It serves as a 'table setter' for the last section by defining and demonstrating the predictable configurational effects of particular compositional strategies in American cities. The last section, **Spatial Configuration**, focuses on analysis of the urban spatial network in representative examples of historical and contemporary American settlements. Detailed information about sources and credits for illustrations used throughout are available at the end of the book.

Part I, *Formal Composition*, will review the history of regular grid planning in the world from the Indus Valley Civilization of Ancient India to colonization of the New World. It also discusses prevailing thought about the regular grid in the field of urban studies and introduces the concept of 'generic function' to suggest possible reasons for widespread use of the regular grid in settlements, especially for colonization activities. In this context, generic function means the ramifications for the most fundamental aspects in human use of space (occupation and movement) for the locating of settlements (Hillier, 1996b). It goes on to discuss the formal design parameters of regular grid planning – linear, cross-axis, orthogonal, offset, radial – in the context of precisely defining the terminology used in this book. This section concludes by reviewing the findings of a survey of formal composition in more than 700 American historical town plans in order to more better characterize the tradition of regular grid planning in the United States, principally before the 20th century (Major, 2015a).

Chapter 1, *The Regular Grid as Historical Object*, briefly summarizes the history of regular grid planning in settlements before the 19th century with an emphasis on when and where. This includes the early influences most commonly cited by historians in giving shape to the American urban landscape such as the Spanish Laws of the Indies, medieval European *bastides* (i.e. fortified towns), Thomas Jefferson's Land Ordinance of 1785, and William Penn's 1682 plan for Philadelphia, Pennsylvania. It argues the regular grid has been a standard part of the town planning vocabulary for more than 4,500 years. There is clear evidence for distinctive and separate traditions of regular grid planning in the Indus Valley Civilization of Ancient India and Pre-Columbian Mesoamerica. Some even argue for separate traditions in Ancient Egypt, Greece, Italy, and the Orient, though the evidence these are truly distinct is inconclusive. These traditions in Ancient India and Pre-Columbian Mesoamerica indicate the generic qualities of the regular grid as an artifact of physical arrangement – that is, as a general consequence to the act of humans placing dwellings in a settlement – are a contributory factor for its widespread use in so many settlements around the world. Finally, the chapter concludes by arguing the importance of William Penn's 1682 plan for Philadelphia on the American town planning tradition lies in its size instead of its composition. Penn's plan demonstrated town planning could occur on a previously unimaginable scale in the abundant lands of the New World.

Chapter 2, *The Regular Grid as Historical Subject*, briefly reviews the literature about regular grid planning in settlements with an emphasis on why. The objective is to establish at a basic level the reasons for its widespread use in so many different societies in different parts of the world over time. The chapter argues the answer lies in both the generic and utilitarian qualities of the regular grid. First, its generic qualities as an artifact of physical arrangement; namely, its quick adaptability to differing topographical conditions for the efficient division and/or allocation of land. Second, its utilitarian qualities (meaning of practical use) as a planning tool, which has been transmitted from one generation to another – and even from one society to the next – over time. This is because it is ideally suited to *facilitate* – not determine – certain social outcomes such as colonization in the broadest sense of the word, i.e. not only colonization of a people or place but also of the land itself. By implication, this includes promoting political control of territories in colonization activities and mercantile/free market capitalism, especially land speculation in the American experience. Because of this, widespread use of the regular grid in American cities represents the culmination of both its generic and utilitarian aspects in the history of town planning.

Chapter 3, *The Essential Right Angle*, examines the basic concepts of formal composition, meaning how the plan of the urban object is composed of geometrical elements, in the American town planning tradition. This is necessary before analyzing configuration, meaning how those elements are topographically interrelated in space syntax terms, to understand the effect of plan composition on the urban spatial network in later chapters. The purpose is narrow; namely, to avoid confusion and misconception by clarifying the parameters and terminology used for the geometrical description of American urban grids in this book. Using notional plans and historical examples, the chapter argues there is a finite set of concepts combined in regular grid planning, principally rectangularity of blocks and parallel/perpendicular streets based on the right angle. However, despite the simplicity of these concepts, regular grids are robust mechanisms for generating a seemingly infinite variety of plan compositions in real world examples. This has the effect of embedding consistencies and covariations – general to all, unique to each – in most American urban grids. Based on this investigation, the book principally utilizes geometrical descriptions such as linear and cross-axis (or crossroads) settlements, and deformed, orthogonal, offset, and radial grids. 'Regular' and 'regular grid' are general terms meant as inclusive of orthogonal, offset, and radial grids. The book defines suburban-type layouts in a later chapter because it is not necessarily formal design that most distinguishes such layouts but rather their process effect on spatial configuration (Allen et al., 2001).

Chapter 4, *The Regular Grid in America*, reviews the findings of a survey of regular grid planning in a historical record of American town plans (Major, 2015a). A broadly representative sample of more than 700 American town plans from 1565 to 1961 – a large majority from the 18th and 19th centuries – was compiled from various sources for this survey (Major, 2015a). A significant portion is associated with more than a quarter of all urban areas populated by 40,000 or more people in the United States today, including a large majority of the 50 largest. The purpose is to qualify the extent and frequency of regular grid planning in the United States by identifying the formal composition of American settlements as recorded in town plans over time and space, i.e. from early colonization to westward expansion. The chapter argues town planning in America was predisposed to regularity from the very beginning of colonization in the New World. This was due to extensive use of the bastide model in early colonial settlements as well as colonization occurring during the European Renaissance and Age of Enlightenment, which emphasized order concepts in town planning. The regulatory framework imposed by 1785 Land Ordinance for the practical division and distribution of land only served to *intensify* the American predisposition towards regularity. In this sense, the American town planning tradition represents the epitome of the Renaissance city ideal, what Boyer (1983) characterizes as the American dream of a rational city.

Part II, **Form and Space**, will begin with an analysis of 20 contemporary American urban grids controlled for size to establish a quantitative baseline about their metric and spatial characteristics using space syntax. This analysis builds on the findings from a previous study comparing 20 American and European urban grids using the same methodology (Major, 2015c). Hillier's principles of *centrality*, the tendency for formal compactness to maximize internal relations, and *linearity*, the tendency for formal extension to maximize relations to the outside world, for urban systems will be introduced (Hillier, 1996b). The local physical moves – grid expansion and deformation, manipulation of block size, street extension, and discrete separation – for design of the regular grid and their predictable effects on configuration in American cities are then demonstrated. It will be argued these design methods and their process effects on spatial structure are necessary to resolve the tension between centrality and linearity during urban growth.

Chapter 5, *The Spatial Logic of American Cities*, examines consistencies and covariations in the metric and spatial parameters of 20 contemporary American urban grids, focused on urban centers and controlled for axial size (i.e. number of axial lines). It builds on the methodology and findings of previous studies comparing and contrasting American and European urban grids (Major, 1997b and 2015c). In these studies, it was demonstrated that widespread use of the regular grid in American cities results in larger blocks and fewer, longer streets. Because of this, the urban layout of American cities tends to integrate at much higher levels while encompassing a much more expansive land area. This leads to a scale of urban space in the horizontal dimension of American cities that is a magnitude greater in terms of composition and configuration than typically found in other models of urbanism, especially in Europe (Major, 2015c). This appears to be a fundamental attribute of spatial configuration in American cities because all cities have a fractal dimension – or a degree of self-similarity – at all scales of the built environment, which tends to persist even as the scale of the urban pattern upsizes during the evolution of urban growth (Carvalho and Penn, 2004; Shpuza, 2014). The purpose of this chapter is two-fold: first, to see if these results hold in a larger sample of contemporary American urban grids incorporating a greater area of the urban fabric and, second, to see if we can better understand how American urban grids are differentiated from each other. The chapter argues this is the case. Specifically, larger block sizes and fewer, longer streets serve to differentiate American cities in a broadly similar manner to how these characteristics distinguished American and European urban grids from one other (Major, 2015c). This chapter also broadly defines the formal composition of American suburban layouts as three types (*repetitive deformity*, *asymmetrical regularity*, and *geomorphic* variations of each) in which departure from the large–scale grid logic of their surrounding context is the common denominator.

Chapter 6, *The Grid as Generator*, introduces Hillier's (1996b) principles of centrality and linearity in urban form. A brief review of the literature demonstrates that prevalent models of city growth in urban studies – concentric zone, sector, and multi-nuclei theory – take different approaches to account for the tension between centrality and linearity in settlements. Using space syntax, the chapter then examines the local physical moves for designing the regular grid, arguing there are well-defined design methods for its formal composition. These serve as instrumental tools with predictable process effects on spatial configuration in resolving the tension between centrality and linearity during the evolution of the urban form in American cities. They do so by differentiating parts and privileging the center within the pattern of the urban whole in a manner consistent with regular grid planning principles. The chapter shows how these design methods – grid expansion and deformation, street extension, and manipulation of block sizes – have an effect on the spatial pattern of American urban grids. It also examines the spatial effect of 20th century suburban layouts on the urban pattern, which we characterize as *discrete separation by linear segregation*. These design methods and spatial processes are still active today in the planning and development of American cities. Because their spatial effect is a predictable consequence to local design decisions, better and more effective intervention in the American urban fabric is possible while still approaching American cities as problems in "organized complexity" (Jacobs, 1961; 453).

Part III, **Spatial Configuration**, will analyze spatial structure in historical and contemporary American settlements in terms of their emergent pattern. Spatial structure will be probabilistic – or emergent – based on *laws of spatial emergence*; that is, predictable "global spatial effects" that arise from purely "local physical moves" in the design of the urban grid (Hillier, 1996b; 5). It is also subject to *laws of spatial convergence*, which are "processes whose rules… converge on particular global types which may vary in detail but at least some of whose most general properties will be invariant" (Hillier, 1996b; 245). According to Hillier (2002), "human beings are bound by these laws in the sense that they form a system of possibilities and limits within which they evolve their spatial strategies" (154). This section will analyze: block manipulation, street extension, and grid deformation in New Haven, Connecticut from 1638 to 1852; and, expansion of the orthogonal grid in the 'ward plan' of historic Savannah, Georgia from 1733 to 1856. It will then conclude by analyzing spatial structure in two contemporary American cities primarily characterized by their lack of a large-scale orthogonal super grid (Baltimore, Maryland and Seattle, Washington) and two that do possess a large-scale orthogonal super grid (Chicago, Illinois and Las Vegas, Nevada) to demonstrate emergence-convergence in the American urban object.

Drawing upon the historical record and theoretical models discussed in the previous chapter, Chapter 7, **Order and Structure in the Regular Grid**, examines the formal composition and spatial configuration of two basic plan concepts that appear to lay at the heart of the American planning tradition. The first is the Roman *plan castrum* model of an orthogonal grid in a 4 x 4 block layout with central cross-axis streets bisecting the layout into four quadrants as outlined in Vitruvius' *Ten Books of Architecture*. The second is the plan model of an orthogonal grid in a 3 x 3 block layout with dual cross-axes defining the perimeter streets of a central square as outlined in the Spanish Laws of the Indies. The chapter then examines the 'ward plan' model of James Oglethorpe's design for Savannah, Georgia. It argues Savannah's 'ward plan' represents a synthesis of these Roman and Spanish models in combination with the American tendency for elongated, rectangular blocks (nominally, to increase the number of lots). The chapter concludes by using space syntax to analyze the historical growth of the Nine Square Plan in New Haven from 1638 to 1852 and Savannah ward plan from 1733 to 1856. Block manipulation, street extension, and deformation of offset grids primarily characterize the former while grid expansion does so for the latter. This analysis demonstrates that the patterning of urban growth over time tends to conserve – and function with – the micro-scale spatial structure underlying these basic plan concepts; the Spanish model in the case of New Haven and the innovative 'ward plan' model in Savannah.

Chapter 8, *Complexity and Pattern in the City*, investigates how widespread use of the regular grid gives rise to an emergent spatial structure that is complex but filled with information based on the patterning of the urban grid for movement in contemporary American cities (Anderson, 1986; Hillier, 1996b). The chapter briefly introduces the concept of *cities as movement economies* and the phenomenon of *grid intensification* in differentiating local 'parts' such as areas and neighborhoods within the configurational pattern of the urban whole (Hillier, 1996b; Hillier, 1999a). It argues grid intensification is equally relevant for American cities as previously found in other cities of the world. However, the expansive, spare urban fabric of American cities has profound implications for network analysis. The chapter then examines emergence–convergence in two contemporary American cities lacking a large–scale orthogonal super grid: metropolitan Baltimore and Seattle. This analysis demonstrates grid expansion and deformation, street extension, and discrete separation play a crucial role in shaping the emergent spatial structure of these cities. Baltimore represents a quintessential example of emergent spatial structure converging on the near invariant of the ortho-radial grid in urban form. In contrast, a trio of integrated cores (two urban, one suburban) characterizes emergent spatial structure in Seattle due to the acute topographical conditions, effect of the Interstate Highway System in overcoming these conditions, and 20th century suburbanization in that city. In both cases, and despite these differences, emergent spatial structure tends to conserve the primacy of the center in the form of the CBD and/or historical area to resolve the tension between centrality and linearity during the evolution of urban form.

Chapter 9, *Learning from the Grid*, further investigates the process of emergence and convergence in American cities. The focus of this analysis is two contemporary American cities primarily characterized by large–scale orthogonal super grids: metropolitan Chicago and Las Vegas. It identifies a 'strip effect' along the prime activity axes or capital routes of these two American cities (Major, 1997a; Karimi et al., 2005). This phenomenon of linear or *strip intensification* is a variation on grid intensification discussed in the previous chapter whereby a long street and its immediate connections – instead of an area or neighborhood – patterns pervasive centrality into the urban grid. It then argues there are subtle differences between emergent spatial structure in Chicago and Las Vegas, despite possessing a large–scale orthogonal grid logic, which, in both cases, is the material manifestation of the national grid system imposed by the 1785 Land Ordinance. Both cities demonstrate particular approaches to conserving the primacy of the center in the form of the CBD/historical area by varying street length and connections in a manner consistent with regular grid planning principles. However, emergent spatial structure in Chicago is symptomatic of the 19th century land speculation process described by Reps and others (Reps, 1965 and 1979; Kunstler, 1993). In contrast, emergent spatial structure in Las Vegas is more indicative of the segregation of land uses and modes of movement associated with Euclidean zoning and modern transportation planning in the United States during the post-war period. In many ways, Chicago and Las Vegas represent quintessential examples of American town planning during the 19th and 20th century, respectively.

Finally, *The Tapestry Being Woven*, briefly summarizes the key findings of the book and discusses the implications for scholarly inquiry about the American planning tradition, public policy in the development of American cities, and urban research about cities in general, and American cities, in particular. The initial predisposition toward regularity in settlement form during the first three centuries of urban development in America, and the 1785 Land Ordinance in establishing a conceptual geometric order for land division in the United States, continue to be profound factors in shaping the future development and growth of American cities. A distinctive spatial structure emerges from a continual process of amalgamating towards and fragmenting from conceptual order during urban growth in American cities even as these cities tend to converge on the familiar model of the ortho-radial grid. The chapter concludes by suggesting that we begin to see our cities more clearly as complex spatial systems that are constantly being woven in the tapestry of the American urban object.

Introduction Notes

[1] Hillier (2005b) cites Center for Spatial Analysis (CASA) working papers "Network Geography," 63 (2003), "A New Theory of Space Syntax," 75 (2004a), and "Distance in Space Syntax," 80 (2004b) for these quotes from Michael Batty.
[2] This description of the space syntax approach is summarized from lecture notes accompanying the 'Representing' module taught by the author from 1997 to 1999 for the M.Sc. in Architecture: Advanced Architectural Studies program at The Bartlett School of Graduate Studies, University College London. Dr. Julienne Hanson originally wrote these notes, which were later revised by the author. The most comprehensive material about the principles and methods of space syntax is available in *The Social Logic of Space* (Hillier and Hanson, 1984), "The Architecture of Community" (Hanson and Hiller, 1987), "Ideas are in Things" (Hillier et al., 1987), *Space is the Machine* (Hillier, 1996b), and *Decoding Homes and Houses* (Hanson, 1998).

1 The Regular Grid as Historical Object

"Geometry is the means, created by ourselves, whereby we perceive the external world and express the world within us. Geometry is the foundation."
- Le Corbusier

This chapter briefly reviews the history of regular grid planning in human settlements before the 19th century with an emphasis on when and where. The objective is to establish at a basic level how regular grid town planning in other parts of the world and different periods of history influenced its eventual application in the American context. This includes early influences most commonly cited by historians in giving shape to the American urban landscape such as the Spanish Laws of the Indies, medieval European *bastides* (i.e. fortified towns), Thomas Jefferson's Land Ordinance of 1785, and William Penn's 1682 plan for Philadelphia. The chapter argues the regular grid has been a standard part of the town planning vocabulary for more than 4,500 years. There is evidence for the emergence of distinctive and separate traditions of regular grid planning in the Indus Valley Civilization of Ancient India and Pre-Columbian Mesoamerica. Some argue for distinct, separate traditions in Ancient Egypt, Greece, Italy, and the Orient, but the evidence is inconclusive. The emergence of regular grid planning traditions in Ancient India and Pre-Columbian Mesoamerica indicates the generic qualities of the regular grid as an artifact of physical arrangement – that is, as a general consequence to the act of humans placing dwellings in a settlement – is a contributory factor for its widespread use in so many settlements around the world. The chapter concludes by arguing the importance of William Penn's 1682 plan for Philadelphia on the American town planning tradition lies in its size, not its composition. Penn's plan demonstrated town planning could occur on a previously unimaginable scale in the abundant lands of the New World.

From Ancient India to the Roman Empire

The regular grid has been a standard part of the town planning vocabulary in human settlements for more than 4,500 years. Some suggest its arrival in the New World is an example of historical diffusion, which is the sequential influence of (or cultural transmission from) one society to another, which can be reliably traced over time and space. Stanislawski (1946) argues "despite its apparent obviousness, it would seem (the regular grid) was not put into practice by any except those who had known it previously or who had access to regions of its occurrence" (112–113). According to Stanislawski (1946), regular grid town planning first originated in Ancient India, diffusing in a well-defined manner over time along trade routes to Assyria, then Greece and Rome, Western Europe, and eventually into the New World. According to Reps (1965), the use of the regular grid in the New World was more due to "functional requirements rather than historical imitation" (2). Stanislawski (1946) and Kostof (1991) trace the earliest example of regular grid town planning in the world to the Indus Valley Civilization of Ancient India, specifically the city of Mohenjo-Daro located in modern day Pakistan approximately 2,500 years before the birth of Christ.[1] According to archaeologists, Mohenjo-Daro probably had around 35,000 residents at its height (Kenoyer, 1998).

The excavated plan of Lower Town in Mohenjo-Daro appears only suggestive of an underlying geometrical logic to its layout. However, the vertical dimension of its archaeological remains makes the geometric foundations of the city layout more readily apparent (**Figure 1.1**). It is likely a process of building and rebuilding in the city over a thousand years of habitation caused the plan to deviate from its initial geometric logic. This is quite common. Rossi (1982) describes this as the urban dynamics of "destruction and demolition, expropriation and rapid changes" (22).

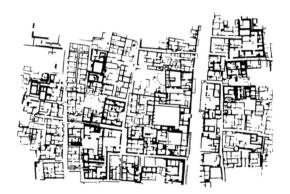

Figure 1.1 – Ancient India: (left) excavated plan of Lower Town in the city of Mohenjo-Daro founded circa 2,500 BC in modern day Pakistan (Image: © 2017, Trustees of the British Museum); and, (right) excavated remains at the Mohenjo-Daro UNESCO World Heritage Site.

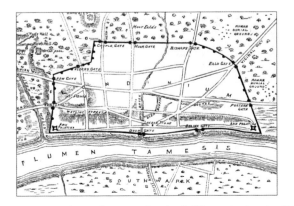

Figure 1.2 – The Transformation of London: (left) Roman London after 62 AD (various sources are cited for the creation of this plan but it should be considered illustrative and not factual); and, (right) Norden's 1593 map of the City of London.

The City of London provides an excellent example of this process at work. The Romans founded the City of London (*Londinium*) as a civilian settlement based on a regular grid circa 50 AD (Wacher, 1974).[2] As building and rebuilding occurred in the city over time, the plan of London took on the characteristics of a deformed grid (**Figure 1.2**).

Others point out the Egyptians were using orthogonal grid planning for the city of Kahun in the Old Kingdom around 3000–2500 BC (Fairman, 1949; Gallion and Eisner, 1963; Mumford, 1961; Owens, 1991). However, more accurate archaeological dating indicates Kahun (originally named Hotep-Senwosret or "Senwosret is Satisfied") was built in the 12th Dynasty of the Middle Kingdom during the reign of Pharaoh Senusret II (also known as Senwosret II or Sesostris II) from 1897 to 1878 BC. Kahun was a city built for administrators, priests, artisans, and workers assigned to construct the Pyramid at El-Lahun and maintain the funerary cult of Senusret II after his death.[3] The streets of Kahun were aligned to the cardinal points of the compass and the pyramid complex of Senusret II (**Figure 1.3**, left)(Badawy, 1966; Kemp, 1989). While Stanislawski's (1946) hypothesis of regular grid town planning principles diffusing along trade routes from Asia to the Near East and then presumably to Egypt cannot be entirely discounted, it would also not be surprising if a separate tradition of regular grid town planning arose in Ancient Egypt. The earliest Egyptian pyramid (Pyramid of Djoser designed by the architect Imhotep) was constructed around 2630–2611 BC, or about the same time as the founding of Mohenjo-Daro in Ancient India. Others have documented the skill and precision of Ancient Egyptian surveying techniques, some of which endured in practice into the early 20th century (Rossi, 2004). Because of this, historians cannot reliably discount the emergence of a separate tradition of regular grid town planning in Ancient Egypt.

Stanislawski (1946) provides an illuminating review about the history of regular grid town planning, beginning in Mohenjo-Daro, then to Assyria with the founding of the new capital at Magganuba in the 8th century BC, and the eventual introduction of the regular grid in the Mediterranean Basin. The Ancient Greeks made widespread use of the regular grid in town planning activities during the Hellenic or Classical Period from 500 to 300 BC (Stanislawski, 1946; Gallion and Eisner, 1963; Rykwert, 1988). Some historians credit Hippodamus, a 5th century Greek, with 'invention' of the orthogonal grid system

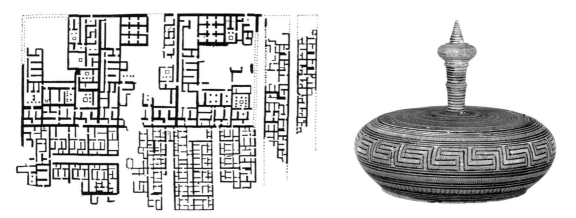

Figure 1.3 – *(left) Orthogonal layout in the city of Kahun during the 12th Dynasty of the Middle Kingdom in Ancient Egypt circa 1,900 BC; and, (right) Geometric Period Greek Pyxis (box with lid) in terracotta, mid-8th century BC.*

(Stanislawski, 1946; Rykwert, 1988; Owens, 1991). However, this is a fallacy since there is ample evidence for regular grid town planning at least two millennia before its widespread application in the Mediterranean Basin. According to Gallion and Eisner (1963), it is not even accurate to suggest Hippodamus was responsible for its reemergence during the Hellenic period. The rebuilding of Greek cities destroyed by the Persians near the end of the Archaic Period (800–500 BC) utilized the orthogonal grid system. Finally, Greek art during the Homeric or Dark Age (1100–800 BC) is commonly characterized by geometric motifs in vase painting (i.e. Geometric Period). At the very least, it indicates the Greeks were adept at handling geometrical concepts almost 400 years before the life of Hippodamus (**Figure 1.3**, right on previous page).

The best surviving record of Hippodamus comes from Aristotle, who credits him with planning Piraeus, the port town of Athens. This is probably the only plan that can be reliably attributed to him (Owens, 1991). It was possible he was involved in the planning of the Greek town Miletus (Miletos) in Anatolia (modern day Turkey) circa 479 BC. However, Owens (1991) argues this is pure conjecture. Several historians suggest 5th century BC is when the regular grid began to become a standard part of the town planning vocabulary. Owens (1991) states, "Hippodamian gridded cities... were a widespread feature of the Greco-Roman world" (6). This was due, in no small part, to the expansive military conquests and town-founding activities of Alexander the Great from his ascension to the Macedonian throne in 336 BC to his death at Babylon in 323 BC

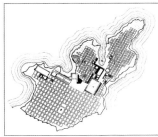

Figure 1.4 – *Greek Town Planning: (left) speculative illustration of Hippodamus' plan for the Athenian port town of Piraeus; (middle) Hippodamian orthogonal grid in Miletus (Miletos) on the western Aegean coast of Anatolia (modern day Turkey) circa 479 BC; and, (right) orthogonal grid in the Alexandrian city of Priene on the western Aegean coast of Anatolia (modern day Turkey) circa 323 BC.*

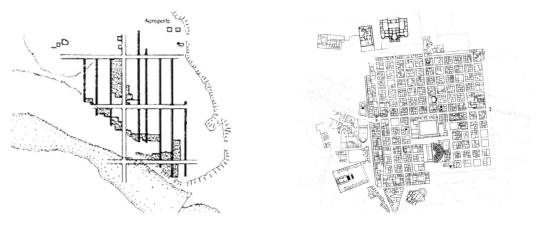

Figure 1.5 – *Town Planning in Ancient Italy: (left) 6th century Etruscan town plan of Marzabotto in the Po Valley of Northern Italy; and, (right) town plan of Timgad (Thamugadi) founded in North Africa during the reign of Trajan around 100 AD.*

(Stanislawski, 1946; Gallion and Eisner, 1963; Rykwert, 1988; Owens, 1991). Stanislawski (1946) offers the Alexandrian city of Priene as probably the best example of Greek regular grid town planning (**Figure** 1.4).

Stanislawski (1946) argues the Roman version of the regular grid is a transformation of the Greek model, co-opted primarily for military purposes. Owens (1991) comments on this, stating, "the Romans introduced new ideas which were adapted to their standardized, but nonetheless flexible, approach to town planning" (120). However, some argue for a separate tradition emerging with the Etruscans during the 6th century BC in Italy (Owens, 1991). If true, this might mean the generic nature of the regular grid for the physical arrangement of space was self-evident to the Etruscans instead of culturally transmitted from the Greeks via the Etruscans to the Romans. However, Owens (1991) goes on to assert the more likely explanation is the Greeks influenced the Etruscans, given the extent of Greek colonization efforts throughout the Mediterranean Basin including southern France and Italy beginning around 800 BC. According to Owens (1991), "axial grid planning became the characteristic feature of Roman colonies and towns through Italy… undoubtedly built upon the achievements of the Greeks and Etruscans… the combination of adaptability within a standardized arrangement laid the foundations for the urbanization of the Roman Empire in succeeding centuries" (118–120). The best surviving example of Roman regular grid town planning is probably Timgad (Thamugas or Thamugadi). It was a military camp established during the reign of Emperor Trajan circa 100 AD and located in modern day Algeria (**Figure** 1.5).

From Medieval Europe to Pre-Columbian Mesoamerica

Stanislawski (1946) argues the time from the fall of the Western Roman Empire in 476 AD until the late medieval period circa 1200 AD represents a period of disuse for regular grid town planning, He argues this was due to the decline of centralized political power in Europe. He sees the reemergence of regular grid town planning during the 13th century in Europe as a natural consequence to the reemergence of centralized political power in the form of absolute monarchy. A large number of planned towns used the regular grid during the late medieval period (Lilly, 1998). The most comprehensive review of town planning during this period is Maurice Beresford's *New Towns of the Middle Ages: Town Plantation in England, Wales and Gascony* (Beresford, 1967). He identifies 97 towns with surviving evidence of a regular grid layout. Of these: 26 are located in England including Liverpool; 26 in Wales including Cardiff; and, 45 in western Normandy of northern France. Beresford (1967) points out most of these towns were military or commercial bastides, each having "their own variation on the theme of rectangularity" and often with a central market square in the plan (10). He suggests the use of the regular grid

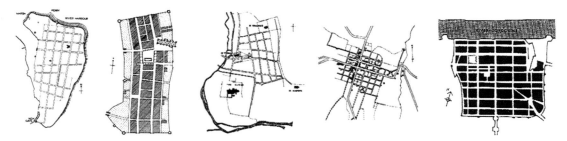

Figure 1.6 – Medieval planned towns: (from left to right) New Winchelsea, Sussex, England; Beaumont de Périgord, France; New Salisbury, Wiltshire, England; Ste. Foy la Grande, Gironde, France; and, St. Denis, Aude, France.

for these medieval bastides was because the plan "was a flexible one. It could be adapted to a square site as well as a long, narrow site; rectangles of different size could be laid together to cover hill sites such as Monségur or Dommen where the natural features did not leave a neat rectangular level space" (Beresford, 1967; 147) (**Figure 1.6**).

Several historians also point out there was a regular grid planning tradition in the Orient and Pre-Columbian Mesoamerica. Kostof (1991) cites the orthogonal grid layout in the Japanese city of Heijokyo (present day Nara) founded in 710 AD. Moholy-Nagy (1968) reviews some other examples including the royal city of Kyoto, Japan founded circa 792 AD by Emperor Kammu and Ch'ang-an in China founded during the Han Dynasty circa 195 BC (**Figure 1.7**). Like others, Moholy-Nagy (1968) views the regular grid planning tradition in the Orient as further evidence for the cultural expression of centralized military/political power and control. It is unclear if these Orient examples truly represent a separate tradition from the one emerging at least two millennia earlier in the Indus Valley Civilization of Ancient India (Major, 2015a).

In Pre-Columbian Mesoamerica, Kubler (1993) points to the 'native grids' of the Aztec city Tenochtitlán founded circa 1325 AD and Olmec city Cholula founded circa 600–700 AD. Both Tenochtitlán and Cholula were located in present day Mexico. Mesoamerica is a term referring to a region of the Americas that extends approximately from central Mexico to Belize, Guatemala, El Salvador, Honduras, Nicaragua, and Costa Rica where a number of Pre-Columbian societies flourished before Spanish colonization of the region during the 16th and 17th centuries. Kubler (1993) argues there is ample evidence for a separate regular grid planning tradition flourishing in Mesoamerica at least 800 years before the arrival of the Europeans. Moholy-Nagy (1968) views the use of orthogonal grid planning in Tenochtitlán (located in modern day Mexico City) as further evidence for its applicability as a means of military/political control in town planning activities. Gasparini (1993) points to other examples of regular grid planning in Mesoamerica and South America predating the arrival of the Spanish in the New World, which he describes as the Pre-Hispanic Grid. He goes further by suggesting the possibility that the Spanish tradition of regular grid town planning in the New World was influenced by Pre-Columbian urban centers instead of the Greco-Roman tradition. He argues the Spanish Laws of the Indies represents the merging of two separate planning traditions (Pre-Columbian and European) instead of the imposition

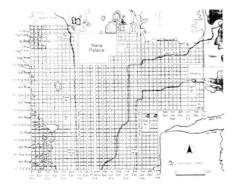  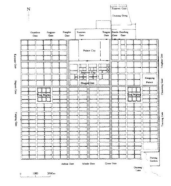

Figure 1.7 – Oriental regular grids: (left) Heijokyo (contemporary Nara, Japan) founded in 710 AD; (middle) Royal city of Kyoto, Japan founded circa 792 AD; and, (right) Ch'ang-an in China founded during the Han Dynasty circa 195 BC.

of a rational European Renaissance model on a primitive New World landscape. His argument is based on reconstruction of Pre-Columbian plans and how constituent elements were later incorporated after the arrival of the Spanish into the urban fabric of contemporary settlements (Gasparini, 1993). However, this seems unlikely given the extensive history of Greco-Roman colonization of the Iberian Peninsula since 800 BC, almost 2,300 years before Columbus' journey of discovery to the New World in 1492. It is more probable the Spanish simply found the generic aspects of physical arrangement in both the European Renaissance and Pre-Columbian traditions largely consistent with one another. The question of whether the Spanish Laws of the Indies is a merging of two separate traditions, the co-opting of one into the other, or the subjugation of the Pre-Columbian one by the European Renaissance tradition seems, for the most part, a rather esoteric debate. Nonetheless, it is a debate Kostof (1991) describes as "unresolved" (114). The well-established evidence for a separate and distinct regular grid planning tradition in Pre-Columbian America seems far more significant. Like Moholy-Nagy, Gasparini (1993) argues Pre-Columbian societies used the regular grid as a tool of territorial dominance in the same manner as the Europeans. He points to the Inca settlements Chucuito, Hatunqolla, and Paucarqolla in Peru, in addition to the Olmec city Cholula and Aztec city Tenochtitlán, as relevant examples (see **Figure A.16** in Chapter 7).

The regular grid in the New World

No other part of the world provides such a pervasive example of regular grid town planning as America (Batty and Longley, 1994).[5] Batty and Longley (1994) indicate this is because "urban growth in the cities of the New World has invariably followed a more geometric pattern, usually based on the grid, than in cities elsewhere, especially in Europe" (s38). The most comprehensive review of American (e.g. United States) town planning history is John Reps' two books, *The Making of Urban America: A History of City Planning in the United States* (1965) and *Cities of the American West: A History of Frontier Urban Planning* (1979). Reps (1965) sought to discover the "extent city planning was rooted in the nation's tradition" and trace "the main influences that have governed the form of America's cities for some four hundred years" (xv). He indicates the early history of American town planning was essentially a two-fold process. During the early years of colonization, the plans of villages and towns – and their surrounding agricultural lands – were consistent with, if not outright copies of, those traditionally found in Britain. Later, the medieval bastide plan was more influential (Reps, 1965 and 1979). Rybczynski (1996) echoes this assessment that "the first generation of American towns... reflected the traditional English preference for informality and improvisation, and a casual approach to planning" (66). The 1640 platting of Wethersfield, Connecticut provides a typical example of a New England town plan and the pattern of land

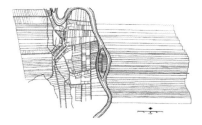  

Figure 1.8 – *Early Colonial America: (left) 1640 platting of Wethersfield, Connecticut showing the town plan and pattern of land division in the surrounding agricultural lands.; (middle) fortified town of New Orleans, Louisiana in 1759; and, (right) fortified town of Detroit, Michigan in 1764.*

The basics of representation

Space syntax uses representations. It is a fact. For a few, it is an odd criticism. Architects, urban designers, and planners use representations as a matter of course during most days of their education and career. Drawings and models are representations. Some of the most iconic architectural and urban visions in human history were only representations, such as Ville Radieuse or Broadacre City (**Figure A.3**). We never constructed these projects, yet we cannot deny their subsequent influence as mere representations.

A representation begins with a point in space, the simplest notion on which to build a geometry. A *point* has no size, only position. The number of points in any space will be infinite without a resolution, i.e. defining the bounds of space and a 'size' for the points. For the built environment, a reasonable resolution for a point is the physical area of an average human standing stationary, which is about 3 square feet (SF) or 0.28 square meters (m^2). A reasonable bound is the walls of a building. For a 3,000 SF house (e.g. the typical size of new American home with a two-car garage today), this translates into 1,000 points in space. It is a lot but manageable for the processing power of today's computers. However, measuring the relationship of every point to all others in this way using topology is excessive for a couple of reasons. First, a large subset of points will be largely redundant to adjacent ones. Move over 1 foot from where you are reading this book and look around. Did it make any discernible difference? For most people, it will not. Repeat and, eventually, it will. Second, only four to five people (based on the classic definition of a 'nuclear family' with two parents and 2.5 children) will use this house, probably less. Practically, an alternative description of space would make more sense to better understand it as a built environment. Space syntax does this by aggregating points in space into simple descriptions tied to human use; at its most basic for moving, staying, and seeing. Hillier, Hanson, Alan Penn, and others developed descriptions of space obeying the real constraints that the

Figure A.3 – *(left) Le Corbusier's perspective drawing of Ville Radieuse; (right) Frank Lloyd Wright's model of Broadacre City (Photo: Skot Weidemann © 2017 Frank Lloyd Wright Foundation).*

built environment places on visibility and movement (Hillier and Hanson, 1984; Hillier et al., 1987; Hillier, 1996b; Hanson, 1998; Turner and Penn, 1999) (**Figure A.4**).

Movement tends to be linear because humans are bipedal, forward-facing creatures bound by gravity. One of the most important representations in space syntax is the *line* (aka axial line, axis, or line of sight). A line is a set of points having a length but no width or depth. It represents an idealization, such as the lines in architectural or planning drawings. The matrix of the longest and fewest lines of sight and access completely covering all spaces of a built environment is the axial map. This is what most people typically regard as a space syntax model, especially for cities. The occupation of space tends to be convex so everyone can see and be seen by everyone else, such as a group of people gathered in a circle. In a *convex space*, all points are visible to all others. The collection of the fattest two-dimensional lumps of convex space in a built environment is the convex map. Often, a convex map is the space syntax model for buildings, i.e. discrete spatial layouts with a well-defined difference between inside and outside. The potential for seeing and moving is a *visual field*, which is all visible and accessible space from which we might see or move as defined from a particular set of points in the plan (Benedikt, 1979; Conroy Dalton and Bafna, 2003). The most extensive portions of some visual fields in cities will tend to approximate a 'fat' line (see below). A matrix of all visual fields from a gridded set of points to all others in a built environment is a visibility map (Turner and Penn, 1999). Space syntax usually defines visual fields at eye level. Today, average human height is about 5'4". Eye level is between 5" and 5½" from the top of the head for most people, so eye level is usually set at 5 feet (or 1.5 meters). Visual fields can be set at knee level to accommodate access, typically at 19–20" or 0.5 meter. A person can step on/over a bench in a museum space or the wall of an office cubicle by moving vertically, e.g. using the bench or desk as a step. Most people are too polite to do so. We can safely ignore such scenarios as statistically rare.

Space syntax uses combinations of these simple descriptions – point, line, space, field – to create layered representations of the built environment. These descriptions are "a natural and necessary spatial geometry describ(ing) some aspect of how buildings and cities are organized… as a vital aspect of how we create them, use them and understand them" (Hillier, 2005b; 5).

Figure A.4 – *(left to right) point, line, convex space and visual field (from a single point) at an intersection in Mid-Wilshire, Los Angeles.*

division for the surrounding agricultural areas during the early colonial period. In these New England agricultural settlements, the colonists often lived in town but traveled to work their agricultural lands. Sometimes, this was simply a matter of accessing agricultural lands to the back of a dwelling (**Figure 1.8**, left on page 27). After harvesting the land, residents could bring any produce not required for day-to-day subsistence or winter to market for sale in town (Reps, 1965).

Many historians point to the influence of the medieval European bastides in southern France, northern Spain, Ireland, and Wales for the emergence of the regular grid in America (Stanislawski, 1946; Reps, 1965 and 1979; Moholy-Nagy, 1968; Goldfield and Brownell, 1979; Gandelsonas, 1999). Goldfield and Brownell (1979) describe bastides as "small towns with gridiron street patterns and elaborate fortress walls" (25). It is not surprising "these provided one model of urban design in the virgin and often hostile territory of the Americas" (Goldfield and Brownell, 1979; 25). According to Reps (1965), "the bastide plan met the requirements of... stern conditions" (2) (**Figure 1.8**, middle and right on page 27).

Several historians trace the origins of the regular grid in America to the Spanish Laws of the Indies as a historical progression from the medieval bastides and planning principles of the European Renaissance (Stanislawski, 1946; Reps, 1965 and 1979; Moholy-Nagy, 1968; Gandelsonas, 1999). According to Stanislawski (1946), the Laws of the Indies placed the physical layout of streets and arrangement of plots in Spanish colonies into regulatory law. Kostof (1991) describes the standard layout codified by the Spanish Laws of the Indies: "The grid with two main axes intersecting… the plaza was the key to the entire settlement; its size regulated the makeup of the grid. The blocks immediately surrounding the plaza… divided into four equal sections (*solares*) and (were) assigned to the leading settlers. Sometimes the blocks were oriented with their corners facing the cardinal points at such an angle that prevailing winds might not sweep the length of the town – as recommended by Vitruvius" (115). Kostof (1991) proclaims the Spanish Laws of the Indies as "a genuine product of Renaissance thought" inspired by the "Classical treatise of Vitruvius, which had been translated into Spanish first in 1526" (114). The earliest Spanish colony in North America to apply the Laws of the Indies was Santa Domingo, West Indies in the present day Dominican Republic. The best surviving historical record of the town planning principles outlined in the Spanish Laws of the Indies can probably be found in the 1730 plan for the pueblo of San Fernando de Béxar, which is present day San

Figure 1.9 – *Spanish Laws of the Indies: (left) Santo Domingo, Dominican Republic, West Indies was the earliest settlement to apply the laws in North America, shown here in 1586 under siege by Sir Francis Drake and the English; (middle) Pueblo of San Fernando de Béxar (modern day San Antonio, Texas in the United States) circa 1730; and, (right) contemporary satellite view from 750 m of Old Town Fernandina, Florida.*

Antonio, Texas. However, the best preserved example on the ground is the Town of Fernandina, Florida (commonly referred to as Old Town Fernandina), which was the last town founded according to the requirements of the Spanish Laws of the Indies in the Western Hemisphere in 1811 (**Figure 1.9**).

Widespread use of the regular grid in the United States was further facilitated by the 1785 Land Ordinance, written by Thomas Jefferson and adopted by the U.S. Congress under the Articles of Confederation, which was the first constitution of the United States drafted by the Second Continental Congress in 1776. Under the Articles, Congress did not have the power to raise revenue by direct taxation of citizens. The immediate goal of the 1785 Land Ordinance was to raise money by the sale of land in the largely unmapped territories west of the original 13 colonies. The newly independent United States acquired this land in the 1783 Treaty of Paris, which ended the Revolutionary War. The Land Ordinance established a national grid system across all lands west of the Appalachian Mountains to the Mississippi River. Congress later extended this national grid system to the Pacific Ocean after the Louisiana Purchase in 1803, also an initiative of then-President Thomas Jefferson.[5] Over three-quarters of the land area in the continental United States eventually came under the rectangular survey of the national grid system (Treat, 1910; Carstensen, 1988). This grid system divided land into a series of townships measuring 36 square miles in area (or 6 miles by 6 miles). The system further subdivided each township into 36 sections measuring 1 square mile (**Figure 1.10**). Typically, owners would further subdivide these sections using this grid system, which led to the creation of thousands of rectangular tracts across the landscape. When these tracts were purchased, it was expedient to lay out streets parallel to the property lines of the tracts and rural roads were usually located at the boundaries of sections or townships (Reps, 1965 and 1979; Carter, 1983). In this way, the 1785 Land Ordinance embedded within government regulation the "paramount principle that land was first and foremost a commodity for capital gain" (Kunstler, 1993; 26).

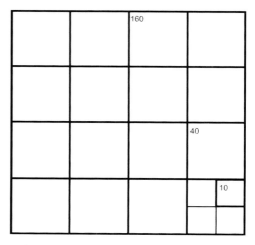

Figure 1.10 – *1785 Land Ordinance: (left) General Land Office (now the U.S. Bureau of Land Management) plan for numbering sections of a standard township, adopted May 18, 1796; and, (right) schematic of a typical subdivision of a section within the parameters of the national grid system.*

Reps (1965) argues the effect of the 1785 Land Ordinance was to "reinforce the natural inclination for the gridiron street system, the easiest of all to lay out when speed or the desire for land speculation guided the hand of the surveyor… section lines became rural roads… (and) later federal legislation establishing half-section town sites of 320 acres perpetuated the rectangular street system for the overwhelming majority of American cities" (217). However, he goes on to suggest "perhaps the rectangular survey pattern for the west was the only system that could have resulted in speedy settlement and the capture of the continent for the new nation, but its results in city planning were dullness and mediocrity" (Reps, 1965; 217). "The gridiron plan stamped an identical brand of uniformity and mediocrity on American cities from coast to coast… we now view most of these gridiron street plans with distaste… their lack of beauty, their functional shortcomings, their overwhelming dullness, and monotony cause us to despair" (Reps, 1965; 314). Of course, the latter opinion is open to interpretation. However, the 1785 Land Ordinance did establish the regulatory and practical framework for the division and distribution of land in the United States, which would foster widespread use of the regular grid in giving shape to American urbanism.

A new vision for a New World: New Haven and Philadelphia

In a sense, American settlements represent the epitome of the Renaissance city ideal, what Boyer (1983) characterizes as the American dream of a rational city, due to the cumulative influence of the bastide model, Spanish Laws of the Indies, and the 1785 Land Ordinance. The most important examples in early American history are the Nine Square Plan of New Haven and William Penn's plan for Philadelphia. The 1641 plan of New Haven incorporates nine square-shaped blocks (**Figure 1.11**). There is a public green in the center and eight blocks subdivided into lots surround this public green with eight streets in a 4 x 4 alignment. It is an English variation on the planning principles in the Spanish Laws of the Indies. The Nine Square Plan is perfectly symmetrical but only in the abstract. Construction of the town in real world conditions establishes an asymmetrical relation to the topography. This includes the New Haven Harbor to the south, and the tributaries of the Quinnipiac River along the perimeter to the south and west. The periphery blocks/land tracts do not adhere to the symmetry of the Nine Square Plan, nor does the subdivision of blocks into individual lots. In New Haven, the streets are parallel and perpendicular (more or less) to tributaries of the Quinnipiac River in existence at the founding of the town but since built over.[6] In terms of scale, each block is 16 acres (or 6.5 hectares) in size. In this plan, there is subdivision of the blocks adjacent to the public green into 87 lots (or 8–13 lots per block) with an average lot size of nearly 1.5 acres (or 0.6 hectare). The surrounding land tracts were in single ownership except for the two irregular shaped blocks adjacent to the river tributaries in the south. The block immediately adjacent to the Nine Square Plan appears to be roughly 12 acres in size with an average lot size of approximately

Figure 1.11 – *Nine Square Plan and division of land ownership in New Haven in 1641.*

three-quarters of an acre, or less than one-third of a hectare.[7] The Nine Square Plan incorporates 16 street intersections at right angles, either in four directions around the public green or three or two directions along the perimeter streets. Alignment of the blocks and/or land tracts around the perimeter of the Nine Square Plan orients to the topography of the river tributaries while still maintaining connections to the four streets intersecting internally within the Nine Square Plan. However, none of the streets in the periphery intersect at a right angle with those streets defining the perimeter of the Nine Square Plan itself.

Penn's 1682 plan for Philadelphia is composed of 176 blocks of varying size and shape laid out in an 8 x 22 alignment (**Figure 1.12**, left). All but 20 are rectangular-shaped blocks longer in one dimension than the other. There are 16 square blocks (including the green spaces in each quadrant of the plan) and 4 L-shaped blocks that form a public square at the intersection of the two central, cross-axis streets (the most central street in a north-to-south dimension and the adjacent one to the most central street in the east-to-west dimension). The northerly L-shaped blocks are slightly larger than the southerly ones. There are nine streets running in an east-to-west direction, perpendicular to the Delaware and Schuylkill Rivers. There are 23 streets running a north-to-south direction parallel to the topography of the rivers at this location in a 9 x 23 alignment, so there are 32 streets in total. The plan incorporates 207 intersections at a right angle with 60 three-way intersections and 4 two-way intersections (at the corners) along the perimeter of the layout. Sixty-nine percent (69%) of the street intersections (143 in total) are four-way intersections internal to the layout.

In his plan, Penn also provided a scheme for the subdivision of the blocks into lots (**Figure 1.12**, right). According to Reps (1965), most of the blocks in Penn's plan measured "between 425 feet by 675 and 425 feet by 500 feet," which indicates this scheme was devised for lots of approximately 1/3 acre, 1/2 acre, 3/4 acre and 1 acre in size (163). The plan maintains a consistent geometric logic even though it utilizes two different street widths, three different block shapes (square, rectangular and L-shaped), five public spaces or parks, and fifteen different block sizes. All street intersections occur at a right angle. Finally, the plan has a bilateral symmetry along the central cross-axis street in only the north-to-south dimension of the plan.

Many historians cite the influence of Penn's Philadelphia plan for the eventual widespread use of the regular grid in America. This includes Reps (1965), who observes,

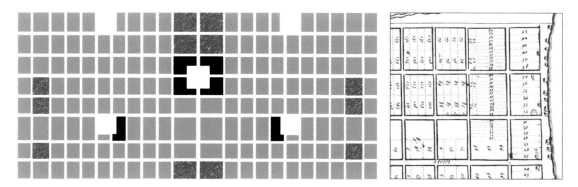

Figure 1.12 – *William Penn's Philadelphia: (left) pattern of block shape with rectangular blocks in light gray, L-shaped blocks in black, and square blocks in dark gray. The square shaped public spaces in each quadrant of the plan and the central square are shown in white as part of the street network; and, (right) close-up of block subdivision scheme into 1/3 acre, 1/2 acre, 3/4 acre and 1 acre lots.*

Figure 1.13 – *Comparison of scale in the original plan of: (left) New Haven; and, (right) Philadelphia. The boundary of the original plan is shaded in white on a satellite image of the contemporary urban fabric in both cities from 5.5 km.*

"Philadelphia, as the first large American city to be laid out on a grid pattern has always been identified, usually unkindly, as the inspiration for the great era of rectangular grid planning throughout the last two and half centuries. For many of the towns that were built later during the westward march of urbanization, Philadelphia served as the model… the regular pattern of streets and one or more public squares were features that became widely imitated" (172–174). He even wonders if "Philadelphia must share the blame for the ubiquitous gridiron" (Reps, 1965; 174). Reps (1965) argues "the single open square in the center of the town became the typical expression of the Philadelphia plan as it was transplanted west" (174); what is today generally regarded as the prototypical model of small town America, especially in the Midwest. However, that model is more consistent with the Nine Square Plan of New Haven and the town planning principles outlined in the Spanish Laws of the Indies. Other American towns rarely duplicated the variation of block size/shape and subdivision of lots in Penn's plan for Philadelphia in the same manner. Reps (1965) can only cite a few possible examples – most in Pennsylvania – but goes on to assert there was "a strong psychological motivation to duplicate a familiar community element in the midst of unfamiliar surroundings" to explain the influence of Penn's plan (174). However, it seems far more likely Philadelphia's influence mainly lies in being "large by (previous) colonial standards" (Reps, 1965; 172). Philadelphia demonstrated town planning could occur on a previously unimaginable scale in the abundant lands of the New World. For example, the area of Penn's plan for Philadelphia was more than four times the size of New Haven's Nine Square Plan founded only 40 years earlier (**Figure 1.13**). Philadelphia showed the realm of the possible for town planning in the virgin lands of the New World. In this sense, it was truly visionary.

Chapter 1 Notes

[1] Using the common designations of Anno Domini (abbreviated as AD) and Before Christ (abbreviated as BC) in the Gregorian calendar.

[2] For the date of founding for Roman London, see English Heritage archaeological evacuations at Number 1 Poultry, London EC4 in *Archaeology Review* 1995–96 (http://www.eng-h.gov.uk/archrev/rev95_6/poultry.htm).

[3] Archaeological evidence brings into question the commonly held belief that slaves constructed the Great Pyramids of Egypt (Shaw, 2003).

[4] From this point forward in the book, the terms 'America' and 'American' generally refer to North America and, specifically, the United States.

[5] Thomas Jefferson may be the most significant figure in American history due to his involvement in the 1776 Declaration of Independence, 1785 Land Ordinance, and 1803 Louisiana Purchase. The cumulative effect of these three events – practically and symbolically – in giving shape to the emerging national identity of the United States and its egalitarian mythos of equality and opportunity for all is immeasurable.

[6] The course of the southern tributary of the Quinnipiac River in the 1641 plan matches the path of a modern highway in contemporary New Haven (refer to Figure 1.13, left).

[7] The subdivision of the other irregular shaped block adjacent to the river tributary is illegible.

The Regular Grid as Historical Subject

"Geometry is not true, it is advantageous."
- Robert M. Pirsig

This chapter briefly reviews the literature about regular grid planning in human settlements with an emphasis on why. The objective is to establish at a basic level the reasons for its widespread use in so many different societies in different parts of the world over time. The chapter argues the answer lies in both the generic and utilitarian qualities of the regular grid. First, its generic qualities as an artifact of physical arrangement; namely, its quick adaptability to differing topographical conditions for the efficient division and/or allocation of land. Second, its utilitarian qualities (meaning of practical use) as a planning tool, which has been transmitted from one generation to another – and even from one society to another – over time. This is because it is ideally suited to *facilitate* – not determine – certain social outcomes such as colonization in the broadest sense of the word, i.e. not only colonization of a people or place but also of the land itself. By implication, this includes promoting political control of territories in such activities and mercantile/free market capitalism, especially land speculation in the American experience. Because of this, widespread use of the regular grid in American cities represents the culmination of both its generic and utilitarian aspects in the history of town planning.

Why the regular grid?
Based on the brief review of the previous chapter, we can trace the history of regular grid town planning to at least 2,500 years before the birth of Christ. More importantly, we cannot exclusively attribute the evolution of regular grid town planning principles to a process of historical diffusion, which Kostof (1991) argues no one believes anyway. At the very least, the historical record indicates the emergence of distinct, separate traditions in the Indus Valley Civilization of Ancient India and Pre-Columbian Mesoamerica. It is also feasible separate traditions arose in Ancient Egypt, the Orient, or perhaps even Italy. However, the evidence is inconclusive. In any case, this suggests there is a generic quality about the regular grid that lends itself to human settlement (Martin, 1972). On the other hand, it also appears well-established that regular grid town planning principles were widely used

in the Mediterranean Basin beginning in Egypt and the Near East, then with the Greeks and Romans, later in the fortified towns of medieval Europe, and eventually in the European Renaissance tradition during colonization of the New World. This suggests there must be something about the utilitarian qualities of the regular grid lending itself to widespread application by means of cultural transmission since so many different societies adopted – and adapted – its use in different parts of the world over the last 4,500 years. The literature about the history of regular grid town planning is largely consistent in answering this question with reference to both its generic qualities in terms of simple, physical arrangement and utilitarian qualities as a planning tool to foster certain political, social, and economic outcomes. In terms of generic qualities, the most commonly cited reasons are adaptability and efficiency (Stanislawski, 1946; Mumford, 1961; Reps 1965 and 1979; Beresford, 1967; Kostof, 1991; Owens, 1991; Kunstler, 1993; Rybczynski, 1996). In terms of utilitarian qualities, there are three reasons most commonly cited in the literature. First, use as an aspect of centralized power for the purposes of military/political control of society (Stanislawski, 1946; Beresford, 1967; Moholy-Nagy, 1968; Kostof, 1991; Gasparini, 1993; Rybczynski, 1996). Second, use in colonization activities for the control of territory (Stanislawski, 1946; Mumford, 1961; Reps, 1965 and 1979; Kostof, 1991; Owens, 1991; Rybczynski, 1996). Lastly, use in the promotion of economic activity and mercantile/free market capitalism (Stanislawski, 1946; Beresford, 1967; Moholy-Nagy, 1968; Barth, 1975; Reps 1979; Carter, 1983; Davis, 1990; Kostof, 1991; Kunstler, 1993; Rybczynski, 1996).

Adaptive and efficient qualities of the regular grid

By adaptive, it usually means the regular grid can be used anywhere under the most extreme circumstances. Stanislawski (1946) refers to "its greatest virtue is the fact that as a generic plan for disparate sites it is eminently serviceable" (106). However, adaptability is not a quality exclusive to the regular grid. For example, the regular grid layout of San Francisco, California in the United States and the deformed grid layout of Ragusa, Sicily in Italy both incorporate acute topographical conditions in the settlement (**Figure 2.1**). In San Francisco and Ragusa, the vertical construction of dwellings adapts to the topographical conditions of a local site in particular ways. In the case of San Francisco, this occurs by steeply adapting finished floors so they step up or down in section with the topography, which serves to maintain the conceptual logic of the regular grid imposed on the acute elevation changes in that settlement. In Ragusa, the logic of the deformed grid emerges from a local process of aggregating dwellings (Hillier and Hanson, 1984). During this process, finished floors are adapted to contours of the topography for specific sites so changes in elevation tend to be gradual instead of steep. In this way, the layout literally incorporates the local topographical

Figure 2.1 – (left) Satellite (from 1 km) and street view of the regular grid layout in the Nob Hill area of San Francisco, California in the United States, and (right) satellite (from 1 km) and aerial view of the deformed grid layout of the Sicilian town of Ragusa in Italy.

conditions into its functional pattern. This is the basis for Moholy-Nagy (1968) describing such layouts as geomorphic. What this means is elevation changes in movement through the street network of San Francisco tend to be more steep but shorter whereas in Ragusa these changes tend to be more gradual but longer in terms of time and distance. In any case, this brief comparison of San Francisco and Ragusa suggests both regular and deformed grid layouts are highly adaptable as settlement forms. Adaptability, in itself, is not a unique characteristic of the regular grid. There must be something else that lends the regular grid to widespread use around the world.

Efficiency is another quality commonly cited in the literature. By efficiency, it means achieving maximum productivity with minimum wasted effort or expense in town planning activities. According to Reps (1979), the regular grid is efficient because it is "easy to design, quick to survey, (and) simple to comprehend" (x). This echoes Beresford's (1967) assessment: "the simplest way of setting out building plots and streets was in a rectilinear grid, which made no more demand on techniques of measurements than the ability to set out a straight line, to divide it into equal proportions, and to set another at right angles to it" (146). Stanislawski (1946) also summarizes the efficient qualities of the regular grid. He argues the flexible extension of local parts can occur without alteration to the conceptual pattern of the whole, the generation of rectangular plots easily fits into a scheme incorporating squares and plazas, it is intuitive either in drawing or built form, and it is easily surveyed even under the most primitive of conditions. He is explicitly referring to the overall concept of the plan when he discusses the flexible extension of local parts. However, we can also expand this explanation to include the replication of horizontal and vertical construction methods and materials, what Kunstler (1993) refers to as the regular grid promoting "good economy of building" (30). Indeed, the regular grid appears ideal for the modern industrial era with its emphasis of mass production based on the standardization of parts. It is not surprising that historians often cite standardization as another reason for its widespread use (Stanislawski, 1946; Mumford, 1961; Reps, 1965 and 1979; Carter, 1983; Kostof, 1991; Owens, 1991; Rybczynski, 1996).

In this sense, they usually discuss standardization in egalitarian terms about the equal distribution of property, which the chapter covers in a subsequent section about the regular grid planning tradition in the United States. However, of more practical concern than the social implications for the equal division of property was *expedient distribution*. The purely abstract Cartesian geometry of the regular grid helps to enable agreement on land ownership at a distance for planned settlements in the absence of detailed surveys about topographic features, contours, etc. The crown controlled property in those territories held by particular colonial powers (England, Spain, France, Holland) before American independence. The distribution of property based on simplified surveying using regular grids was efficient and practical at a long distance. All the colonial powers in North America adopted this model (the English in New Haven, the Spanish in St. Augustine, the French in New Orleans, and the Dutch in New Amsterdam/New York). However, if we assign 'invention' based on which colonial power first broke through the barriers for successful settlement of North America, the Spanish are primarily responsible since Santo Domingo in the Dominican Republic (1498) and St. Augustine in Florida (1563) both used regular grids. However, the 'invention' of using regular grids to distribute property at a distance in colonization activities can be traced, at least, to the Greeks in Asia Minor and Italy during the Classical Period and probably even further back in time. In any case, it appears the generic nature of the regular grid on several levels intimately ties together efficiency, standardization, and adaptability as assets since the standardization of parts makes it efficient to design and survey. It is this efficiency, which allows the regular grid to be *quickly* adapted to different topographical conditions. This is one of the reasons for its widespread use in so many different societies and regions of the world.

As a tool of the military, colonization, and economy
Stanislawski (1946) argues the regular grid helps to foster military control of a town and its hinterland. Rybczynski (1996) agrees with this assessment, stating, "grid planning has often been associated with colonization, since standardized, orderly, rational layouts appeal to the military mind; grids can also be devised in advance and imposed on different terrain" (44). The use of the regular grid in the layout of Roman military encampments is well established, which often formed the basis for the subsequent town plan of numerous Roman colonies (Owens, 1991). How does the regular grid lend itself to application by the military? Kostof (1991) suggests the answer lies in the "advantages of straight streets for military purposes" (95). More specifically, the regular grid lends itself to military use precisely because of its generic qualities, since it is efficient to design, survey, and quickly adapt to different topographical conditions. The standardized layout is also easy for soldiers to comprehend. Different camps may be in different locations but the standardized layout remains, more or less, the same for hundreds or even thousands of soldiers.[1] The regular grid layout also facilitates ease of movement for troops; not only in case of attack by allowing for the efficient movement of soldiers to the fortified perimeter of the camp but also in the ordinary, day-to-day tedium of camp life. However, more than this, the selection of highly strategic and tactical (or defensible) positions for encampments based on local topographical conditions is usually perceived as standard practice for the military; at least historically. It is not surprising these locations served the same function for colonial towns and often proved strategic for colonization and commercial activities. For example, it appears the location of many fortified towns in early colonial America, in combination with the use of a regular grid inside the fortifications, may have been for the same reason. In particular, rapid movement to the town fortifications in defense against potential attacks, principally inland of the settlement from hostile Native American tribes or naval attacks from competing colonial powers (**Figure 2.2**).

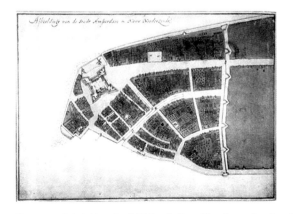
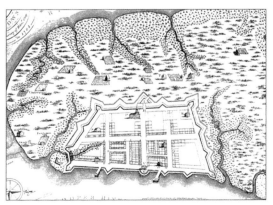

Figure 2.2 – Colonial America: (left) Castello Plan of New Amsterdam (later New York) by Jacques Cortelyou in 1660; and, (right) plan of Charles Towne (later Charleston) in 1704.

This is a characteristic of what Hillier (1996b) defines as "generic function, by which is meant the spatial implications of the most fundamental aspects of human use of space, that is the fact of occupation and the fact of movement" (5–6). He details this concept specifically about buildings but generic function is equally applicable to settlements. Topographical conditions generate *a priori* arrangements in space that makes some locations better suited for the purposes of human settlement than others. It is important to point out that site selection, in itself, is the first conscious act of design in town planning. This act rarely, if ever, occurs in an intellectual vacuum, even under extreme circumstances; for example, the earliest European colonies in the New World during the 16th century. In the case of settlements, generic function refers to movement and the basic human requirements for occupation, i.e. food, water, and shelter. Barter and defense are more specialized aspects of these basic requirements (Penn, 2005). At this generic level, the functional requirements of water, shelter, movement, and defense (for example, in a military camp or a colonial town) necessitate a location that is spatially viable for those functions. This is often responsible for what most settlements have in common. To directly adapt Hillier's (1996b) terminology from *Space is the Machine*, generic function is the first filter between the field of possibility and urban actuality. The second filter is then the specific urban functions of that settlement. The third filter is the idiosyncrasies of structure and cultural expression, which distinguishes that settlement from all others. The passage from the possible to the real passes through these filters. Without an understanding of each, we cannot decipher the relationship between form and function in settlements. For example, all aspects of generic function are transformed via the 'second filter' of functional requirements into specialized urban functions such as portable water and sanitary sewer infrastructure, housing and government administration, retail and commercial trade, and transportation in the form of public transit and ports. Most of all, without a knowledge of generic function and its spatial implications, we cannot understand that the spatial structures of all settlements already have much in common. Settlements are profoundly influenced by human use of space, nominally before even a single building is constructed. This suggests generic function is an important aspect for selecting strategic and tactical locations to establish a settlement. This is also the key to widespread use of the regular grid by the military and, by implication, promoting colonization and commercial activities in colonial towns.[2]

The historical record of human geography is replete with examples of settlements established adjacent to or near water bodies in order to provide a readily available source of drinking water, transportation and trade, and even recreation (Cooley, 1894; Harris and Ullman, 1945). For example, more than 50% of the total population in the United States today lives in coastal communities along the Atlantic and Pacific Oceans, Caribbean Sea, or the Great Lakes/St. Lawrence River and Seaway (Source: U.S. National Oceanic and Atmospheric Administration). This statistic does not even include cities along major North American rivers such as the Mississippi, Ohio, Missouri, or Colorado.

Historians generally accept the four largest settlements in colonial America before the Revolutionary War in 1775 were (from largest to smallest in terms of population) Philadelphia, New York, Boston, and Charleston. Usually based on 19th century sources, population estimates vary but it is generally accepted approximately 2,400,000 people lived in the American colonies in 1775. About 600,000 or one-quarter were slaves. Approximately 30,000–40,000 people lived in Philadelphia, 25,000 in New York, 16,000 in Boston;

Probability, not determinism

We shape built environments. It is why we have professions for the built environment, i.e. architects, urban designers, city planners, landscape architects, and so on. Nonetheless, it does not determine what a single individual will do in a building or city. It does create the preconditions for what many people will *tend to do* by allowing certain possibilities and limiting, even denying, others. It is common sense.

Built environments shape us. Design intent is always social, even when paradoxically claimed otherwise, i.e. a lack of social intent *is* a social intent. People input social intentions into their design strategies for the physical geometries of our buildings and cities. We have built for 10,000 years, at least; much longer for the simplest dwellings. We replicate strategies that facilitate our everyday practical and social use of buildings and cities. We discard those that do not, usually through neglect and demolition. For buildings, we recognize the most common strategies as 'vernacular' even if originally innovative. For cities, we recognize them as 'traditional urbanism.' Generally, this means before the 20th century, Modernism, and/or World War II depending on the topic under discussion, i.e. auto mechanics, theory, regulatory, etc. This purposeful process of adoption and adaptation, abandonment and obsolescence in buildings and cities, in turn, shapes society and us. Again, it is common sense. Otherwise, why choose one design strategy over another? Cost and profit are social intents too, albeit economic ones.

Space syntax does not predict what a single individual will do in a building or city. It does not try to or claim to. Space syntax does *forecast* what aggregate populations will tend to do in a building or city. Space syntax forecasting of movement levels is typically accurate in a statistical range from 60% to 80%. This accuracy is similar to weather forecasts of the U.S. National Weather Service. People plan ahead their day or week (even vacations) based on the weather forecast and adjust accordingly as required by the reality. People need to do the same for their buildings and cities in the years and decades ahead, where the costs, benefits, and consequences are much more significant than a rained-out picnic. However, some people find this alarming. A few criticize space syntax as environmental or physical determinism. It is curious on several levels. It has the merits of vagueness. Few people understand 'determinism' but most have a general sense of its association with institutionalized racism and eugenics, so it sounds bad. In architecture and urbanism, 'determinism' is tantamount to an accusation of racism or fascism; easy to make, impossible to disprove *in absentia*. In the United States, this criticism inextricably relates to a now-deeply ingrained professional and societal reaction ('less is a bore') against the worst follies of Modernism, mistakenly perceived as scientific in nature where Mies van der Rohe's maxim of 'less is more' is akin to Occam's Razor ('other things being equal, the simplest solution is usually the correct one'). Such criticism manages to grossly misunderstand Modernism, science, and space syntax all at once. Like many theories about architecture and cities, Modernism is normative, i.e. conjectures of intuition based on experience. Walter Gropius conjectured natural light and airflow would promote public health so he prescribed a relationship between building setbacks and heights (**Figure A.5, left**). At the time, it made intuitive sense. There was no scientific evidence to support it. To many people, it still makes sense today. There is still little evidence to support it except for hospitals. Late 19th century social reformers, later associated with *The London Society*, conjectured a green belt around London would promote public health by improving air quality and retarding urban sprawl. At the time, it made intuitive sense. There was no scientific evidence to support it. By 1944, Patrick Abercrombie included a 6 mile wide green belt in the Greater London Plan. By the late 1990s, the Centre for Transport Studies at University College London had the scientific evidence. London's Green Belt worsened urban sprawl and air quality due to large increases in commuting distances via automobiles to new towns like Harlow, Hemel Hempstead, Basildon, and Milton Keynes. *The London Society* conceded in a 2014 position paper by Jonathan Manns that "green sprawl" (now 35 miles wide around London) was inadvisable (**Figure A.5, right**). However, urban planners persist in proposing and aggregating parcels for green belts in cities around the world. The point should be clear.

Modernism often borrowed the language of science to promote normative theory. By any measure, it was not analytical theory based on scientific evidence. It is nonsensical to react against the scientific basis of space syntax due to the failures of Modernism or determinism. For the record, environmental determinism asserts the natural biophysical environment, including climate and geography, determines the development trajectory of a people, society, and state. Physical determinism asserts a *complete* description of the physical state of the world at any given time and a *complete* statement of the physical laws of nature together determines physical events after that time. People discredited the first whereas the second is hotly debated, largely for the same reasons. Both deal in certainties. Space syntax deals with the probabilities of aggregated populations, not the certainties of an individual person or concept.

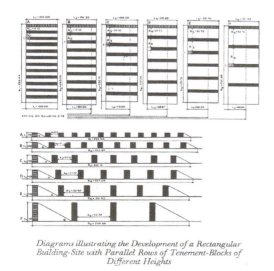
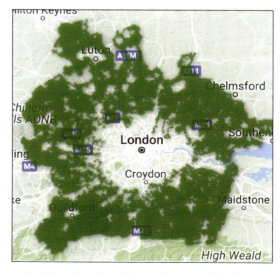

Figure A.5 – *(left) Gropius' diagram "illustrating the development of a rectangular building-site with parallel rows of tenement-blocks of different heights;" (right) London's Green Belt (in dark green) today.*

and, 12,000 in Charleston (excluding slaves and Native Americans). The estimated population in Boston fell to less than 7,000 during the British occupation of 1775–76 (Source: U.S. Census Bureau). British forces also occupied Philadelphia, New York, and Charleston at various stages of the war. Historians estimate approximately 500,000 people (20% of the total population) were Tories – loyal to the British crown – who fled the country after the war. This suggests there was a pause in growth for several American settlements during the Revolutionary War (1775–83) or, at least, a reduction in the growth rate (Elson, 1904; Green and Harrington, 1932; Middlekauff, 2005).

These four settlements are important deep-water ports on the east coast for the transportation of trade to European markets (**Figure 2.3**). Boston founded at the conflux of the Charles and Mystic Rivers into a natural harbor (later known as Boston Harbor) on the Shawmut Peninsula of the Massachusetts Bay estuary (**Figure 2.4**, left). New York (originally named New Amsterdam) founded on Manhattan Island at the conflux of the Hudson and East Rivers into a natural harbor at Upper New York Bay (**Figure 2.2**, left). Philadelphia founded on the banks of the Delaware River near the conflux of the Schuylkill River into the Delaware River, approximately 30 miles upriver from its major estuary outlet into Delaware Bay and the Atlantic Ocean (**Figure 2.4**, right). William Penn laid out his famous plan for Philadelphia in this location because the depth of the Delaware River was still sufficient to serve as a port, what he referred to "by reason of situation must in all probability be the most considerable for merchandize, trade and fishery" (Reps, 1965; 160).[3] Charleston (originally named Charles Towne) founded on a peninsula at the conflux of the Cooper and Ashley Rivers into a natural harbor (later known as Charleston Harbor) on the coast of South Carolina (**Figure 2.2**, right). All four colonial settlements are excellent examples of generic function at work. Local topographical conditions established *a priori* arrangements of space making these locations ideal for a settlement, primarily for defense and water transportation of trade to European markets. Historically, colonization is a means for a country, nation, or group of people to project political, economic, and/or military power over distance to a territory originally not their own. This occurs by sending settlers to take political control over a territory and appropriate it for their own use. In fact, the term colonization derives from the Latin *colere*, which means, "to inhabit, cultivate, frequent, tend, practice, guard, (and) respect" (Rockman, 2003). This Latin term is appropriate since it is inclusive of all aspects of colonization including its economic, military, and political dimensions. Based on the historical record, the Greeks and Romans used

Figure 2.3 – *Historical map of Colonial America in 1775.*

the regular grid during extensive periods of colonization in several parts of Europe and the Mediterranean Basin as did the Europeans in colonization of the New World (Owens, 1991; Reps, 1965 and 1979; Kostof, 1991). The generic qualities of the regular grid allowed these colonial powers to quickly and efficiently survey and lay out a town in a strategic and tactical location (evaluated on the basis of generic function) and then inhabit/occupy that town. This could occur much more quickly using the regular grid than relying on a purely local process of aggregating dwellings, which can often take years and does not take into account the immediate tactical situation of the settlement. Of the four largest colonial American settlements in 1775, Boston is the only town to take this approach. The tactical location of the colonial town and its regular grid layout facilitated defense of the town, which made it more difficult to expel the colonists. In turn, this tended to establish their political control over the area. The strategic location of the town would also be ideal to foster commercial activities and trade with the larger region, which tended to reinforce the political control of the colonists over the territory of the town and its hinder regions, as suggested by Stanislawski (1946).

In discussing medieval bastides, Beresford (1967) suggests the openness found in the regular grid layout also facilitated commercial activity. He argues regular grid towns served as a contrast for visitors to older European towns with their "oligarchic structure" mirrored in the deformed grid layout, which "gave less encouragement to newcomers" and tended to "assert the characteristic rights of Insider against Outsider" (59). While there might be some truth to this, it is probably of less consequence than the act of quickly establishing and inhabiting a strategic and tactical location. For example, the phenomenon of 'insider' and 'outsider' is just as prevalent in small American towns with regular grid layouts. It appears to be more a function of population and settlement size. In a small town, there is simply a greater probability of knowing or being casually acquainted with one's neighbors and fellow residents. Insiders are more easily able to identify a visitor to town as an outsider. In large cities, there is the contrasting phenomenon of anonymity in that there is a much larger population so there is less probability of being readily identified as an 'insider' or 'outsider.' This embeds the individual with a certain amount of social freedom in an urban setting that is usually lacking in a small town. In small settlements, it is easier to see and be seen. In large cities, it is easier to go about unnoticed. This is putting aside the phenomenon of ethnic populations locating in specific urban areas by choice or market/regulatory

 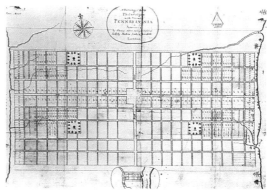

Figure 2.4 – *Colonial America: (left) Captain John Bonner's historical survey of Boston, Massachusetts in 1722; and, (right) William Penn's plan for Philadelphia in 1682.*

restrictions such as the now illegal practice of covenant restrictions in American housing during the early-to-mid 20th century. Examples of these types of urban neighborhoods often operate as enclaves. In such cases, definition of 'insider' and 'outsider' tends to shift from internalized information ("I do not know this person") to external factors ("You are different because you don't look or talk like me"). In any case, Beresford (1967) sees the regular grid layout in European bastides as an important aspect of increased commercial production and trade during the medieval period since several did not even have fortifications.

What appears more significant for a colonial town to become a center of commercial activity and trade is the selection of a strategic and tactical location. This is initially based on the evaluation of local topographical conditions in terms of generic function so to best site the town and then occupy/inhabit that town to quickly establish political and economic control over the area. In this sense, the process of colonization is reminiscent of the old common law idiom associated with adverse possession, e.g. possession is nine-tenths of the law. The regular grid as a utilitarian tool is ideally suited for colonization in that it can quickly facilitate the physical founding of a town, possession, and then establish political and economic control over the territory associated with that town. There are many examples in the historical record of military forts or fortified towns that later evolved into larger settlements and centers of commercial trade and activity and, eventually, into major cities (Reps, 1965; Kostof, 1991). However, though it appears the regular grid can help to *facilitate* this evolution, it does not – in itself – determine or embed military power, political control, or economic activity. This is why the historical record is equally replete with examples of colonial towns with regular grid layouts occupied by foreign invaders as it is those without any history of foreign occupation at all. For example, Persian dominion over Greek colonies in Asia Minor during the late Archaic Period (circa 500 BC) or British occupation of Charleston and Philadelphia during the Revolutionary War in colonial America. Ultimately, the outcome is dependent upon human action.

As a tool of land speculation

Another reason commonly cited by historians for widespread use of the regular grid in America is the division of land into rectangular plots of standardized size helps to facilitate the process and economics of land speculation. According to Reps (1979), land speculation gave shape to hundreds of American towns and cities during the 19th and 20th centuries, especially west of the Mississippi River. Kunstler (1993) suggests government legislation promulgated this outcome, specifically the 1785 Land Ordinance discussed in the previous chapter. This legislation took as its "paramount principle that land was first and foremost a commodity for capital gain… speculation became the primary basis for land distribution. Indeed, the commercial transfer of property would become the basis of American land use planning, which is hardly to say any planning at all… somebody would buy a large tract of land and subdivide it into smaller parcels at a profit… a process that continues in our time" (26). Moholy-Nagy (1968) argues that, "to the founding fathers, land was a commodity to be sliced, weighted and sold to the highest bidder" (192). Kunstler (1993) asserts that today, as in the past, many American cities flourish solely as centers for the real estate business. Reps (1979) suggests the success of these cities is representative of the power of free market capitalism whereas the failure of numerous towns in American history to survive beyond their initial plot division is equally representative of the role that chance, error, and corruption played in patterning the American urban landscape.

Barth (1975) argues Americans founded cities in the main "as sources of commercial opportunities and economic ventures" in contrast to the Europeans, who created their towns for political and social reasons as well as economic ones (153). Moholy-Nagy (1968) proposes there is a common basis for all planning traditions using the regular grid. She sees use of the regular grid as an exercise in the realization and perpetuation of social myths, whether of military, religious, or economic origin. In her opinion, the regular grid layout of American settlements was "called upon to visualize the myth of unlimited free enterprise" (83). Generally, Hillier (2002) seems to agree with this assessment, namely "an orthogonal grid town is one in which the local cultural process is in the spatial image of the global economic process, as in medieval planted towns or early American towns" (175). "Even in the case of American cities, where one of the main factors in creating the more uniform American grid is thought to be the need to parcel up land as quickly and easily as possible to facilitate economic development, we note that the grid was prior to economic development. (It) should therefore be seen as a 'spatial cultural' decision to create and use space in a certain way" (Hillier, 2002; 157). Reps (1965) views the regular grid as a tool of land speculation in the American planning tradition rather more acidly. This is based on "its intrinsic use in surveying, its adaptability to speculative activities, and its simple appeal to unsophisticated minds" (294) and that "in the frenzy of trading in town sites that characterized so much of the nineteenth century, the standardized grid became the playing board of the clever and the unscrupulous land speculator" (324). In the same way, Barth (1975) argues use of the regular grid in the American planning tradition primarily arises from its generic aspects of adaptability and efficiency (he uses the term expediency) tied to the economics of land speculation. Kostof (1991) describes this culmination of expediency and economics in land planning as fostering "good old speculative greed" (11). Rybczynski (1996) describes this as "surveying rather than town planning; the chief virtue of this approach was simplicity and speed of execution" (69). Many cite the pervasive orthogonal grid logic in Chicago as the best example of urban growth driven by land speculation activities during the 19th century (Reps, 1965). Today, cities in Florida and southern California as well as Las Vegas, Nevada probably best exemplify the real estate frenzy commonly associated with late 20th century boomtowns (Davis, 1990) (**Figure 2.5**).

Does the regular grid have egalitarian qualities?

Historians usually cite similar reasons for use of the regular grid in America as in other parts of the world. However, they often offer an additional explanation for its pervasive use in America, which is its egalitarian

Figure 2.5 – *Satellite image from 25 km of the contemporary urban fabric in: (left) Chicago, Illinois; and, (right) Las Vegas, Nevada.*

nature in promoting the equal distribution of property (Stanislawski, 1946; Mumford, 1961; Reps, 1965 and 1979; Carter, 1983; Kostof, 1991; Rybczynski, 1996). Equal distribution of property refers to the standardized layout of the regular grid generating lots where the dimensions of length, width, and depth are equal to those dimensions for all other lots similarly arranged in the layout. Reps (1979) describes the regular grid as "offering all settlers apparently equal locations for homes and businesses within its standardized structure" (x), whereas Stanislawski (1946) argues, "if equitable distribution of property is desirable, there is hardly any other plan conceivable" (106). According to Carter (1983), the American regular grid is a "testimony to an egalitarian system which made no distinction between men other than their ability to compete… that competition was best organized on the grid, on the basis of which transactions were most easily carried out" (121).

American self-identity is intimately bound to this idea since egalitarian principles are the basis for the radical American experiment in representative government. "All men are created equal, that they are endowed by their Creator with certain unalienable Rights, that among these are Life, Liberty and the pursuit of Happiness" as expressed by Thomas Jefferson in the 1776 Declaration of Independence and later given political form by James Madison in the 1787 U.S. Constitution and 1791 Bill of Rights (e.g. the first ten amendments to the U.S. Constitution). Whatever your condition in life – rich or poor, first generation American or recent immigrant, and so forth – there is equal opportunity or promise of the possibility for prosperity and success "each according to ability or achievement" in the United States (Adams, 1931). In addition, property is a protected right in the U.S. Constitution under the fourth and fifth amendments of the Bill of Rights. Citizens often see property as a means and/or realization of prosperity in the United States as part of the mythos of the American Dream. Adams (1931) describes this as the "dream of a land in which life should be better and richer and fuller for every man, with opportunity for each according to ability or achievement. A dream of social order in which each man and each woman shall be able to attain to the fullest stature of which they are innately capable, and be recognized by others for what they are, regardless of the fortuitous circumstances of birth or position" (214–215). By frequently citing equal distribution of property, some historians imply the standardization found in the regular grid is a means to create this social equality because the size of lots is similarly equal. This is a myth. However, it is an exceptionally powerful one. While all men are created equal, not all property is created equal as shown by a cursory review of any American settlement. The intrinsic logic of parallel/perpendicular streets and rectangular blocks in layout is a shared characteristic of many cities but the length and width of blocks – and, by implication, the dimensions of length, width, and depth of lots subdivided within those blocks – often vary greatly not only from settlement to settlement but also within any settlement. Finally, the well-known real estate mantra of "location, location, location" plays a critical role in differentiating property values in terms of cost and value. In a June 26, 2009 issue of his online *New York Times* blog, "On Language," columnist William Safire attributes the origins of this phrase to a 1926 real estate advertisement in the *Chicago Tribune*.

The egalitarian qualities of the regular grid as an explicit tool to generate those same qualities in American society and/or its citizens may be a myth. However, the power of that myth in contributing to the emergence of a distinctive American identity is undeniable. At best, the standardization found in the regular grid appears merely symbolic of the egalitarian principles on which the nation was founded. In this, the regular grid did help to perpetuate the American mythos of equality and opportunity for all.

For other historians, the allocating of land equally to all on *a priori* grounds by means of the regular grid actually implies no preferred social order (Stanislawski, 1946). Carter (1983) argues both views are simplistic and problematic since it is not just a characteristic of the regular grid planning tradition in America. He points out during "medieval times the equal division of land was the consequence of a landlord providing urban sites in return for money or services" (Carter, 1983; 119). This indicates the regular grid might lend itself more as a utilitarian tool for economic activity – mercantile capitalism in the case of medieval Europe and free market capitalism in the case of America – rather than as an egalitarian framework for creating or shaping a democratic society. In short, the regular grid is the simplest, cheapest, and quickest way to exploit the land (Carter, 1983). In this regard, it seems likely one of the contributing factors for its pervasive use in the United States is the expansive availability of land in the country. The land area of the contiguous United States (i.e. the lower 48 states excluding Alaska and Hawaii) is approximately 1.9 billion acres or 770 million hectares. Population estimates from 2010 for the lower 48 states was 305 million people, or an approximate population density of only one person per 7 acres (Source: U.S. Census Bureau).

The answer to 'why the regular grid' lies in both its generic and utilitarian qualities. First, its generic qualities as an artifact of physical arrangement; namely, its *quick* adaptability to differing topographical conditions for the efficient division and distribution of land. Second, its utilitarian qualities as a practical planning tool, which has been transmitted from one generation and society to another over time. This is because it was ideally suited to *facilitate* – not determine – certain social outcomes such as colonization in its broadest sense. By implication, this includes promoting political control of territories in colonization activities and mercantile/free market capitalism, especially land speculation in the American experience. Widespread use of the regular grid in America represents the culmination of both its generic and utilitarian aspects in the history of town planning.

Chapter 2 Notes

[1] For example, the typical size of a Roman legion varied over time though, generally, it would number around 10,000 troops, approximately half of which were legionaries supported by an equal number of auxiliary troops, see: Goldsworthy, A. 2003. *The Complete Roman Army*. London: Thames & Hudson, Ltd; Holder, P. 1980. *Studies in the Auxilia of the Roman Army*. British Archaeological Reports; and Elton, H. 1966. *Frontiers of the Roman Empire*. Indiana University Press.

[2] An absurd example of the role of generic function in site selection is it might be technologically feasible to construct a deep-water port in the middle of an arid desert. However, it would not be practical in terms of cost and effort. There are other readily available locations where topographical conditions are better suited for a port (for example, an inlet on the coast or via a river).

[3] Reps (1965) cites this quote from "Proposals by the Proprietors of East Jersey… for the Building of a Town on Ambo Point…," Smith, S. 1877. *The History of the Colony of Nova-Casesaria, New Jersey*. Trenton: W. S. Sharp, 544.

3

The Essential Right Angle

"The right angle is the essential and sufficient implementation of action because it enables us to determine space with an absolute exactness."
- Le Corbusier

This chapter examines the basic concepts of formal composition, meaning how the plan of the urban object is composed of geometrical elements, in the American town planning tradition. This is necessary before analyzing configuration, meaning how those elements are topographically interrelated in space syntax terms, to understand the effect of formal composition on the urban spatial network in later chapters. The purpose is narrow; namely, to avoid confusion and misconception by clarifying the parameters and terminology used for the geometrical description of American urban grids in this book. Using notional plans and historical examples, the chapter argues there is a finite set of concepts combined in regular grid planning, principally rectangularity of blocks and parallel/perpendicular streets based on the right angle. However, despite the simplicity of these concepts, regular grids are robust mechanisms for generating a seemingly infinite variety of plan compositions in real world examples. This has the effect of embedding consistencies and covariations – general to all, unique to each – in most American urban grids. Based on this investigation, the geometrical descriptions principally used in this book are linear and cross-axis (or crossroads) settlements, and deformed, orthogonal, offset, and radial grids. 'Regular' or 'regular grid' are general terms meant as inclusive of orthogonal, offset, and radial grids. We define suburban-type layouts in a later chapter because it is not necessarily formal composition that most distinguishes such layouts but rather their process effect on spatial configuration (Allen et al., 2001).

Geometrical descriptions
A cursory review of satellite imagery readily available for contemporary cities of the United States demonstrates the physical composition of American urban space is incredibly diverse (**Figure 3.1**). This occurs despite the layouts of most American settlements sharing several characteristics. Most commonly, this is a tendency to utilize rectangular blocks and parallel/perpendicular streets intersecting at right angles. There are many others but these are the most prevalent. Different American cities appear to combine a finite number of compositional characteristics, which leads

to a seemingly infinite variety of settlement patterns that are, at once, consistent to all and unique to each. We need to initially focus on better understanding this before we can investigate the relationship, if any, to the spatial configuration of American cities. To do so, we need to clarify and define the parameters and terminology used in this book for geometrical descriptions of the American urban object based on the formal composition of the plan. In doing so, we initially separate form (composition) and process (configuration) to focus on the former before reuniting with the latter through the application of space syntax (Marshall, 2005). It is accepted as a given that American settlements may not have been – and often were not – precisely realized on the ground as initially planned. It is also accepted as a given that streets and blocks in urban grids are differentiated in the third dimension by vertical construction. However, plans are a vital physical record of historical processes in a city as documented at any particular point in time. Rossi (1982) argues these processes in the city, "destruction and demolition, expropriation and rapid changes in use and as a result of speculation and obsolescence, are the most recognizable signs of urban dynamics" (22).

Geometrical descriptions are particularly relevant due to widespread use of the regular grid in American urbanism. This is because the basis for our geometrical descriptions of urban form is often order concepts, which are "a set of principles based on some generally accepted notion of sameness; repetition, geometry, rhythm, symmetry, harmony and the like" (Hanson, 1989; 22). These descriptions may be explicit because of a readily apparent geometric logic to the physical arrangement of streets and blocks in plan such as orthogonal, regular, gridiron, gridded, checkerboard, axial grid, patchwork, rectilinear, radial, and so on. These descriptions may also be implicit due to a seeming lack of a geometric logic in plan such as organic, geomorphic, deformed, and so on. Precision about our terminology is necessary to avoid confusion or misconceptions. The geometrical descriptions of urban grids principally relied upon in this book are linear, cross-axis, deformed, orthogonal, offset, and radial. 'Regular' or 'regular grid' are general terms meant to be inclusive of orthogonal, offset, and radial grids. However, we also use the terms 'radial' and 'diagonal' for the geometrical description of individual streets. Later chapters discuss and define suburban layouts in more detail. This is because there are generally three types of suburban layouts in terms of formal design. However, what is most common to suburban layouts is not formal design but their process effect on spatial configuration (Allen et al., 2001). Before discussing

Figure 3.1 – *Satellite view from 12 km: (left) New York, the most populous city in the United States (2000 metropolitan population: 18,323,002); (middle) Los Angeles, the second most populous city in the United States (2000 population: 12,365,627); and, (right) the national capital Washington, D.C. (2000 population: 4,796,183) (Source: U.S. Census Bureau).*

and defining the different types of regular grid patterns in American settlements, we begin with the right angle itself to demonstrate several things. First, there are a limited number of possibilities for formal composition when exclusively using the right angle in town planning. Second, despite this, many different urban patterns arise from this relatively simplistic, limited set of possibilities. Lastly, this discussion serves as the heuristic basis for reviewing the qualitative classification of more than 700 American historical town plans from a previous study in the next chapter (Major, 2015a).

The right angle

When it comes to the right angle, there is a finite set of possibilities where there is correspondence between connection, as defined in space syntax methodology, and intersection as commonly defined in the planning profession. In space syntax, a connection is the point where only two axial lines (i.e. lines of sight) intersect with each other. An intersection is a two-dimensional convex space defined by building facades in plan that encompasses all of the connections between two or more streets (or axial lines) in a node. This correspondence appears relevant for defining regularity in an urban grid. In this section, we use theoretical models to illustrate the limited possibilities for layouts based on the right angle and begin to define the compositional parameters we are particularly interested regarding American settlements. For the purposes of characterizing formal composition of the plan in this chapter, we are only interested in how streets relate to the intrinsic logic of the layout itself and not to the outside world.

First, a simple right angle connection between two streets where only two directions are feasible in terms of the layout itself (either in defining the perimeter of the layout or internally within it) is a two-way intersection. In the case of two-way intersections, where one street terminates is where another one begins. A right angle connection between two streets where only three directions are feasible in terms of the layout itself is a three-way intersection. In the case of three-way intersections, one street terminates where another street continues. Like two-way intersections, a three-way intersection can also define the perimeter of the layout due to being the termination point of a street at the edge. Lastly, two streets that connect with each other at a right angle to form a cross-axis where four directions are possible is a four-way intersection because the streets continue beyond the connection in four directions (**Figure 3.2**). A simple layout composed of four rectangular blocks with a central cross-axis is the minimal requirement for a crossroads settlement. A linear settlement is one where buildings are gathered along a single street and a block structure defined by crossing streets has not been established yet, usually due to a lack of growth. In these minimal conditions for a cross-axis (or crossroads) settlement, it is

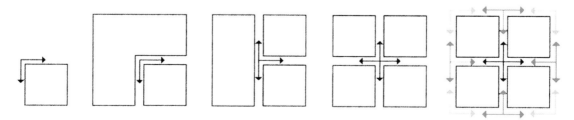

Figure 3.2 – *Right angle street intersections: (left to right) two-way intersection along the perimeter of a layout; two-way intersection internal to a layout; three-way intersection internal to a layout; four-way intersection forming a cross-axis; and, 1 four-way intersection, 4 three-way intersections, and 4 two-way intersections in a simple 3 x 3 street (or 2 x 2 block) layout with 9 right angle intersections.*

composed of nine connections: 1 four-way intersection for a cross-axis at the center of – and internal to – the layout; 4 three-way intersections at the termination of the cross-axis streets on the periphery; and 4 two-way intersections for the streets defining the corners of the layout at the perimeter. Accessing more than four directions from a connection based on a right angle is not feasible since the intersection of more than two streets with each other in a node would require, by definition, that one of those connections occur at something other than 90 degrees or change direction using right angles (i.e. left, then right or vice versa).

A layout entirely composed of two-way intersections at right angles would be an outward facing block since four streets define the perimeter of the layout (**Figure 3.3**, left). The block is, by definition, oriented to its perimeter and the outside world. A layout composed of two-way intersections at right angles internal to that layout is only possible in a closed system since successive right angle intersections would be composed of parallel paths internal to and along the perimeter, and neither network would be accessible to the other except via the block itself. This plan concept actually should be familiar. For example, this is the basic layout in many modern office buildings with office spaces defining the perimeter of the building around an internal mechanical core and between which is the primary circulation system on each floor of the building (**Figure 3.3**, middle) (Penn and Hillier, 1992).[1] This is also the basic concept for many historical forts and Spanish presidios in North America. The difference is often there was not an internal block but rather an open space to marshal troops for defense of the presidio, allow for multi-directional internal movement, and use as a market square in commercial activities (Reps, 1965 and 1979). This can been seen more clearly in the 1820 plans for the Spanish presidios in San Francisco and San Diego, California (**Figure 3.3**, right and **Figure 3.4**, left).

This may also explain what Reps (1965) describes as the unusual plan for the French Huguenot settlement of Manakin, Virginia circa 1700 (**Figure 3.4**, middle on next page). He describes this plan as something of "a mystery" because "its details and scale" are unclear (440). However, he suggests the "four-corners of the square were reserved for public uses (with) gardens between a double row of houses on two sides of the square fronting the woods and the river on the other two sides. As the danger from the Indians passed and the Huguenots became familiar with their surroundings, the original compact settlement gradually disappeared" (443). Reps (1965) does not provide any description for

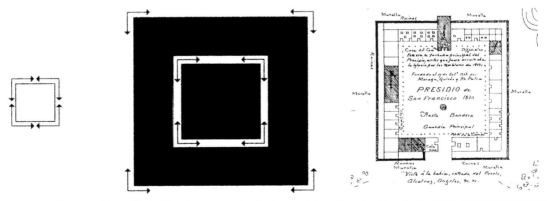

Figure 3.3 – (left) Outward facing block with perimeter streets forming two-way intersections at right angles; (middle) two blocks with internal and perimeter streets forming two-way intersections at right angles in a closed system; and, (right) Spanish presidio prototype in 1820 plan for San Francisco, California.

what the elongated lines (some dotted) represented at the 'entrance' of this settlement. In the plan, they are along the alignment of cross-axis streets. However, in comparison to the presidio plans in San Francisco and San Diego, it suggests the Huguenots designed this layout to transform into a closed system for defensive purposes much in the same manner. The row of outward facing houses would actually form the fortifications of the settlement. If this were the case, then it would seem a less than ideal version of the Spanish model with row houses serving as a compromise for the construction of fortifications. This would make residents of the outward facing houses more vulnerable during an attack (they would have to get inside before the gates were closed) than those occupying the row houses facing inward towards Nicholson Square. Finally, if residents sought refuge within Nicholson Square during an attack, they would be sacrificing any personal property in the outward facing houses after closing the gates. However, the Huguenot settlement survived and eventually thrived so the defensive capabilities of this modified presidio plan were either effective or never tested.

A simple layout composed of 2 two-way intersections along a single path that deviates at successive right angles internal to a layout and 4 two-way intersections at the corners of the perimeter is feasible. However, 2 three-way intersections form where the path passing through the layout terminates at the perimeter. A regular grid layout composed almost entirely of three-way intersections except 4 two-way intersections for the perimeter streets at the corners of the layout would generate a 'brickwork pattern.' Such a layout could also still be predominantly composed of three-way intersections but prioritize the central cross-axis streets by utilizing 1 four-way intersection and introducing 2 two-way intersections in the upper left and lower right quadrants or vice versa. Finally, it could still be predominantly composed of three-way intersections and prioritize only a single street of the central cross-axis by introducing 4 two-way intersections in each quadrant of the layout. This would have the effect of loading intersections onto a single cross-axis street whilst eliminating all intersections to the other except for the four-way intersection of the cross-axis streets themselves (**Figure 3.5**, next page). All of these plans are regular grids because parallel/perpendicular streets and intersections occurring at a right angle characterize the layouts except for the first, which is just two L-shaped blocks oriented to each other. However, there were not any historical plans remotely similar to these layouts in a sample of more than 700 American town plans from a previous study (Major, 2015a). The key difference in these layouts is the absence or deficiency

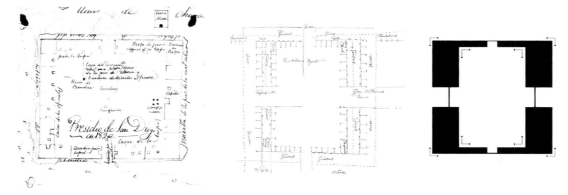

Figure 3.4 – (left) Spanish presidio prototype in 1820 plan for San Diego, California; (middle) plan of Manakin, Virginia circa 1700; and, (right) model for Manakin consisting of L-shaped blocks with row houses forming rudimentary fortifications for the settlement. The principal right angles shown in the layout are a visual reference to the closed system model in Figure 3.3.

of four-way intersections at a right angle compared to that typically found in American settlements. The brickwork layouts in Figure 3.5 bear some resemblance to the reconstructed plan for the Aztec city Tenochtitlán in Pre-Columbian Mesoamerica (see **Figure A.16** in Chapter 7). This suggests the layout in Tenochtitlán may have maintained the rectangular shape of dwellings to the exclusion of locating those dwellings to generate four-way street intersections except for the ceremonial axes themselves, which would have prioritized these longer streets in the layout (Hillier, 1996b and 2009b). This is in contrast to the American planning tradition where block size and shape varies greatly and four-way intersections at right angles to form a parallel/perpendicular street logic is the primary consideration in the manner shown for the orthogonal grid layout to the far right in Figure 3.5.

All of these layouts are regular grids utilizing 16 blocks. Seventy-five percent of the blocks in the second layout shown (excluding the first layout of two L-shaped blocks oriented to each other) are the same size and shape. Fifty percent of the blocks in the third and fourth layouts are the same size and shape. All of the blocks in the orthogonal layout are the same size and shape. This difference helps to define efficiency for surveying the regular grid as discussed in the previous chapter. For the brickwork layouts in Figure 3.5, surveying 21 or 22 streets is necessary. For the orthogonal layout in Figure 3.5, surveying is necessary for only ten streets. An orthogonal grid layout utilizing the maximum number of four-way street intersections at right angles for the minimum number of streets requires less than half the amount of surveying work. Therefore, it is twice as efficient (or more so) than those layouts predominantly composed of three-way intersections at right angles. Finally, two-, three- and four-way street intersections at right angles are not exclusive to the regular grid. For example, the 1640 plan of Boston makes use of four- and three-way intersections at right angles even though it is a deformed grid layout. It is the repetitive use of four-way street intersections at a right angle to form a parallel/perpendicular street network that principally defines the geometric logic of the regular grid.

The grid pattern

Hillier (1999a and 2009b) argues the deformed grid layout of organic cities actually possesses a consistent geometric logic. The geometry characterizing deformed grids is near right angle connections usually within 15 degrees of a right angle and very obtuse angles usually within 15 degrees of a direct continuation with angles near to 45 degrees occurring less frequently. The result is principal streets tend to be composed of successive lines of sight that terminate on building facades at an open angle (i.e. greater than 90 degrees) and serve to indicate the continuation of that street. Secondary streets tend to connect to principal streets at or near right angles. A deformed grid layout tends to emerge from a local process of aggregation in a settlement; that is, the aggregating of dwellings based on simple, purely local rules (Hillier and Hanson, 1984). However,

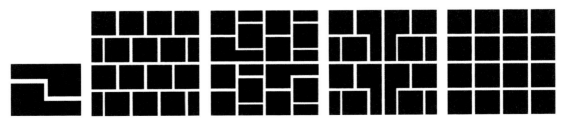

Figure 3.5 – Layouts using right angles (left to right): two-way intersections along a single internal path; brickwork layout composed almost entirely of three-way intersections; brickwork layout prioritizing both streets of the cross-axis; brickwork layout only prioritizing one cross-axis street; and, orthogonal grid layout entirely composed of internal four-way intersections.

during the evolution of urban form in a deformed grid layout, streets also tend to become straighter and wider and blocks larger in size to varying degrees, more so in European settlements (Hanson, 1989) and less so in Middle Eastern ones (Karimi, 1997 and 1998). Boston, Massachusetts is probably the best example of a city with a deformed grid layout in the United States (**Figure 3.6**).

An orthogonal grid is composed of similar blocks and streets laying and intersecting at right angles to each other, which form a regularly spaced layout defined by the intrinsic parallel/perpendicular logic between those streets and blocks. Settlements with orthogonal grids often maintain this intrinsic logic to the exclusion of other factors such as topography or function. This usually occurs initially during the early stages of growth but also potentially for a significant amount of time. Orthogonal grids may also vary block size or shape and street widths as long as the intrinsic logic of parallel/perpendicular streets intersecting at right angles is consistent. Many orthogonal grids also possess an order in their formal composition beyond that of parallel and perpendicular streets; for example, plan symmetry. Stewart and Golubitsky (1992) define symmetry as "not a thing, it's a transformation… that leaves (the object) apparently unchanged… we say apparently because, although after the transformation the overall form of the object is the same as it was before, the object itself has moved" (28). This is actually of secondary importance in defining the characteristics of an orthogonal grid. However, it is useful to briefly demonstrate the principles of plan symmetry for later discussions about the 17th century Nine Square Plan of New Haven and 18th century 'ward model' plan of Savannah.

Figure 3.7 (top, next page) shows an orthogonal grid utilizing one block size and shape (a square) composed of 16 blocks in a 4 x 4 layout. It is composed of 10 parallel/perpendicular streets of the same length and width in a 5 x 5 layout with 25 intersections, all of which are at a right angle. This layout is completely symmetrical in plan. It can be rotated and remain the same. It possesses a bilateral symmetry along its central axis in the horizontal and vertical dimensions where one half of the layout can be folded and remain perfectly reflective of the other. The same is true along a diagonal axis from any corner to its opposite (Stewart and Golubitsky, 1992). **Figure 3.7** (middle, next page) shows the same orthogonal layout except for differentiating the street widths of the cross-axis

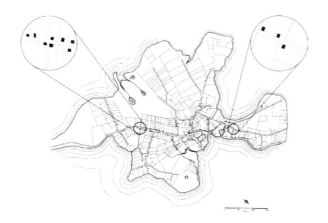 

Figure 3.6 – *Boston, Massachusetts: (left) four- and three-way street intersections at right angles in the deformed grid layout of Boston in 1640; and, (right) contemporary street view of Washington Street illustrating lines of sight terminates on building facades at an open angle.*

streets. This layout is also perfectly symmetrical in plan. **Figure 3.7** (bottom) shows an orthogonal layout where three block sizes and shapes (square, rectangle, and L-shaped) are differentiated in addition to the wider width of the cross-axis streets. It is composed of 24 blocks in a 4 x 6 layout and 12 streets in a 5 x 7 layout with 35 intersections, all at a right angle. This layout only possesses bilateral symmetry along its central axis streets in the horizontal and vertical dimensions. All of these layouts are orthogonal grids because the intrinsic logic of parallel/perpendicular streets intersecting at a right angle is consistent. However, they are also subtly different from each another due to variations in block size and shape, street width, and/or the total number of streets and intersections at a right angle.

Figure 3.8 (left) shows another layout that does not vary in block size or street width. Highlighted in gray is an area consistent in size and shape with the top layout in Figure 3.7. This provides a reference for clarity in the subsequent illustrations of this chapter. The blocks defining the edges of this layout eliminate any symmetry in plan because street lengths are now varied. By definition, the perimeter of a settlement will be multi-directional with reference to the outside world in its undifferentiated periphery. However, at this point in clarifying our terminology, we are only interested in the intrinsic relationship of streets and blocks in the formal composition of the layout itself. A layout like this may occur *a priori* in designing the plan for a settlement before it is founded but, most often, in aggregating blocks of similar size and shape in a manner consistent with the pre-existing logic of the original grid during subsequent growth. In terms of composition, this is still an orthogonal grid because the intrinsic logic of parallel and perpendicular streets intersecting at a right angle is consistent. **Figure 3.8** (middle) shows a similar but larger layout where blocks defining an edge of the plan

are irregular in shape. This is due to local topographical conditions such as a river. For our purposes, the terms 'topography' and 'topographical' are used in this book in a broader sense to mean the study of place rather than the more common – and narrower – definition in the United States as the study of elevations and contours. Pervasive application of the orthogonal grid logic leads to streets and blocks terminating at the riverbank. In this case, the geometrical order of plan ignores the topography of the river. This is not unusual. Lot lines often extend into partially submerged lands. Owners fill the submerged portion of the property in order to make the lot rectangular in shape and, hence, more buildable. The narrowing of the width of rivers in several major cities across the world over time (for example, the River Thames in London) is a characteristic of this phenomenon. Beachfront lots in Florida today often extend several hundred feet into

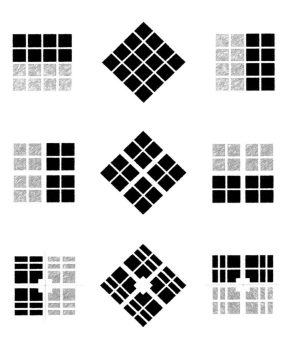

Figure 3.7 – Orthogonal layouts: (top) no variation in block size/shape and street length/width; (middle) width of cross-axis streets is different from others; and, (bottom) block size/shape and width of cross-axis streets are varied. The blocks shaded in gray are a visual reference to demonstrate the symmetry of the plan along central cross-axis streets in the horizontal and vertical dimension.

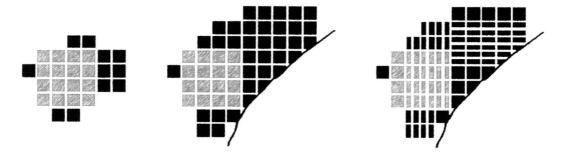

Figure 3.8 – Orthogonal grid layouts where: (left) only variation is street length due to edge definition; (middle) irregular block shapes/sizes emerge from pervasively realizing the orthogonal grid logic of the plan despite local topography; and, (right) additional variations in block size/shape and street width.

the submerged waters of the Atlantic Ocean, which is the result of soil erosion, i.e. the shoreline of the beach was further out at the time the lots lines were originally platted. Despite the irregular shaped blocks adjacent to the riverbank, this layout is still an orthogonal grid since all street intersections occur at a right angle. **Figure 3.8** (right) shows the same layout but with more variations in block size and shape, and street widths. This is an orthogonal grid, too.

All orthogonal grids are regular grids but not all regular grids are orthogonal grids. Even if you formulate a regular grid in which the pattern of streets in either dimension is randomly distributed so no two urban blocks have the same size and shape, it is still a regular grid because the orthogonal nature of the grid is defined by the intersection of all streets at a right angle. A regular grid is also principally composed of blocks and streets laying and intersecting at right angles to each other to form a regularly spaced layout. However, the intrinsic parallel and perpendicular logic is only consistent between some but not all streets and blocks in the layout since it is composed of offset grids. Offset grids are multiple orthogonal grids laid out along different alignments to each other in the same settlement. This type of regular grid tends to have greater variety in the size and shape of blocks, and the length and width of streets, than an orthogonal grid. **Figure 3.9** (left) shows a layout similar to that presented in Figure 3.8. However, the orthogonal grid logic of the plan terminates before the blocks and streets reach the topographical boundary of the riverbank. This has the effect of generating a diagonal street, which runs parallel to the riverbank to define that edge of the layout. This street aligns, more or less, at a 45-degree angle to all other streets in the settlement. The introduction of this single diagonal street at the edge of the layout is important. First, every street in the layout is parallel and perpendicular to each other, except for the diagonal. Second, the overwhelming majority of blocks are rectangular and street intersections are at a right angle. Lastly, the diagonal only defines one edge instead of internal to the layout.

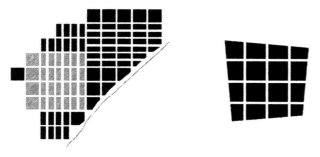

Figure 3.9 – Orthogonal grid where: (left) streets/irregular shaped blocks stop short of topographical boundary and a diagonal street defines the edge; and, (right) irregular edge definition with perimeter streets along a different alignment to the internal logic of parallel/perpendicular streets in the layout.

The basics of configuration

Space syntax represents built environments using the line, convex space, and visual field. All are a set of points in space bound in a particular way related to human use, i.e. moving, occupying, and seeing. What is configuration? Configuration is a relational system using topological graph theory where any *local* change in a system can have *global* effects across that system (Hillier, 1993 and 1996b).

Take two objects, say a cube; one marked 'a' and the other 'b' in a vacuum. They are in a mathematical relationship to each other so 'a' is to 'b' as 'b' is to 'a' (**Figure A.6**). When we establish this relationship to a third object, say the surface of the Earth (marked 'c'), it becomes a configurational relationship. As long as the objects remain distinct, then the mathematical relationship is 'a' is to 'c' as 'b' is to 'c' but, in order to reach 'a' from 'b' or *vice versa*, we have to pass through 'c'. The corresponding topological graph makes this clear, treating each object as a *node* and their relation (e.g. *vertices*) as a line; 'c' is shallower or more accessible to 'a' and 'b' than either are to each other. The *depth* of 'a' and 'b' is three, whereas the depth of 'c' to the others is only two and total depth is eight in this system of objects. We can place 'a' and 'b' next to each other to explicitly introduce the idea of permeability or *connection*. Now, this system of objects is in a symmetrical relationship where all spaces are equally *shallow or accessible* to each other, so 'a' is to 'b' as 'b' is to 'c'. In this case, the depth of any object to all others is two and total depth is six in the system. We can place 'b' on top of 'a' to establish an asymmetrical relationship to the surface of the Earth ('c'), like floors in a building. You have to pass through 'a' to reach 'b' from 'c'. However, it is unnecessary to pass through 'b' to go from 'c' to 'a' or *vice versa*. In this case, the depth of 'b' and 'c' is three and the depth of 'a' is only two in the system. Total depth in this asymmetrical relationship is eight (Major, 2000b). According to Hillier (2005b), "space syntax seeks to formulate mathematically the configurational properties of space that we intuit, as manifested in the way… we construct real spatial patterns through building and cities" using topological graph theory to measure these spatial properties (6).

The topological graph is the basis for calculating a relativized mean depth for every space to every other in the network of the layout for whichever selected representation, e.g. line, convex space, visual field; relativized

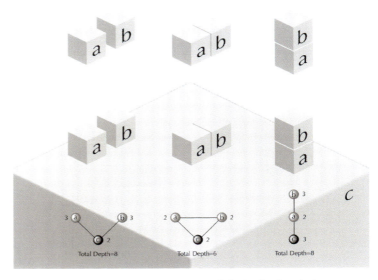

Figure A.6 – *The basics of configuration in space syntax.*

because as built environments become larger, a continuous sequence like a labyrinth or maze becomes increasingly improbable.

Today, space syntax software 'virtually' draws topological graphs from every space and calculates a variety of measures for networks using sophisticated algorithms. Generations of programmers, beginning with Coates and Czapski through Dalton to Alasdair Turner and Tasos Varoudis, are responsible for the evolution of these algorithms over the years. However, students of space syntax still learn the rudimentary drawing of the topological graphs and the calculating of relativized mean depth. Some continue to do so for the smallest buildings (typically, houses) because the graphs, in themselves, are often fascinating. We can justify or order graphs from a common space (i.e. entry, living, kitchen, bedroom) across a set of particular housing types (e.g. architect, style, region, historical period, and so on). For example, for comparing rings of circulation in Peter Eisenman's constructed House III to the almost continuous sequence of spaces in his unbuilt House IV (Major and Sarris, 1999 and 2001) (**Figure A.7**). Justified graphs can provide an illuminating picture of domestic functions from a particular point of view (i.e. visitors, men, women, children, servants) as designed and embedded in the spatial organization of the house (Hanson, 1998). More importantly, calculations based on topological graphs provide quantitative measures about the characteristics of architectural and urban space (via the mechanism of *connection*) common to all buildings and cities, not unique to a particular architectural style, geographical region, economic system, or planning method. This provides an objective, mathematical foundation for the scientific investigation of built environments.

Urban street networks are too large and complex to make effective use of topological graphs in this graphical manner. Nonetheless, topological graphs underlie every representation (most usually, lines in the axial map of a city) as the basis for quantitative measures of the configurational network at the urban level. In doing so, space syntax provides a powerful means to objectively investigate and understand the design and dynamics of urban space in neighborhoods, cities, and metropolitan regions.

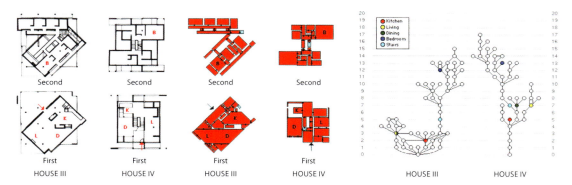

Figure A.7 – *(from left to right) Floor plans, convex maps and justified graphs from main entry space in Peter Eisenman's House III and House IV. All indicate the location of principal domestic functions (e.g. entry space, living, kitchen, dining, stairs and master bedroom).*

Another key difference is that connection as defined in space syntax methodology and intersection, as commonly defined in planning as a node where two or more streets intersect, do not necessarily correspond with each other any longer in this plan. A tendency for connection and intersection to correspond with one another in a layout is a characteristic of the orthogonal grid. As demonstrated in Figure 3.9, it is debatable whether edge definition in itself is sufficient to characterize the layout as anything other than an orthogonal grid. It depends on whether we are talking about composition or configuration (Marshall, 2005); or, if you like, the difference between design intent and the real world impossibility of mathematical purity in the physical object. The same distinction applies to edge definition as determined by street alignments. This is because if taken to its logical conclusion, then no layout could ever be accurately described as an orthogonal grid.[2]

The regular grid
Figure 3.9 (right, page 59) shows a 4 x 4 block layout composed of 16 blocks, of which only 4 (or 25%) are rectangular. The rest of the blocks are irregular in shape. It is also a 5 x 5 street layout composed of 10 streets and 25 intersections, of which only nine intersections (or 36%) are at a right angle. Six of the streets (or 60%) are parallel and perpendicular to each other in the layout. This is still an orthogonal grid even though only 9 street intersections (or 36%) are at a right angle because all of these right angle intersections are internal to the layout. In fact, we can determine

on this basis the minimum parameters for the formal composition of an orthogonal grid. It is a 3 x 3 layout with 9 blocks comprising a 4 x 4 layout of 8 streets and 16 intersections where a minimum of 4 parallel and perpendicular streets are internal to the layout. This is the basic plan model outlined in the Spanish Laws of the Indies and used for the Nine Square Plan of New Haven (see Chapter 1). This suggests the parallel/perpendicular relationship of streets and their connection via a right angle *internal* to the layout – more so than propensity of rectangular blocks or street intersections at right angles in sum – is what most defines the geometrical nature of a regular grid.

Figure 3.10 (left) shows an example of a layout composed on offset grids. The boundary between the grid sections generates a diagonal street that runs from edge-to-edge of the layout – parallel/perpendicular to one layout but not the other – and along which street intersections occur at something other than a right angle. Diagonal streets such as these often become functionally important in settlements composed of offset grids (Clay, 1973). This layout is composed of 120 blocks, the overwhelming majority of which are rectangular in shape, and 40 streets, the overwhelming majority of which intersect at a right angle. About half

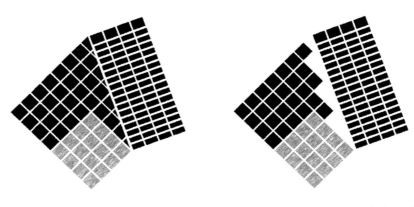

Figure 3.10 – *Offset grid layout where: (left) orthogonal grids along different alignments to each other and boundary between forms a diagonal street from edge-to-edge of the settlement; and, (right) orthogonal grid logic defines regularity for majority of streets/blocks in the settlement.*

of the streets run parallel/perpendicular to each other in one grid but not to those in the other half. An offset grid layout usually occurs in response to external factors such as topography and/or the division of the land in a parent tract along a similar alignment. This layout is still a regular grid because it is predominantly defined in geometric terms by the intrinsic logic of parallel/perpendicular streets and intersections occurring at a right angle, which comprises the majority of the layout though it now takes place along two different alignments. **Figure 3.10** (right) shows this more clearly with all of the non-rectangular shaped blocks removed from the layout.

The rapid growth of San Francisco offers a good example of offset grids in the planning of an American settlement. San Francisco was founded on the farthest tip of a peninsula surrounded by the Pacific Ocean and San Francisco Bay. The first orthogonal grid laid out in 1847–48 was to the east of the Spanish presidio in the area of Bay Street. Due to the California Gold Rush in 1848, San Francisco became a boomtown over night and there was an explosion of growth in the settlement (Reps, 1965 and 1979). The layout rapidly grew to the south and east along the same alignment of the original grid until the planning of a new gridiron section along a different alignment to the south in 1849 (**Figure 3.11**). These two grid sections encompass almost the entire northeast area of the peninsula. The boundary between them is Market Street, which "served as the dividing line between these two sections of the city. Today that broad street and the larger blocks to the southeast confine the (central) business district centering on Union Square to the older portion of the city. The compactness and convenience of the San Francisco business district is largely due to this happy accident originating in a scramble to lay out streets and blocks in the competition of real estate development" (Reps, 1965; 304). Hillier (1996b) argues examples such as these are "unlikely to have occurred by chance" (337). Market Street aligns from the eastern shoreline of the peninsula towards the southwest where there was more raw land at the time, which was soon developed. This new alignment for the grid section and Market Street was likely for two reasons. First, there was the potential of lengthening Market Street to the southwest to exploit undeveloped land on the peninsula. Second, to generate rectangular blocks for waterfront lots on San Francisco Bay at the eastern edge of the new grid section due to local topographical conditions of the shoreline at that location. Today, Market Street remains one of the most important streets in San Francisco (Reps, 1965). **Figure 3.11** (right) shows the early stages of growth for the

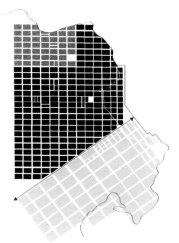

Figure 3.11 – (left) 1849 plan of San Francisco, California; and, (right) drawing showing the earliest orthogonal grid layout (shaded in dark gray), growth of this orthogonal grid logic (in black), and the new 1849 grid section along a different alignment (in light gray) from the original layout.

San Francisco urban grid. Adjacent to the Spanish Presidio, the first orthogonal was laid out (in dark gray). Initial rapid growth of the town occurred along this orthogonal grid logic (in black) before the new grid section was laid out in 1849 along a different alignment (in light gray). A line with arrowheads indicates the diagonal street generated as the 'seam' between these offset grids, i.e. Market Street (Clay, 1973). We can also see the effect of human intervention in shaping the shoreline of the San Francisco peninsula (shown as a sequence of black and white lines in Figure 3.11 but more readily apparent in the 1849 plan).

A regular grid may also incorporate radial streets along which intersections occur at something other than a right angle. **Figure 3.12** (left) shows the same layout as in Figure 3.9 but incorporating radial streets through a central square to the edges of the settlement. The radial streets are aligned, more or less, parallel and perpendicular to the riverbank and the diagonal street defining that edge of the layout. Most blocks are rectangular and the overwhelming majority of street intersections occur at a right angle. What defines the radial nature of these streets – and hence the plan itself – is their alignment at 45 degrees to the orthogonal logic in the rest of the layout. **Figure 3.12** (right) shows this more clearly with all of the non-rectangular shaped blocks removed from the layout. We often describe this type of layout as a radial plan but it is also a regular grid because of deploying radial elements within a predominant orthogonal grid logic. This variation on regularity can occur *a priori* in designing a radial plan before the founding of the settlement; for example, most famously in Pierre Charles L'Enfant's plan for the national capital in Washington, D.C. **Figure 3.13** shows the 1792 plan for Washington, D.C. (left) and the block structure with all of the non-rectangular blocks removed (right). This demonstrates several interesting things about L'Enfant's plan. First, non-rectangular shaped bocks arise from both radial planning principles and local topographical conditions, which mostly define the east, west, and south boundaries of the plan. Second, despite this, two-thirds of the urban blocks in the plan are still rectangular. Third, the cumulative effect is to generate orthogonal grid 'clusters' (some large, some truncated) formally defined by radial streets and non-rectangular blocks at their edges. Fourth, this effectively 'internalizes' rectangular blocks within these clusters of the plan. Lastly, of notable interest, is the degree of variation L'Enfant introduces by varying the length or width of rectangular blocks throughout this plan. Historians are effusive in their praise of L'Enfant's grand plan for Washington, D.C. but often silent about assessing this block structure, content to allow the looming historical figures (Pierre Charles L'Enfant, Thomas Jefferson, and George Washington, in particular) involved in the planning of the National Capital to speak for themselves through their written records (Reps, 1965; Moholy-Nagy, 1968; Kostof,

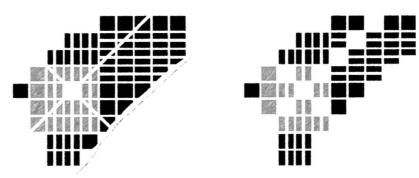

Figure 3.12 – *Regular grid layout where: (left) radial streets run from a central public space to settlement edges; and, (right) radial nature defined with reference to the orthogonal grid logic in the rest of the layout with the non-rectangular blocks removed.*

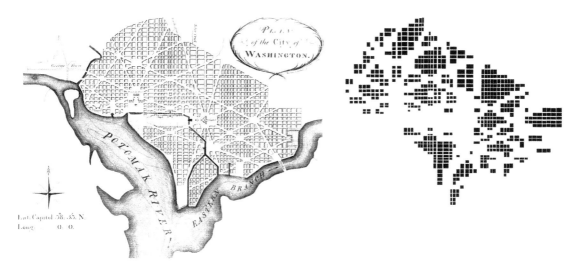

Figure 3.13 – *Washington, D.C.: (left) Pierre L'Enfant plan for the national capital in Washington, D.C. as revised by Andrew Ellicott in 1792; and, (right) with the non-rectangular blocks removed.*

1991). It is possible this complicated block structure – in combination with the less than ideal local topographical conditions for city building, e.g. Ronald Reagan's 1983 comment to "drain the swamp" of big government in Washington, D.C. has a long political history in the United States, which seems intimately tied to the origins of building the national capital – played a contributory role in the long gestation period (relative to the rapid growth of other American boomtowns) before urban growth accelerated in the national capital during and after the U.S. Civil War. The population of Washington, D.C. grew 75.4% from 1860 to 1870; the largest period of population growth in the city after the initial decade of its founding (Source: U.S. Census Bureau). This complicated block structure was simply less efficient to survey based on the terms defined in this chapter. In any case, the radial planning variations on regularity can also occur by extensive interventions in the existing urban fabric. For example, Daniel Burnham's proposals for several American cities including Chicago and San Francisco during the City Beautiful Movement of the late 19th/early 20th century or Haussmann's renovation of Paris during the mid-19th century (Reps, 1965 and 1979). In defining and examining these basic concepts of formal composition in the plan of the American urban object, we have laid some necessary groundwork before analyzing configuration so we can better understand the effect of plan composition on urban spatial networks in later chapters. There are a finite set of concepts combined in regular grid planning, principally rectangularity of blocks and parallel/perpendicular streets based on the right angle. However, despite the simplicity of these concepts, regular grids are robust mechanisms for generating a seemingly infinite variety of plan compositions in real world examples.

Chapter 3 Notes

[1] Most dwellings – or even a room – are nothing more than a built environment with a layout that can become a closed system by securing the door, as long as there is one to close.
[2] In fact, there is no such thing as a perfectly orthogonal grid. There will always be some geometrical deviation to the built form in the real world.

4

The Regular Grid in America

"Order and chaos are seen as two opposites,
poles upon which we pivot our interpretations of the world."
- Ian Stewart

This chapter briefly reviews the findings for a survey of regular grid planning in a historical record of American town plans (Major, 2015a). For this survey, a broadly representative sample of more than 700 American town plans from 1565 to 1961 – a large majority from the 18th and 19th centuries – was compiled from various sources (Major, 2015a). A significant portion is associated with more than a quarter of all urban areas populated by 40,000 or more people in the United States today, including a large majority of the 50 largest. The purpose is to qualify the extent and frequency of regular grid planning in the United States by identifying the formal composition of American settlements as recorded in town plans over time and space, i.e. from early colonization to westward expansion. The chapter argues town planning in America was predisposed to regularity from the very beginning of colonization of the New World. This was because of extensive use of the bastide model in early colonial settlements as well as colonization occurring during the European Renaissance and Age of Enlightenment, which emphasized order concepts in town planning. The regulatory framework imposed by the 1785 Land Ordinance for the practical division and distribution of land only served to *intensify* the American predisposition towards regularity. In this sense, the American town planning tradition represents the epitome of the Renaissance city ideal, what Boyer (1983) characterizes as the American dream of a rational city.

American town plans

A historical record of more than 700 town plans was compiled for qualitative analysis from a multitude of secondary sources in a previous study (Major, 2015a). The majority is in the digital collections of the University of Texas Perry-Castañeda Library Map Collection, University of Georgia Hargrett Library Rare Map Collection, Texas State Library and Archives Commission, and John Reps' two books, *The Making of Urban America* (1965) and *Cities of the American West* (1979). Several are topographical maps accurately depicting streets and/or building footprints in a settlement at the date of the plan's creation by the U.S. Geological Survey after its establishment in 1879.

A significant portion of the town plans is associated with more than a quarter of all urban areas populated by 40,000 or more people in the United States in the 2000 census, including a large majority of the 50 largest urban areas. The U.S. Census Bureau defines an urban area as contiguous census block groups with a population density of at least 1,000 inhabitants per square mile (386 people/km^2), with any census block groups around this core having a density of at least 500 inhabitants per square mile (193 people/km^2). The U.S. Census Bureau delineation of urban areas, urbanized areas (i.e. population over 50,000), and urban clusters (i.e. population less than 50,000) does not account for political boundaries. According to this definition, there are a little over 500 urban areas with a population of at least 40,000 people in the United States (excluding Alaska, Hawaii, and Puerto Rico) based on the 2000 census (**Figure 4.1**). The sample of historical town plans is representative of 140 or 27% of these urban areas. The Census Bureau considers several settlements for which plans are included in the sample as part of larger urban areas. For example, Tacoma (plans dated 1869, 1873, and 1880) and Fort Worth (plan dated 1894) are part of the Seattle and Dallas urban areas, respectively. The suburbs Lake Forest (plan dated 1857) and Riverside (plan dated 1869) are part of the Chicago urban area. About 70% of the plans compiled are associated with the 140 urban areas represented in the sample. About 30% of the plans in the sample are located in non-urban areas as defined by the U.S. Census Bureau (i.e. fewer than 40,000 people). Finally, the sample includes historical plans for 44 of the 50 largest urban areas in the United States today. This includes several plans for some of the largest urban areas at various times such as eleven plans for Charleston from 1672–1885, twelve plans for Philadelphia from 1682–1898, ten plans for New York from 1660–1838, twenty-two plans for New Orleans, Louisiana from 1720–1954, and twenty plans for Savannah from 1733–1900. The six urban areas not represented in the sample of historical plans are (in rank order according to population size from largest to smallest): Miami, Florida; Minneapolis-St. Paul,

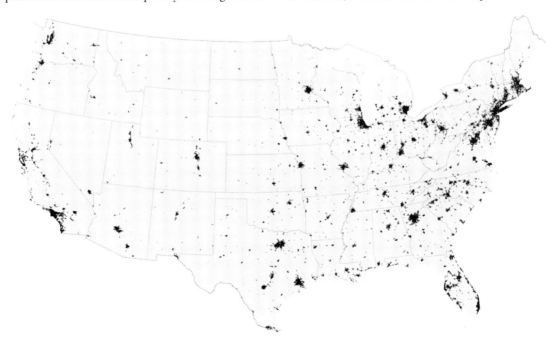

Figure 4.1 – *U.S. Census Bureau map of urban areas and urban clusters (in black) in the contiguous United States in 2000.*

Minnesota; Tampa-St. Petersburg, Florida; Riverside-San Bernardino, California; Virginia Beach, Virginia; and Charlotte, North Carolina. This is due to mere unavailability of plans for whatever reason.

The purpose of this heuristic exercise is to qualify the extent and frequency of regular grid planning in the United States by identifying the formal composition of American settlements as recorded in their town plans over time and space, i.e. from early colonization to westward expansion. In particular, how really widespread was historical use of regular grids in American settlements? To understand this, we need to determine the degree to which the best characterization of a historical town plan is regular or deformed, or some other kind of layout. Of additional interest is the degree to which the 1785 Land Ordinance affected the frequency of regularity in this historical record of American town plans, if at all. The parameters and terminology defined in the previous chapter serve as the basis for evaluating and classifying the formal composition of the town plans. Namely, the propensity for street intersections at or near right angles based on a consistent logic of parallel/perpendicular streets across the entirety or large portions of the layout in settlements over time. For the purposes of characterizing plan composition in this review, we are again primarily interested in the intrinsic logic of streets in the layout itself, not to the outside world. Finally, the focus of this review is the record of town plans *en masse* instead of the composition or growth of any particular settlement, though multiple plans of some settlements at different times are included in the sample. The chapter does not provide a traditional historical narrative of the people and factors shaping town planning in the United States, though such information is occasionally offered to illustrate a particular point or provide historical context.

Several criteria were the basis for including a plan in the sample (Major, 2015a). First, there is a reasonably accurate and readable representation of street widths and/or block sizes in plan to sufficiently determine details of the layout. For example, panoramic or bird's eye view representations of a town and its plan, a popular means of promoting towns in 19th century America, are not included. Second, the plan depicts the entirety or a significant portion of the layout in a settlement. Third, the settlement is/was located in the territory of the contiguous United States. Settlements in Alaska, Hawaii, and overseas U.S. territories are not included. Fourth, the selection emphasizes plans dated before 1926. This is the year of the landmark case, *Village of Euclid, Ohio v. Ambler Realty Co.*, in which the U.S. Supreme Court upheld zoning as a constitutional exercise of police power. The post-war period after 1945 generally marks the beginning of rapid suburbanization in American settlements. The nearly 20 years between the *Euclid* decision and the end of World War II represents a sufficient amount of time before the effects of the legal precedent established could be fully realized in town planning activities, given the turmoil of the Great Depression from 1929–1940 and World War II from 1941–45. Because of this, it is best to be cautious about drawing any conclusions about the few plans dated between 1926–1945.

Plans depicting road centerlines without accurately showing blocks and street widths are not included, except for the 1961 road centerline plan of Las Vegas from Venturi et al.'s (1972) *Learning from Las Vegas*. Nonetheless, it was double-checked against 1952 and 1992 topographical maps of Las Vegas to ensure accuracy and comparability. Any plan grossly exaggerating street widths to provide an unrealistic representation of block size is not included, such as street maps typically designed for the purposes of wayfinding. This is very much a judgment call driven principally by the characteristics of block size in any particular settlement. A settlement with a tendency for small block sizes suggests there is greater exaggeration of street widths in the wayfinding map so it would be less reliable. A tendency for large block sizes suggests the wayfinding map may be somewhat more reliable since street widths are less exaggerated. Finally, the selection process did not discriminate based on whether the layout could be reasonably described as a deformed or regular grid, or something else. This is because whatever the nature of the plan at any particular point in time, it is possible the settlement would incorporate regular grid sections at some point during its evolution. For example, historical town plans of Boston are included in the sample even though its layout is generally regarded as a deformed grid.

There were 761 historical town plans in total for the sample (Major, 2015a). This includes 2 ideal town plans independent of any specific location and 22 unrealized town plans. Some historical town plans were never constructed as originally designed for whatever reason. However, in some cases, there is still a settlement (whether it is a small village or rural community) bearing the name of the planned town in that location today. If this is the case, then it is included in the sample. For example, the 1793 plan for Asylum, Pennsylvania remains unrealized but there is a small rural village in the same location bearing the same name today. For our purposes, an unrealized historical plan is not included if there is a lack of historical or contemporary evidence for a built environment ever constructed at the location where originally planned, which is the case for a couple of Mormon town plans. In contrast, the historical plan of a contemporary 'ghost town' (a town that once thrived as a settlement but was later abandoned) such as Aurora, Nevada is still included. There are several examples of American ghost towns, especially in the western United States.

There are also plans for 12 Spanish presidios (five in Texas, five in California, and one each in Arizona and Louisiana). The sample does not include bastides, fortified towns, and presidios in the compiled data if the plan represents only fortifications and nothing about the internal layout.

Town plans over time

The historical plans date from a reconstructed 1565 plan of St. Augustine, Florida (the oldest, continually inhabited settlement in the United States) to the road centerline plan of Las Vegas in 1961 (Venturi et al., 1972). The plans are grouped together by date based on the following periods: before 1701, 1701–1785, 1786–1865, 1866–1900, 1901–1945, and after 1945. The first period covers 135 years from the founding of St. Augustine to the end of the 17th century. The second period covers 85 years from the dawn of the 18th century to the year the U.S. Congress adopted the Land Ordinance, which includes 8 years of warfare during the American Revolutionary War (1775–1783). The third period covers 79 years following adoption of the Land Ordinance until the end of the U.S. Civil War (1861–1865), which includes 4 years of warfare on American soil between Union and Confederate forces. Fighting destroyed several American towns during the Civil War including Atlanta in Georgia, and Richmond and Fredericksburg in Virginia. The fourth period covers only 34 years from the end of the Civil War until the end of the 19th century. The fifth period covers 45 years from the dawn of the 20th century until the end of World War II, which includes 6 years of warfare during World War I (1917–1919) and World War II (1941–1945). The sixth and last period covers only 15 years of the post-war period until 1961. There are three reasons for grouping the town plans based on these periods. First, to demonstrate the post-*Euclid* plans are an insignificant portion of the sample. Second, to determine if there are any temporal biases in the sample. Third, to establish the extent to which the 1785 Land Ordinance truly influenced the use of regular grids in American town planning activities.

Only 2% of the plans are from the post-war period after 1945. Only 3% of the plans are dated after the *Euclid* decision in 1926. Less than 4% of the plans date before the 18th century though this notably includes plans of Boston, Charleston, New York, Philadelphia, St. Augustine, and New Haven. Nearly 12% of the plans are from 1701 to 1785 whereas 14% are from 1901 to 1945. This means 68% of the historical plans in this sample cover the 114 years from 1786 to 1900. This time is roughly consistent with the period beginning with the territories west of the Appalachians coming into the possession of the United States in the 1783 Treaty of Paris, which ended the Revolutionary War. It roughly ends with the opening of the last Native American territories to homesteaders under the Dawes Act from 1889 to 1895, also known as the Oklahoma Land Rush (Carlson, 1981). For comparison, the entire sample covers a period of 396 years. The 17th century sample accounts for 34% of that time span. The 1701–1785 sample covers 21% and the 1786–1865 sample is 20%. The 1866–1900 sample accounts for nearly 9% and the 1901–1945 sample only 11%. The post-war sample covers only 4% of that time span.

The estimated land area of the original 13 colonies was approximately 239 million acres or 97 million hectares. Contemporary land area data for the first 13 states plus Maine, Vermont, and West Virginia (each originally part of Massachusetts, New Hampshire, and Virginia, respectively) is the basis of this estimate (see Figure 2.3). The contemporary land area data had to suffice since the exact boundaries of the original 13 colonies are difficult to determine. This was due to imprecise/incomplete surveying and competing land claims between the colonies over territory westward of the settled coastal areas at the time. During 1783–1900, the land area of the United States increased over eight times in size to almost 2 billion acres or 750 million hectares. The town plans compiled for all periods after 1785 represent approximately five and a half times the number of plans compiled for the 220 years from 1565 to 1785, and over seven times the number of plans in the 18th century only before 1785.

There does appear to be some bias in the sample for the period after the Civil War until the end of the 19th century (1866–1900), since plans dated during these 34 years constitute 31% of the sample. By comparison, 37% of the plans cover more than twice the amount of time from 1785 to 1865. This bias is probably due to three factors. First, a large number of plans are found in John Reps' *Cities of the American West* (1979), which focuses on town planning during westward expansion in the United States. Second, a large number of plans are topographical maps created by the U.S. Geological Survey established in 1879. Lastly, better record keeping in local, State, and Federal government during this period meant the survival of more plans. The end of the Civil War to the beginning of the 20th century does typically mark the period most commonly associated with settlement of the Old American West. This apparent bias warrants caution in drawing any definitive conclusions based solely on the gross number of plans from 1866 to 1900 in the sample. However, the sample as a whole appears broadly representative of the intensity of town founding activity in the United States after Independence and during the 19th century in America. This would seem to ably demonstrate Reps' contention that the 19th century represented a remarkable period of city founding in the United States (Reps, 1965 and 1979).

What is natural movement?

Early studies in the 1980s suggested the potential of space syntax models to reveal important functional characteristics about architectural and urban space. One of the seminal events in the history of space syntax was construction of the axial map of Greater London within the North and South Circular Roads in the late 1980s. The axial map represents the most optimal line of sight passing through every accessible space in the street network until accounting for all spaces (Penn et al., 1998; Turner, 2005 et al.). A line might represent a series of 'named' streets. Two or more lines might also represent a single 'named' street. Names are arbitrary but visibility is not. However, usually, there is enough commonality between a line and street in cities so we can dispense with the distinction, simply calling them streets. Urban space tends to be linear with streets, boulevards, avenues, and alleys but only occasional convex elements such as squares and parks (Hillier, 2005b). At the time, Greater London was the largest space syntax model in the world by a wide margin, representing about 10,000 streets. In the late 1990s, models of metropolitan Chicago, Illinois (70,000+ streets) and Tokyo, Japan (140,000+ streets) surpassed this size standard. Successive generations of algorithmic innovations and faster processing speeds expanded the capabilities of space syntax software. This includes automatic generation of lines, mapping using road centerlines, relativizing for angular route choice, and incorporating Cartesian or metric distance (Peponis, 1997; Conroy, 2001; Conroy Dalton and Dalton, 2001; Turner, 2001b; Turner et al., 2005; Hillier and Iida, 2005; Turner, 2008; Hillier, 2009c; Turner, 2008 and 2009). Subsequently, there are space syntax models of regions, even entire countries (Hanson, 2009). However, Chicago and Tokyo remain the standard for the most expansive urbanized areas with a sparsity or density of streets in a space syntax model, respectively. It is a fundamental characteristic about both metropolitan regions, not a quirk of the modeling (**Figure A.8** below and **Figure 9.17** in Chapter 9). Today, it requires only minutes to process the configurational calculations underlying space syntax models. In the late 1990s, it took many hours for one the size of Chicago or Tokyo. In the late 1980s, it took days to process for one the size of Greater London.

When the processing was complete, the model identified Oxford Street as the shallowest or most accessible street in Greater London for the pattern of global integration, which measures the configurational relationship of all streets to all others across the entire network. The software automatically colors each street in

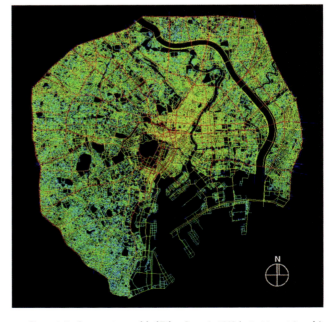

Figure A.8 – *Space syntax model of Tokyo, Japan in 1999 (not set to metric scale).*

a range from most integrated or shallow to most segregated or deep; for grayscale, black through variations of gray to white; and, for color, red through orange, yellow, green, to blue and purple. Then and today, Oxford Street is the busiest shopping street in London (**Figure A.9**). Crucially, the space syntax model did *not* account for other urban functions such as land use, building heights, or population density in any manner. It was a purely mathematical representation of spatial configuration. However, it offered a very realistic picture of the urban street network in London. Soon, this led to a key discovery. There are strong and consistent correlations between pedestrian and vehicular movement flows and spatial configuration of the urban street network *before* ever taking into account the location of attractors or generators of movement (Hillier et al., 1993; Penn et al., 1998). Integrated streets carry larger movement flows than segregated ones. This led to the *theory of natural movement*, which states movement patterns in cities arise naturally from the way the street network organizes the simplest routes to and from locations involving the fewest changes of direction in that network. In this sense, natural movement is akin to a background effect of the street network. Most movement in urban space is through movement, passing along a street on its way from somewhere to somewhere else in the network. The key to measuring and understanding this background effect is spatial configuration.

This does not deny the benefits of attraction. It only places attraction in its proper context. The distribution of activities and land uses has the potential to further intensify – or detract from – the background effects of natural movement (Hillier, 1996b; Peponis, 2004; Hillier and Vaughan, 2007). Here is a simple way of thinking about this: humans were moving long before we were building. Migration (e.g. movement) has been a (perhaps dominant) characteristic of human evolution. By comparison, building is relatively recent. It is the difference between hundreds of thousands of years compared to tens of thousands. Nonetheless, natural movement is a characteristic of the first (e.g. move) and attraction of the second (e.g. build). You *have* to move to build. You do *not* have to build to move. Cities are very much the same.

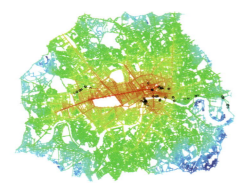 

Figure A.9 – *(left) Space syntax model of Greater London within the North and South Circular Roads in 1999 (Scale=1:800,000); (right) View looking west along Oxford Street, west of Oxford Circus, in London, 2006.*

The regular grid before the Land Ordinance

The results of classifying the town plans across time based on type and geometry are illuminating. **Table 4.1** shows a summary tabulation of the classification data. The sample of plans before the 18th century is very small with only 27 plans for 21 separate settlements. The reasons would seem to be straightforward. First, there were not many established settlements in colonial America by the end of the 17th century. Second, the harsh and dangerous conditions during the early years of colonization frequently led to outposts failing due to weather, illness, or conflict with other European powers. Record keeping was poor and a low priority for colonists. Lastly, what records might have existed were lost for the same reasons as an outpost might have failed.[1] The Lost Colony of Roanoke, Virginia (located in present day North Carolina) is probably the most famous example of an early failed colonization effort. Sir Walter Raleigh financed and organized this colony. English settlers unsuccessfully attempted to establish the colony from 1585 to 1587. People call it "The Lost Colony" because the fate of approximately 120 settlers is still something of a mystery (Kupperman, 1984).

Of these plans, over 30% are bastides, slightly more than half of which possess a geometric logic in the layout though not necessarily an orthogonal grid. Four of the settlements are deformed grids and three are linear settlements, i.e. dwellings located along a single rural road utilizing three-way intersections at or near right angles to access agricultural tracts. All of these are British settlements located in New England. Every plan in the sample has street intersections at a right angle or nearly so, whether in isolation or as part of an overall concept to the layout. Nine plans are bastides or fortified towns, all of which have regular grid layouts including New Amsterdam (New York). The early plans for New Amsterdam demonstrate the fortified town initially possessed a regular grid layout with offset grids at the small-scale in relation to local topographical conditions so some streets could run parallel or perpendicular to the East River (refer to the Castello Plan of New Amsterdam in Figure 2.2).

The small number of plans with a deformed grid or linear layout in the sample (approximately 25%) before the 18th century brings into question the observations of Rybczynski and others that "the first generation of American towns... reflected the traditional English preference for informality and improvisation, and a casual approach to planning" (Rybczynski, 1996; 66 and Reps, 1965). While this was certainly a characteristic of some New England towns, the majority of plans in this admittedly small sample indicate a greater tendency toward regular grid planning. Slightly more than 70% of the plans in the 17th century sample are regular

	Type/Date	Pre-1701	(%)	1701-1785	(%)	1786-1865	(%)	1866-1900	(%)	1901-1945	(%)	Post-1945	(%)	Sub-total	(%)	Not Included
Time	Years	135	34.4	85	21.6	79	20.1	34	8.7	45	11.5	15	3.8	393	100.0	
	Major Warfare	0	0.0	8	9.4	4	5.1	0	0.0	6	13.3	0	0.0	18	4.6	
Model	Bastilles	9	33.3	18	18.4	1	0.4	0	0.0	0	0.0	0	0.0	28	3.7	0
	Ideal/New Towns	0	0.0	0	0.0	0	0.0	2	0.8	0	0.0	0	0.0	2	0.3	(2)
	Presidios	0	0.0	17	17.3	4	1.4	0	0.0	0	0.0	0	0.0	21	2.8	(12)
	Unrealized	0	0.0	2	2.0	14	5.0	4	1.7	2	1.9	0	0.0	22	2.9	(22)
	Settlement	18	66.7	61	62.2	261	92.6	230	97.5	98	95.1	14	93.3	682	89.6	0
	Suburbs	0	0.0	0	0.0	2	0.7	0	0.0	3	2.9	1	6.7	6	0.8	0
	Sub-total	27	3.5	98	12.9	282	37.1	236	31.0	103	13.5	15	2.0	761	100.0	(36)
Geometry	Orthogonal	11	57.9	41	71.9	147	59.0	88	42.3	21	24.4	4	33.3	312	49.4	
	Offset	8	42.1	13	22.8	87	34.9	114	54.8	59	68.6	8	66.7	289	45.8	
	Radial	0	0.0	3	5.3	15	6.0	6	2.9	6	7.0	0	0.0	30	4.8	
	Regular	19	70.4	57	67.9	249	92.9	208	90.4	86	85.1	12	80.0	631	87.0	
	Deformed	4	14.8	14	16.7	11	4.1	17	7.4	3	3.0	0	0.0	49	6.8	
	Crossroads	1	3.7	7	8.3	4	1.5	5	2.2	1	1.0	0	0.0	18	2.5	
	Linear	3	11.1	1	1.2	0	0.0	0	0.0	0	0.0	0	0.0	4	0.6	
	Dispersed	0	0.0	5	6.0	2	0.7	0	0.0	0	0.0	0	0.0	7	1.0	
	Planned Deformity	0	0.0	0	0.0	2	0.7	0	0.0	11	10.9	3	20.0	16	2.2	
	Sub-total	27	3.7	84	11.6	268	37.0	230	31.7	101	13.9	15	2.1	725	100.0	

Table 4.1 – *Classification of more than 700 American historical town plans across time based on type and geometry.*

grids including fortified towns based on the European bastide model. Eleven of the plans are orthogonal grids. Four plans are deformed grids though three are for Boston from 1640 to 1675. This suggests the first generation of towns in colonial America had a greater tendency toward regularity in their layouts.

During the 85 years marking the dawn of the 18th century to adoption of the Land Ordinance, 25 plans in the sample are bastides or Spanish presidios. Three plans of Spanish presidios show only the location of dwellings but not the layout of streets. The positioning of dwellings indicates there might be a geometric logic to the layout in two of these plans but it is best to be cautious due to the scale of the drawings, so all are characterized as dispersed settlements. In the rest of the bastide and presidio plans, the layout orients to the shape of the fortifications so there is a geometric logic with the capacity to become a closed system like the 17th century examples in Manakin, San Diego, and San Francisco shown in the previous chapter. Only the 1770 plan of St. Augustine incorporates streets in a regular grid layout with offset grids aligned parallel/perpendicular to the topography. In this case, the alignment is to an inlet of the Matanzas River providing access to the Atlantic Ocean. The rest have a regular grid layout relying on parallel/perpendicular streets, all with four-way intersections except for the perimeter streets adjacent to the fortifications of the settlement. This includes seven plans for New Orleans from 1720 to 1770 where the shape and alignment of the fortifications and orthogonal grid layout are largely consistent to one another in the settlement (**Figure 4.2**). Eight plans are linear or cross-axis settlements. All utilize street intersections at a right angle in the layout but there are not enough streets or blocks to accurately classify them as regular grids.

Fourteen plans are deformed grid layouts but 11 of these are Boston from 1722 to 1777 and New York from 1731 to 1776. The 17th century plan of New York demonstrates the settlement initially had a regular grid layout with offset grids in relation to the topography of the East River at the southern tip of Manhattan Island. This layout evolved into a deformed grid during the 18th century to become somewhat more characteristic of European towns (similar to the transformation that occurred in London over time from its Roman founding to the medieval period, see Figure 1.2). Fifty-seven plans in the sample are regular grids, 41 of which are orthogonal grids. Another 13 plans utilize a regular grid layout with offset grids in relation to local topographical conditions (**Figure 4.3**, top). The 1718 plan of Annapolis is a regular grid though its layout utilizes radial town planning principles, of which there

Figure 4.2 – *Town Plans of 18th century bastides: (top) St. Augustine in 1770; and, (bottom) New Orleans in 1759.*

are three plans during this period. In Annapolis, there are twice as many street intersections at a right angle than those occurring at open angles due to the four radial streets in the layout (**Figure 4.3**, middle). There is also three times the number of parallel/perpendicular streets compared to radial ones.

The 18th century sample from 1701 to 1785 is over three times larger than the 17th century one. Nearly 75% of the plans are regular grids when including bastides and presidios, which specifically comprise nearly 25% of the sample. Less than 33% of the plans are deformed grid layouts or dispersed, linear, and crossroads settlements, but nearly three-quarters of these are plans for Boston and New York. This suggests the predisposition towards regularity in American town planning activities continued well into the 18th century with little variation, which includes a large number of fortified towns based on the bastide model. The influence of the European bastide model, Spanish presidios, and Laws of the Indies on town planning in colonial America appears evident. However, *in toto*, this predisposition toward regularity indicates the greater importance of town planning in colonial America taking place against the background of the cultural milieu in which colonization occurred. This further suggests the perceived importance of the traditional English approach to town planning during the early colonial period – certainly a characteristic of many New England towns – has been somewhat overstated on the part of some historians (Reps, 1965; Rybczynski, 1996). This is probably because of the small number of 17th century plans available in the historical record and the large amount available for one town in particular, i.e. Boston. It seems likely there is a natural and quite understandable inclination on the part of some historians to elevate the importance of Boston in the nation's planning tradition to a position equal to its undoubted place in history as the birthplace of the American Revolution. In any case, it appears clear the territories of the New World became the experimental laboratory for applying the town planning principles of the European Renaissance and Age of Enlightenment with their emphasis on order and regularity.

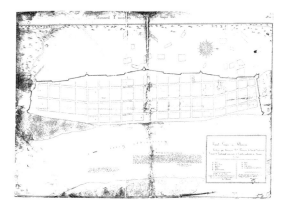

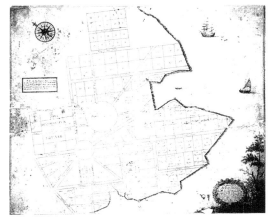

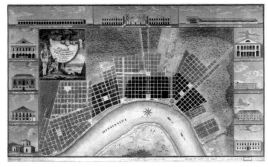

Figure 4.3 – *(top) Offset grids related to the topography of the Mississippi River in Colonel Auguste Chouteau's 1780 plan for St. Louis, Missouri; (middle) Francis Nicholson's plan for Annapolis, Maryland in 1718 utilizing radial town planning principles; and, (bottom) 19th century plan for New Orleans in 1815.*

The regular grid after the Land Ordinance

The sample for the 79 years from 1786 to 1865 is over three times larger than the size of the 18th century sample before adoption of the Land Ordinance, just as that sample size was three times larger than the previous one. Almost 93% of the plans from 1786 to 1865 are regular grids. Of these, 59% are orthogonal grids. Nearly 35% are regular grid layouts with offset grids in relation to some other variable (usually topography and/or land division); for example, in the 1815 plan of New Orleans (**Figure 4.3**, bottom). The rest are regular grid layouts utilizing radial town planning principles within a predominant orthogonal grid logic, most famously in Pierre L'Enfant's 1792 plan for the national capital in Washington, D.C. (see Figure 3.13). The remaining 7% are not regular grids. Eleven are deformed grid layouts but the plans for Boston from 1800 to 1847 and New York from 1797 to 1838 comprise more than half of this number. The famous 1811 Commissioner's Plan for New York City planned an orthogonal grid layout for the rest of Manhattan Island. New York could – and maybe should – count as a regular grid layout after this date based on the parameters defined in the previous chapter (**Figure 4.4**). However, the subsequent plan for New York in 1838 is primarily of the south end of Manhattan Island, which is still strongly characterized by a deformed grid layout. The only other plan of New York during this time period is dated 1797, which is also primarily of the south end of the island. It shows the origins

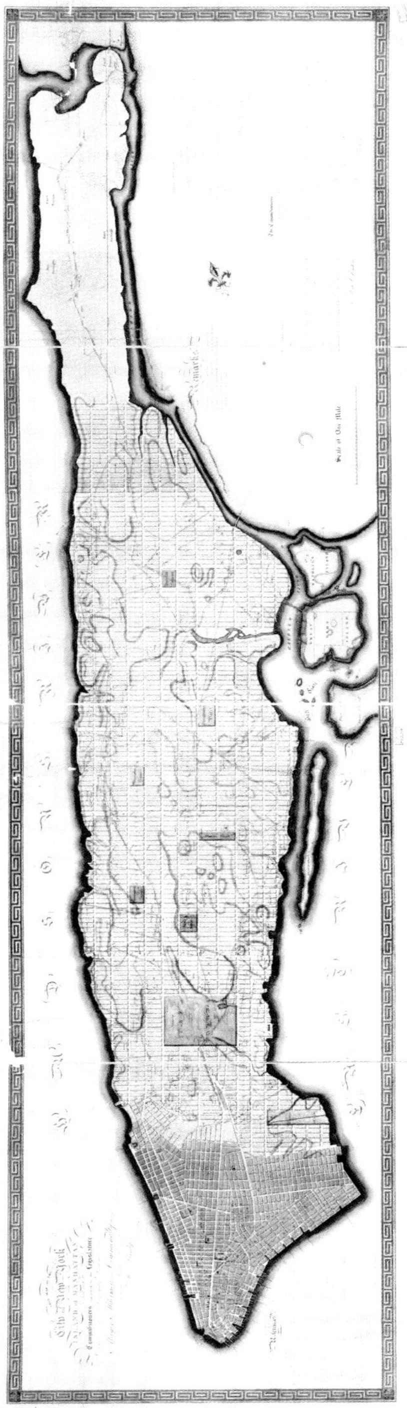

Figure 4.4 – *1811 Commissioner's Plan for Manhattan Island, New York.*

Figure 4.5 – *1797 plan of southern end of Manhattan Island, New York.*

of the Manhattan gridiron predate the famous 1811 plan (**Figure 4.5**, previous page). Finally, there are not any additional plans in the sample for New York after 1838. We characterize all of these New York plans as deformed grids. If we did classify New York as a regular grid after 1811, it would only reinforce the findings of the survey.

Two plans are suburbs: Lake Forest in Chicago and Llewellyn Park in Trenton, New Jersey. Only two of the plans are dispersed or linear settlements. Finally, four plans are Spanish presidios in California and one plan is the fortified town of New Orleans in 1798, which did not possess offset grids at this time. The small number of plans for presidios and bastides suggests this settlement model fell into disuse after the founding of the United States. This is only partially true. In fact, Americans built hundreds of forts and trading posts during westward expansion, many of which were a hybrid of the European bastide model and Spanish presidios (Lamar, 1977). The disappearance of this settlement model from the American landscape was more gradual than suggested by the sample. Many of these forts/trading posts would later become towns; for example, Fort Leavenworth, Kansas and Fort Lincoln, Nebraska.

The sample from 1866 to 1900 has almost as many plans for a 35-year period as the previous period, which covered nearly 80 years. Slightly more than 90% of the plans in this period are regular grid layouts, of which only 3% are radial plans, 42% are orthogonal grids, and 55% are regular grids with offset grids. Less than 8% of the plans are deformed grid layouts and only five can be considered linear or crossroad settlements. The sample size for the 45 years from 1901 until the end of World War II in 1945 is less than half the size of the preceding one. Slightly more than 85% of the plans are regular grid layouts. More than 68% are regular grid layouts with offset grids and only 24% are orthogonal grids. This represents a 50% decrease in orthogonal grid layouts in the early 20th century compared to the previous 114 years. Mostly, this is the effect of using offset grids in relation to the original plan of an existing town during subsequent growth. Attoe and Brownell (1989) describe this transformation: "Cities based overall on a grid pattern, however, often come to have a variegated patchwork pattern as a result of land development by subdivision. The patchwork of American cities provides opportunities for diversity within the regularity of the overall circulation pattern… the juxtaposition creates legible boundaries defining neighborhoods and districts… thus an American city can be a collection of diverse rather than uniform parts held together by the underlying physical or conceptual order of the grid" (126). Only 7% of the plans from 1901 to 1945 are regular grid layouts utilizing radial planning principles. Only three plans are deformed grids and one plan is a crossroad settlement (the 1908

Figure 4.6 – *The dawn of American suburbia in the 1929 plan for Radburn, New Jersey.*

plan of Las Vegas, see Figure 9.2). Over 10% of the plans are examples of suburban layouts. Most have a layout composed of a formal element discretely replicated over and over during the design process to generate the overall plan for the development. This element is often a curved street or a residential pod, i.e. the layout of a few lots and/or homes around a single street such as a cul-de-sac. In this sense, the conceptual basis of these layouts is *repetitive deformity*, which is vastly different from a deformed grid. Hillier (1999a) describes the deformed grid of European cities as having a hidden geometrical logic, which differentiates principal streets and local streets from each other in a consistent manner. One of the most renowned examples of repetitive deformity is the influential suburb of Radburn, New Jersey, outside of Newark (**Figure 4.6**). **Figure** 4.7 shows all the residential pods removed from this 1929 plan of Radburn and re-oriented so the curb cut of each road is located at the base of the drawing. This clearly shows there is very little variety in the formal design of Radburn. Of 72 residential pods, cul-de-sacs define 69 of them and all that differentiates them are minor variations in road design, siting of dwelling units around this cul-de-sac, and, in a few cases, the overall shape due to siting of dwelling units on main roads adjacent to the cul-de-sac. This effectively demonstrates the repetitious nature of formal design in these types of suburbs. In the sample, only three of the plans from 1901 to 1945 are suburbs within a larger urban area. The rest of the plans

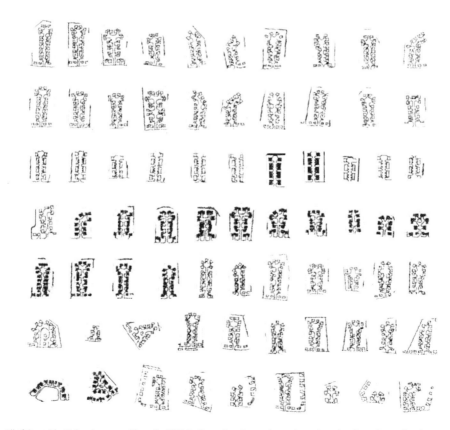

Figure 4.7 – *All of the residential pods removed from the 1929 Radburn, New Jersey plan and re-oriented so the curb cut of each entry road is oriented to the bottom of the drawing.*

are new towns utilizing repetitive deformity in the layout; eight in all, but three are plans for Kingsport, Tennessee. There are only a few isolated examples of suburban development in the periphery of settlements with regular grid layouts during this period. Suburbs are not unique to the American town planning tradition. As Owens (1991) points out, suburbs were "an integral aspect of the city itself" in ancient Greece and Rome (152).

In any case, this review of a large historical record of American town plans clearly demonstrates the effect of the 1785 Land Ordinance in a cultural milieu already predisposed to the order concepts of Renaissance town planning, what Kostof (1991) refers to as "merely extending the well-established rectilinear habits of late Colonial America to the unsettled territories" (116). During the period from adoption of the Land Ordinance to the end of World War II, an average of nearly 90% of all town plans in the sample are regular grids. This represents a nearly 37% increase in the use of the regular grid *after* adoption of the Land Ordinance in 1785, above and beyond when about 70% of all American towns were already using regular grid planning principles. It also demonstrates the gradual emergence of the first developments during the late 19th century and early 20th century, which would come to characterize suburbanization during the post-war period in America (Fishman, 1987; Duany et al., 2000). The sample of plans in the post-war period is far too small (only 15) to draw any definitive conclusions, but 75% have evidence of suburban development in the periphery of the settlement. This occurs even though 80% of the plans in this period are still predominantly regular grids. Finally, one plan in the post-war sample is the 1952 plan for Levittown, Pennsylvania (**Figure 4.8**). Levittown became the archetypal model for mass production of the American suburb in the post-war period. According to Bryson (1994), "in 1945 America needed, more or less immediately, five million additional homes as… millions of young couples settled down to start a family. The simplest and cheapest solution was for a developer to buy up a tract of countryside within commuting distance of a city and fill it with hundreds – sometimes thousands – of often identical start homes. The master of the art was Abraham Levitt, who began scattering the eastern states with his Levittowns in 1947. By making every home identical and employing assembly-line construction techniques, Levitt could offer houses at a remarkably low cost. At a time when the average house cost was $10,000, Levitt sold houses for just $7,900, or $65 a month, with no down payment, and they came equipped with major appliances" (408). The construction techniques pioneered by Levitt – including for horizontal construction of the site such as the clear-cutting, site fill, and replanting of trees – became the standard business model for the home-building industry in the United States from this point forward to the present day.

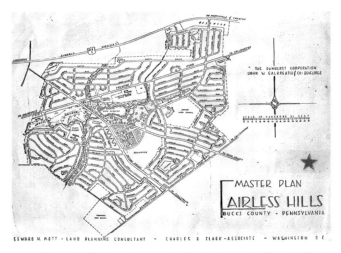

Figure 4.8 – *The dawn of mass production development and home building in American suburbia, i.e. 1952 plan for Levittown, Pennsylvania.*

Chapter 4 Notes

[1] According to a timeline of North American colonization on Wikipedia, there were nine attempts by the French, Spanish, and English to establish permanent settlements in the 17th century. All but one failed, i.e. Spanish settlement in St. Augustine. It lists 53 mostly British colonies established during the 18th century. This timeline does not cite any references/sources so it is only illustrative of the difficulties for early colonization: see http://en.wikipedia.org/wiki/Timeline_of_the_colonization_of_North_America.

5 The Spatial Logic of American Cities

"You come upon the horizontal infinite in every direction... you will never have encountered anything that stretches as far as this before. Even the sea cannot match it, since it is not divided up geometrically."
- Jean Baudrillard

This chapter examines consistencies and covariations in the metric and spatial parameters of 20 contemporary American urban grids, focused on urban centers and controlled for axial size (i.e. number of axial lines). It builds on the methodology and findings of previous studies about American and European urban grids where it was demonstrated that widespread use of regular grids in American cities results in larger blocks and fewer, longer streets (Major, 1997b and 2015c). Because of this, the urban layout of American cities tends to integrate at much higher levels while encompassing a much more expansive land area. This leads to a scale of urban space in the horizontal dimension of American cities that is a magnitude greater in terms of composition and configuration than typically found in other models of urbanism, especially in Europe (Major, 2015c). This is a fundamental attribute of spatial configuration in American cities since all cities have a fractal dimension – or a degree of self-similarity – at all scales of the built environment, which tends to persist even as the scale of the urban pattern upsizes during the evolution of urban growth (Carvalho and Penn, 2004; Shpuza, 2014). The purpose is two-fold: first, do these results hold in a larger sample of contemporary American urban grids incorporating a greater area of the urban fabric and, second, can we better understand how American urban grids are differentiated from each other? The chapter argues this is the case. Specifically, larger block sizes and fewer, longer streets differentiate American cities in a broadly similar manner to how those characteristics distinguished American and European urban grids from each other (Major, 2015). This chapter also broadly defines the formal composition of American suburban layouts as three types (*repetitive deformity*, *asymmetrical regularity*, and *geomorphic* variations of each), where departure from the large-scale grid logic of their surrounding context is the common denominator, especially in terms of connectivity.

The American city as subject and object
The American city has often been the source of scholarly speculation. Sometimes, this speculation takes as its subject what the physical form of the American city might mean or symbolize about American society itself, usually within

the framework of a dichotomy comparing American and European cities. For example, this is prevalent in the writing of post-modern French sociologist and philosopher Jean Baudrillard in his book, *America*. Baudrillard (1988) observes the concept of space in America appears radically different when compared to Europe, as distinctly realized in the built environment of their cities. He states, "clouds spoil our European skies… compared with the immense skies of America and their thick clouds, our little fleecy skies and little fleecy clouds resemble our fleecy thoughts, which are never thoughts of wide-open spaces. In Paris, the sky never takes off… it doesn't soar above us… it remains caught up in the backdrop of sickly buildings, all living in each other's shade, as though it were a little piece of private property… it is not, as here in the great capital of New York, the vertiginous glass facade reflecting each building to the others. Europe has never been a continent... you can see that by its skies... as soon as you set foot in America, you feel the presence of an entire continent – space there is the very form of thought" (16). In contrasting street life in Europe and the United States (again, specifically Paris and New York), Baudrillard argues "they say the streets are alive in Europe but dead in America… they are wrong… in Europe, the street only lives in sudden surges, in historic moments of revolution and barricades. The American street has not, perhaps, known these historic moments, but it is always turbulent, lively, kinetic, and cinematic, like the country itself, where the specifically historical and political stage counts for little" (Baudrillard, 1988; 18). Finally, in speculating about the meaning of the urban pattern in cities such as Los Angeles compared to those of Europe, he comments "…you come upon the horizontal infinite in every direction …you will never have encountered anything that stretches as far as this before… even the sea cannot match it, since it is not divided up geometrically. The irregular, scattered flickering of European cities does not produce the same parallel lines, the same vanishing points, the same aerial perspective either… they are medieval cities. This one (Los Angeles) condenses by night the entire future geometry of the networks of human relations, gleaming in their abstraction, luminous in their extension, astral in their reproduction to infinity" (Baudrillard, 1988; 51–52) (**Figure 5.1**). In this way, Baudrillard (1988) compares and contrasts space, street life, and urban form in American and European cities in an explicit effort to find social meaning. He calls this a search for "astral America" (27), by which he means the nonphysical social realm of existence in which the physical can be seen as its counterpoint or reflection. His search takes place within the context of a clear dichotomy, which is Europe and America in general but European and American urban space in particular, i.e. organic and regular cities.

On the other hand, there is an urban legend common to most American cities, probably originating with Los Angeles, that "thanks to the freeways, everything is

Figure 5.1 –*Los Angeles By Night (Photo: André M. Hünseler)*.

twenty minutes away" (Rachlis, 2001; 6). Rachlis (2001) points out, "always at the center of that fantasy is the freeways" or more specifically, the automobile (6). This is probably true at some point during the evolution of most American cities, including Los Angeles, which helps to explain why the legend is so prevalent in urban America. However, is this legend solely about the role of the automobile and freeway systems in American society? By their very nature, freeways or interstates are limited access highways designed to facilitate the movement of vehicular traffic and quickly distribute that traffic from one location to another in the urban network. Los Angeles is commonly considered to have the most expansive freeway system in the United States. Interstate 405 (I-405) in Los Angeles has the highest traffic volumes (390,000 vehicles per day) in the United States based on a 2006 estimate (Source: Federal Highway Administration). Locally known as the northern segment of the San Diego Freeway, I-405 runs approximately north-to-south in Los Angeles from Irvine to San Fernando. However, a freeway system in even a city such as Los Angeles cannot directly connect all locations to all others (**Figure 5.2**). That is the role of the urban grid.

In *The Image of the City*, Lynch (1960) argues the Los Angeles "grid pattern is an undifferentiated matrix" (33), which seems to accurately characterize the common perception about that city (Banham, 1971; Warner, 1972; Davis, 1992). Despite this, the expansive nature of the Los Angeles urban grid does characterize that city as much as – if not more so than – its freeway system (see Figure 3.1). The same appears true for most American cities. So there must be something about the American urban grid itself – independent of its interstates, freeways, and highways – that contributes to this urban legend, even if the specifics of the legend are not exactly accurate. In particular, it suggests there is something fundamental about the nature of accessibility in the American city. Accessibility is an attribute often associated with American cities in the town planning literature. For example, Warner (1972) describes the American city as having a "high degree of spatial freedom" (136). Banham (1971) discusses this in *Los Angeles: The Architecture of Four Ecologies*: "The point about this giant city, which has grown almost simultaneously all over, is that all of its parts are equal and equally accessible from all other parts" (36). In this, Banham is specifically referring to the effect of the freeway system in shaping the urban environment of Los Angeles, which is one of his four ecologies. However, the idea of American urban space as a neutral background to the social life of the city – and therefore egalitarian in nature since "all of its parts are equal and equally accessible" to all others due to widespread use of the regular grid – is an *a priori* assumption (Banham, 1971; 36). His four ecologies of Los Angeles – beach, freeways, flatlands, and foothills – discounts the urban grid itself as something worthy of investigation, which he explicitly states is because

Figure 5.2 – *Los Angeles in the Age of the Automobile: (left) traffic in 1947 (Photo: Loomis Dean/Image: © Christopher Dean); (middle) interchange between Interstate 105 and 110; and, (right) contemporary traffic on Interstate 5 approaching Interstate 10 east of downtown Los Angeles.*

"Los Angeles has no urban form at all in the commonly accepted sense" (Banham, 1971; 75). As previously discussed, this is an idea often at the heart of the literature about American cities that is either implicitly implied or explicitly stated. For example, the otherwise excellent Davis (1992) review of social, economic, and political factors shaping the development of Los Angeles in *City of Quartz: Excavating the Future in Los Angeles* analyzes these factors independently of city form in a manner consistent with the prevailing social science paradigm of urban studies. Others are clearer about seeing accessibility in American cities as a function of both the macro-scale highway network and micro-scale street network of the urban grid itself (Fishman, 1994; Woodroffe et al., 1994).

There is a contraction inherent in much of this scholarly speculation about American cities. First, a certain degree of 'bigness' characterizes the American city so, by definition, everything is further apart from everything else. Second, a "certain degree of mutual accessibility" characterizes the American city so by definition everything is equally accessible to everything else (Blumenfeld, 1982; 483). How it is possible for the American city to be both expansive and accessible by its very nature? Certainly, the automobile plays a role. The extremely high number of vehicles in the United States today appears to demonstrate this fact (**Table 5.1**).[1] The vehicle per capita rate in the United States is 21% greater than the country with the next highest rate (Luxembourg) and more than 50% greater than the average (548 per 1,000 people) for 16 European countries. However, six of the ten largest metropolitan regions in the United States today in terms of land area (as defined by the U.S. Census Bureau) were founded during the 17th or 18th century (**Table 5.2**). The remaining largest metropolitan regions of Chicago,

VEHICLES PER CAPITA
(Per 1,000 people)

Rank	Country	Amount
1	United States	842
2	Luxembourg	697
3	Iceland	658
4	Australia	619
5	Puerto Pico	617
6	Italy	571
7	Canada	563
8	New Zealand	560
9	Austria	558
10	Germany	558
11	Finland	543
12	Japan	543
13	Ireland	542
14	Malta	539
15	Switzerland	539
16	Norway	494
17	France	494
18	Slovenia	488
19	Belgium	486
20	Spain	479
22	United Kingdom	458
23	Netherlands	457
51	Russia	213
52	Mexico	209
65	Brazil	156
78	Chile	97

TEN LARGEST METROPOLITAN REGIONS BY LAND AREA IN THE UNITED STATES TODAY

Rank	City	km²	Square miles	Founded
1	New York	8,683.2	3,352.6	1625
2	Chicago	5,498.1	2,122.8	1803
3	Atlanta	5,083.1	1,962.8	1843
4	Philadelphia	4,660.9	1,799.5	1682
5	Boston	4,496.7	1,736.2	1630
6	Los Angeles	4,319.9	1,667.9	1781
7	Dallas	3,644.2	1,407.0	1841
8	Houston	3,354.7	1,295.3	1837
9	Detroit	3,267.1	1,261.4	1701
10	Washington, DC	2,996.0	1,156.8	1790
	MEAN	**4,150.7**	**1,776.2**	**1753**

Tables 5.1 and 5.2 – (left) Vehicles per capita rate/ranking of 26 countries. Note: Puerto Rico is a commonwealth territory of the United States though listed separately in this table.[1] The line represents the mean for the cases in this table; and, (right) table showing the city, land area (in square kilometers and square miles), and date of the founding for the ten largest metropolitan regions in the United States today (Source: U.S. Census Bureau).

Atlanta, Dallas, and Houston are 19th century cities, the founding of which predates by at least seven decades Henry Ford's release of the Model-T in 1908 and the associated production line innovations by 1914, which manufactured Model-Ts every 3 minutes (Flink, 1988). This generally marks the birth of the modern automobile age in the United States (**Figure 5.3**). This suggests accessibility in the American city is not a product of the automobile itself but rather something else for which the automobile was well suited.

The American urban grid

The answer to this contradiction lies in the regular grid itself, namely the effects of larger block sizes on formal composition and longer streets on spatial configuration. Previous studies demonstrate larger blocks and widespread use of regular grids led to longer, fewer streets characterizing the American city (Major, 1997b and 2015c). This suggests the physical form of American cities was ideally suited for the new technology of the automobile and, in hindsight, made the American urban grid remarkably innovative well before its time, which Kunstler (1993) attributes to "four-way intersections at every block allowed for flexible traffic patterns" (30). The automobile later modified the American city through implementation of the 1956 National Interstate and Defense Highways Act passed by the U.S. Congress and signed into law by President Dwight D. Eisenhower. However, the

Figure 5.3 – *Unfinished Model Ts rolling on assembly line circa 1913.*

primary determinant for the expansive and sparse nature of American urban grids in terms of their formal composition is larger block sizes (Major, 2015c). The primary determinant for the mutually accessible nature of American urban grids in terms of their spatial configuration is longer street lengths, which tends to intensify connectivity using regular grids (Major, 2015c). Because of this, the American city represents the 'invention' of a new scale in the horizontal dimension for town planning, borrowing from the terminology of Gandelsonas (1999), in terms of composition and configuration.

We can further demonstrate this by searching for consistencies and covariations among a family of metric and spatial parameters in a sample of 20 contemporary American urban grids, focused on urban centers and controlled for axial size (i.e. number of axial lines or k-lines), using space syntax. The axial maps for 16 of the 20 largest urban areas in the United States today in terms of population are included in the sample. These 20 axial maps also represent 48% of the largest 42 urban areas in the United States today, with Salt Lake City being the least populated. The methodology for the analysis in this chapter is the same as the previous study of 20 American and European urban grids (Major, 2015c). Briefly, this methodology pairs American urban grids of comparable axial size, focusing on the urban street network (i.e. park pathways and highways removed from the axial map) within well-defined physical boundaries (topography, railroad lines, streets, and so on). The author constructed each axial map with the exception of Seattle (constructed by Paul Bottege in 1994), Baltimore (Shah, 1996b), and New Orleans (Bone, 1996). The author double-checked, updated, and revised each axial map in 2002 based on topographical maps produced by the U.S. Geological Survey. The characterizations of the axial maps in this chapter are as of the date of model construction. The

The nitty-gritty of measurement

Space syntax developed dozens, perhaps hundreds of different ways of measuring spatial configuration over the decades. Occam's Razor tells us 'other things being equal, the simplest solution is usually the correct one.' The same is true for space syntax measures, too. The most basic are often the most powerful ones. They have the merits of simplicity and validity. Most people easily understand them. They are even intuitive. They also have a long record of success.

This chapter principally relies on 11 measures or parameters in comparing averages across a sample of American urban grids. The rest of the book relies on these same measures (some more so than others) in models of individual American cities. They represent a small subset of those available in the space syntax toolkit. There are four metric parameters: area, line length, line segment length, and line density. At the time, the author attributed these metric characteristics to the space syntax models. Nowadays, they are included as a matter of course. There are seven configurational or spatial parameters: axial size, global integration, connectivity, local integration, mean depth, intelligibility, and synergy. The first five are first-order measures based on the topological graph. The last two are second-order measures, which are expressions of the linear relationship between first-order parameters.

Metric parameters
'Area' is the two-dimensional span (e.g. length by width) of the axial map measured in terms of square kilometers (sqkm or km^2). Line length ('Length') is the metric extent of a line measured in meters (m). The metric parameter of line length is the basis for discussing street length. Street and line length are not always consistent in cities. For example, a 'named' street might be composed of multiple lines. In contrast, a single line might have different street names along its length; perhaps even thought of as different streets from a planning point of view in terms of land use variations along its length. The opposite might be true as well in either case. This is accepted as a given. Nonetheless, we often use the terms 'street length' and 'line length' on an interchangeable basis for simplicity's sake. More often than not, a line and street will tend to correspond. Line or street segment length ('Segment') is the sum total of metric lengths divided by the sum total of connections for all lines in the axial map in meters (m). It is the basis for calculating average block sizes in American urban grids based on previously established methodology (Major, 1997b; Major, 2015c). Line or street density is the average number of lines per square kilometer ('k/sqkm') in the axial map. It is a measure of the density or sparsity of streets in an urban fabric. We express the majority of data about Cartesian distance based on the metric system. However, there are several instances where we translate this information into the English system for American audiences, e.g. feet, miles, square feet, acres, etc.

Spatial parameters
Axial size ('K-lines') is the number of lines in the axial map. Global integration ('Global'), or *betweenness* in topological terms, is a relativized measure of mean depth of a line to all other lines in the axial map. We can most easily understand global integration in this way: you are standing in a street; how accessible or shallow is that street

in relation to all others in the entire network of the city? Connectivity ('CN') is how many lines are directly accessible from a single line. Connectivity is simple: you are walking along the length of a street; how many other streets can you directly access from it? Local integration ('Local'), or *choice* in topological terms, is a relativized measure of mean depth of a line to all others up to only two connections away in the axial map. We can most easily understand local integration in this way: you are standing at an intersection of multiple streets (two or more) and you look in all directions to see what other streets might be directly accessible along their lengths. Local integration measures this 'collective picture' for you. The built environment also tends to reinforce the pattern of local integration for us. It does so in the third dimension of building (e.g. heights, intensity of land uses, and so on), actual observable usage (e.g. road widths, how many people and cars, and so on), and even urban design features (e.g. provision or lack of signage, street trees, on-street parking, and so on). Depth is the mean number of connections from the most integrated line to all others in the axial map. We can most easily understand depth as: what does the rest of the spatial network in the city look like from *only* this single street? You can measure depth from any line in an axial map. However, for this book, we limit ourselves to only the most integrated street.

Space syntax software automatically colors each line in a most-to-least range for all of these measures; for grayscale, black through dark-to-light variations of gray to white; and, for color, red through orange, yellow, green, to blue and purple. Because there are multiple parameters, there are also multiple ways to measure the linear relationship between first-order parameters in second-order measures. For our purposes, the most important are Intelligibility ('Intell'), which is the relationship between global integration and connectivity, and 'Synergy,' which is the relationship between global and local integration. There are even more ways to interrogate the data and models. It is only a matter of what you are trying to better understand.

In the early 2000s, space syntax adjusted its terminology for global and local integration to *betweenness* and *choice*, respectively. These are precise mathematical terms in the study of topology. However, as formulated, these terms are somewhat alien and difficult to intuitively understand for the built environment professions. In architecture, betweenness even has

Figure A.10 – *View south down Market Street from the Ferry Building in San Francisco, California, 1926.*

unhelpful connotations with phenomenology such as Christian Norberg-Schulz's (1985) ideas about the 'beingness' of buildings and places. Like this book, many space syntax people continue to use the terms global and local integration. Space syntax most often engages with the built environment professions. They more easily understand and intuit the meaning of these terms, i.e. this street is globally integrated or accessible, you are locally integrated or shallow, and so forth. (For a detailed description of the quantitative measures of space syntax including their mathematical basis, see: Hillier and Hanson, 1984 and 1986; Hillier et al., 1987; and Hillier, 1996b.)

The jargon monster
English is a redundant language; equally wonderful and frustrating. There are three principal forms (e.g. American, British, Australasian) and over three-dozen dialects in the world. Many words mean the same thing, more or less, depending on context. The thesaurus has 15 synonyms for 'word.' 'Term' has another 16, which are completely different, including 'terminology.' Ironically, English is both easy to use with a minimal vocabulary *and* difficult to master as a second language; some might say as a first language, too. Most space syntax researchers and practitioners write articles and books in English even if it is not their first language; not all, of course, but most. There are also space syntax publications in French, Greek, Spanish, Italian, German, Portuguese, Mandarin Chinese, Hebrew, Arabic, and others. However, most space syntax terms originate in English. This is understandable. Space syntax began in The Bartlett School of Architecture and Planning at University College London in the United Kingdom.

A keen reader might notice 'or' is one of the most used words in space syntax publications, including this book. This is because there is an inherent paradox at the heart of research and dissemination about the built environment. Scientific research requires, even demands, precision. However, most people have only a cursory foundation in the preferred language of science, i.e. mathematics. At the same time, dissemination requires generalities. The subject matter is the built environment. People of many fields with diverse backgrounds in different parts of the world have an interest in the built environment. The result is space syntax people tend to over-explain things while trying to serve the genuine interests of both research precision and knowledge dissemination. For example:

- Configurational or topological or spatial
- Global or 'at the large-scale' or whole and local or 'at the small-scale' or subsystem or part, all relative to size
- Global integration or *betweenness* or relativized mean depth or relative asymmetry, or the truly ponderous but now largely disused relative asymmetry asymmetry (RAA) (see *The Social Logic of Space*)
- Integrated or accessible or shallow with adjective variations (highly, moderately, etc.)
- Segregated or inaccessible or deep with adjective variations (poorly, somewhat, etc.)
- Local integration or *choice* or the slightly different but related 'control'
- Angular choice or changes in direction
- Global choice or (the now obsolete) radius-radius integration, an intermediate measure between global and local integration based on mean depth from the most integrated space, which mediates

for 'edge effect,' e.g. spaces at the edges of space syntax models are segregated by virtue of their location on the edge (**Figure A.11**)
- Lines or axial lines or axes or lines of sight or streets in the axial map
- Convex spaces or convexity in the convex map, often associated with rooms though not always
- Visual field or isovist (point or linear or convex, at eye level and visible or at knee level and visible *and* accessible) in a visibility map or visibility graph analysis (VGA)
- Space syntax or configurational or spatial model or topological graph or justified graph.

Next, layer in measurements of Cartesian distance for two widely used systems (Metric and English). Then, add common terms in architecture, urban design, and planning; many often the subject of intense debate about their meaning in academia and professional practice with varied uses by different specialists. Word meaning also evolves over time. In today's interconnected world of mass media and rapid communications, it can happen relatively quickly, even occasionally overnight.

Then, mix together and try to explain the same concepts and ideas to laymen, who have little or no background in the built environment except for their everyday experience of it. They understand how to use built environments. They

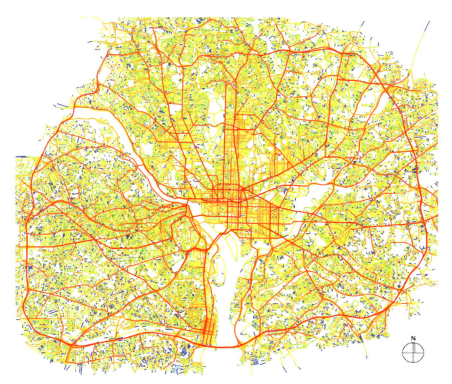

Figure A.11 – *Space syntax model of global choice in Greater Washington, D.C. within Interstate 495 (Scale=1:375,000).*

struggle to explain their use in precise terms. Hillier (1996b) calls this non-discursive use of the built environment, i.e. people are good at the former but not the latter. Finally, we might purposely select a word in English for its nuances of meaning, which is lacking in a different language or *vice versa*, i.e. selecting one word translated into another language with unintended nuances of meaning. It is a recipe for a metaphorical explosion of jargon.

However, most space syntax ideas and principles fall under the purview of common sense. The multitude of terms does not represent a conscious (or even subconscious) effort on the part of researchers and practitioners to make space syntax confusing or opaque for the uninitiated. It might seem so to some. It does represent a struggle to find the best words to describe things so they broadly resonate with the largest possible audience. It is doomed to failure due to the very nature of language itself, especially English. Nonetheless, the struggle is constant. Non-space syntax people sometimes ask, why lines? They mean why use axial lines or lines of sight as the principal representation for urban streets in space syntax models. One of the best answers achieves that precious rarity of precision and poetry. Modernist artist Paul Klee once said, "A line is a dot that went for a walk." Of course, Klee was discussing artistic composition. However, in architecture and city planning terms, it ably explains the line in space syntax if you think of the 'dot' as a person (**Figure A.12**).

The 'or' explanations in space syntax mean similar things, or nearly so with some nuances. As such, they are largely consistent with one another. The fact is a person can go a very long way towards understanding space syntax and what it has to tell us about the built environment relying on a few terms. These are *integrated* or *segregated* and *global* or *local*; or, even simpler, *shallow or deep in the network* and *whole or part of the network*. Consider everything else 'window dressing' until you develop a broader and deeper knowledge about space syntax through mere exposure and repetition.

Figure A.12 – *Trafalgar Square in central London was remodeled in the late 1990s using space syntax (Photo: David Iliff)*.

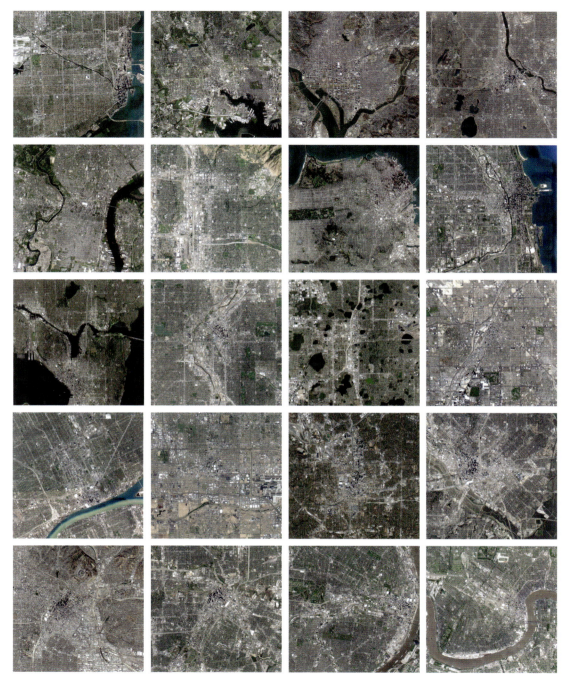

Figure 5.4 – Satellite views from 15 km of approximately 110 square kilometers or 42 square miles area of urban fabric in 20 American cities (left to right by row): (top row) Miami, Florida; Baltimore, Maryland; Washington, D.C.; Minneapolis, Minnesota; (second row) Philadelphia, Pennsylvania; Salt Lake City, Utah; San Francisco, California; Chicago, Illinois; (third row) Seattle, Washington; Denver, Colorado; Orlando, Florida; Las Vegas, Nevada; (fourth row) Detroit, Michigan; Phoenix, Arizona; Atlanta, Georgia; Dallas, Texas; (bottom row) Los Angeles, California; Houston, Texas; St. Louis, Missouri; and, New Orleans, Louisiana. Satellite views are organized based on axial size for the paired samples from smallest to largest (left to right and downward). The two smallest axial maps are Miami and Baltimore (first row, upper left) and the largest are St. Louis and New Orleans (bottom row, lower right).

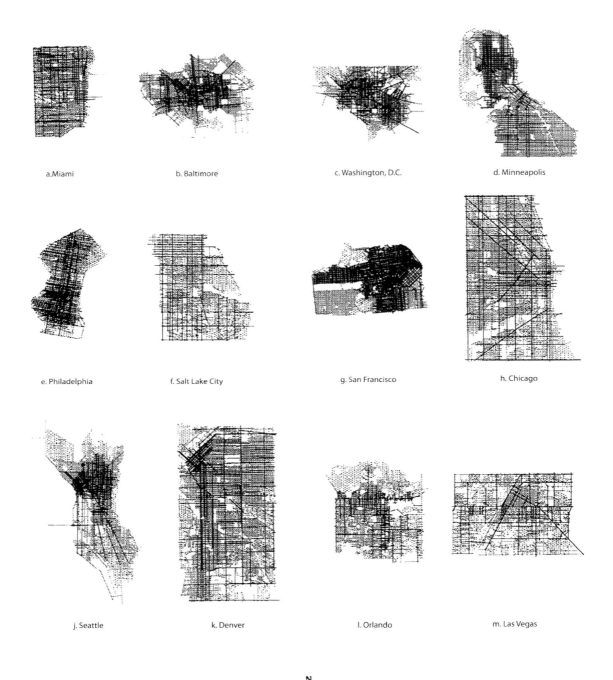

Figure 5.5a–m – *The pattern of (log) global integration in the axial map of 20 American urban grids grouped by pairings of comparable axial size from smallest to largest (by row, left to right and then top-to-bottom of each page) (Scale=1:375,000).*

Figure 5.5n–u – *The pattern of (log) global integration in the axial map of 20 American urban grids grouped by pairings of comparable axial size from smallest to largest (by row, left to right and then top-to-bottom of each page) (Scale=1:375,000).*

axial maps on average encompass an additional 25% of land area whilst utilizing 10% fewer axial lines than the American urban grids of the previous study (Major, 2015c).

Figure 5.4 (page 93) shows a satellite view covering approximately 110 square kilometers or over 42 square miles of the urban fabric in the American cities of the sample. At first glance, three things are readily apparent. First, all American urban grids are characterized by some degree of regularity in their urban layout. Second, either a large-scale orthogonal logic (most clearly in Chicago, Detroit, and Las Vegas) or an offset logic (as in San Francisco, St. Louis, and New Orleans) tends to define this regularity. Third, interruptions and deviations "continually qualifies the morphological regularity of the gridiron concept" in either type (Tremonto, 1993; 27), so that the American urban object "is blemished in its realization" (Stonor, 1991; 1). Lastly, the large-scale effect of topographical conditions in limiting the potential for patterning of the urban grid is readily apparent, most clearly in the satellite views of Philadelphia, San Francisco, Chicago, Orlando, and especially Seattle. This is only more apparent if we examine the pattern of (log)global integration in the sample of 20 American urban grids, organized based on comparable axial size of the pairings in the sample (**Figure 5.5**, pages 94-95). The logarithmic transformation of global integration is merely for visual purposes since it allows for the configurational structure of the urban grid to be clearer in a grayscale range from black (most integrated) through gray to white (more segregated). American cities characterized by offset grids possess a 'deformed wheel' structure with an enlarged integrated core composed of the largest offset grids. Hillier and

Sample	AREA (SQKM)	K/SQKM	MAX LENGTH	MEAN LENGTH (M)	MEAN SEG (M)
Philadelphia	27.7	55.6	10879.0	724.9	97.3
Miami	29.1	39.5	10061.8	775.3	113.6
Washington, D.C	32.1	40.4	7600.0	670.3	99.3
Baltimore	37.5	34.0	9200.0	842.3	114.1
San Francisco	40.7	43.5	7297.6	684.3	95.3
Orlando	47.0	48.0	9563.3	488.7	115.6
Seattle	49.4	39.1	7390.2	639.4	113.1
Salt Lake City	51.2	31.1	11832.3	622.9	137.9
Minneapolis	51.4	26.2	9325.6	901.3	121.1
Atlanta	53.9	50.3	9738.6	473.2	100.7
Las Vegas	59.6	40.9	13100.0	514.6	119.8
New Orleans	81.5	40.9	7460.5	693.6	103.2
Phoenix	84.4	30.9	16417.2	730.3	143.9
Chicago	88.3	20.6	18771.3	1182.1	140.8
Dallas	92.8	29.6	9289.4	701.8	132.5
St Louis	101.7	31.5	7800.0	749.8	140.0
Denver	102.2	20.0	17823.2	1121.4	154.7
Houston	102.7	29.9	12719.6	794.8	140.0
Los Angeles	105.0	28.8	13416.5	881.2	139.4
Detroit	105.6	24.3	14199.9	975.6	144.6
Mean	67.2	35.3	11194.3	758.3	122.4

Table 5.3 – *Metric area, line density, maximum and mean line length, and mean segment length for 20 American urban grids (rank ordered from smallest to largest in terms of area).*

		First-order								Second-order	
Sample	K-LINES	MAX GLOBAL	MEAN GLOBAL	MAX CN	MEAN CN	MAX LOCAL	MEAN LOCAL	MAX DEPTH	MEAN DEPTH	INTELL.	SYNERGY
Miami	1147	4.1	2.3	109	6.9	8.3	3.6	12	3.9	.32	.77
Baltimore	1274	4.0	2.1	96	8.0	8.0	3.7	11	4.1	.33	.70
Washington, D.C	1294	3.0	1.7	63	6.8	7.2	3.2	12	4.6	.35	.68
Minneapolis	1349	2.3	1.3	77	6.9	8.2	3.1	13	5.4	.24	.53
Philadelphia	1541	4.9	2.6	117	8.1	8.3	4.0	9	3.6	.35	.74
Salt Lake City	1595	3.8	2.1	88	4.4	7.8	2.9	8	4.1	.17	.67
San Francisco	1772	2.2	1.4	82	6.6	8.8	3.1	17	5.7	.23	.57
Chicago	1819	5.8	3.1	142	8.6	8.6	4.3	5	3.4	.47	.86
Seattle	1929	2.6	1.5	61	5.6	7.2	2.9	11	5.2	.28	.53
Denver	2046	4.1	2.2	128	7.6	8.7	3.5	10	4.1	.38	.79
Orlando	2259	2.7	1.5	60	4.2	7.1	2.6	12	5.1	.12	.45
Las Vegas	2436	3.5	1.8	98	4.1	8.0	2.5	9	4.5	.23	.67
Detroit	2564	3.9	2.2	130	7.3	8.6	3.8	8	4.2	.19	.60
Phoenix	2607	4.6	2.5	123	4.9	8.4	3.2	9	3.9	.27	.85
Atlanta	2712	2.3	1.4	64	4.8	7.2	2.7	13	5.8	.23	.56
Dallas	2744	2.4	1.4	60	5.6	7.2	3.0	16	5.8	.16	.41
Los Angeles	3026	3.6	2.0	120	6.7	8.3	3.6	10	4.5	.16	.57
Houston	3067	2.3	1.4	78	6.9	7.7	3.3	12	5.9	.17	.31
St. Louis	3200	2.0	1.2	49	5.4	6.7	2.9	17	6.5	.15	.34
New Orleans	3334	2.0	1.2	73	6.7	8.7	3.1	14	6.5	.20	.37
Mean	2186	3.3	1.8	91	6.3	8.0	3.2	11.4	4.8	.25	.60

Table 5.4 – *Spatial parameters in the sample of 20 American urban grids for: axial size (k-line); maximum and mean global integration; maximum and mean connectivity; maximum and mean local integration; maximum and mean depth from the most integrated line (first order); and, intelligibility and synergy (second order).*

Hanson (1984) describe a 'deformed wheel' structure as a convex-shaped integration core forming the axles of the wheel, diagonal lines radiating from center-to-edge like spokes, and portions of the edge forming the ring of the wheel itself in the urban grid. These offset grids form a large, highly integrated core with the diagonal streets (usually defining the boundary between offset grids) radiating from center-to-edge of the urban spatial network. American urban grids more characterized by a large-scale orthogonal logic have a super grid structure more or less connecting from edge-to-edge across the urban spatial network. This super grid of streets tends to define what Karimi et al. (2005) characterize as the capital routes of the city.

The effect of block size

There does not appear to be any readily apparent effect of overall size on the data in the sample. Metric area in the sample ranges from nearly 30 square kilometers in Philadelphia and Miami to 105 square kilometers in Los Angeles and Detroit (**Table 5.3**). Axial size ranges from nearly 1,200 axial lines in Miami to a little over 3,300 axial lines in New Orleans (**Table 5.4**). In terms of comparable axial size, there is an average size difference of approximately 78 axial lines (less than 4%) per pairing of urban grids. There is a clear relationship between axial size and metric area ($R^2=0.5776$, $p<0.001$), but axial size is unrelated to any other metric parameter in the sample.

We can discern several things by examining the metric parameters in comparison to the American sample in the previous study (Major, 2015c). First, line density is 25% less and line density in this sample ranges from about 20 axial lines per square kilometer (km^2) in cities strongly characterized by a large-scale orthogonal logic such as Chicago and Denver to nearly 56 per km^2 in Philadelphia. An orthogonal grid also characterizes Philadelphia but its mean segment length is about 50% shorter than the average of Chicago and Denver. Second, mean street length is over 20% greater than in the American urban grids of the previous study (Major, 2015c). Given these axial maps incorporate about 25% more of the urban fabric and there is strong correspondence between axial size and metric area, it would only be surprising if this were not the case. Mean street length increases to an average of over 750 meters or nearly 2,500 feet in this sample. Third, average maximum street length in this sample is over 11,000 meters or nearly 37,000 feet, with Chicago and Denver having the longest axial lines due to the large-scale orthogonal logic in these urban grids (approximately 18,000 meters, 60,000 feet, or 11.5 miles). Conclusions about maximum street length are suggestive rather than definitive since some lines of maximum length may actually extend even further beyond the boundaries of the axial map. Maximum street length was not a

ESTIMATION OF AVERAGE BLOCK SIZE

City	Meters^2	Acres
San Francisco	9,082	2.2
Philadelphia	9,467	2.3
Washington, DC	9,861	2.4
Atlanta	10,141	2.5
New Orleans	10,650	2.6
Seattle	12,791	3.2
Miami	12,905	3.2
Baltimore	13,019	3.2
Orlando	13,363	3.3
Las Vegas	14,352	3.6
Minneapolis	14,665	3.6
Dallas	17,556	4.3
Salt Lake City	19,016	4.7
Los Angeles	19,432	4.8
Houston	19,600	4.8
St. Louis	19,600	4.8
Chicago	19,825	4.9
Phoenix	20,707	5.1
Detroit	20,909	5.2
Denver	23,932	5.9
MEAN	**15,554**	**3.8**

Table 5.5 – *Average block size estimate in the sample of American urban grids ordered from smallest to largest.*

parameter examined in the study of 20 American and European urban grids (Major, 2015c). Finally, mean segment length has increased about 17% compared to the American urban grids of the previous study (Major, 2015c). Larger blocks, longer streets, and an expansive, sparse urban fabric in the horizontal dimension appears to characterize American cities to an even greater degree when incorporating a greater portion of the urban layout in the axial maps in comparison to the previous study (Major, 2015c).

Based on mean segment length, we can estimate average block size in this sample as 90 x 170 meters (295 x 560 in feet), i.e. over 3.25 acres or more than 15,000 square meters. This is an increase of 1 acre compared to the American urban grids of the previous study (Major, 2015c). **Table 5.5** shows the estimation of average block size in this sample. We can see average block size is larger than 2 acres in every American urban grid up to a high of nearly 6 acres in Denver. **Figure 5.6** shows a comparison of average block size in a selection of American urban grids across the range of sizes in the sample. Average block size in Philadelphia is nearly 9,500 square meters or more than 2 acres, which translates into a block measuring 65 x 145 meters or 215 x 475 feet if the block is rectangular where its length is roughly twice the width. In Las Vegas, it is over 14,000 square meters or more than 3.5 acres, which translates into a rectangular block measuring 90 x 160 meters or 295 x 525 feet. Finally, in Denver, it is nearly 24,000 square meters or nearly 6 acres in size, which translates into a rectangular block measuring 110 x 215 meters or 360 x 705 feet. We adopt very strict parameters for

correlations between variables in this book. Namely, a strong relationship between metric and/or spatial parameters is a linear correlation with a R^2 value of 0.500 or greater where the p value is small, i.e. less than 0.01 or 0.001. When the term 'weak' is used, it means there is a R^2 value between 0.35 and 0.50, where p<0.01. When the term poor is used, it means the same as no relationship, i.e. R^2 value of less than 0.35.

As in the previous study, average block size strongly relates to metric area (R^2=0.6512, p<0.001) (Major, 2015c). Interestingly, mean street length in this sample inversely relates to street density, and maximum line length (i.e. the length of the longest street in the urban network) strongly relates to block size but the opposite is not true.[2] Mean street length has a poor relationship to average block size, as does maximum street length to street density. This suggests a couple of things. First, the longest streets in the urban layout are more a result of block size rather than the average length of all streets. Second, whether the urban grid is dense or sparse for line density, it is a function of street lengths across the entire urban layout rather than merely its longest streets. According to Hillier (2002), this is predictable since "as settlements grow... the proportion of lines that are long relative to the mean for the settlement becomes smaller but the lines themselves get longer" (158–159). Maximum and mean street length are weakly or poorly related to every other metric parameter in this sample, including each other. Average block size inversely relates to street density, which indicates the role of larger block sizes across the entire urban system in contributing to whether the urban grid is dense or sparse.

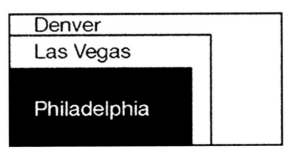

Figure 5.6 – *Scaled diagram of average block size in Philadelphia, Las Vegas, and Denver in the sample of 20 American urban grids. The sample mean is only slightly larger than average block size in Las Vegas.*

Taken together, this seems to confirm one of the most remarkable characteristics about the American city is its expansive size in the horizontal dimension, which arises due to widespread use of the regular grid incorporating larger blocks and longer streets. This pattern is repeated over and over again – facilitated by the national grid system established in the 1785 Land Ordinance – through either expansion of the orthogonal grid logic at the large-scale of the urban grid, aggregation of multiple orthogonal grids along differing alignments in the form of offset grids, or both. The cumulative effect is that the expansive nature of the American city is of a magnitude that is both remarkable and unique in the annals of town planning. Gandelsonas (1999) argues this represents the invention of a new scale rather than a new type of layout. Baudrillard (1988) eloquently describes this as Americans "have not destroyed space, they have simply rendered it infinite… hence these infinitely extendable cities" (99). Using a large database of space syntax models of urban layouts from around the world, including several of the axial maps included in this book, Carvalho and Penn (2004) were able to demonstrate that the spatial configurations of all cities have a fractal dimension. This means all urban spatial networks have a degree of self-similarity at all scales of the built environment. Shpuza (2014) also demonstrated in a sample of small Adriatic settlements that this characteristic of self-similarity tends to persists during the evolution of urban growth even as block sizes and street lengths become metrically larger and longer in mediating the relationship between the city and its expanding edges. According to Batty (2008), "cities are classic examples of fractals in that their form reflects a statistical self-similarity or hierarchy of clusters" (770). In the context of these findings, this means American cities represent a magnitude increase in the scale of city building in the history of town planning.

As seen in Chapter 1, this can be traced to the very beginning of town planning activity in America during the colonial period, initially in the 1641 Nine Square Plan for New Haven and achieving full expression in William Penn's 1682 plan for Philadelphia. Pierce (1998) argues this has been a defining, historic characteristic of American urbanism: "Americans… spread out in a pattern with rare historical precedent. Consider the older city of St. Louis, one of the nation's great industrial centers… between 1950 and 1990, the population of St. Louis and the surrounding counties in the state of Missouri and Illinois rose by 35 percent… but the amount of land consumed by development – for housing subdivisions, new commercial centers, factories and industrial parks – soared by 355 percent. (From) 1970 to 1990… the Chicago region's population inched up 4 percent, but its land use increased by 46 percent… Los Angeles, a fast growth area, added 45 percent more people – but consumed 300 percent more land" (28).

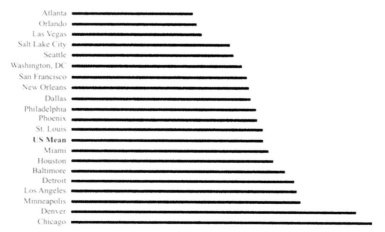

Figure 5.7 – Comparison of mean line length in the sample of American urban grids arranged from shortest to longest mean line length set to a common scale.

The effect of street length

The previous study argued the effect of street length and connectivity on spatial configuration is how American cities overcome building on such a grand scale in the horizontal dimension, where, by definition, everything has to be further away from everything else (Major, 2015c). The longer a street, then the more it tends to be connected. This is a fundamental characteristic that tends to distinguish the urban grid of most cities. It is also how different American urban grids vary from each other. We can illustrate this in a similar manner as block size in the previous section. **Figure 5.7** (previous page) compares mean street lengths in the sample set to a common scale. Chicago and Denver represent the extreme cases with the longest mean street lengths. Both possess a large-scale orthogonal logic in the urban grid. The urban grids with the shortest mean line length are Atlanta, Orlando, and Las Vegas. In all three cases, this is reflective of the propensity for 20th century suburban development in these cities, despite all possessing a large-scale orthogonal logic in the urban grid (Orlando and Las Vegas more so than Atlanta). The same is true for Salt Lake City, which has the next lowest mean street length. In Atlanta, the large number of offset grids in the downtown area only accentuates the effect on mean street length of suburban developments in its periphery, which causes the Atlanta urban grid to have, on average, the shortest streets in the sample.

If a comparison of maximum street length is similarly set to a common scale (in this case, ten times the scale in Figure 5.7), then the extreme differences for the longest streets in the 20 contemporary American urban grids are readily apparent (**Figure 5.8**). Based on the average maximum street length in the sample, the most typical urban grid is Philadelphia. Offset grids characterize all eight cities with the shortest maximum street length. The urban grids of the three cities with the longest maximum street length all possess a large-scale orthogonal logic (Phoenix, Denver, and Chicago). Orlando is the only urban grid characterized by a large-scale orthogonal logic that falls into the bottom half of the sample as a whole for maximum street length. The reason is the impetus for explosive urban growth in Orlando over the last half-century was Walt Disney's announcement of the construction of the Disney World theme park in 1965, which opened in 1971. The population of Orlando was 99,000 people in 1970. It now has a metropolitan population of more

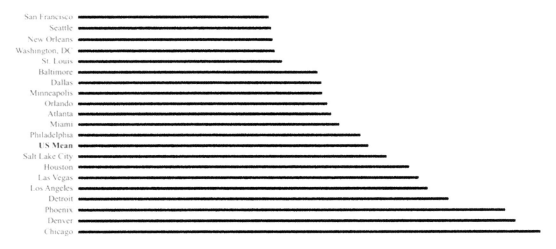

Figure 5.8 – *Comparison of maximum line length in the sample of American urban grids arranged from shortest to longest mean line length set to a common scale.*

than 2 million people (Source: U.S. Census Bureau). This occurred after adoption of the 1969 National Environmental Quality Act (NEQA) and 1972 Federal Clean Water Act (CWA). These laws placed significant limits on development due to environmental regulations for protecting water bodies/wetlands and stormwater management. It eliminated opportunities to extend the conceptual order of the orthogonal grid in the region.

The constraints on development imposed by these Federal regulations in Orlando are considerable since the local topography is mostly wetlands. Other cities experiencing explosive growth after 1972 such as Las Vegas and Phoenix have fewer constraints on development because of local environmental conditions. For example, there are not any protected water bodies/wetlands in the Phoenix area at all and only one protected wetland in Las Vegas (associated with the Desert Wetland Park, shown in green to the extreme lower right in **Figure 5.9**, left). This is not surprising since both cities are located in the subtropical arid climate of the Sonoran and Mojave Deserts, respectively. Orlando is located in a tropical/sub-tropical climate where there are a large number of protected water bodies/wetlands associated with lakes and swamps in the area, as can be seen in the National Wetlands Inventory map in **Figure 5.9** (areas in dark and light blue and green). Some American land speculators and developers circumvent the most restrictive requirements of these Federal laws by literally building their cities – according to Kunstler (1993) tending to flourish solely as centers for the real estate business – in a desert. At the same time, they enjoy the financial windfall associated with reduced short-term costs of planning and building suburban layouts in these locales where there is no physical or environmental need (as there is in Orlando) but only socioeconomic ones such as residential exclusivity and managing vehicular traffic flows. Seen in this light, American cities such as Las Vegas and Phoenix might flourish, in part, because government regulations introduce a 'perversion' into the methods of city building established over the preceding 5,000 years of human history. We can say perversion because some of these cities do not have the local resources (water being the most obvious with Los Angeles being another example) to sustain themselves in terms of generic function (Banham, 1971; Davis, 1992). American land speculators and developers are quick to exploit this regulatory perversion in dogged pursuit of the largest profit margins, which seems to strike at the fundamentals of urban sustainability and traditional, common sense ways of building (Mouzon, 2010). In fact, given the effect of these regulatory constraints, the existence of a large-scale orthogonal logic in the Orlando urban grid at all is even more

Figure 5.9 – National Wetlands Inventory maps of: (left) Las Vegas; (middle) Orlando; and, (right) Phoenix. Blue colors indicate protected water bodies and green colors are protected wetlands (Scale: 1:250,000) (Source: U.S. Fish and Wildlife Service).

remarkable. Its maximum street length is 37% and 72% shorter than cities such as Las Vegas or Phoenix, respectively. Orlando provides a contrast to the other Floridian city (e.g. Miami) in the sample. Miami experienced substantial urban growth beginning in the 1920s, which continued into the post-war period. It already had a metropolitan population of more than 2 million people at the time of adoption of the Federal NEQA and CWA (Source: Real Estate Center at Texas A&M University). Orlando is also instructive because its large-scale orthogonal logic was as much a result of the pattern of land division imposed by the national grid system of the 1785 Land Ordinance as any overall conceptual plan prepared by regulatory agencies for that city. The State of Florida did not adopt its Growth Management Act until 1985, which required local governments to prepare comprehensive plans for projected urban growth. This law did not carry much legal weight until the Florida Supreme Court's decision in *Board of County Commissioners of Brevard County v. Snyder* in 1993 (Dawson, 1996). In *Snyder*, the Florida Supreme Court ruled certain land use decisions are quasi-judicial in nature and subject to strict scrutiny rather than simply a matter of policy, which is subjective in nature and open to opinion (Dawson, 1996). In any case, 20th century boomtowns such as Las Vegas, Orlando, Phoenix, and Salt Lake City demonstrate the enduring impact of the national grid system on American urbanism. Reps and others describe this orthogonal grid logic as emerging from a well-defined subdivision process during land speculation activities in many 19th century cities (Reps, 1965). However, these distinctly 20th century boomtowns demonstrate this process is alive and well today.

The effect of configuration

The spatial parameters of the sample were previously shown in **Table 5.4** (page 96). The table organizes the data from smallest to largest in terms of axial size.

Interestingly, there is less variation for the spatial parameters in this sample of American urban grids compared to the previous study (Major, 2015c). Global integration ranges from the most integrated urban grid in Chicago, characterized by a large-scale orthogonal logic, to the least integrated urban grids of St. Louis and New Orleans, both characterized by offset grids. Overall, Chicago is the most connected urban grid in the sample whereas St. Louis has the lowest maximum connectivity. Despite also possessing a large-scale orthogonal logic, Las Vegas has the lowest mean connectivity. This is due to suburbanization in so many 20th century boomtowns such as Las Vegas, Orlando, Phoenix, and Salt Lake City, all of which have the lowest mean connectivity values in the sample despite also possessing a large-scale orthogonal logic.

In terms of formal composition, there are generally three types of suburban layouts in American cities. First, there is *repetitive deformity*, whereby the designer replicates a formal element such as a curved street or a residential pod over and over again to generate the

Figure 5.10 – *Suburban-type layout in a 2006 development for over 250 town homes in a major city of Florida, which shows a typical plan tailored to environmental regulations for protected wetlands (in light gray) and stormwater management (in dark gray) with only one street connection (southeast corner) to the urban context.*

overall plan. Second, there is *asymmetrical regularity*, whereby the designer designs the plan based on order concepts so there is a readily apparent geometric logic such as parallel/perpendicular streets or circular roads, but these are poorly related to the large-scale grid logic of the surrounding urban context, especially in terms of connectivity. Hence, there is an asymmetrical relationship in the scale of the geometric logic at macro- and micro-levels of the urban grid. Third, there are *geomorphic* variations of each – borrowing from Moholy-Nagy's (1968) terminology – whereby the designer tailors a layout based on repetitive deformity or asymmetrical regularity to local topographical constraints, usually due to environmental protection regulations associated with the Federal NEQA and/or CWA. However, formal design generates elements of the plan (streets, blocks, etc.) in the same manner as the others (**Figure 5.10**). For example, this occurs in several areas of the Orlando urban grid due to restrictive wetland protection and stormwater management regulations in the State of Florida. In all three cases, designers typically terminate streets at the perimeter of the development so they remain internal to the development. There are minimal connections (e.g. inter-connectivity) to the context. Repetitive deformity will also often minimize the number of internal street connections as well (e.g. intra-connectivity). Despite these formal differences, the spatial effect is the same. Connections are broken to discretely separate these developments by segregating them at the local scale within the large-scale pattern of the urban grid at the global scale in terms of spatial configuration. The key to this type of layout is minimal connections. The breaking of lines of sight by use of curvilinear roads has a secondary effect, though less so than one might expect due to expansive street widths, which are typical in most American settlements. In spatial terms, these types of suburban layouts tend to only relate to themselves. Pope (1996) describes this as "grid erosion… the subtle distortion of urban convention" (59) whereby "these settlement layouts operate as almost discrete elements within the urban fabric but which are singularly attached to the main gridlines" (64). Suburban layouts have a profound effect on mean street length and connectivity in the spatial structure of American cities with a propensity for such development such as Las Vegas, Orlando, Phoenix, and Salt Lake City.

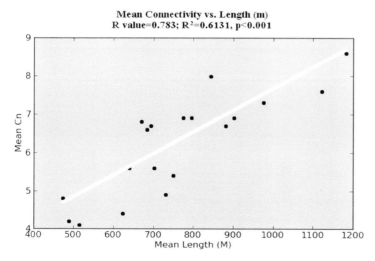

Figure 5.11 – *Correlation between mean connectivity (CN) and street length (m) in the sample of American urban grids.*

There is some variation for local integration values in the sample. San Francisco has highest maximum local integration but all of the urban grids have a value above 7.0 with the exception of St. Louis. Chicago has the highest mean local integration whereas Orlando has the lowest, despite both possessing a large scale orthogonal logic. Chicago also has the highest values for intelligibility and synergy, which is reflective of being the shallowest urban grid in terms of depth from the most integrated line. Orlando is the least intelligible, whereas Dallas has the lowest value for synergy.

By examining the relationship between the spatial parameters, we can see maximum and mean global integration are nearly perfectly related, and both measures strongly relate to maximum connectivity.[3] Maximum connectivity is also strongly related to maximum and mean local integration, depth, and synergy but only weakly related to mean connectivity and intelligibility. Mean connectivity strongly relates to only one other spatial parameter, which is mean local integration. This is not surprising since both are local measures of spatial structure.[4] Maximum and mean depth are strongly related to each other, mean depth is strongly related to synergy, and intelligibility and synergy are again strongly related to each other.[5] There is no relationship between any other spatial parameters.

Axial size has no relationship to any of the spatial parameters, or only weakly so in the case of mean depth, intelligibility, and synergy. However, axial size does relate to metric area ($R^2=0.5761$, $p<0.001$) but not to any other metric parameter. Segment length and street density are unrelated to any spatial parameter. Maximum street length strongly relates to global integration as well as maximum connectivity and depth.[6] Mean street length is strongly related to mean connectivity (**Figure 5.11**) and it is only weakly related with maximum connectivity. Mean street length is also strongly related to mean local integration but not to any other spatial parameter.[7] Again, this is not surprising because mean street length and mean connectivity are strongly related, and connectivity and local integration are both local measures of spatial structure.

Figure 5.12 shows the percentage distribution of connected streets for three U.S. urban grids (relative to their axial size) at the low, intermediate, and high range of mean street lengths in the sample. Since mean street length and mean connectivity are strongly related in the sample, this is extremely instructive because the urban grids at the high and low end of the range of mean line lengths, Chicago and Las Vegas, respectively, are characterized by a large-scale orthogonal logic. The urban grid near the mean for the entire sample (St. Louis) is characterized by offset grids. This chart effectively demonstrates the spatial pattern of Las Vegas is one of extremes when it comes to street length and connectivity. It has a higher percentage of streets with ten or more connections than the most integrated, shallowest urban grid with the highest values for maximum street length and maximum connectivity in the sample, i.e. Chicago. At the same time, Las Vegas has a much higher percentage of two-connected streets than the urban grid with one of the lowest values for

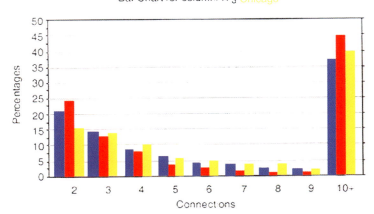

Figure 5.12 – Bar chart of percentage distribution of connected lines in three U.S. urban grids at the low (Las Vegas in red), intermediate (St. Louis in blue), and high (Chicago in yellow) range of mean line lengths in the sample.

maximum street length and the lowest value for mean connectivity, i.e. St. Louis. This is entirely due to 20th century suburbanization in the interstitial areas of the Las Vegas super grid, which effectively drags its mean street length to the bottom of the range despite having a maximum street length more comparable to those American urban grids with some of the longest streets (e.g. Houston, Los Angeles, Detroit). While approximately 40% of the streets in the Chicago urban grid have ten or more connections, this chart also effectively demonstrates both Chicago and St. Louis pattern connectivity (and, by implication, street length) across the entire spatial network. Both Chicago and St. Louis have a higher percentage of streets possessing three to nine connections than Las Vegas. The offset grid layout of St. Louis has a higher percentage of streets with three-to-nine connections than Chicago, and an equivalent percentage of streets with six, seven, or nine connections. Streets in Las Vegas tend to be either extremely long/highly connected or extremely short/poorly connected. Streets in Chicago tend to be extremely long/highly connected or moderately long/connected. Streets in St. Louis tend to be moderately long and connected across the entire spatial network.

This effect of intensifying and accentuating street lengths and connectivity in the regular grid gives rise to a spatial configuration that is highly integrated and shallower from all locations in the city to all others compared to other models of urbanism such as in Europe (Major, 2015c). The degree of accessibility commonly attributed to the American city by some scholars is a direct consequence of spatial configuration, as reflected in the high values for intelligibility and synergy found in American regular grids. We can describe this as the American regular grid *overcoming metric separation by means of linear integration*. The conceptual order of parallel/perpendicular streets of the regular grid in combination with the effect on spatial configuration appears to make American urban grids more readable for movement. This is especially true for those cities possessing a large-scale orthogonal logic in their street network oriented to the cardinal directions. Where you are and where you can go is intuitive and easy to understand. It is the regular grid that enables American cities to overcome their expansive nature in terms of metric area. 'Space is the machine' for overcoming this metric separation through the intensification of linear integration in the urban spatial network of the American city and the key is connectivity (Hillier, 1996b).

Chapter 5 Notes

[1] Data on vehicles per capita compiled from multiple national sources available on Wikipedia at http://en.wikipedia.org/wiki/List_of_countries_by_vehicles_per_capita.
[2] Mean line length vs. K/km^2 (R^2= -0.558, p<0.001); and maximum line length vs. average block size (R^2=0.5432, p<0.001).
[3] Maximum global integration versus: mean global integration (R^2=0.9920, p<0.001) and maximum connectivity (R^2=0.7534, p<0.001). Mean global integration vs. maximum connectivity (R^2=0.7569, p<0.001).
[4] Mean connectivity vs. mean local integration (R^2=0.7903, p<0.001).
[5] Maximum depth vs. mean depth (R^2=0.6790, p<0.001); mean depth vs. synergy (R^2=0.8245, p<0.001); and intelligibility vs. synergy (R^2=0.5837, p<0.001).
[6] Maximum line length versus: maximum global integration (R^2=0.5417, p<0.001); mean global integration (R^2=0.530, p<0.001); and, maximum depth (R^2=0.5595, p<0.001).
[7] Mean line length vs. mean local integration (R^2=0.6131, p<0.001).

6 The Grid as Generator

"The human heart likes a little disorder in its geometry."
- Louis de Bernières

This chapter introduces Hillier's (1996b) principles of centrality and linearity in urban form. A brief review of the literature demonstrates prevalent models of city growth in urban studies – concentric zone, sector, and multi-nuclei theory – take different approaches to account for a tension between centrality and linearity in settlements. Using space syntax, the chapter then examines the local physical moves for designing the regular grid, arguing there are well-defined design methods for its formal composition. These serve as instrumental tools with predictable process effects on spatial configuration in resolving the tension between centrality and linearity during the evolution of the urban form in American cities. They do so by differentiating parts and privileging the center within the pattern of the whole in a manner consistent with regular grid planning principles. The chapter shows how these design methods – grid expansion and deformation, street extension, and manipulation of block sizes – have an effect on the spatial pattern of American urban grids. It also examines the spatial effect of 20th century suburban layouts on the urban pattern, which we characterize as *discrete separation by linear segregation*. These design methods and spatial processes are still active today in development of the American city. Because their spatial effect is a predictable consequence to local design decisions, better and more effective intervention in the American urban fabric is possible while still approaching American cities as problems in "organized complexity" (Jacobs, 1961; 453).

Hillier's principles of centrality and linearity
Interruptions and deviations from the conceptual order of the regular grid characterize the American urban pattern as much as the conceptual order of the regular grid itself. Several argue this is the key to understanding the American city (Clay, 1973; Whyte, 1988; Attoe and Logan, 1989; Gandelsonas et al., 1991; Pope, 1996). Clay (1973) contrasts the complexity that deviations, interruptions, and interfaces between offset grids introduce against the common perception of the American city as "unvarying and monotonous in its addiction to the grid" (42).

He finds the common perception lacks substance. Clay (1973) urges looking beyond the conceptual order of the individual gridiron to how "breaks" from that order introduce variation into the urban grid (45). Similarly, Pope (1996) argues, "because of the grid's formal simplicity, its inherent complexity often remains unacknowledged. Common assumptions… are often based on the reading of its strong categorical and prescriptive order… yet beyond these qualities, it is apparent that the grid is… also a benign apparatus capable of bringing out of an undifferentiated flux an inclusive, heterogeneous field of almost unlimited complexity. The qualities of the grid as an enabling apparatus are too often overlooked and too easily dismissed in a rush to criticize its order as reductive… seldom are its 'weak' tendencies towards complexity… reconciled to the 'strong' predictable and rigid order that is commonly associated with the orthogonal grid geometry. It is precisely in the area that lies between the heterogeneous and the prescriptive that accounts for the grid's unique power. The grid is not only predictable but indeterminate, not only prescriptive but ambiguous… it is capable of sustaining an order (urban or otherwise) that is simultaneously strong and weak" (19–21). In *The Urban Text*, Gandelsonas et al. (1991) demonstrates this graphically by drawing a Chicago grid section and then 'peeling' off those streets inconsistent with the orthogonal logic to reveal the underlying variations (**Figure 6.1**).

The conceptual order of the regular grid as well as 'breaks' from that order appear to work together to resolve Hillier's (1996b) principles of centrality and linearity. He argues there is a tension between centrality and linearity that has to be resolved during the evolution of urban form. This tension arises because the most internally integrating shape is circular but the most externally integrating shape is linear. By definition, circular shapes tend towards compactness in maximizing internal integration whereas linear shapes tend towards extension in maximizing external integration. Hillier (1996b) uses the term 'axiality' in identifying this paradox since axial lines are representations of the longest line of sight. However, the term 'linearity' is equally applicable, especially as a more broadly understood planning concept. In this sense, axiality and linearity are interchangeable terms. "Urban form must then overcome two paradoxes. It must create external integration for the sake of relations to the outside world as well as internal integration for the sake of relations amongst locations within… It must pursue both compactness and linearity, the former for the sake of trip efficiency, the latter for the sake of visibility and intelligibility" (Hillier, 1996b; 268). He argues the resolution of this tension is detectable in all cities because they tend to calibrate new developments to conserve existing spatial structure during urban growth (Hillier, 1996b). American urban grids tend to have longer streets, larger blocks, and a sparse, more expansive urban fabric in the horizontal dimension

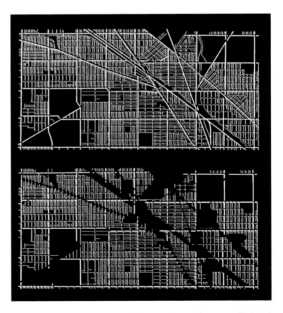

Figure 6.1 – *The Chicago Gridiron: (top) Gandelsonas et al.'s (1991) drawing of a grid section; and, (bottom) streets inconsistent with orthogonal logic peeled off to reveal the variation in the urban grid.*

compared to other models of urbanism (Major, 2015c). At first glance, it seems apparent the entire basis for the conceptual order of the regular grid lies in privileging linearity at the expense of centrality – to varying degrees – in urban form. However, deviations from that conceptual order are also crucial for patterning the urban layout to resolve this tension between centrality and linearity in American cities. This is because they introduce variations to the length of streets and their number of connections in terms of spatial configuration, which patterns centrality into the spatial structure of the American urban grid in varying ways. In this sense, diagonal streets in radial plans such as Washington, D.C. or Annapolis introduce centrality into the urban grid. Though these diagonal routes are themselves, by definition, linear elements, they tend to bisect across predominantly orthogonal grid layouts to pattern centrality in the urban grid at the global scale of space. These routes typically radiate from the center toward the edge in some fashion, thereby maximizing internal integration in terms of centrality while simultaneously maximizing external integration to the outside world in terms of linearity. The effect is similar for the incorporation of old trails and rural roads over time to form diagonal streets across the predominantly orthogonal grid layout of cities such as Chicago and Las Vegas. 'Breaks' between offset grids also tend to assume this role in American cities, depending on the scale of the offset grids and length of the 'seam' streets in relation to the urban whole (Clay, 1973). This can also occur in a less readily apparent manner by varying the length of streets and their connections within a large-scale orthogonal logic. The result is some streets become privileged over others in the urban pattern, transforming the strong prescriptive order of the regular grid into a well-structured spatial network, and striking a balance between the practical benefits of formal composition (efficiency, adaptability, and standardization) and functional benefits of spatial configuration (connectivity, readability, and intelligibility).

The growth of the city

The tension between centrality and linearity in urban form is often present in the literature about cities. This sometimes leads to competing, confusing, or even contradictory perspectives because these "properties are theoretically opposed to each other" (Hillier,

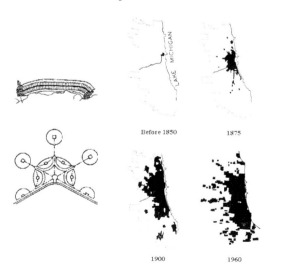
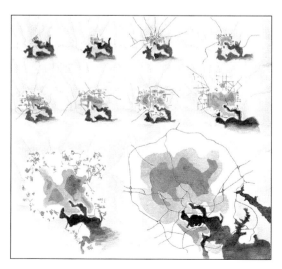

Figure 6.2 – (top left) Linear model of Soria y Mata; (bottom left) diagrammatic scheme of concentric city and satellite towns by Raymond Unwin; and, urban growth of (middle) Chicago, 1850–1960 and (right) Baltimore, 1745–1979.

1996b; 268). For example, Gallion and Eisner describe Utopian ideals of the late 19th to early 20th century as a competition between linear and concentric models of the city. They contrast Soria y Mata's 1882 theory of *La Ciudad Linear* ("The Linear City") with those of Ebenezer Howard and Raymond Unwin for a city surrounded in a concentric fashion by satellite towns as part of the Garden City Movement (Howard, 1898; Gallion and Eisner, 1963). Properties of centrality and linearity are also often apparent in representations of urban growth over time. For example, in Chicago and Baltimore showing linear development along routes into and out of these cities contrasted with concentric patterns of growth from the initial settlement in relation to its ever-expanding edges (**Figure 6.2**, previous page). There is also evidence of this tension at work in prevailing theories about the growth of the city. According to Goldfield and Brownell (1979), there are three principal models of city growth, which are historically prevalent in the field of urban studies: concentric zone, sector, and multi-nuclei theory (Park and Burgess, 1925; Hoyt, 1939; Harris and Ullman, 1945; Fyfe and Kenny, 2005) (**Figure 6.3**). Each attempts to resolve this tension by taking different approaches to the problem in either elevating one property to the exclusion of the other (concentric zone), better incorporating both properties (sector), or separating them out altogether (multi-nuclei) to hypothesize a model of city growth. Concentric zone theory is the work of Park and Burgess at the University of Chicago, outlined in their 1925 text, *The City: Suggestions for Investigation of Human Behavior in the Urban Environment*. Park and Burgess worked in the then-embryonic field of sociology and contributed to the emergence of human ecology as a new field of study. They describe human ecology as the "study of the spatial and temporal relations of human beings as affected by the selective, distributive and accommodative forces of the environment. Human ecology is fundamentally interested in the effect of position, in both time and space upon human institutions and human behavior" whereby position means "the place relation of a given community to other communities, also the location of the individual or institution within the community itself" (Park and Burgess, 1925; 63–64). They argue the physical form of the city should be the initial starting point of scholarly inquiry. Specifically, they refer to the natural advantages and disadvantages of geography in shaping the framework of the urban plan to facilitate or hinder transportation. In this, Park and Burgess built on Charles Cooley's (1894) earlier work to account for the location of cities. Martindale summarizes Cooley's (1894) argument: "While in the past cities were located by proximity to a religious establishment or fort and while some cities have at all times been located by political considerations, the primary reason for the

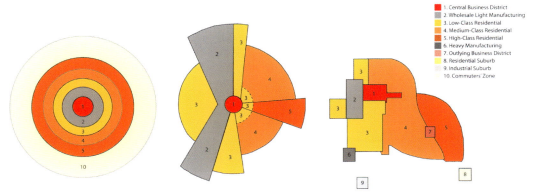

Figure 6.3 – *Models of City Growth: (left) concentric zone, (middle) sector, and (right) multi-nuclei models of city growth.*

location of cities is found in transportation. It is at the mouth of key points of rivers, meeting points on hills and plains, and other such areas that city formations appear" (Martindale, 1958; 16).

Using Chicago as a case study, Park and Burgess (1925) postulate the urban environment patterns ecological and economic factors, which translate into social organization. Based on this pattern, they propose a general model of city growth derived from the differentiation of land uses. They saw land use as a characteristic of this social organization, especially in terms of how populations in different socioeconomic classes (i.e. rich, middle class, poor) come to locate in one residential area or another. Their model is a series of successive rings of concentric growth from the center of the city (i.e. the Central Business District or CBD) outward to its edges. It represents an ideal picture of the tendency for "any town or city to expand radially from its central business district" (Park and Burgess, 1925; 50). They describe these rings as "successive zones of urban extension" and areas with similar land uses become "differentiated in the process of expansion" from each other (Park and Burgess, 1925; 50). They acknowledge the importance of linear development in the form of transportation routes for this social organization. "The axial or skeletal structure of a community is determined by the course of the first routes of travel and traffic. Houses and shops are constructed near the road, usually parallel with it… with the accumulation of population and utilities, the community takes form, first along one side of the highway and later on both sides. The point of junction or crossing of two main highways, as a rule, serves as the initial center of the community. As the community grows, there is not merely a multiplication of houses and roads but a process of differentiation and segregation takes place as well… residences and institutions spread out in centrifugal fashion from the central point of the community… and a fairly well-differentiated structure is attained" (73–74). Their use of the term 'highway' here means a main ground-level road, not a limited access highway in the sense of the Interstate Highway System in the United States today. In any case, this linear nature is not explicitly included in their concentric zone model so one property (centrality) appears elevated in importance above the other (linearity).

A few years later, the economist Hoyt (1939) attempted to address this aspect of concentric zone theory. He argues different land uses and social groups cluster together in wedge-shaped sectors of the city based on the location of main roads and transportation routes. His sector theory of city growth is a variation of concentric zone theory, clearly building upon its foundations (Goldfield and Brownell, 1979; Fyfe and Kenny, 2005). He also uses Chicago as a case study and suggests an upper class residential sector evolved outward along the desirable Lake Michigan shoreline north of the CBD (i.e. The Loop) while industry extended southward (i.e. South Chicago) in sectors that followed railroad lines. Higher levels of access meant higher land values so many commercial functions remain in the CBD while manufacturing functions develop in a wedge surrounding transportation routes. Residential functions also grew in wedge-shaped patterns with a low-income housing sector bordering those for manufacturing and industry because these areas were less desirable due to traffic, noise, and pollution. Sectors for middle- and high-income households locate furthest away from manufacturing and industrial functions for the same reason. In devising sector theory, Hoyt attempts to better incorporate the nature of linear development in the city, which Park and Burgess (1925) acknowledge but exclude from their model (Hoyt, 1939; Fyfe and Kenny, 2005). According to Smith (1962), Hoyt's sector

Contextual modeling, contextual thinking

Configuration has profound implications for the built environment. One of the most important is *context*. Simply put, relational systems require relations. If you want to understand how a site might function, you need to understand its larger neighborhood; a neighborhood, then a large part of the city, or a city center, then the whole city. If you want to understand how a room might function, you need to understand the floor on which it is located; the floor, then the building, and so forth. For example, the most revealing evidence about visitor use at the Tate Gallery Millbank (now Tate Britain) in London during a mid-1990s study was movement traces of a typical 100 people from the main entry during the first 10 minutes of their visit; that is, from outside to inside (Hillier et al., 1996). This demonstrated building layout itself principally shaped visitor use of the museum, not the attraction of particular exhibits. Of course, there were attractor effects, most notably for the special exhibit area and a famous Salvador Dali painting. However, the effects of attraction were temporary and secondary to layout. Space syntax modeling accounted for the natural biases of use designed into the building (**Figure A.13**).

Contextual modeling leads to a contextual understanding, which leads to contextual thinking and solutions for the built environment. Designing for context is crucial for realizing the benefits of natural movement in urban environments. Designing solely based on attraction is akin to swimming without regard for the current. You might find yourself swimming with the current as a matter of chance. You might even struggle against the current and achieve the objective but it is unnecessarily difficult, usually measured in greater costs. It is not the square, neighborhood, or city center itself but how it relates to the larger neighborhood, urban surroundings, or entire city, respectively. This does not discount the importance of urban design or land use planning for a square,

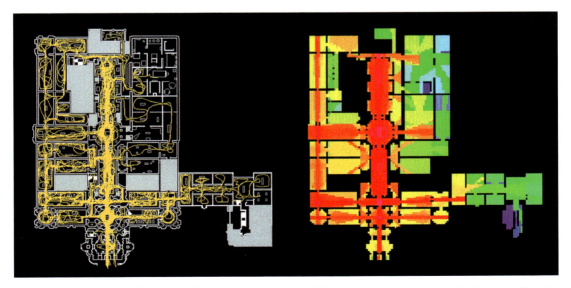

Figure A.13 – *Tate Gallery Millbank in London: (left) movement pattern of a typical 100 people from main entry during the first 10 minutes of their visit; (right) visibility graph analysis of the building layout (Images: Space Syntax Laboratory, University College London).*

neighborhood, or city center. They are important. The 'devil is in the details' but we discount or ignore the details of context at our peril. Natural movement is the door to socioeconomic and functional success. Context is the key for unlocking that door.

'Rules of thumb' about an appropriate urban context for space syntax models evolved over time. No one ever wrote down these rules, not precisely. It is learnt knowledge. This is because the problem of context is paradoxically contextual. It depends. Configurational models require clear *physical* boundaries. These typically include large-scale roads (i.e. major thoroughfares, highways, and so on), urban barriers (i.e. highway structures, railroad lines, and so on), and 'holes' in the urban fabric (i.e. parks, rivers or waterways, shorelines, and so on). Clearly, these will be different for all cities so it is difficult to specify 'hard and fast' rules in Cartesian terms, e.g. so many square kilometers or acres. The King's Cross, London project in the late 1980s established a widely used rule of thumb about urban context for space syntax models. Namely, a 10–15 minute walk in all directions from the study focus (e.g. site or neighborhood), adjusted for clear physical bounds in the urban fabric. This is a temporal rule about context tied to a means of locomotion, i.e. how far would a typical person walk in 10–15 minutes. In the built environment professions, this type of pedestrian shed is quite common. Pedestrian sheds are a way of conceiving context 'as the crow flies' with catchment areas measured in terms of distance or time, usually 0.25–2-miles and 5–30 minutes, respectively (**Figure A.14**). For European cities – with their smaller block sizes, shorter streets, more route choices, and hence, greater walkability – this rule of thumb proved appropriate time and time again (Major, 2015c). However, this rule is unintentionally detrimental for researching American cities using space syntax.

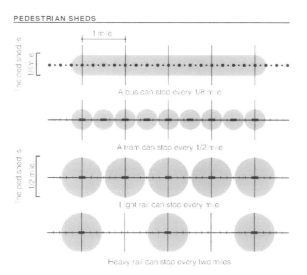

Figure A.14 – *Pedestrian shed examples tied to different modes of locomotion (e.g. buses, trams, light rail, heavy rail) in terms of Cartesian distance (Image: DPZ).*

They have larger block sizes. They have longer streets. They have more highly connected streets. In terms of configuration, American cities are much shallower while, paradoxically, more expansive in area. Our conception of scale is different and larger in American urban space. Our conceptions about context must correspond. A reasonable rule about specifying context for space syntax models of American cities is a 10–15 minute drive in all directions from the study area, adjusted for clear physical bounds at the large-scale. This rule is *not* because Americans designed their cities for automobiles. Halfway through this book, it should be clear that Americans did not; at least, not explicitly before the post-war period. Instead, it is a function of the American regular grid, even for those nominally tailored for automobile usage in the post-war period. This is counter-intuitive. Space syntax researchers have used pedestrian sheds to define context for their area of study focus in constructing models of American urban areas. Many of these studies produced only suggestive or even unclear findings for one reason. The models were too small, applying a rule about context appropriate for European cities but inadequate for American ones. This is a methodological problem for space syntax to correct. Advances in computer processing power have already gone some way in resolving this issue, i.e. the computer is faster so people build larger models. This book represents an intentional attempt at an intellectual correction. A good corollary rule is 'better to model too big than too small.' It is easier to pare down a larger model to a smaller one, calibrating for an optimal urban context. Sincere but misguided attempts to do *vice versa* can lead to methodological flights of fancy.

Architects, urban designers, and city planners have done much the same in conceiving of catchment areas using pedestrian sheds for design and/or policy interventions in American cities. The substantial progress of the New Urbanism and Smart Growth movements over the last two decades has only accelerated the use of pedestrian sheds. In itself, there is nothing wrong with this instinct. It is even helpful for promoting walkable neighborhoods if it results in the design of smaller block sizes for new developments. However, it also points to a potential 'gap' between intent and reality for some developments and/or policies. These catchment areas might provide some insight about the large-scale urban context, depending on the nature and scale of the sheds, development, and even the city itself. In this case, something *is* better than nothing. However, in the absence of a more comprehensive picture based on spatial configuration, the design sensibilities of a particular professional governs these contextual relations. They can be quite expansive in area for American cities; even those characterized by relatively small-scale, offset grid patterns (**Figure A.15**). Designers and planners are people, too. Some are better about intuitively understanding relations than others. This can introduce an element of risk into a project for a client. Some might conclude it represents too big of a financial risk for a multi-million dollar development or our urban environments in general. Contextual solutions promote natural movement through urban areas. Smaller block sizes promote walkability in urban areas. Both promote vibrant urbanism but work better together than either separately.

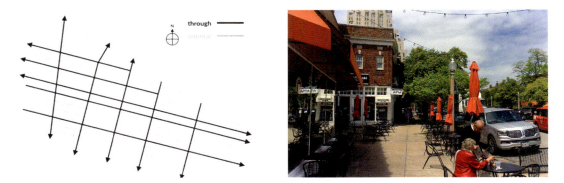

Figure A.15 – *(left) Diagram of through, internal, and boundary routes; and, (right) street view of the Central West End in St. Louis.*

theory attempts to characterize a broad principle of urban organization. The sector model does appear to better represent the type of spatial differentiation regularly occurring in cities due to development along transportation routes while still recognizing centrality as an important aspect of urban form.

Park, Burgess, and Hoyt were primarily interested in the socioeconomic characteristics of populations in different residential areas of Chicago. In their 1945 article "The Nature of the Cities," geographers Harris and Ullman (1945) took a different approach in two ways to theorize about city growth. First, they are primarily interested in economic processes and a range of economic activities "to assist in planning the future of cities" (Fyfe and Kenny, 2005; 18). Gandelsonas (1999) characterizes this approach as taking the flow of money as the subject of scholarly inquiry to develop urban policy independent of physical form. Second, they implicitly divorce the properties of centrality and linearity characterizing urban form into different subjects of scholarly inquiry by proposing "two general categories of patterns and relationships for analysis – systems *of* cities and systems *within* cities (our emphasis)" (Fyfe and Kenny, 2005; 17). In taking this approach, Harris and Ullman argue a city contains more than one center around which activities evolve, so they devised multi-nuclei theory. Particular nodes attract some activities while others try to avoid them. For example, the university node may attract well-educated residents, pizzerias, and bookstores whereas the airport may attract hotels and warehouses. Incompatible land use activities avoid clustering in the same areas, which helps to explain why heavy industry and high-income housing rarely exist in vicinity to one another. Crucially, Harris and Ullman's theory introduces the concept of segregating incompatible land uses – rather than mere differentiation of different types – into the discussion about urban form and growth. This is consistent with the dictates of Euclidean zoning, ruled constitutional by the U.S. Supreme Court in 1926 and gaining widespread use at the time.

In part, multi-nuclei theory is also an attempt to explain the phenomenon of leapfrog development in cities. This type of development does not seem to proceed in an orderly fashion along transportation routes but instead 'leaps' existing land uses to locate further and further into the periphery. Harris and Ullman (1945) attribute this phenomenon to people having greater mobility due to increased car ownership. This increase in spatial freedom allows for the specialization of regional centers, i.e. heavy industry, business park, and so on. However, Rybczynski (1996) points out "the edges of American cities were easily movable… well before the automobile" (80). Indeed, it is the availability and cost of land (i.e. an economic transaction) that appears to drive leapfrog development in cities. Often, under the auspices of Euclidean zoning, it is simply more profitable to convert low-cost agricultural land into high-value urban land than purchase land already zoned for urban uses at a higher cost. According to Fyfe and Kenny (2005), the problem with multi-nuclei theory is that other than the CBD, there is very little predictability about where different land uses and social groups locate in the city. This approach is convenient for paradigmatic and practical reasons. In paradigmatic terms, it is consistent with the a-spatial perspective of the city dominating American urban studies since the mid-20th century. In practical terms, if there is no predictability to the pattern of urban functions then policy makers, developers, and planners can – and often do – randomly insert almost any function into the city in the name of economic development (Boyer, 1983). However, such development is only leapfrog in the sense of the real estate transaction itself and the non-adjacent location of the land in relation to existing land uses. Such development has to connect back into the city in some fashion via existing transportation infrastructure, which is usually a road or highway. Otherwise, the developer has to construct out of necessity – or as required by regulatory agencies – improvements to the existing transportation infrastructure, new infrastructure, or often both in order to service the development. Because of this, leapfrog development appears fundamentally related to the property of linearity in urban form, at least during its initial stages.

The fact is well-defined local design methods – easily replicated with eminently predictable, global process effects on spatial configuration – are deployed to resolve this tension between centrality and linearity during the evolution of urban form in all cities in general, and American cities in particular. We can describe these as grid expansion and deformation, block manipulation (upsizing and subdivision), street extension, and discrete separation (**Figure 6.4**). Discrete separation in American settlements tends to occur by repetitive deformity, asymmetrical regularity, or geomorphic variations of each in suburban layouts. The real 'genius' of the regular grid lies in these design methods and their process effect on configuration being easily observable in its formal composition; perhaps to the point where some historians and theorists too easily dismiss the American regular grid as repetitive and monotonous on the assumption that the 'answer' has to be more complicated and less obvious.

In the following sections, we deploy grid expansion and deformation, block manipulation (upsizing and subdivision), street extension, and discrete separation to 'grow' two notional settlements using space syntax. In doing so, we demonstrate American cities are also characterized by *laws of spatial emergence* like other cities of the world. By emergence, we mean predictable "global spatial effects" arising from purely "local physical moves" in design of the urban grid (Hillier, 1996b; 5). The first example utilizes grid expansion, street extension, block manipulation, and discrete separation based on asymmetrical regularity to pervasively realize an orthogonal grid (that is, streets connecting at only right angles) in a layout. The second utilizes grid deformation, street extension, block manipulation, and discrete separation based on repetitive deformity to pervasively realize an offset grid (that is, streets connecting at more than right angles). In the first case, emergent spatial structure at the global scale is an enlarged and highly integrated orthogonal center that includes not only the CBD/historical area but also those parts of the urban grid most crisscrossed by streets of a super grid oriented to cardinal directions. In the second case, emergent spatial structure at the global scale is a pattern of integration that radiates from the center to the edges of the urban grid. In both cases, we can say the spatial structure tends to *consolidate* – because any intervention in the city has to be correspondingly large in scale to significantly alter this emergent pattern – and converge on an invariant type,

Figure 6.4 – *Local design methods and global spatial processes in the American city: (from left to right) grid expansion; manipulation of block sizes; grid deformation; street extension; and, discrete separation of suburban-type layouts.*

i.e. the ortho-radial grid. This is clear and present in the offset grid example of this chapter but less readily so in the orthogonal grid one, though it will become clearer with the real world examples examined in subsequent chapters. Because of this, American cities are also subject to *laws of spatial convergence* like other cities of the world. By convergence, it means "processes whose rules… converge on particular global types which may vary in detail but at least some of whose most general properties will be invariant," usually an ortho-radial grid (Hillier, 1996b; 245).

Expansion, extension, and block manipulation
Topography can also play a role in allowing, limiting, or even denying certain possibilities for patterning of the urban grid, which Park and Burgess (1925) characterize as the natural advantages or disadvantages of geography for shaping the framework of the urban plan in facilitating or hindering certain activities such as movement. Given the massive scale of American cities in the horizontal dimension, topography often plays a correspondingly large role in shaping these possibilities for generating an emergent spatial structure. However, we can also consciously design the regular grid for this purpose. The rest of the chapter illustrates this in a series of ideal layouts using space syntax to demonstrate the process effect of these design methods on spatial configuration. All of these layouts begin with the layout shown in **Figure 6.5**, which defines the existing spatial structure of a small orthogonal grid at the micro-scale in terms of visual integration and universal (or Cartesian) distance based on 'all lines' axial analysis. The definition of an isovist or visual field at eye level (refer to the

Introduction) articulated by Conroy Dalton and Bafna (2003) makes clear the term 'all lines' is a misnomer since there are an infinite number of lines passing through any point in space. The next chapter discusses this micro-scale structure in more detail. However, for now, this adequately demonstrates the spatial structure we want to conserve in subsequent design and growth of the layout, i.e. cross-axis spatial structure connecting from the geometric center to the center of the edge, and from the center of the edge to the corners.

Hanson (1989) and Hillier (1996b) point out in a layout such as this, each line will have the same integration value in the axial map using least line axial analysis. This is because each are equally connected to exactly half of the total number of lines. If the orthogonal grid is elongated in one dimension, then all lines in that dimension will share a higher integration value whereas all lines in the other will share the lower one (Hanson, 1989). Initially, universal distance and visual integration (as well as generic function, though it is not a consideration in these notional layouts) have to work together to establish the rudimentary spatial structure of a regular grid. Otherwise, the urban object would be subject to a kind of 'ping pong' where the focus of the spatial structure (i.e. its integration core) shifts first here and then there based on wherever and whenever growth is aggregated to the layout. The initial growth rate of many American cities was rapid (Reps, 1965 and 1979). In these cities, any effect from shifting of the initial spatial structure is often brief, sometimes marginal, and often permanent. In Chapter 4, we discussed a historical example of shifting spatial structure during

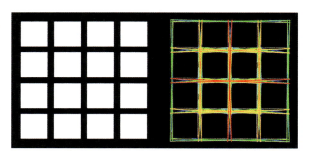

Figure 6.5 – *Micro-scale spatial pattern in: (left) perfect orthogonal grid layout: and, (right) the center-to-edge pattern of visual integration generated by 'all lines' axial analysis.*

the initial growth of San Francisco from 1847 to 1849. This can now be demonstrated using space syntax. **Figure 6.6** shows the pattern of global integration in the plan of San Francisco from 1847 to 1849 using least line axial analysis. The historical plan previously shown in Figure 3.11 serves as the basis for constructing the 1849 model of San Francisco. **Figure 6.7** shows the historical plans serving as the basis for the 1847 and 1848 models of San Francisco. Through a quirk of dating, these plans are actually dated in reverse order. However, given that we know San Francisco became a boomtown almost over night, it is reasonably safe to conclude that the city rapidly grew – instead of contracting – in the manner shown in the axial analysis (Reps, 1965 and 1979). **Figure 6.6** (top left) shows integration initially focuses on the east–west streets defining the north–south edges of Portsmouth Square. This is due to the effect of the shoreline interrupting streets in both directions at the northern edge of the layout as well as modeling the opportunities for diagonal movement across Portsmouth Square itself. The pattern of visual integration using 'all lines' axial analysis is available below this plan as a reference. The center-to-edge/center-of-edge to the corners micro-scale spatial structure arising from visual integration and universal distance is perhaps less apparent than in Figure 6.5 but nonetheless still present. Integration is much more strongly focused on the most central east–west streets, which is due to elongation of the overall geometric shape of the plan in an east–west direction as well as interruptions to the geometric logic of the layout at the northern shoreline. **Figure 6.6** (middle) shows grid expansion occurring to the east and south of the original layout in the settlement. Integration remains focused on the same east–west streets defining the northern/southern edges of Portsmouth Square for the same reasons as before though they are now the most centrally located streets in the north–south dimension of the plan. **Figure 6.6** (right) shows the effect of additional grid expansion and large-scale

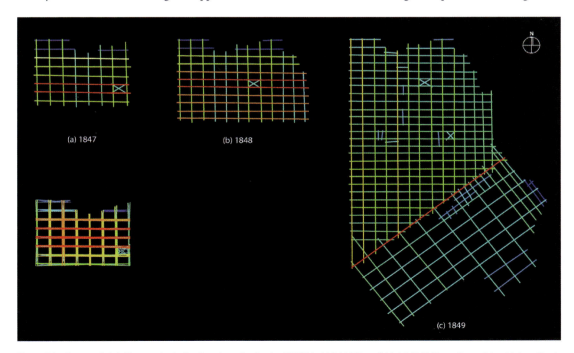

Figure 6.6 – Pattern of global integration in San Francisco plan for: (top) 1847; (middle) 1848; and, (right) 1849. The pattern of visual integration in the 1847 plan of San Francisco is shown to the bottom left.

deformation with the introduction of the new offset grid section along a different alignment to the original settlement. The 'seam' street between these regular grids (i.e. Market Street) becomes the most integrated street in the enlarged settlement, and integration in general shifts southwards toward a new integration core focused on Market Street.

One way to mitigate for this shifting effect is the manipulation of block sizes. Hillier (1996b) argues this is a fundamental characteristic of American cities in that "some lines are internally stopped at right angles by built forms, while others continue from local actions on blocks" (354). This occurs by either block subdivision in the original layout, the upsizing of new blocks added in the periphery of the settlement, or often both. **Figure 6.8** (left, next page) shows an example of grid expansion to the north and west from the original layout (shaded in the plan and outlined in white on the axial map based on the plan in Figure 6.5) with upsized block sizes in the periphery. This upsizing of blocks privileges the cross-axis and perimeter streets of the original layout within the spatial structure of the enlarged settlement. **Figure 6.8** (middle, next page) shows a similar effect where the orthogonal logic expands *in toto* to the north and west whilst block subdivision occurs in the original layout. Finally, the effect of both upsizing block sizes in the periphery and subdividing blocks in the original layout intensifies the privileging of the cross-axis and perimeter streets – and the original layout as a whole – in the enlarged settlement (**Figure 6.8**, right on next page). In each of these cases, mean connectivity intensifies on average along all streets passing through the original layout in relation to the enlarged settlement to varying degrees. However, the spatial effect is the same, i.e. to privilege the original layout. In each case, the north–south streets of the integration core share the same values for length, connectivity, and integration in the axial map. Similarly, the east–west streets of the integration core also share the same values. Because of this, the pattern of visual integration will only marginally shift to the northwest quadrant of the original layout based on grid expansion in those directions (Major, 2001). More importantly, intelligibility in the original layout is 0.99 (+10%) compared to 0.90 for the settlement as a whole. The manipulation of block sizes is quite common during the evolution of urban form. The upsizing of new blocks in the periphery is typically the result of a landowner subdividing a parent tract of land into

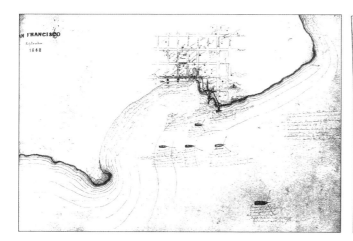 

Figure 6.7 – *Historical plans of San Francisco serving as the basis for space syntax analysis in (left) 1847; and, (right) 1848. NOTE: The orientation of these plans in terms of cardinal directions is reversed, i.e. north at the bottom of the page and south at the top.*

parcels and selling them. Later, these parcels may be further subdivided and sold again as developable raw land or surveyed lots. A similar process for block subdivision takes place in the previously surveyed and platted settlement. Siksna (1997) argues there is "a clear trend for larger blocks to be broken down into smaller sub-blocks (whereby) building forms may… cause lots to be subdivided" and the layout is "considerably modified by the addition of street and alleys, creating smaller blocks and sub-blocks" (22–25). This constant upsizing and subdivision of blocks – and back again over time – is one of the most recognizable characteristics of what Rossi (1982) describes as the essential dynamic of cities.

Another method to pattern the regular grid is street extension. In this case, a strategic street in the existing layout – often one of the cross-axis or perimeter streets in the original plan shown in Figure 6.5 – extends into the periphery as the main road into and out of town in defining the settlement's relationship to the outside world. Lots and land uses then attach to this extended street in the manner described by Park and Burgess (1925). In practical terms, this may occur within the conceptual order of grid expansion whereby initial focus of vertical construction is along the most strategic street in relation to the original layout (i.e., the main road out of town). In spatial terms, the effect is to privilege this street for length, connectivity, and integration above all others in the layout as shown in **Figure 6.9** (left, next page). Both cross-axis streets of the original layout can also be extended in order to privilege not only these streets but also reinforce the existing spatial structure of the original layout for the pattern of integration in all cardinal directions (**Figure 6.9**, right). In the first case, this spatial structure is a characteristic of linear settlements and, in the second, of cross-axis (or crossroads) hamlets. In both cases, it is irrelevant whether or not there is a geometric logic to the layout since only multiple connections to the central street(s) is what matters for patterning the layout in spatial terms. The manipulation of block sizes tends to only vary the degree of privileging for the strategic street(s) but not the spatial structure as whole.

According to Hoyt (1939), higher levels of access tend to mean higher land values. The relation between access and land value is not only a characteristic of linearity along transportation routes within the urban pattern at the global scale. It also appears to be a characteristic of centrality by virtue of adjacency in terms of universal distance and visual integration at the local scale (refer back to the spatial pattern using the 'all lines' axial analysis in Figure 6.5). Because of this, land located in or near the center tends to be more accessible at both the global and local scale of space. Therefore, it also

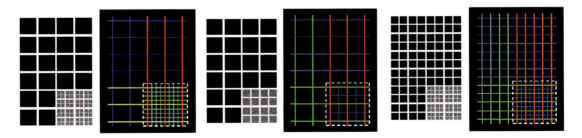

Figure 6.8 – *Integration in an orthogonal layout based on: (left) grid expansion and upsizing of block sizes in the periphery; and, (middle) grid expansion and subdividing of blocks in the original layout; and, (right) grid expansion, subdividing of blocks in the original layout, and upsizing of block sizes in the periphery.*

tends to have a higher land value in the present and the future (Desyllas, 1997 and 1999). In part, this explains why land values in the center of cities are usually higher – actually, much higher – than in the periphery. For example, according to one contemporary estimate, the average price of land for sale in Chicago today is more than $3 million per acre (Source: www.landandfarm.com). This average price is based on over 100 properties available for sale in Chicago as of April 2011 near the end of the Great Recession. Chicago is located in Cook County where the average price of land for sale at the same time was nearly $650,000 per acre, making the average price in Chicago nearly 400% greater than in Cook County in general.

In this sense, the phenomenon of leapfrog development is a cost-value business calculation of the real estate speculation process. Reduce costs in the present (i.e. cost of the land today) in order to reap the financial benefits of land appreciation in the future (i.e. value of the land tomorrow). However, leapfrog development has to locate in a strategic manner in order to be accessible in the manner described by Hoyt (1939). When a settlement is small, locating such development in terms of accessibility at the global scale and near adjacency at the local scale is more feasible. It also appears more profitable in gross terms over the long haul based on the comparison of average land values in the City of Chicago and Cook County. As the settlement grows larger, near adjacency in terms of location – and universal distance and visual integration – is less feasible because the land in the city center becomes more expensive over time. Accessibility in terms of configuration at the global scale then becomes much more important for the success of leapfrog growth, which is why such development tends to project further and further into the periphery in order to find cheap land to be profitable. In part, this is what Reps (1965) means by "the pattern of rural land holdings helped to shape the expansion of the (American) city" (73). We can demonstrate there is a spatial effect. We add this type of development to the notional grid in **Figure 6.8** by leapfrogging over available raw land adjacent to the existing layout, and projecting further into the periphery to the north, south, and west (**Figure 6.10**, next page). Leapfrog development has to connect back into the urban fabric in some fashion. In this case, it occurs by extension of the most integrated streets in the existing spatial structure, i.e. the cross-axis and perimeter streets of the original layout (outlined in white). The effect is to further accentuate the privileging of the original layout in the spatial structure of the newly enlarged settlement. Intelligibility in the original layout is 0.93 (+8%) compared to 0.86 for the whole settlement. Even though these developments are further away from the original layout in terms

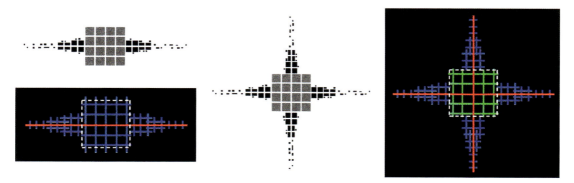

Figure 6.9 – Pattern of integration for street extension of orthogonal grid based on: (left) privileging along the length of a single street; and, (right) privileging along the length of cross-axis streets.

of metric distance, they still have a high degree of accessibility in terms of spatial configuration. Whether it is an existing main road or an interstate highway that is used – or even a newly constructed arterial/collector road – the design principles behind this type of growth are the same. The difference is the scale at which such development occurs in the horizontal dimension of the city. This changes over time as well as the infrastructure required to provide sufficient accessibility within the emergent spatial structure of the city.

In time, successful leapfrog development spurs more economic activity near the immediate vicinity when real estate developers, adverse to the initial financial risks involved with such land speculation, capitalize on the potential for additional urban development. The results are eventually absorbed into the urban fabric of the city during subsequent growth. In this case, the orthogonal grid logic often expands at the large-scale due to the pattern of land division imposed by the national grid system, especially in cities of the western United States (Reps, 1965 and 1979). This can give rise to a super grid in the emergent spatial structure of some American cities. Sometimes the orthogonal logic also continues at the fine scale of the urban grid. Sometimes interruptions or deviations occur due to barriers caused by topography and/or transportation infrastructure such as railroads, limited access highways, and so forth. Perhaps as often, local agents in a conscious act of design can also deviate from conceptual order of the regular grid. For example, it occurs by discretely separating the layout of new developments at the local scale from the grid logic at the global scale, which is what typically occurs in suburban layouts. **Figure 6.11** (next page) shows an example of this phenomenon in the areas to the extreme north, west, and south of the layout. These areas maintain the orthogonal logic but the streets tend to be short, poorly connected, and internal to the interstitial areas defined by the super grid (i.e. asymmetrical regularity). The design decisions in our initial sequence of notional orthogonal grids to privilege the original layout (now the historical area and/or CBD) has conserved its strategic importance by privileging the streets passing through it within the emergent spatial structure of the enlarged whole. When introducing suburban developments based on asymmetrical regularity into periphery areas of the urban fabric, the effect is to further consolidate the

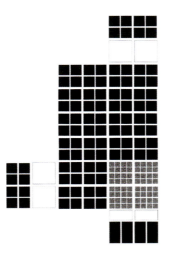
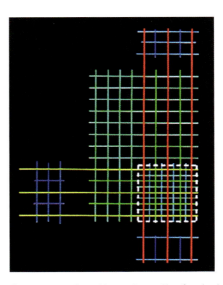

Figure 6.10 – *Pattern of integration in orthogonal grid based on street extension, grid expansion, and leapfrog development.*

emergent spatial structure of the city. In this case, intelligibility in the original layout is 0.78 (+32%) compared to 0.59 for the settlement as a whole.

Deformation in offset grids

The methods for designing the regular grid in layouts characterized by offset grids are broadly the same as for large-scale orthogonal grids. However, there are some differences. Principally, a large-scale super grid does not emerge in the spatial pattern. Instead, street extension of diagonal/radial routes is more important in patterning the relationship from center-to-edge during the evolution of urban form. Sometimes, these are old rural and trails roads incorporated into the urban grid over time: for example, in cities such as Chicago and Las Vegas (Reps, 1965 and 1979). Often, they can also emerge along a street defining the boundary (e.g. break or seam) between offset grids. Kostof (1991) is somewhat dismissive of their importance, saying these diagonals are "actually nothing more than the meeting line between two independently laid out segments of town" (233). On the other hand, Clay (1973) and others argue this is crucial for a better understanding of the American city (Pope, 1996). During "rapid expansion, American cities have shown the results of change more clearly than have those of Europe, and these breakpoints – or gear-shifting zones – tell us a great deal about the larger scene. As special, geometric epitome districts, they offer quick insights into the larger dimensions of the city… a break… occurs where there is an abrupt, visible switch in the direction and/or design of streets – especially where the pattern shifts diagonally. It occurs where… the original gridiron of one settlement… clashes with an adjoining street network… from this clash, there usually emerges a series of awkward, irregular and angular street junctions along the fracture zone where the grids encounter each other" (Clay, 1973; 42). Finally, orthogonal streets of extreme length – consistent with an orthogonal grid but extending far beyond the portion of the urban fabric pervasively realizing this logic – can also sometimes operate in a similar manner to diagonals by patterning from the center to the edge.

We can describe this process as deformation. Grid deformation often occurs due to the pattern of land ownership in a settlement (for example, downtown Atlanta as previously discussed). It also occurs in response to local topographical conditions to ensure the most valuable parcels or lots are rectangular in shape; for example, adjacent to or near a water body. According to Reps (1965), "the curving of the bank suggested a new orientation for the grid plan of these city extensions, a change in street directions that could

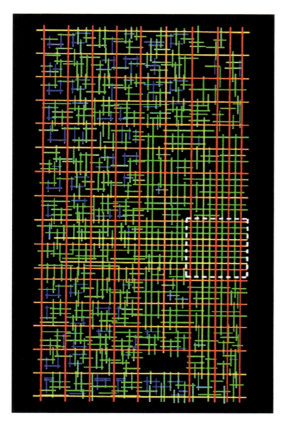

Figure 6.11 – *Pattern of integration in orthogonal grid based on grid expansion and discrete separation due to asymmetrical regularity in peripheral developments.*

be disastrous except for the skill with which these were connected to the streets of the old city" (84). The purpose is what Kunstler (1993) characterizes as an efficiency of construction method for the most valuable property. Due to deformation, irregular shaped blocks emerge along the street at the boundary between these grids, internalized within the layout, and sometimes at the edge of a new grid section furthest away from the most valuable lots in the parcel. Deformation has a well-defined spatial effect in patterning the urban grid and conserving the existing spatial structure of a settlement during growth. Initially, spatial structure can shift based on where growth aggregates to the existing layout. However, in the same manner for settlements characterized by an orthogonal grid layout, universal distance and visual integration (as well as generic function, but, again, not a consideration in this chapter) work together to initially establish the rudimentary spatial structure to conserve during subsequent growth.

When deformation first occurs in a settlement, the perimeter street of the original layout where an offset grid is aggregated becomes privileged within the enlarged whole. Often, upsizing blocks in the new grid section and subdividing blocks in the original layout can marginally mediate for the shift to this street. As more offset grids are aggregated around the perimeter of the original layout, spatial structure in the original layout tends to stabilize. This is because the spatial effect of deformation around the entire perimeter (or nearly so) of the original layout is to privilege all streets passing through it. Attoe and Logan (1989) observe the outcome is a "variegated patchwork pattern as a result of land development by subdivision. The patchwork of American cities provides opportunities for diversity within the regularity of the circulation pattern. The juxtaposition creates legible boundaries defining neighborhoods and districts… thus the American city can be a collection of diverse rather than uniform parts held together by the underlying or conceptual order of the grid" (126). **Figure 6.12** (left) shows the effect of deformation in offset grids around the original layout (again, shaded in the plan and outlined in white in the axial map) in privileging it as a whole but especially its perimeter streets. The effect of block subdivision in the original layout only intensifies the emergent spatial structure at the global scale (**Figure 6.12**, right). In this ideal layout, the streets forming the boundary between offset grids to the north and east connect into the cross-axis streets of the original layout at its perimeter whereas they do not to the south and west. This demonstrates we can pattern the regular grid to not privilege (or, at least, less so) a boundary street between offset grids within the enlarged layout. It can be a conscious design decision, if permitted by the pattern of land ownership.

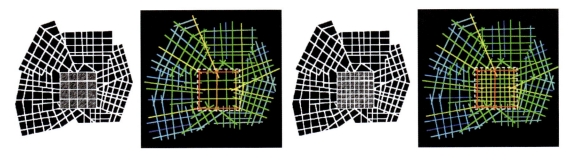

Figure 6.12 – Pattern of integration in regular grid based on: (left) deformation in the form of offset grid without block subdivision in the original layout; and, (right) deformation in the form of offset grid with block subdivision in the original layout.

If it is impossible to offset grids around the entire perimeter (or nearly so) of the original layout – for example, due to topography – then the shifted spatial structure tends to become a permanent feature of the settlement. For example, as previously seen along Market Street in San Francisco. Due to deformation, integration in San Francisco permanently shifted in a very short period (about a year) to Market Street because of its relationship to the original layout and raw land to the southwest, which was soon developed. Today, Market Street remains the most integrated street in San Francisco. The example of Market Street also indicates the role (even potentially) that street extension can often play in patterning the regular grid during urban growth. Another effect of deformation is to privilege some diagonal streets in the new grid sections of the periphery over other streets (**Figure 6.13**). In this case, the opportunity for expansion of the orthogonal logic in the original layout is lost without large-scale remedial intervention. Instead, the privileged diagonals of the new grid sections tend to extend further into the hinterlands of the settlement. Development then aggregates along the length of these streets, which provides a high degree of accessibility back into the original layout. Because of this, new development in the periphery tends to be geometrically oriented (usually based on the right angle) to the alignment of these diagonal streets rather than the orthogonal logic of the original plan. The spatial effect is to further conserve existing spatial structure in the original layout of the settlement and intensify privileging of these extended diagonals for global integration and connectivity. Intelligibility in this layout as a whole is 0.64 whereas it is 0.73 (+15%) for the streets composing the original layout. According to Hillier (1989), this is standard practice in urban systems whereby they "grow by privileging a few lines which form a kind of super grid" (238). Blumenfeld (1982) describes this as "the stellar or finger metropolis… it fingers in all directions… each finger would retain the center and the thrust out would be… comparable to a linear city" (490). This is a view echoed by Schwartz (1982) who describes this as metropolitan outreach composed of corridors.

Discrete separation in 20th century suburbanization

As previously discussed, the types of layouts associated with 20th century suburbanization are more characterized by deviation from the grid logic of their larger urban context. Suburban layouts are often based on either repetitive deformity, where a formal element

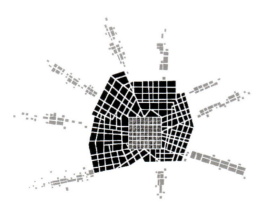
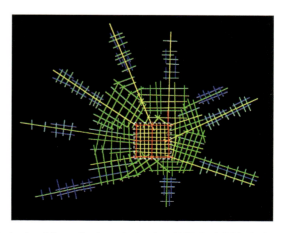

Figure 6.13 – *Patterning of regular grid based on deformation and street extension of diagonal routes center-to-edge with block subdivision in the original layout.*

is replicated over and over again to generate the plan, or asymmetrical regularity whereby the geometric order of formal design tends to remain intrinsic to the site itself. In either case, the formal logic is sometimes geomorphic, meaning adapted in some fashion to local topographical conditions of the site to meet environmental protection regulations. The primary effect of such layouts is on spatial configuration. This is because what is common to suburban layouts, first and foremost, is the minimizing of connections to perimeter streets and thus to their larger surrounding context. Internal streets also tend to be short and poorly connected relative to this context (Peponis et al., 2007a). However, the key is breaking connections to the surroundings. We can describe the spatial effect of many suburban layouts as *discrete separation by linear segregation*. During the 20th century, interstitial areas of the urban grid are often in-filled with these suburban developments. The streets of the large-scale super grid in the city tend to define these interstitial areas. It does not matter if the super grid possesses an orthogonal logic connecting edge-to-edge or offset grids with diagonal routes radiating from center-to-edge at the global scale of space. First, the suburban layout introduces an intensified form of spatial segregation into the urban grid, more so than normally occurs simply by virtue of being located at the edges of the urban spatial network. Second, this intensification of segregation (usually in the periphery) tends to consolidate the existing spatial structure at the global scale of the city. **Figure 6.14** shows a close-up example (in color) of suburban layouts in interstitial areas of the Las Vegas and Chicago axial maps in Chapter 5.

We can demonstrate this effect by introducing a series of short, poorly connected streets around the entire perimeter of the orthogonal grid layout in Figure 6.5. In this ideal layout, we incorporate streets based on repetitive deformity for similar reasons that asymmetrical regularity was deployed in the interstitial areas of the ideal layout in Figure 6.11. We can see this is not the consequence of any geometric order but rather spatial configuration (**Figure 6.15**, left on next page). The effect is to intensify the privileging of the orthogonal grid layout for integration and connectivity to a high degree.[1] This privileging occurs because the most direct routes from all locations to all others tend to pass through the center. We can similarly introduce repetitive deformity into the interstitial areas formed by the diagonal routes radiating from center-to-edge in the ideal layout of Figure 6.13 (**Figure 6.15**, middle on next page). The effect is the same except the diagonal routes connecting back through them to the original layout also become highly privileged for integration and connectivity. The original layout and offset grids surrounding it form an enlarged integrated core within the pattern of the urban whole, which we previously saw in some axial maps in the sample of 20 American urban grids (such as Baltimore and Houston, see Chapter 5). Suburban development further consolidates spatial structure in the settlement at the global scale because, as before, only a large-scale intervention can significantly alter this emergent pattern.

However, several things also seem evident. First, in highly connected and shallow spatial systems such as American cities, in order to effectively introduce segregation into the urban grid for a desired social outcome (for example, residential exclusivity or

Figure 6.14 – *Pattern of local integration for suburban developments in interstitial areas of: (left) Las Vegas; and, (right) Chicago.*

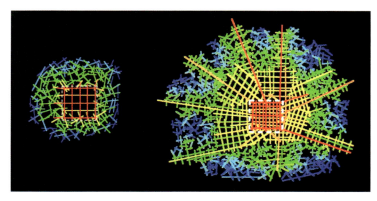 

Figure 6.15 – *Pattern of integration introducing repetitive deformity: (left) around the perimeter of orthogonal grid layout; (middle) in interstitial areas defined by diagonal routes from center-to-edge; and, (right) satellite view of Olmsted's Riverside suburb in Chicago today.*

reduced traffic flows), then you have to intensify the degree of segregation relative to the typical shallowness found in the overall urban spatial network. This is why the breaking of connections is more prevalent today than merely using shorter streets in suburban layouts. For example, Frederick Law Olmsted's Riverside suburb in Chicago uses a curvilinear road system composed of shorter lines of sight (**Figure 6.15**, right). However, there are approximately 20 connections from the suburb to its perimeter streets. Because of this, and proximity to the city's integration core, Riverside still moderately integrates into the Chicago urban grid. This appears to be one reason why the earliest garden suburbs with origins in the 19th century Garden City and City Beautiful movements such as Chicago's Riverside, Atlanta's Inman Park, Jacksonville's Riverside-Avondale, and London's Hampstead Garden Suburb tend to remain highly attractive urban neighborhoods. These orbital picturesque schemes still maintain a degree of connectivity to the surrounding urban context. This is also the design model typically aspired to by the Congress for New Urbanism; at least, ideally (Talen, 1999). The development presented in the Introduction (see Figure 0.2) represents an example of perverting New Urbanism ideals to 'fit' the suburban prototype. In contrast, when suburban development becomes profit-driven based on cost reduction, the elimination of external connections serves to reduce infrastructure costs and intensify segregation of the development. Second, as more and more connections are broken in suburban developments, it introduces more discrete separation by linear segregation into the urban grid. In effect, this tends to abuse the instrumental power of the regular grid to overcome metric distance by linear integration in terms of spatial configuration to achieve a desired and contradictory social outcome (i.e. exclusivity of location or traffic flows). All of these design methods and spatial processes – both their positive and negative connotations for American urbanism – remain active in the growth and development of American cities today.

Chapter 6 Notes

[1] There is another factor related to the color range in the axial map. By extending the range towards segregation, it emphasizes red at the integrated end even if these spaces do not necessarily become more integrated. The way to resolve this is to set the scale from the most integrated of the most integrated system to the most segregated of the most segregated system in comparisons across types of cities.

Order and Structure in the Regular Grid

"The decision to parcel the private development areas in a certain way... established local patterns that transformed the original arbitrary geometry into a structure filled with information."
- Stanford Anderson

Drawing upon the historical record and theoretical models discussed in previous chapters, this chapter examines the formal composition and spatial configuration of two basic plan concepts that appear to lay at the heart of the American planning tradition. The first is the Roman *plan castrum* model of an orthogonal grid in a 4 x 4 block layout with central cross-axis streets bisecting the layout into four quadrants as outlined in Vitruvius' *The Ten Books on Architecture*. The second is an orthogonal grid plan model in a 3 x 3 block layout with dual cross-axes defining the perimeter streets of a central square as outlined in the Spanish Laws of the Indies. The chapter then examines the 'ward plan' model of James Oglethorpe's design for Savannah, Georgia. It argues Savannah's 'ward plan' represents a synthesis of these Roman and Spanish models in combination with the American tendency for elongated, rectangular blocks (nominally, to increase the number of lots). The chapter concludes by using space syntax to analyze the historical growth of the Nine Square Plan in New Haven from 1638 to 1852 and the Savannah ward plan from 1733 to 1856. Block manipulation, street extension, and deformation of offset grids primarily characterizes the former while grid expansion does so for the latter. This analysis demonstrates that the patterning of urban growth over time has tended to conserve – and function with – the micro-scale spatial structure underlying these basic plan concepts; the Spanish model in the case of New Haven and the innovative 'ward plan' model in Savannah.

The elemental cross-axis
Based on our review of the historical literature and record – as well as the theoretical models used in the previous chapter to demonstrate the process effect on spatial structure of expanding and attaching growth to an orthogonal grid – we can now propose there are two basic plan concepts at the heart of the American planning tradition. Both fundamentally relate to Renaissance planning principles via Leon Battista Alberti's *The Ten Books on Architecture* published in 1452, which itself was a reformulation of Vitruvius's similarly titled treatise written during reign of the

Roman Emperor Augustus during the 1st century BC (Alberti, 1452; Vitruvius, 1960). The first is the Roman *plan castrum* model of a 4 x 4 block layout with central cross-axis streets dividing a town into four quadrants (northeast, northwest, southeast, and southwest if the streets are oriented to cardinal directions, which is contrary to Vitruvius' recommendations due to prevailing winds) (Vitruvius, 1960; Kostof, 1991). The second is the plan concept outlined in the Spanish Laws of the Indies of a 3 x 3 block layout with 'dual' cross-axes defining the perimeter streets of a central green or square (**Figure 7.1**). Kostof (1991) argues "the grid with two main axes intersecting, and the large public square at the intersection, were standard" for Spanish settlements of the New World (115). Reps (1965) cites both Vitruvius and Alberti as sources for the planning principles outlined in the Spanish Laws of the Indies. "We have every reason to believe from internal evidence that the Spanish planners and colonial administrators drew heavily on Vitruvius in formulating their own regulations for town development" (Reps, 1965; 31). Whereas "another possible source, and one closer in time to the period of Spanish colonization, was the great work on architecture by Alberti (which) contained a summary of the suggestions by Vitruvius" (Reps, 1965; 31).

In spatial terms, what distinguishes these two plan concepts from one another is not the central square or green (though this is an obvious difference in terms of formal composition) but the even- or odd-number of blocks in the plan. We can demonstrate it by analyzing the pattern of visual integration in both layouts (**Figure 7.2**, next page). As briefly discussed in the previous chapter, Hillier (1996b) identifies a well-defined spatial structure in small, highly ordered layouts using 'all lines' axial analysis. This structure radiates from center-to-edge and from the center of the edge to the corners based on the pattern of visual integration. Visual integration is the configurational relationship of all spatial locations that are visible to all others in a layout in terms of multiple, overlapping lines of sight based on the extension of lines from the vertices of every block to every other block (Turner et al., 2001). Both of these layouts in least line axial analysis "would give each line the same integration value because all are equally connected to exactly half of the total (but) the integration structure in the 'all line' axial analysis distributes integration from edge to center. The central bias in the integration core arises because, in addition to the global structure of lines, as would be found in the axial map of the grid there are also everywhere a large number of lines of every length specified by pairs of vertices which can see each other, including a large number of lines only a little longer than the blocks of built form" (Hillier, 1996b; 271). Conroy Dalton and Bafna (2003) later articulate a revised definition of an isovist as a visual field at eye level composed of "the sum of the infinite number of lines of sight" passing through a single point in space (6). This makes clear the term 'all lines' for this type of analysis is a misnomer because there are an infinite number of lines passing through any point in space. By definition, the spatial information available along the length of most of

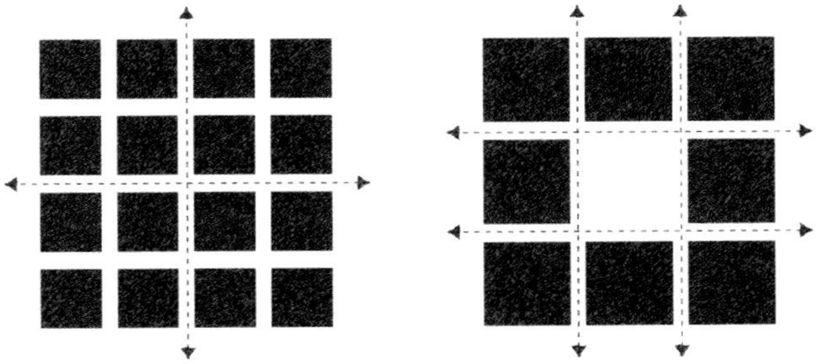

Figure 7.1 – *Basic plan models of the American regular grid: (left) Roman plan castrum of a 4 x 4 block layout bisected by cross-axis streets dividing the town into four quadrants; and, (right) Spanish Laws of the Indies model of 3 x 3 block layout with dual cross-axes defining the perimeter streets of a central square or green.*

these lines is largely redundant to a neighboring line, what Hillier (2003) appears to refer to as "information theoretic redundancy" (13). In effect, least line axial analysis filters out spatial redundancy by focusing on the fewest, most strategic lines of sight necessary for movement. There might be numerous ways that humans use redundancy to their advantage in urban space; signage and streetscape design being the most obvious examples. Redundancy could prove an important characteristic of urban space since this begins to tie into our phenomenological experience of space (Norberg-Schulz, 1985; Hillier, 2005a; Seamon, 2007).

The micro-scale spatial structure emerging from this type of analysis begins to pick up characteristics of metric integration or universal distance. Universal distance is "the distance from each origin to all possible destinations in the system, and so from all origins to all destinations" measured in Cartesian terms (Hillier, 2009b). Today, space syntax calculates universal distance as the average length from the middle of a street segment to the middle of every other street segment (Hillier and Iida, 2005). The topological modeling of universal distance will always tend towards the geometric center based on the overall shape of any representation. 'All lines' axial analysis begins to pick up this bias. According to Hillier (2003b), "cities are shaped by a subtle and complex interplay between visual and metric factors, and in a key sense one will… lead to the other" (4). **Figure 7.2** (far left) shows a micro-scale spatial structure focused on central cross-axis streets bisecting the Roman model into four quadrants as precisely described by Vitruvius. **Figure 7.2** (middle left) shows a micro-scale spatial structure focused on dual cross-axes defining the perimeter streets of the central space in the Spanish model. Crucially, this dual cross-axes spatial structure will remain largely consistent whether there is a central space or urban block in the plan (**Figure 7.2**, middle and far right).

We can say the Roman *plan castrum* serves as the model for the "unending and relentless gridiron pattern" of many American town plans because its cross-axis spatial structure is an elemental function of spatial configuration and universal distance (Reps, 1979; 23). This is because even if we elongate the square blocks into rectangular ones to increase the number of lots, as done in many American settlements, the cross-axis spatial structure remains a consistent factor (Major, 2013). **Figure 7.3** (far left, next page) shows a version of the *plan castrum* composed of lots measuring 55 x 110 feet or 1/8 acre in size. All street widths are 55 feet. Eight lots compose each urban block so the average block size in this layout is a little over one acre (1.11 ac). This block size is more typical of European cities (Major, 2015c). There are 128 lots in this plan. **Figure**

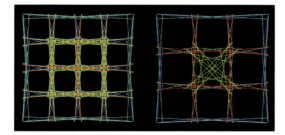  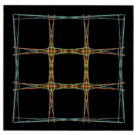

Figure 7.2 – *Pattern of visual integration in; (far left) Roman plan castrum model of a 4 x 4 block layout bisected by cross-axis streets dividing the town into four quadrants; (left middle) Spanish Laws of the Indies model of 3 x 3 block layout with dual cross-axes defining the perimeter streets of a central square or green; (right) 3 x 3 block layout of the Spanish model using a central block instead of a square or green, showing the dual cross-axes spatial structure remains consistent with the central block.*

7.3 (middle) shows the same layout but eliminates the two, least central north–south streets to generate more lots using elongated, rectangular blocks. It is still composed of lots measuring 55 x 110 feet or 1/8 acre in size and street widths remain the same. However, each urban block is now composed of 20 lots. The layout is composed of eight urban blocks, each averaging nearly 3 acres in size (2.78 ac). As seen in Chapter 5, this corresponds to average block size at the lower range of the American urban grids in our sample. Average block size in the sample of 20 American urban grids ranged from 2.2 acres in San Francisco to 5.9 acres in Denver, with a sample average of 3.8 acres. This layout is now composed of 144 lots. However, the pattern of visual integration for this altered layout remains characterized by the cross-axis spatial structure (**Figure 7.3**, right). At first glance, it appears this alteration has 'degraded' the clarity of this structure in the east–west dimension. However, this is a function of the only internal, north–south street becoming much more important and integrated within the overall layout; not the internal east–west streets becoming less important and integrated. These east–west streets remain similarly privileged for spatial configuration and universal distance within the layout. Nonetheless, it is an interesting effect. We will see in a subsequent section about historical growth of the Savannah 'ward plan' that there is a clever and subtle manner to compensate for this effect on spatial structure, which is not only true for Savannah but for many American settlements using elongated, rectangular blocks in this fashion. In any case, what truly distinguishes the Roman *plan castrum* model and Spanish model from each other is the number of blocks. An even number of blocks (or odd number of streets) in one dimension tends to focus along the singular, most central cross-axis streets. An odd number of blocks (or even number of streets) in one dimension tend to focus along the two most central streets, i.e. dual cross-axes. As discussed in the previous chapter, if growth does not consistently expand in all directions, then the cross-axis spatial structure (whether singular or dual) will shift in the direction of that growth. One way to compensate for this effect and conserve existing spatial structure is block manipulation and deformation, otherwise such shifting tends to become a permanent feature of the settlement (for example, in San Francisco). In the next section, we examine a clear example in New Haven where the patterning of urban growth tends to maintain – and reinforce – this micro-scale spatial structure over time.

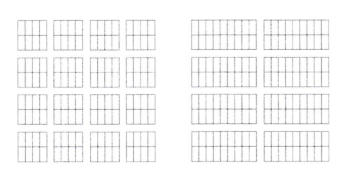 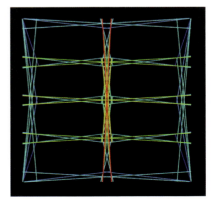

Figure 7.3 – (left) 4 x 4 block layout composed of lots measuring 55' x 110' or 1/8 acre and urban blocks a little over 1 acre in size; (middle) 2 x 4 block layout composed of similarly-sized lots but with urban blocks nearly 3 acres in size by eliminating the two, least central north–south streets in favor of additional lots; and, (right) pattern of visual integration in the 2 x 4 block layout.

Historic growth of New Haven's Nine Square Plan

We previously introduced the Nine Square Plan of New Haven in a comparison of scale with William Penn's 1682 plan for Philadelphia. English Puritans founded a theocracy at New Haven in 1637–38. They were part of the main body that originally established Massachusetts Bay Colony around Boston and Salem in 1628. They located the town on what would become New Haven Harbor at the northern shore of the Long Island Sound estuary of the Atlantic Ocean between Connecticut to the north and New York to the south. John Brockett surveyed the original town plan of a 3 x 3 block layout with a central green (New Haven Green), with each block and the green measuring 16 acres in size (Reps, 1965 and *Records of the Colony and Plantation of New Haven, from 1638 to 1649*).

Though the Nine Square Plan is much larger, its formal composition is the same basic concept outlined in the Spanish Laws of the Indies; even to the point where the plan is offset to the cardinal directions as recommended by Vitruvius. Kostof (1991) views the plan of New Haven as an oddity, arguing "the strict grid pattern (was) almost unknown" in New England and "may have been made in advance in London" in order to explain its existence (115–116). In this, he appears to adopt Reps' (1965) own argument "that the form and dimensions of New Haven had been determined well in advance" though he suggests this occurred in Massachusetts, not London (129). Kostof and Reps make these arguments despite the founders of New Haven being part of the original Massachusetts Bay Colony, which begs the question about why this plan did not make a previous appearance in the historical record of that colony (Reps, 1965; Kostof, 1991). More likely, their arguments are consistent with the idea that "the first generation of American towns... reflected the traditional English preference for informality and

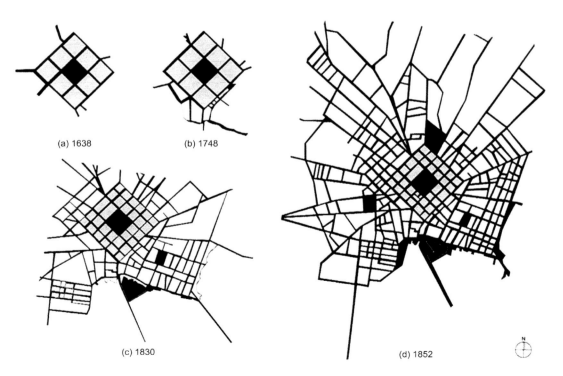

Figure 7.4 – *Growth of New Haven from 1638 to 1852 with the blocks of the original Nine Square Plan shaded in gray.*

From design intent to the designed reality

Space syntax offers objective, quantifiable descriptions of architectural and urban space. Built environments are an integral factor in human society; one of the oldest and most pervasive ones. Because of this, space syntax is relevant for a wide range of fields from archaeology to urban planning, perhaps even 'a-to-z' with zoology; at least, tangentially. Zoologists have not used space syntax. A few space syntax researchers have examined theme parks. A zoo is one of the earliest forms for a theme park, albeit with a longer history than Disneyland; significantly so if you include *menageries*, which have been around since Ancient Egypt. Basically, a zoo is a more sophisticated kind of theme park with a scientific and educational grounding since the early 19th century for the study and care of living specimens including creation and maintenance of habitats tailored to their particular ecosystem. It is easy to envision a scenario where a space syntax study of park layout, exhibit and retail locations, and visitor use might prove enlightening about such places as the London, San Diego, or St. Louis Zoos. Of course, this is not really zoology. It is park and landscape design but it is a sufficient basis for a speculative leap to the end of the disciplinary alphabet.

One of the most fruitful areas for space syntax lies in bridging the humanities and social sciences such as archaeology, anthropology, geography, and history; much like architecture itself. We could fairly describe some of the earliest space syntax studies about the built environment by Hillier, Hanson, and others as socio-spatial exercises in archaeology (i.e. spatial) and anthropology (i.e. social) (Hillier and Hanson, 1984). Such studies can also provide a more rigorous training ground for architects, urban designers, and city planners in the history of the built environment. Many students bring their interest about a historical topic along with them to their studies at one of the space syntax research programs in universities around the world (UCL, Georgia Tech, and so on). For example, a UCL student in the late 1980s studied tribal villages in Sub-Saharan Africa (Salah-Salah, 1987). Several people have studied the Aztec city of Tenochtitlán, which has also been a topic of fascination to Bill Hillier for many years (Hillier, 1996b; Morton et al., 2012; Bermejo Tirado, 2015) (**Figures A.16** and A.17).

 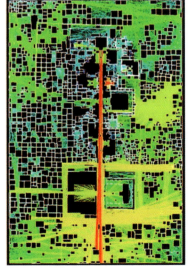

Figure A.16– *(left) Reconstructed plan; and, (right) 'all lines' axial analysis of Tenochtitlán, Mexico.*

Indeed, we might even go so far as to state this is the essential function of space syntax. It understands the past to build a better future for the built environment. We use buildings and cities right now. By definition, we built them in the past. The only real difference lies in whether we still use them (i.e. anthropology) or they still exist today (i.e. archaeology), and then conjecturing future design solutions (i.e. architecture, urban design, and planning). Archaeologists and historians were some of the first non-built environment people to realize the potential of space syntax for their studies. The reason seems apparent. Often, they are dealing with a minimal or even manifest lack of recorded documentation while possessing a relative abundance of physical evidence including buildings, foundations, and so forth for a specific people and culture at a particular time. With space syntax, they are able to generate quantitative descriptions of spatial layouts based on this physical evidence. Essentially, it generates data where little or none existed before and provides an objective foundation to conjecture about their use in the past based on universal traits of being human. After all, our distant ancestors were bipedal, forward-facing organisms bound by gravity, too. Space syntax enables these humanities disciplines to focus on the generic attributes common to all human use for a very long time. In doing so, they can discount more fanciful theories by grounding their studies in the social science of the built environment. Other uses of space syntax by archaeologists include Native American built environments in the American Southwest (Bustard, 1997; Shapiro, 1997 and 2005) and Canadian Arctic (Dawson, 2006). Space syntax allows us to make the link from design intent to designed reality about the:

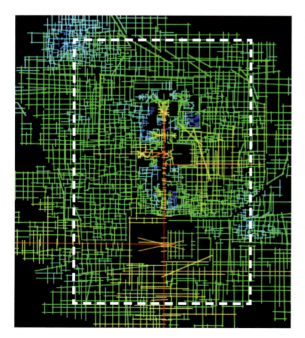

Figure A.17 – *Space syntax model of Tenochtitlán, Mexico. The area of 'all lines' axial analysis on the opposite page is indicated in white.*

- Recorded intent of a particular architect;
- Unrecorded intent of a collective people;
- Constructed reality of individual or collective action;
- Unbuilt or reconstructed reality as recorded in drawings, plans/plat, surveys, and so on.

It is a diagnostic tool for evaluating how a built environment might function in the past, present, and/or future.

It is not surprising that many perceived theoretical and practical problems associated with the socio-spatial functioning of built environments today are often rooted in this 'gap' between design intentions and designed realities (Hillier, 1986 and 1996b; Major et al., 1999; Shu and Hillier, 1999; Hillier and Stutz, 2005).

improvisation, and a casual approach to planning" (Rybczynski, 1996; 66). However, as demonstrated by our survey of a large historical record of American town plans, this is, at best, a questionable idea about the American planning tradition. In fact, Reps (1965) is blistering (in academic terms) in dismissing the idea that the Nine Square Plan had anything to do with town planning principles outlined in Vitruvius' *The Ten Books on Architecture*. He points out that Anthony Garvan advances this argument in his 1951 book, *Architecture and Town Planning in Colonial Connecticut*, which Reps deems "at best tortured, and demonstrat(ing) more ingenuity than sound historical judgment" (Reps, 1965; 128). By implication, Reps' criticism also excludes Leon Battista Alberti's 1452 book outlining Renaissance town planning principles based on Vitruvius as a possible influence for the Nine Square Plan (Alberti, 1452). Reps' (1965) assessment appears incorrect, though he admits "the plan of New Haven was perhaps the most striking of the early New England geometric compact villages" (130).

Over 214 years, block manipulation in the Nine Square Plan itself and street extension/deformation of offset grids in relation to the Nine Square Plan – mostly tailored to local topographical conditions – characterizes historical growth in New Haven. **Figure 7.4** (page 133) shows the stages of growth in New Haven in 1638, 1748, 1830, and 1852. These plans were in the sample of the historical record of American town plans compiled for a previous study as the basis for Chapter 4 (Major, 2015c). The bibliographic references are available in the Illustration Credits. The blocks composing the original Nine Square Plan are shaded gray in each plan. We can see from the 1641 plan of New Haven in Figure 1.11 that initial surveying of property on the periphery of the Nine Square Plan offsets in relation to the Quinnipiac River to the

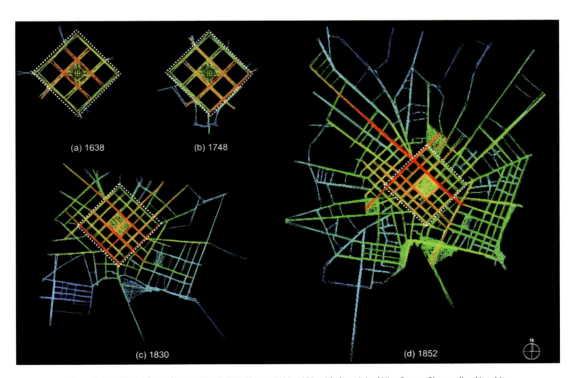

Figure 7.5 – *Pattern of visual integration in New Haven, 1638–1852, with the original Nine Square Plan outlined in white.*

south and west. This eliminated the potential for grid expansion of the formal geometric order in the Nine Square Plan around its entire periphery from the very beginning of the settlement. We can also see in Figure 7.4 that the Nine Square Plan accommodated most of the growth in New Haven during the first 100 years of the settlement until the American Revolutionary War (comparing the 1638 and 1748 plans), and no block subdivision occurred in the Nine Square Plan during this time. Settlement growth then accelerated after American Independence, especially during the 19th century.

We can use space syntax to analyze these historical plans and demonstrate the effect on visual integration (and, by implication, universal distance) and connectivity in tailoring urban growth to conserve the initial micro-scale spatial structure of the Nine Square Plan over time. **Figure 7.5** (previous page) shows the pattern of visual integration using 'all lines' axial analysis during each stage of urban growth in the settlement. A white outline identifies the blocks composing the original Nine Square Plan in each plan. In the 1638 plan, we can see the characteristic dual cross-axes spatial structure seen in Figure 7.2, which focuses on the streets defining the perimeter of New Haven Green. In the 1748 plan, this spatial structure is, more or less, intact though it marginally shifts to the south due to the deformation of offset grids in relation to the Quinnipiac River to the south and west. In the 1830 plan, the marginal shifting to the south remains as the majority of growth is attached to the south and west in offset grids. However, the pattern of integration has intensified in the Nine Square Plan itself due to block subdivision. Integration focuses on the perimeter streets defining the west, south, and east of New Haven Green as well as the perimeter streets of the Nine Square Plan to the south and west. The

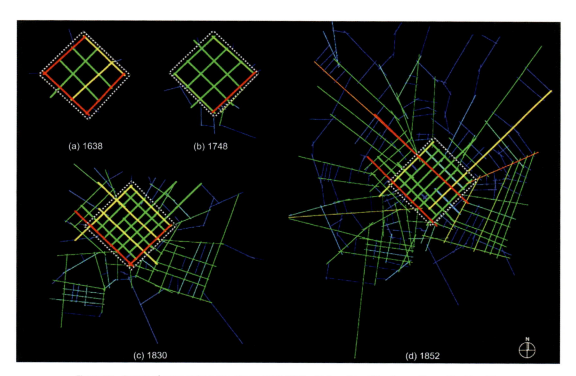

Figure 7.6 – *Pattern of connectivity in New Haven, 1638–1852, with the original Nine Square Plan outlined in white.*

spatial pattern also picks up Temple Street, which runs through the center of New Haven Green today. The marginal shifting to the south and west is again due to the deformation of offset grids on the periphery of the Nine Square Plan in those directions. However, urban growth is beginning to emerge on the northern and western edges of the Nine Square Plan by 1830. By 1852, this spatial pattern re-orients to the north and east streets (College Street and Elm Street) defining the perimeter of New Haven Green and the perimeter street (York Street) defining its northern edge. It also picks up the long extension of Elm Street (relative to the overall size of the settlement) into the expanded periphery of the settlement to the north.

We can now turn to least line axial analysis to examine the effect on connectivity in the macro-scale spatial structure of the settlement, especially the relationship between connectivity in the original Nine Square Plan and the enlarged settlement during this process of growth. **Figure 7.6** (previous page) shows the pattern of connectivity in New Haven for each plan based on least line analysis. A white outline again identifies the streets composing the Nine Square Plan in each plan. **Table 7.1** shows the mean syntactic parameters for each axial map in the left column. It also shows the mean connectivity and intelligibility values of all streets passing through the original Nine Square Plan for each date in bold at the right of this table. For this analysis, we are primarily interested in the mean values for connectivity and intelligibility (shaded in gray) for the Nine Square Plan and the overall settlement, respectively.

There is very little difference in the layout from 1638 to 1748. The pattern of connectivity shifts around the perimeter streets based on where rural roads connect into the Nine Square Plan. It is likely this was less important in this small settlement than the pattern of visual integration (and universal distance), which tends to focus on the streets defining the perimeter of New Haven Green at the heart of the Nine Square Plan. What little development there is over the first 100 years occurs on the periphery skewed towards the waterfront lots associated with the inlet from the Quinnipiac River to the south. Mean connectivity in the layout as a whole is 3.8 and intelligibility is 0.81, whereas within the Nine Square Plan, it is 6.4 and 0.92. By 1830, several offset grids aggregate around the perimeter of the Nine Square Plan, with the largest ones located to the south and east around the river inlet.

According to Clay (1973), "sharp breaks tend to occur at the edges of the central business district" in this manner (44). Only a few streets are aligned (principally in the northern grid section) to the orthogonal logic of the Nine Square Plan. Instead, the majority of new streets in the periphery align at a right angle to the diagonals connecting from the perimeter streets of the Nine Square Plan into the periphery (i.e. street extension). Seven streets passing through the Nine Square Plan extend for varying lengths into the new grid sections. The longest is Orange Street towards the northeast, which serves to privilege the Nine Square Plan. Otherwise, privileging of the Nine Square Plan

NEW HAVEN, 1638–1852

Year	k-lines	Global	Max CN	New Haven Whole Mean CN	Local	Depth	Intel.	Original "Nine Square" Plan Mean CN	Intell.
1638	13	2.0	5	3.7	2.2	2.4	0.90	**5.0**	**0.90**
1748	24	1.8	10	3.8	2.2	2.6	0.81	**6.4**	**0.92**
1830	100	1.7	16	5.5	2.8	3.5	0.56	**10.0**	**0.69**
1852	210	1.8	22	5.7	2.9	3.6	0.54	**11.0**	**0.73**

Table 7.1 – *Mean syntactic values for New Haven from 1638 to 1852 for the whole layout (to the left) and connectivity and intelligibility in the original Nine Square Plan (far right) within the enlarged settlement.*

occurs by direct connection to its perimeter streets within the enlarged settlement. The axial size of the 1830 plan is 100 streets. Mean connectivity in New Haven has increased to 5.5 and intelligibility has fallen to 0.56 but mean connectivity for the streets passing through the Nine Square Plan has increased to 10.0 (+82% compared to the whole) and intelligibility is 0.69 (+23%). This is due to street extension into the periphery and subdivision of almost every block in the Nine Square Plan between 1748 and 1830. This generates a spatial pattern that privileges the center within the pattern of the whole.

Only 22 years later, the urban grid had more than doubled in axial size and metric area. The extended routes connecting from and through the Nine Square Plan into the periphery have become the organizing mechanism for the formal composition of development in the periphery, usually based on the right angle (**Figure 7.7**). Orange Street extends further to the northeast, more than double in length, as did Elm Street (nearly so) due to its extension to the northwest. Elm Street deviates slightly and then continues along its new alignment further to the northwest. Subdivision occurs in only two additional blocks of the Nine Square Plan between 1830 and 1856. Mean connectivity in New Haven has risen slightly to 5.6 whereas intelligibility marginally falls to 0.54 but mean connectivity rises to 11.0 (+96%) and intelligibility actually increases to 0.73 (+35%) for the streets composing the Nine Square Plan. Broadly-speaking, the pattern of connectivity using least line axial analysis tends to mimic the pattern of visual integration using 'all lines' axial analysis during the process of growth in New Haven (compare Figures 7.5 and 7.6).

This brief example of New Haven effectively demonstrates the patterning of urban growth to an orthogonal grid to conserve – and even reinforce – micro-scale spatial structure in that layout over time. The elemental cross-axes defining the perimeter streets of New Haven Green initially brought definition to the micro-scale spatial structure of the town as a function of visual integration and universal distance. This 'anchored' the spatial pattern of New Haven until emergence of a macro-scale spatial structure defined by the fewest, most strategic lines of sight. In the next section, we will examine expansion of an orthogonal grid to demonstrate how other factors of urban function can come into play during the process of growth to reinforce micro-scale spatial structure until the emergence of one at the macro-scale in a strongly geometric, highly ordered regular grid. The case study is the 'ward plan' of Savannah, Georgia and the other factor at work in that settlement is constitution, i.e. the location of dwelling entrances.

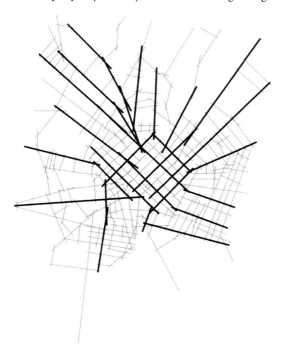

Figure 7.7 – Principal street alignments defining the formal composition of offset grids in the periphery of the 1852 plan for New Haven.

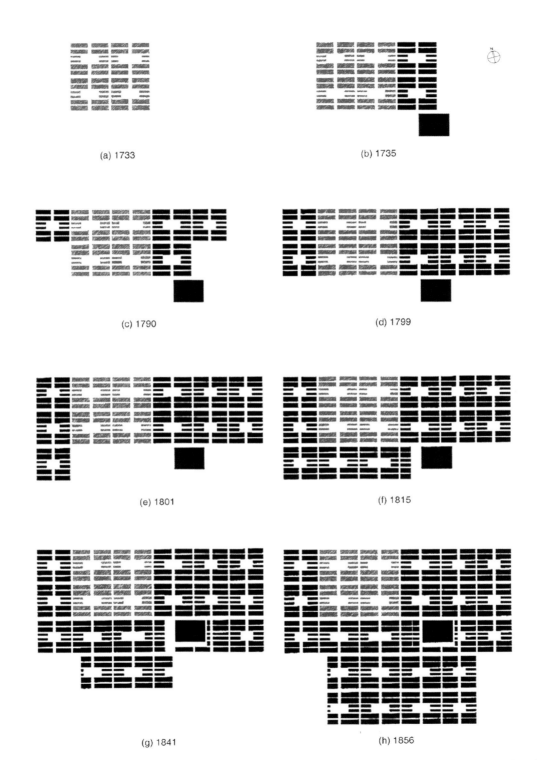

Figure 7.8 – *The Historic Growth of Savannah's Ward Plan, 1733–1856, based on John Reps' 1959 drawing of the same (Reps, 1965; 201). The earliest wards are shaded.*

Savannah: a brief overview

There are few town plans in the world as widely discussed as James Oglethorpe's 'ward plan' for Savannah, Georgia (Gallion and Eisner, 1963; Reps, 1965; Moholy-Nagy, 1968; Clay, 1973; Bacon, 1976; Kostof, 1992; Anderson, 1993, Major, 2001; Wilson and Shay, 2014). Kostof (1991) succinctly describes Oglethorpe's plan: "The city grid was organized into wards, each with its own square measuring some 315 x 270 feet (96 x 82 meters). On the east and west sides of each square, lots were set out for public buildings like churches and stores. The other two sides were divided into forty house lots… The tythings were grouped in two rows of five house lots, back to back, sharing a lane or alley" (96). **Figure 7.8** shows the historical growth of Savannah's ward plan from 1733 to 1856 based on Reps' (1965) famous and often replicated 1959 drawing of the same (Anderson, 1993; Major, 2001). In this figure, the earliest wards are shaded in gray. Despite widespread discussion, others argue the details of the Savannah town plan "are not widely understood" and "(have) not been widely replicated" in real world conditions (Wilson and Shay, 2014; 32). Reps (1965) concurs, saying "one of the great misfortunes of American town planning was that the Savannah plan seemingly exercised no influence on the design" of significant towns in the rest of the country (Reps, 1965; 202). He can only point to the nearby town of Brunswick, located 80 miles to the south, suggesting "had Savannah been located, as were Philadelphia and New York, on the main routes leading to the interior, at least some of our Midwestern cities might have achieved part of the charm and urbanity still retained in Oglethorpe's Savannah" (Reps, 1965; 202). According to Wilson and Shay (2014), "one reason…is that its design elements are unfamiliar to designers and developers," namely each ward plan being composed of tything blocks and trust lots, which makes Savannah "more complex than conventional grids" (32) (**Figure 7.9**). Wilson and Shay (2014) even argue that modern application of the Savannah plan "seems risky" since "a design (without) a proven track record… is difficult to sell to lenders who look to past financial success stories for guidance" (32). This seems an odd argument since – putting aside terminology – each ward layout is an orthogonal grid composed of streets, blocks, and a square, and Savannah has a proven record of success covering nearly 300 years.

We can fairly argue the Savannah ward plan is an English synthesis of the basic models prescribed in the Roman *plan castrum* and the Spanish Laws of the Indies combined with the American tendency for elongated, rectangular blocks (nominally, to increase the number of developable lots though this is not the case in Savannah; at least, initially). We can demonstrate this by means of a simple transformation using the lot and block layouts in Figure 7.3. **Figure 7.10** (far left, next page) shows the Roman *plan castrum* composed of 128 1/8–acre lots in a 4 x 4 block layout, each bock measuring 1.1 acres, with a central cross-axis of streets as previously described. Next, we eliminate the two least central, internal north–south streets as before to produce elongated,

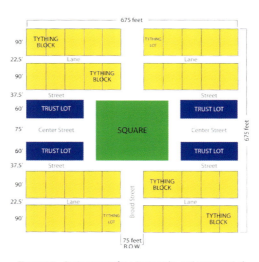

Figure 7.9 – *Basic concept for a Savannah ward composed of tything blocks and trust lots around a central square including typical right-of-way dimensions.*

rectangular blocks measuring nearly 3 acres in size (2.78 ac) in a 2 x 4 layout composed of 144 lots (**Figure 7.10**, middle left). **Figure 7.10** (middle right) shows the introduction of a central square consistent with the Spanish model, which also has the effect of eliminating nearly 28% of the lots. Finally, to recover the lost lots, we incorporate additional blocks to the north and south and attached at the eastern/western edges of all urban blocks in order to 'square off' the ward (**Figure 7.10**, far right). As we saw in Figure 7.8, Savannah wards typically – though not always – tend towards an overall square shape. The widths of right-of-ways can then be adjusted accordingly whilst approximating the overall shape of a square for each ward. Of course, there are more lots in this layout (320 lots measuring 1/8 acre in size) than in the other layouts of Figure 7.10 because it encompasses a larger area (1,815 feet x 1,815 feet or a little over 75 acres compared to 1,155 feet x 1,115 feet or a little over 30 acres including the perimeter streets). Average block size is nearly 4 acres (3.7 ac), which is nearly the same as the average block size (3.8 ac) in the sample of 20 American urban grids in Chapter 5. This is nearly three times larger than the typical ward size of 675 x 675 feet indicated by Wilson and Shay (2014). The Savannah ward plan utilizes through lots approximately 60 x 90 feet (or nearly 1/8

acre in size) instead of the double-loaded lots in our example, so there are only 40 lots per ward (excluding the trust lots). In our example, we could utilize 1/4 acre lots to reduce the number of lots to 160, which is still 11% more than the orthogonal grid without a central square in Figure 7.10. In any case, the principles of formal composition underlying this synthesis and transformation of the Roman *plan castrum* and the Spanish Laws of the Indies model via the American tendency toward elongated, rectangular blocks into the Savannah ward model appears fundamentally sound. If we examine the pattern of visual integration in the ward model, then we can see that integration focuses on the only north–south street passing internally through the layout and central square (**Figure 7.11**). In a similar manner to Figure 7.2, integration of the east–west cross streets through and at the edges of the central square appears 'degraded' (in comparison to the *plan castrum* and Spanish models of Figure 7.2) but this is an artifact of the north–south street becoming more integrated and connected, not the east–west streets becoming less so. Nonetheless, this is still interesting because street widths in Savannah's wards vary in accordance with universal distance, i.e. the most central cross-streets have wider road widths than those streets defining the edges of the square. As we shall see in the next section,

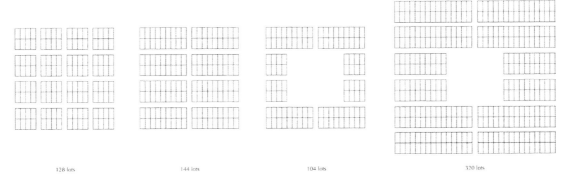

Figure 7.10 – *The Transformation of Savannah's Ward Model:* (far left) Roman plan castrum *composed of 1/8 acre lots in a 4 x 4 block layout; (middle left) elimination of least central, internal north–south streets to produce elongated, rectangular blocks; (middle right) introduction of central square consistent with the Spanish model; and, (far right) introduction of additional blocks to the north and south, and additional lots at the east/west edges of all blocks, to 'square off' the plan to generate the basic concept for a Savannah ward.*

the loading of the east–west streets defining the edges of the square also tends to cleverly compensate for this effect by means of constitution (i.e. location of dwelling entrances).

Reps (1965) cites – and sometimes discounts – numerous possible sources of inspiration for Oglethorpe's ward plan. These include William Penn's 1682 plan for Philadelphia, Nine Square Plan of New Haven, 17th century English planning of Ulster Plantation towns in Northern Ireland, Robert Castell's *Villas of the Ancients*, Sir Robert Mountgomery's Margravate plan of Azilia in Georgia/South Carolina, and private residential squares in London such as Covent Garden, Bloomsbury Square, etc. (Reps. 1965). Wilson and Shay (2014) cite Anthony Ashley Cooper's 1670 plan for Charles Towne (Charleston) and William Penn's 1682 plan for Philadelphia. Kostof (1991) suggests the Savannah ward plan echoes the urban design theories in Pietro di Giacomo Cataneo's 1554 treatise, *I Quattro Primi Libri di Architettura*, and Richard Newcourt's design for London after the Great Fire of 1666. Like others, Gallion and Eisner (1963) cite William Penn's 1682 plan for Philadelphia as a source of inspiration for Savannah but Kostof (1991) explicitly discounts this possibility. Few explicitly connect the Savannah ward plan with 'the usual suspects,' i.e. Vitruvius and the Roman *plan castrum* and/or Alberti and the Spanish Laws of the Indies. Moholy-Nagy (1968) does make, in part, this connection by drawing upon Turpin B. Bannister's article "Oglethorpe's Sources of the Savannah Plan" (Bannister, 1961). She argues Oglethorpe "carried the plan of the Renaissance army camp into the wilderness of America (as) nice proof of historical continuity and of conceptual identity that Oglethorpe did what the Romans had done when they conceived of the castrum plan" (191).

In fact, there appears to be some confusion in the literature about the Savannah plan. This is odd because it seems, on the surface, a relatively simple plan to understand. The reasons for this confusion are multi-faceted. For example, "the plan was the blueprint of a political system" (Kostof, 1992; 96). The Savannah ward plan appeals to urban theorists interested in the planning of society because the political order of the community appears embedded within the formal order of the plan. However, the nature of this political order is open to debate. Wilson and Shay (2014) attribute the Savannah ward plan to Utopian vision, "the order and harmony of Oglethorpe's design was coupled with a social and economic plan for a model yeoman republic similar to the one later envisioned by Thomas Jefferson" (35). However, Gallion and Eisner (1963) argue, "aristocratic paternalism… was reflected in the plan of Savannah" (53). Moholy-Nagy (1968) ascribes the nature of the Savannah plan to the "modular order of military planning" (191). It seems likely part of the confusion arises from the fact that a royal land grant by the British monarch, George II, founded the Georgia Colony and Savannah itself, American Independence and founding of its representative government occurred only 40 years later, and

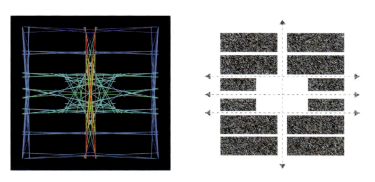

Figure 7.11 – *Savannah ward model with: (left) pattern of visual integration; and, (right) most central cross-axes indicated.*

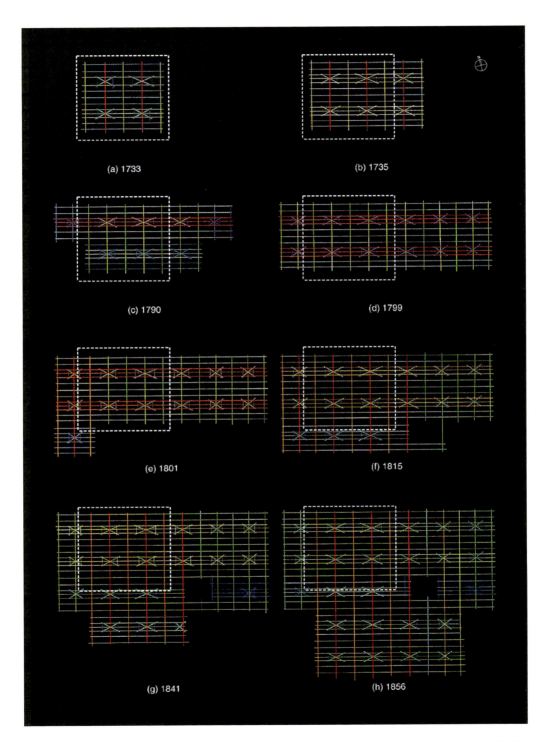

Figure 7.12 – *Pattern of global integration during the historic growth of Savannah's ward plan, 1733–1856. The earliest wards are outlined in white.*

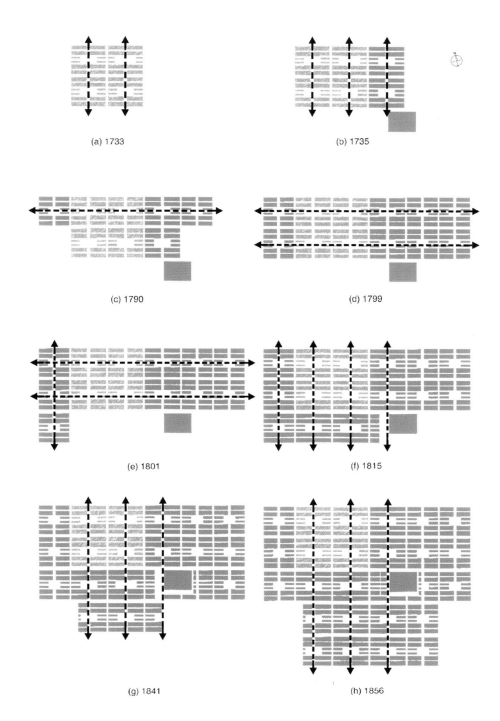

Figure 7.13 – *Diagram showing the most integrated streets in Savannah's ward plan from 1733 to 1856. The earliest wards are shaded in light gray.*

Savannah's prominent role in the slave trade during both periods until 1798 (Eltis et al., 1999). On the other hand, there is Stanislawski's (1946) argument that the regular grid implies no preferred social order at all. Despite the seemingly tidy synthesis between formal and political order in the Savannah plan, a careful review of the planning and historical literature demonstrates this argument lacks consistency as well as a certain depth. This suggests it must be the physical attributes of the plan itself, i.e. the design, which leads to its "splendidly urban and urbane" nature as a settlement (Reps, 1965; 202).

In this, there is some paradigmatic confusion as well. Kostof (1991) points out "the ward unit is repeatable" (96). Wilson and Shay (2014) also argue Savannah's ward layout "is replicable and thus in aggregate it becomes simpler as it repeats" (32) but that "the unique ward design creates an efficient hierarchy of streets" and "streets separating wards can be designed to meet additional purposes, thereby adding new levels to the street hierarchy" (33). Wilson and Shay's (2014) repeated use of the terms 'street hierarchy' and 'hierarchy of streets' in their 2014 *Planning Magazine* article about Savannah's ward plan is unclear but seems to be an attempt to refer to managing vehicular traffic flows without explicitly stating so. This emphasis on repetition and hierarchy in the literature is interesting. Given the emphasis on these concepts in the design of post-war developments in the United States (see the discussion about Radburn, New Jersey in Chapter 4), it seems likely these easily identifiable aspects of Savannah's ward plan might appeal to modern architects and planners on this basis. However, as we shall see in the next section, the hierarchy embedded in the formal and spatial nature of the Savannah ward plan in infinitely richer and subtler. It predates the invention of the automobile, but is eminently adaptable and serviceable for the traffic management of moving vehicles (though not so much for the storing of stationary ones), and tied to the micro-scale spatial structure of any individual ward.

Historic growth of Savannah's ward plan

Figure 7.12 (page 144) shows the pattern of global integration for least line axial analysis of Savannah's ward plan from 1733 to 1856 based on the plans in Figure 7.8, weighing for the squares by modeling the opportunity to move diagonally across them. **Figure 7.13** (previous page) shows a diagram of the lines forming the one, two, three, or four most integrated streets depending on the spatial pattern during each stage of growth. We can see that shifting principally characterizes the macro-scale spatial structure of Savannah's ward plan over its first 123 years of growth; first, focusing on north–south streets, then shifting to east–west streets, and finally back again to north–south streets. Two factors drive this shifting of the spatial structure: first, the weighing of the squares for diagonal movement tends to focus integration on the streets passing through the squares in either direction; and second, the location of additional wards attached during the process of grid expansion. If we examine the pattern of visual integration for 'all lines' axial analysis of Savannah's ward plan from 1733 to 1856, then we can see the micro-scale spatial structure is also characterized by shifting, principally based on the location of new urban growth (**Figure 7.14**). This spatial pattern tends to focus on the north–south streets over time and only picks up east–west streets depending on the lateral attachment of additional wards at the edges of the plan.

On the surface, this is perplexing because it is easy to understand the formal composition of Savannah's ward plan but difficult to discern how it functions in terms of configuration at either the macro- or micro-scale of space. There is very little deviation from the block and

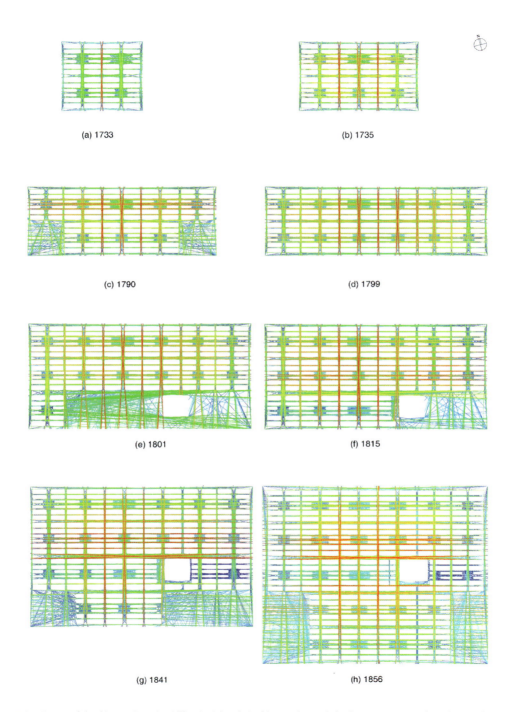

Figure 7.14 – *Pattern of visual integration using 'all lines' axial analysis of Savannah's ward plan from 1733 to 1856. The earliest wards are outlined in white.*

street layout of the ward model. The size of blocks and squares tends to only vary in an east–west direction. For example, Johnson Square is marginally larger than any other square and consequently Derby Ward, where it is located, is marginally larger than all other wards. The exceptions are Percival Ward, which is adjacent and aligned to Derby Ward to the immediate south, and those later wards further to the south along the same alignment. However, despite these marginal variations of square, block, and ward sizes in an east–west direction (for example, the wards on the eastern and western edges of Savannah's plan are smaller than those more centrally located), it occurs in a manner consistent with the geometric order inherent in the formal composition of the ward model. There is very little block manipulation in the Savannah ward plan until embedding of the cemetery into the urban fabric around 1815 and, consequently, the incorporation of smaller blocks around its edges from this time until the U.S. Civil War. There is not any substantial manipulation of block sizes to privilege certain streets over others and stabilize the spatial structure of this plan during the process of grid expansion in the manner discussed in the previous chapter.

Kostof (1991) implies the answer to this problem of formal composition and spatial configuration in the Savannah ward plan, stating "since the houses *all faced east-west streets* (our emphasis), the wards were united visually, as they were interdependently socially in the shared use of public buildings and the like. So the inner-oriented ward system around squares also had a street-oriented linear reading. The streets linking the squares and the squares themselves were tree-lined fairly early, while the north–south thoroughfares and the small streets within the wards remained treeless"

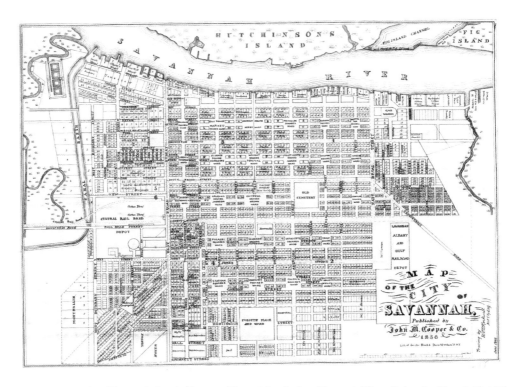

Figure 7.15 – 1856 plan of Savannah, Georgia (Courtesy of Hargrett Rare Book and Manuscript Library/University of Georgia Libraries).

(96). Anderson (1986) explicitly provides the answer in his analysis of Savannah, stating "movement along east–west streets serves for continuous opportunities of access to similar uses; movement along north–south streets provides comparatively rapid access to zones of alternative uses" (275); principally, the port. "What is important to the actual Savannah… is not the specific number of streets or parcel types, but rather the organizational schemata is more differentiated (has a large number of inherent street and parcel types) than is common. Differentiation establishes an energetic coexistence of openness and selective reinforcement by means of various types of location in a patterned array throughout the plan" (Anderson, 1993; 118). "The typology of the wards in relation to the entire city creates alternating centripetal and centrifugal forces – inward to the squares and outward to the streets that are simultaneously a boundary to the wards and the fullest continuity of the larger city structure. The two forces are thus placed in a tense equilibrium that inhibits the city from becoming either a mere collection of independent wards or a system of undifferentiated continuities" (Anderson, 1993; 120–121). Crucially, this happens in an orthogonal grid.

We can effectively demonstrate this by modeling constitution (i.e. the location of dwelling entrances) in the least line axial analysis of Savannah's ward plan. The basis for determining the location of dwelling entrances is the 1856 plan of Savannah, which provides a detailed picture of lot lines in the settlement at that time and we can use to extrapolate backward in time to its earliest plans (**Figure 7.15**). We add a short axial line to represent the front door of a dwelling along the narrowest width of each lot. This represents an 'ideal' model of the street network and constitution in Savannah because of the addition of some dwelling entrances to north–south streets defining the boundary between each ward over time. However, these north–south streets still tend to remain mostly treeless and relatively barren with a propensity for blank walls. At the same time, this model does not reflect the often-repeated but hardly universal tendency in Savannah for double-loaded front doors – even triple-loading with side garden entries – for individual lots on (mostly) east–west streets, i.e. an entry to a ground floor residential unit at (or marginally below) street level with stairs leading to the main house via a second floor entry (**Figure 7.16**). In this, our model represents a 'happy medium' between these two tendencies in Savannah's ward plan. The fact is there are an insufficient number of north–south dwelling entrances to dramatically alter the analysis since the east–west streets are simply longer, and modeling double- and triple-loaded entries on east–west streets would only reinforce the resulting spatial pattern. Finally, in effect, we are making each front door a series of dead-ends off each street. This is interesting because if we were to do the same for a modern suburban development composed

Figure 7.16 – *Savannah Today: (left) view north along Drayton Street at western edge of Brown Ward; (right) street-level entry under stairs to second floor entry on East Charlton Street in Lafayette Ward.*

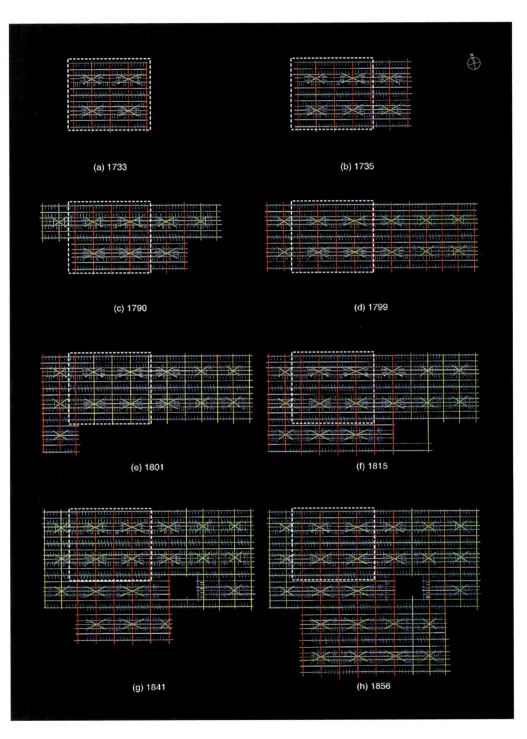

Figure 7.17a – *Pattern of global integration in the street network with building constitution in Savannah's ward plan from 1733 to 1856. The earliest wards are outlined in white.*

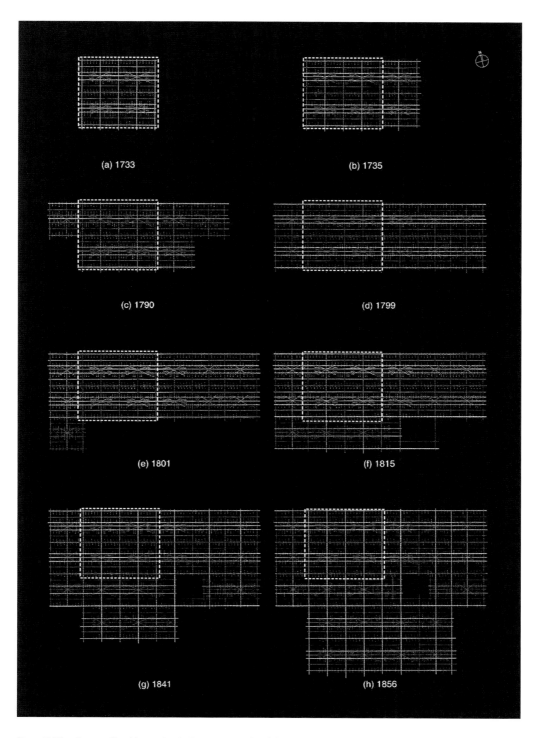

Figure 7.17b – *Pattern of local integration in the street network with building constitution in Savannah's ward plan from 1733 to 1856. The earliest wards are outlined in white.*

of residential pods around a cul-de-sac (such as the Radburn plan), then it would only intensify the degree of spatial segregation in such developments. However, doing so for a highly connected orthogonal grid such as Savannah has a dramatic effect on the macro-scale spatial structure.

Figure 7.17a (page 150) shows the pattern of global integration in the street network with building constitution in Savannah's ward plan from 1733 to 1856. As we can see, global integration stabilizes and focuses on the north–south streets during the process of historical growth (i.e. grid expansion) in Savannah's ward plan. This occurs despite the east–west streets having longer lengths (at least until the addition of the wards at the southern edge in the 1856 plan) and more connections than the north–south streets. This is because the north–south streets are the shallowest spaces in navigating the layout from edge-to-edge. As suggested by Anderson (1986), these streets provide the most immediate access to non-residential land uses in Savannah. Historically, this would have principally meant the port at the riverfront on the northern edge of Savannah's ward plan. **Figure 7.17b** (previous page) also shows the pattern of local integration in the street network with building constitution in Savannah's ward plan from 1733 to 1856. In contrast, local integration permanently focuses on the east–west streets during the growth of Savannah's ward plan. This is because the east–west streets provide the most immediate access to the most dwelling entrances, mainly residential land uses. The east–west streets are the shallowest in terms of moving internally within the layout from one specific location to another as long as those locations tend to not be on the edge. Collectively, this hierarchy of streets and dwelling entrances has the effect of reinforcing the micro-spatial structure of individual wards.

This is a significant finding not only because the layout patterns the relationship between similar (i.e. residential) and alternative (i.e. commercial) land uses, as suggested by Anderson (1986), but also because the plan embeds a spatial hierarchy between insider (i.e. residents) and outsider (i.e. visitors) within the street network and pattern of dwelling entrances itself. Visitors initially tend to enter the Savannah ward plan along the globally integrated north–south streets before

Figure 7.18 – *The City and Harbor of Savannah, Georgia, a 1893 wood engraving drawn by J. O. Davidson.*

changing directions and assimilating into the locally integrated east–west streets. Historically, this used to occur along north–south streets from the port in the north or the interior lands to the south, whether that street passed through the center of a square or defined the boundary between wards. Over time, activities associated with Savannah's port shifted to the west away from the riverfront of the ward plan (**Figure 7.18**). However, traffic management measures implemented during the 20th century in Savannah's ward plan tend to reinforce this spatial hierarchy between north–south and east–west streets. The squares themselves have become enlarged roundabouts for slower moving vehicular traffic in a north–south direction, while the boundary thoroughfares between wards (also north–south streets) accommodate faster moving, higher levels of vehicular traffic. This 'street hierarchy' predates the automobile, being a distinctive characteristic of the ward model from the very beginning due to the elongating of urban blocks in an east–west direction and loading of dwelling entrances onto them. In this sense, Savannah's ward plan (and orthogonal grid) was ideally suited to accommodate the demands of the automobile during the 20th century, at least in terms of moving traffic. In terms of storing stationary vehicles, it appears Savannah's ward plan suffers under the weight of all of these parked cars (**Figure 7.18**, middle). It is also disturbing that some late 20th/early 21st century in-fill developments in Savannah are gradually but systematically deteriorating the formal and spatial differentiation between north–south and east–west streets inherent in the ward plan (**Figure 7.18**, right). In any case, this analysis effectively demonstrates how other factors such as land uses and constitution can come into play to reinforce (or potentially retard) the macro- and/or micro-scale spatial structure of strongly geometrical, highly ordered spatial networks (**Figure 7.19**). Savannah is a case study that brings this symbiotic relationship between formal composition and spatial configuration in the horizontal and vertical construction of American urban space to the forefront of the debate. Finally, and perhaps most importantly, this firmly establishes and intimately ties together the design of Savannah's ward plan with the larger American tradition of regular grid planning.

Figure 7.19 – Savannah Today: (left) view from East Broad Street looking west down East Macon Street, which passes through Troup Square and Lafayette Square further to the northwest where, in the foreground, a contemporary in-fill development loads garages on this east–west street, in effect turning this portion into a back alley whereas, in the background, a contemporary in-fill development loads front doors on this east–west street in a manner consistent with the historical design of Savannah's ward pattern; and, (right) Chatham County Metropolitan Planning Commission offices at the ground level of a 7-story parking garage on Oglethorpe Square.

8 Complexity and Pattern in the City

"Each pattern can exist in the world only to the extent that is supported by other patterns: the larger patterns in which it is embedded, the patterns of the same size that surround it, and the smaller patterns which are embedded in it."
- Christopher Alexander

This chapter investigates how widespread use of the regular grid gives rise to an emergent spatial structure that is complex but filled with information based on the patterning of the urban grid for movement in contemporary American cities (Anderson, 1986; Hillier, 1996b). The chapter briefly introduces the concept of *cities as movement economies* and the phenomenon of *grid intensification* in differentiating local 'parts' such as areas and neighborhoods within the configurational pattern of the urban whole (Hillier, 1996b; Hillier, 1999a). It argues grid intensification is equally relevant for American cities as previously found in other cities of the world. However, the expansive, spare urban fabric of American cities has implications for network analysis. The chapter then examines emergence–convergence in two contemporary American cities lacking a large-scale orthogonal super grid. The focus is metropolitan Baltimore, Maryland and Seattle, Washington. This analysis demonstrates grid expansion and deformation, street extension, and discrete separation play a crucial role in shaping the emergent spatial structure of these cities. Baltimore represents a quintessential example of emergent spatial structure converging on the near invariant of the ortho-radial grid in urban form. In contrast, a trio of integrated cores (two urban, one suburban) characterizes emergent spatial structure in Seattle due to the acute topographical conditions, effect of the Interstate Highway System, and 20th century suburbanization in that city. In both cases, and despite these differences, emergent spatial structure tends to conserve the primacy of the center in the form of the CBD and/or historical area in resolving the tension between centrality and linearity during the evolution of urban form.

The part–whole problem in American cities
A fundamental concept to arise from the theory of natural movement (discussed in "What is Natural Movement?" on pages 72–73) is *cities as movement economies*; namely, it is the pattern of the spatial network as generated by the urban grid rather than the traditional planning emphasis on origin and destination matrices that is the

fundamental thing about the functioning of cities (Hillier, 1996a, 1996b, 1999b, 1999c). The urban grid generates a probabilistic but predictable pattern to the way people move through and occupy spaces in cities. Some spaces receive more movement and use because they are shallower within the urban spatial network whereas others are deeper and receive less. The spatial configuration of the urban grid generates a pattern of "attraction inequalities" whereby land uses tend to locate to exploit these potentials based on the pattern of natural movement (Hillier, 2002; 154). For example, retail will occupy more strategic locations to capitalize on the potential for passing trade. According to Hillier (2005b), "this is not… to deny attraction… it is common sense people make trips because the shops are there… but (attraction) is not fundamental" (11). Space syntax research has consistently found in retail areas there is an exponential increase in movement flows with integration. In non-retail areas, the relationship tends to be linear. The explanation is retail land uses attract a number of additional trips in proportion to the attractiveness of that retail. The retail land uses exhibit a multiplier effect on the basic pattern of natural movement, which results in the exponential growth of movement flows. By contrast, housing is primarily defined by access so it tends to locate in quieter, more segregated locations (Hillier, 1996b). In this way, "the city constructs, in effect, a series of probabilistic interfaces between scales of movement" (Hillier, 2003; 26, originally attributed to Dr. John Peponis in Hillier, 1996b).

"Movement occurs at different scales: some localized and some more globalized. Long journeys will tend to naturally prioritize spaces (that) are globally more integrated, more local journeys those which are more locally integrated… the space system is literally read – and readable – at a different scale. Since different radii of integration reflect different scales of the urban system… the key to understanding parts and whole is understanding the relations between the different radii of integration" (Hillier, 1996b; 127). Hillier (1996b) tests this proposition for some well-established areas and neighborhoods in London such as Soho, Covent Garden, and the City of London – and at the fine-scale of the urban grid for such places as Leadenhall Market in the City itself – in scattergrams. These show the correlation between global and local integration (i.e. synergy) in the urban grid as a whole. The line of correlation comes as close as possible to all points in defining the linear relationship between these parameters (**Figure 8.1**). All axial lines internal to and passing through a local area are then selected to demonstrate how this subsystem of streets relates to the line of correlation for the urban grid as a whole. "The more the set of dark points forms a line crossing the (correlation) line for the whole city but tending to greater steepness, there is more… local integration than global, then the more the sub-area is distinctive. While the more the dark points lie on the… (correlation) line, the more they are simply sets of smaller spaces related to the main grid, but not forming a distinctive sub-area away from it" (Hillier, 1996b; 130).

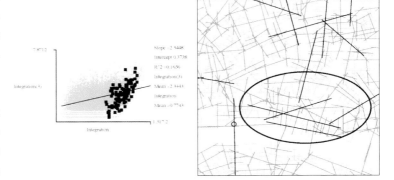

Figure 8.1 – *Local intensification of the grid for: (left) scattergram of synergy for the City (in black) crossing over the regression line for Greater London as a whole (in gray); and, (right) City of London (circled in black) in the space syntax model of Greater London.*

Hillier (1996b) describes this as a "well-structured local intensification of the grid" (130). Yang and Hillier (2007) later refer to it as *embeddedness*. Hillier (2009c) also describes it as "pervasive centrality" in deformed grid layouts (6). "It can both initiate center formation, as in small… shopping streets, but it also happens as a center develops to improve the inter-accessibility of the interdependent facilities" in that center (Hillier, 2005b; 24). According to Hillier (2005b), "grid intensification is essentially a metric process, and it occurs at the local urban scale at which people are able to make reasonable judgments of distance" (25). However, this process works with the local attributes of space in terms of metric characteristics and the global attributes of space, where the geometrical and topological properties of configuration are more critical (Hillier, 2005b; Yang and Hillier, 2007). This phenomenon occurs in several European cities and appears crucial for understanding how "some cities can be put together as cities of parts without losing the sense of the whole (Hillier, 1996b; 130 and Hillier, 1999a). This contrasts to another phenomenon typically found by space syntax research in public housing schemes based on Modernist planning principles, such as those outlined in Le Corbusier's (1925) *The City of To-morrow and Its Planning*. In these public housing schemes, there is an intensification of lines due to the layout and an excess of open space, but these lines have little or no relationship with the larger urban context (Hillier, 1986 and 1996b; Major et al., 1999; Shu and Hillier, 1999; Hillier and Vaughan, 2007). The point of this contrast is that using smaller block sizes as suggested by Jacobs (1961) is simply not enough, even in a geometrical scheme, to generate grid intensification if the streets are not patterned to relate to grid logic of the larger urban context.

Distinctive areas, neighborhoods, and places are certainly as common in American cities as European ones. For example, there are some well-known ones in Chicago such as Lincoln Park and Wrigleyville as well as The Strip in Las Vegas, commonly regarded to be a place in itself. However, in the strongly geometric cities of the United States, there appears to be an inverse problem to the one investigated by Hillier, which is how to distinguish the parts within the conceptual order of the whole. Deviations from and interruptions to that conceptual order are one manner. This differentiates the length of streets and their connections in the American urban grid. Interruptions, usually abrupt ones, such as a railroad line, canal, or an interstate highway tend to form 'edges' as defined by Lynch (1960). Finally, as Clay (1973) points out, the seam streets between offset grids appear to define "special, geometric epitome districts" in distinguishing areas and neighborhoods (42).

However, in seeking to identify the spatial differentiation of local parts within the conceptual order of the American urban grid, there appear to be three problems. The first is local areas and neighborhoods in American cities tend to be composed of streets not exclusively internal to that area, especially in parts of the urban grid planned before 1945. For example, in contrast, the majority of streets in Hillier's (1996b) axial map for the City of London appear internal to the area (as seen in Figure 8.1). Of the roughly 300 lines in this space syntax model, only about 20 lines (or nearly 7%) appear to continue some distance into the surrounding urban context. In a regular grid, some – or even most or all – streets in a local area continue beyond that area, and far beyond for many miles in some cases, to become a part of other areas and neighborhoods. It seems counter-intuitive that a series of streets not exclusively internal to an area can define that area. The conventional wisdom of modern planning is something specifically local to that area must be what makes it unique, such as walking radius, land uses, housing quality and/or types, population demographics, and so on. The first problem appears to be compounded by a second, which is the configurational parameters using traditional space syntax methods are measured for the entire length of an axial line rather than segments of that line passing through a local area (Batty and Rana, 2004). Relatively recent space syntax innovations incorporating line segment measures based on universal distance are an attempt to address this problem (Hillier and Iida, 2005; Turner, 2008; Hillier, 2009c). However, the least line representation of the axial map remains the bedrock of urban network analysis in space syntax. Studies of the forecasting power for movement flows using the new modeling techniques compared to previous findings demonstrate there is significant comparability but none have consistently outperformed the least line representation of the axial map (Hillier et al., 2005). According to Hillier (2003), "the simple least line map, or axial map, is a simpler and truer representation of the properties of the urban grid that give rise of the conceptual picture of the grid as a whole" (18). Turner (2007a) concedes, "the relationship between life and the line may well be fundamental to how we move within the environment" (11). Hillier and Vaughan (2007) state, "least angle analysis is the best predictor of movement, followed *closely* (author's emphasis) by fewest turns, and metric shortest path analysis well back in third place" (8). However, the differences between least angle analysis and fewest turns (traditional axial) analysis available in the public domain appear marginal (Penn, 2001; Turner et al., 2003a; Turner, 2004 and 2007a).

Figure 8.2 – Lynch's elements of city imageability: (from top to bottom) paths, edges, districts, nodes, landmarks.

Due to the long length of streets in American cities, by definition, most – if not all – local trips must utilize segments along these lines rather than the entire length. It seems counter-intuitive the entire length of a street – in terms of its syntactic values represented as an axial line – is more important than line segments exclusively internal to the local area itself. By syntactic values, we mean the family of spatial parameters examined in Chapter 5 for an individual line, a subset of lines, or the mean of all lines within the axial map.

The third problem lies in American urban grids tending to be spatially shallower than other types of urban grids such as those in Europe (Major, 2015c). In those with a large-scale orthogonal logic, it is feasible to move along the length of some streets from one edge of the urban grid to the other with a minimal number of changes of direction. It seems counter-intuitive that local integration is truly 'local' in American cities. At first glance, it seems reasonable to conclude there must be another aspect to the part–whole relationship in American cities than as described by Hillier (1996b). However, the first and second are really aspects of the same problem, which is about our preconceived notions of locality. Our urban development and planning processes unduly focus – both for paradigmatic and practical reasons – on the design of the site itself. For example, in *The Image of the City*, Lynch (1960) argues "the contents of the city image" could "be classified into five types of elements: paths, edges, districts, nodes, and landmarks" (47–48) (**Figure 8.2**). It can be fairly argued that two of these elements (edges and districts) are about defining city form in discrete terms, i.e. you are here and not there or you are inside and not outside. However, what often defines the edge condition of these city elements is a third one, which Lynch (1960) describes as the "predominant elements" of city image (47). These are paths. Lynch's approach is consistent with a predisposition to think of areas/neighborhoods in discrete terms, independent of the larger urban context. Building upon her previous findings about spatial cognition, Conroy Dalton and others have attempted to bring Lynch's findings about city imageability into the same theoretical framework with space syntax (Conroy Dalton and Dalton, 2001; Conroy Dalton and Bafna, 2003). However, the extremely small sample size and subjectivity of Lynch's (1960) original study tends to thwart these attempts.

In any case, if we avoid this 'locality trap,' then it is easy to see it is not the street itself or street segments internal to an area that most defines it in spatial terms. Instead, it is the *connection of streets* in the local area. This interface of streets is unique since, by definition, in terms of their macro-scale linear structure (as lines of sight for visibility and accessibility in movement through urban space) they *cannot* connect anywhere else in the city. Therefore, the global and local relationship of streets measured in terms of spatial configuration for a local area is unique in the real world, even if a conceptual order such as the regular grid characterizes many parts of the city with a degree of sameness in terms of block size/shape or street widths. The connection of these streets in established neighborhoods and places such as Fisherman's Wharf in San Francisco, Lincoln Park and the North Michigan Avenue shopping district in Chicago, the Central West End in St. Louis, and The Quadrangle and Georgetown in Washington, D.C. cannot be replicated anywhere else in the urban grid. If this is accepted, then it does not matter whether a street is exclusively internal to a local area or continues for some distance to become a part of several different neighborhoods. The type and intensity of land uses in a local area then builds upon the spatial potentials established by the patterning of the urban grid for levels of natural movement to further accentuate the uniqueness of that area within the city (Hillier, 1993 and 1996b; Desyllas, 1997 and 1999; Shin et al., 2007).

Given this, it appears simple to resolve the third problem, which is local integration seems insufficiently 'local' in the American city to really define the spatial pattern of a neighborhood or place in terms of the relationship between the global and local scale of space. In some cases, intelligibility (global integration vs. connectivity) appears more suited to detect grid intensification in American cities. This is because connectivity is a more localized parameter of spatial configuration since it measures the immediate connections from an axial line. However, in some cases, synergy (global integration vs. local integration) is better suited. This is simply a function of depth and axial size for any particular American urban grid. As previously seen in Chapter 5, there was a relationship between axial size and mean depth – and mean depth inversely related to intelligibility and synergy – in the sample of 20 American urban grids. This means the larger the axial size and deeper the spatial structure of an axial map, then the more likely synergy is sufficient to detect grid intensification. For example, there is a grid intensification in the Central West End of St. Louis, where axial size is 3,200 lines and mean depth is 5.5. The Central West End is one of the most desirable mixed-use, historical neighborhoods in the city. The smaller the axial size and shallower the spatial structure, then the more likely that intelligibility is required to detect an intensification. For example, there is a grid intensification in The Quadrangle of Washington, D.C.

where the axial size is only 1,294 lines and mean depth is 4.6 (**Figure 8.3**). The reason is a more localized measure such as connectivity is necessary to detect the spatial pattern of an area at the global and local scale of space (i.e. intelligibility) when shallowness characterizes the urban grid. This is because there tends to be greater correspondence between global and local integration. For example, it is possible to move completely across the entire spatial network from edge-to-edge in as little as three or four changes of direction in the models of Chicago, Las Vegas, Los Angeles, Miami, or Washington, D.C. used in Chapter 5. In contrast, local integration is sufficient to detect grid intensification at the global and local scale of space (i.e. synergy) when urban space is characterized by more deepness since there tends to be greater differentiation between global and local integration, for example in St. Louis. This is a direct contrast to Middle Eastern cities, which tend to be distinguished by a great deal of depth in their spatial structure and a greater radius of integration is necessary to define a 'local' measure for streets in the urban spatial network (Karimi, 1997 and 1998). In any case, all of the named local places and neighborhoods in San Francisco, Chicago, and Washington, D.C. previously mentioned in this section do form grid intensifications for either intelligibility or synergy in the manner described by Hillier (Hillier, 1996b; Major, 1997a and 2000a; Yang, 2006).

Implications for network analysis

Collectively, this presents an issue for research into the American urban object. Previous research shows American urban grids on average tend to be twice as expansive in metric area, streets are twice as long, and the urban spatial network more than 25% shallower and twice as sparse as European ones of comparable axial size (Major, 2015c). In the extreme examples, American urban grids can be three times more expansive, streets can be three times longer, and the urban spatial network twice as shallow and three times more sparse (Major, 2015c). In effect, the relationship between street length and metric area is not proportional in two dimensions. Though most streets in American grids are long by comparison to other models of urbanism, a small set of extremely long streets (i.e. the super grid) affects

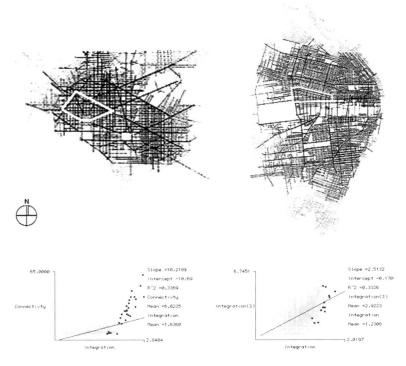

Figure 8.3 – Pattern of (log) global integration in the axial map of: (left) Washington, D.C. with area of The Quadrangle outlined in white (top) and (below) grid intensification of The Quadrangle (in black) in Washington, D.C. (in gray) for intelligibility; and, (right) St. Louis with the Central West End outlined in white (top) and (below) grid intensification of the Central West End (in black) in St. Louis (in gray) for synergy (NOTE: Not set to metric scale).

overall average street length. The same is true for other types of cities, but pervasive use of the regular grid in American cities accentuates this to an extreme degree by using fewer streets to form the entire urban spatial network. This suggests the configurational modeling techniques of space syntax are more susceptible to skewing if a researcher models too small of an area in cities characterized by large-scale regular grids. For example, partial modeling of a very long street skews the syntactic variables so that axial line may not accurately account for the true configurational value of that street within the urban pattern of the whole on the ground, especially in relation to functional data such as movement, land uses, etc. (Stonor, 1991; Raford, 2004; Al Sayed et al., 2009). This could have the additional effect of disrupting the uniqueness of street connections defining a local area or neighborhood in applying space syntax as a design tool for intervention in American cities. This suggests researchers need to be careful about modeling much more of the urban spatial network in American cities than traditionally has been the case. In the case of American cities with a pervasive orthogonal logic (such as Chicago or Miami in Chapter 5), the effect of modeling too small of an area inaccurately skews the spatial parameters of partially modeled streets. It may even be the case that any space syntax model of an American city relying on connectivity as a local measure for differentiating between the global and local scale of space (i.e. intelligibility) is too small of a model (for example, as in Washington, D.C. in Figure 8.3). For such models, it is best to tread carefully in examining the relationship between spatial parameters and other urban functions with a global dimension such as movement and land use. In this regard, some early research findings in the history of space syntax (when computer processing power was insufficient to tackle the particular problems presented by the scale of the American urban object) and a distinctive bias of perspective (due to space syntax first emerging and being extensively applied in an European context) may have unintentionally conspired to limit research results about American cities.

For example, in order to 'calibrate' the space syntax model to successfully predict flows of pedestrian movement in New York, Stonor (1991) slices and dices the Manhattan gridiron into discrete, localized spatial networks independent of a larger urban context. Even then, Stonor (1991) was unable to successfully account for

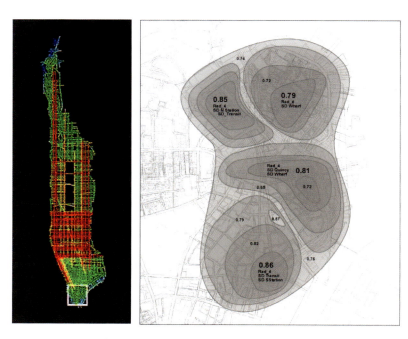

Figure 8.4 – (a) Pattern of global integration in Stonor's (1991) axial map of Manhattan with historical area outlined in white; and, (b) Raford's (2004) correlation contour maps for areas of Boston.

Detecting 'deep structures'

One of the strengths of space syntax lies in the ability of researchers and practitioners to detect 'deep structures' in spatial networks of all kinds. By 'deep structure,' we mean characteristics or subsystems of spatial layouts not intuitively obvious at first glance (e.g. before-the-fact), but which are quite apparent once detected (e.g. after-the-fact); so much so, we might wonder how we missed them in the first place. The problem is not our representations, e.g. drawing, plan/plat, survey, and so on. It is our preconceptions, which blind us to what is right in front of us. Frequently, this is the basis for space syntax telling people the obvious. It is not necessarily a consequence of processing the space syntax model and looking at the results. Sometimes, it comes from constructing the model itself. Today's space syntax software allows for all kinds of automation including the generation of representations, e.g. lines, convex spaces, and visual fields. However, there is value in creating the representations by hand or in the computer without automatic generation. Needless to say, it takes more time but there is a great deal we can learn about a built environment, sometimes nuanced and detailed, before ever processing the 'virtual' topological graphs in the computer. Later, this learnt knowledge informs rigorous interrogation of the space syntax model. This is a matter of technique supported by measurement. There are several examples in this book.

The space syntax models of the historic Savannah ward plan weighting for dwelling entrances (represented as short one-connected lines) in the previous chapter are 'notional' models; conservative ones at that. There is double- and even triple-loading of dwelling entrances on east–west streets most everywhere in historic Savannah today. We could attribute this information to the model numerically in a data table. It is a matter of preference: graphic or numeric. Detecting the 'strip effect' in the next chapter is a technique for selecting a street or streets, measuring depth, and then selecting all streets only one connection away (Major, 1997a). These can be graphically represented in a number of ways, e.g. cutting out of the model as processed (e.g. Halsted Street in Chicago) or re-processing only the local subsystem (e.g. Las Vegas Strip). Hillier (1999b) took this idea to examine dozens of shopping or high streets in European cities, which formed part of the basis for his conjecture about the patterning of *pervasive centrality* in the spatial networks of all cities. Starkly contrasting a measure of depth within a larger model is another technique for showing what is part of a subsystem and what is not (e.g. subsystem from North Seattle in this chapter or from North and Western Avenues in Chicago in the next chapter). Examining second-order measures (e.g. intelligibility and synergy) of sub-systems within their larger urban context is a common means for detecting the spatial distinctiveness of 'named' neighborhoods and places. The next chapter presents another conjecture about modeling technique. If "a city is not a tree," then the idea of 'peeling off' all streets associated with the 1785 Land Ordinance and re-processing the space syntax model of Las Vegas should not have worked (Alexander, 1965; Major 2015a). It did not for a few of the most recent suburban developments in extremes of the city periphery at the time. The fact that it did for the majority of the Las Vegas urban fabric renders more apparent both the hierarchal effect of road classifications during the post-war period and the center-to-edge privileging of Downtown Las Vegas in the collective design of the street network in that city over time. Once detected, quantitative measures help to scientifically ground such findings by describing deep structures in more mathematical terms. This makes it easier to graphically represent such findings in more easily understood ways for people less familiar with space syntax, or not at all. For example, the diagram of boundary, through, and internal streets in the Central West End of St. Louis (page 114 in Chapter 6) graphically represents the deep structure of a 'local area effect' detected using space syntax without resorting to the model or scattergram of synergy (both shown at the beginning of this chapter in **Figure 8.3**). Simply put, the models and their measures are invaluable tools for understanding street networks. However, exclusively relying on them to explain what was understood in the research is not always necessary.

In a similar way, space syntax consultants can interrogate models by running dozens of different design scenarios for a proposed development. This allows for identification and advocacy of the most optimal design solutions on the basis of spatial configuration. It also allows for identification and insurance against the least advisable solutions. All developments involve compromise. Unused space can become abused space, often playing a role in public perception about social malaise and crime (Hillier, 1986 and 1996b; Major et al., 1999; Shu and Hillier, 1999). How and when to compromise or not at all is an important factor. For example, space syntax consultants advocated for an eastern alignment of the London Millennium Bridge, which would allow easier access for pedestrian movement to and from the rest of Southwark in South London. After dropping their initial objections to any bridge at all, opponents began advocating for a western alignment, connecting only the north and south banks, to protect tourist boat views of St. Paul's Cathedral from the River Thames. In the end, there was a compromise with the bridge constructed on axis with St. Paul's Cathedral and nearly so with the new Tate Modern; always the most likely scenario anyway (**Figure A.18**). It is less effective than the optimal alignment but much better than the alternative.

Space syntax helped to defeat an inadvisable concession sought by opponents. Space syntax helps us to understand the best design solutions for conditions on the ground. With this evidence in hand, it is easier to know when a compromise might be less than ideal but acceptable or inadvisable altogether for the long-term spatial functioning and socioeconomic health of a building, development, neighborhood, or city.

Figure A.18 – *London Millennium Bridge from: (left) south of St. Paul's Cathedral in the City of London; (right) south bank on axis with St. Paul's Cathedral at night.*

the spatial phenomenon of Broadway. It is also true that limitations in computer processing power at the time played a large role in constricting the model to only Manhattan Island, independent of the larger urban context of New York. Raford (2004) employs a similar technique for his study of Boston. However, Raford (2004) inverts Stonor's approach by coalescing observed data on movement flows into highly localized subsets that seems to make sense based on previous space syntax studies of European cities. The result is "correlation contour mapping" to define local sub-areas in "fragmented, low intelligibility spatial systems" (Raford and Hillier, 2005; 573) (**Figure 8.4**, page 161). Yang (2006) points out the problem with Raford's approach, namely it "cannot differentiate physical area structure without the data on movement" and it ignores the impact of "the relation between consecutive scales (from local to global) that might play an important role in the formation of sub-areas" (4). Of course, another problem with this approach is the Manhattan gridiron is not a fragmented, low intelligibility system in any conceivable manner to most people. Nor is there any evidence that the manner in which Stonor (1991) cuts up the Manhattan gridiron relates to any recognizable identification for named local sub-areas on the island. Finally, by taking this approach to its logical conclusion if true, it liberates urban designers and planners from having to take into account the larger urban context of a proposed development. This is contradictory to the basic precepts of space syntax and completely in-line with an a-spatial perspective of the city, i.e. the prevailing paradigm of urban studies since the mid-20th century.

We can see in a satellite view of Boston that offset regular grids surround the area of the Raford (2004) study (**Figure 8.5**). A 'Manhattan effect' accentuates this in that, as Manhattan is an island within the larger urban context of New York City, the historical/downtown area of Boston is located on a peninsula. This means the way it connects to the larger urban context appears crucial for understanding how it functions internally. This is because there will tend to be two types of movement at the macro-scale. First, there is movement amongst a series of internal locations. Second, there is movement from the edges of the system, which filters into the local spatial network along the primary routes from the surrounding context. This will occur in terms of step-depth from the perimeter of that system before fully merging to become part of the local spatial network. It is usually easy to identify these primary routes. For example, in New York, they are all of the bridges carrying movement to and from Manhattan Island (Stonor, 1991). In Boston, it is the bridges to the northeast/southeast and surface grid streets/Interstate 93 to the southwest. In effect, it is the not the urban grid that is fragmented but construction of the space syntax model itself (Stonor, 1991; Raford, 2004; Al Sayed et al., 2009).

Figure 8.5 – *Satellite view of Boston showing offset regular grids surrounding the historical and downtown area (on the peninsula to the right) and bridge and road connections to the surrounding context. Interstate 93 to the south is barely visible to the lower right.*

This is not a new principle to space syntax. However, it occurs on a much larger scale in the American urban object compared to other types of cities, especially European ones (Major, 2015c). This is due to the expansive nature of American cities in the horizontal dimension, which, of course, is a product of the regular grid. In these cases, the key determinant for the size of a model should not be the layout at the center of that model and its immediate context, presumably the study area and usually determined by some measurement of walking distance. It should rather be determined by the scale of the regular grid and length of streets within those grids, which surround and feed movement into the study area. This also suggests a few things about American cities. First, a large proportion of movement in any local area will tend to originate from outside that area. Second, planning using gravity models will tend to accentuate and compound the problems associated with a hyper-localized approach to network analysis in those types of cities most characterized by mid-to-late 20th century suburbanization such as Las Vegas, Orlando, and Phoenix because origin and destination modeling on the basis of attraction has difficulties accounting for internal movement capture of mixed-use developments. American suburbia represents an extreme example of this where almost all movement tends to be into or out (or vice versa) of the development with very little internal movement capture. This is not surprising since the planning and permitting of these suburbs occurred in a regulatory framework founded on gravity models, i.e. the outputs constantly reinforce the inputs for a vicious circle. In scientific terms, this is not validation but *manufactured results* (Popper, 1972; Hacking, 1983). Essentially, for a half century, Americans have been designing to improve the predictive power of their traffic models instead of using the predictive power of the models to design better.

Of course, this also represents a problem for urban studies of American cities. The effects of a seemingly 'local' configurational change in one part of the urban grid could potentially have more large-scale effects across the urban spatial network than is normally the case in other types of cities. In a sense, the greater spatial depth typically found in the deformed grid layout of European cities tends to 'inoculate' the urban spatial network against local changes to a certain degree, except for those of a more radical nature. Baron Haussmann's boulevard interventions in the Paris urban fabric during the 19th century are probably the most famous example of a radical intervention in a deformed grid layout. However, in an American city, for those urban functions in which the spatial pattern and levels of natural movement play a critical role (for example, retail land uses), configurational changes that seem purely local in nature could have potentially negative effects on those functions some distance away from the location of an intervention, more so than found in other types of cities. This indicates our typical perspective of neighborhoods and places in the American city has been too narrow, predisposed to treating its parts as discrete elements separated from the rest due to the historical emphasis on formal concepts of order. This does not appear to be the case. Quite the opposite, we need to be more careful when we start to intervene in the American urban object lest we unleash potentially widespread and unforeseen consequences across the urban spatial network by unintentionally altering the pattern of natural movement. Batty (2008) cautions, "that the more we learn about the functioning of such complex systems, we will interfere less but in more appropriate ways" (771).

Baltimore and Seattle: a brief overview
Baltimore was legally founded in 1729 though the Maryland colonial General Assembly created the Port of Baltimore 23 years earlier on Locust Point for the

tobacco trade with England (Krugler, 2004). Locust Point is a small peninsula located on a tidal portion of the Pataosco River, an arm of the Chesapeake Bay allowing water navigation to the Atlantic Ocean. Baltimore is the 20th largest metropolitan area in the United States with a population of nearly 2.7 million people in the 2010 census and one of the largest seaports on the Atlantic Coast of the United States (Source: U.S. Census Bureau and Port of Baltimore). Baltimore quickly grew as a granary for sugar-producing British colonies in the Caribbean during the 18th century (Mountford, 2003). Because the City Planning Department has officially delineated hundreds of districts, Baltimore has taken (or received) a moniker as "a city of neighborhoods," which seems like something of a misnomer being a truism for most cities (Source: City of Baltimore Planning Department) (**Figure 8.6**, top). Reps (1965) has very little to say about the planning of Baltimore. He only states its growth as the "commercial and industrial center for the state happily spared" Francis Nicholson's Baroque plan of Annapolis (see Figure 4.3) from "the destruction that would have accompanied an era of mercantile expansion" (Reps, 1965; 108). He also mentions Baltimore in discussing the influence of Olmsted and Vaux's Central Park in New York for the creation of a public park system in other cities of the United States (Reps, 1965). Kostof (1991 and 1992) limits his discussions about Baltimore to citing the importance of the Land Ordinance on towns predating its adoption and Sherry H. Olson's diagram of ten stages in the city's development in reviewing processes of urban growth (see Figure 6.2).

Figure 8.6 (bottom) shows the 1729 plan for Baltimore north of the harbor in what is now called "Old Town," the port on Locust Point located further to the south. It was mainly a linear settlement composed of 60 lots, each 10 acres in size (600 acres in total) oriented at right angles to Long Street and the seven perpendicular streets or four cross streets running parallel to Long Street. Local topographical conditions on the ground at the time apparently define the boundaries of this 1729 plan. "It was bounded on the west by a deep gully and by the great Eastern road; on the north by the clay hills of Charles and Saratoga streets" (*Baltimore Sun*, 1914). Given the orientation, this presumably means the northwest boundary of this 1729 plan ("Eastern Road") was a portion of the 1,300 mile King's Highway laid out from 1650 to 1735 along the Atlantic Coast from Boston, Massachusetts to Charleston, South Carolina. **Figure 8.7** (top) shows a 1792 French plan of Baltimore and its environs after 63 years of growth, American Independence in 1776, and adoption of the

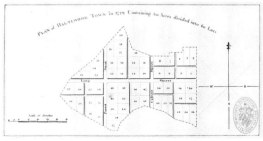

Figure 8.6 – *(top) Official delineation of "neighborhoods" in the City of Baltimore (Source: City of Baltimore Planning Department); and, (bottom) 1729 plan of Town of Baltimore showing 60 lots, each 10 acres in size, on 600 acres (Source: Maryland Historical Society).*

Land Ordinance in 1785. By this time, deformation of offset grids characterizes the plan of Baltimore, mostly in relation to the topography of the harbor and Jones Falls tributary stream (more or less running north–south at the time but later determining the course of Interstate 83, see the satellite image in Figure 5.4, second at top left).

Some offset grids may have been due to ownership patterns (for example, to the northwest). There is also evidence for the planning of a large orthogonal grid aligned to cardinal directions north of Fells Point (center of the image, north of the harbor). By 1836, we can see development of an urban pattern in Baltimore based on offset grids in the oldest areas of the city surrounded on all sides (as the topography allowed) by a series of orthogonal grids oriented to the cardinal directions (**Figure 8.7**, bottom). We can also see several of the 'seam' streets between these offset grids extend to become diagonals running across the parallel/perpendicular street logic of these orthogonal grids.

Like Atlanta (see Figure 5.4, fourth row, second from the right), the urban pattern of Baltimore shows a myriad of factors can come into play to generate an urban center composed of offset grids, which are later surrounded by large-scale orthogonal grids oriented to the cardinal directions. In the case of Baltimore, the offset grid pattern principally arises from topography and, perhaps, colonial land ownership patterns before American Independence. In the case of Atlanta, this almost entirely derives from the pattern of royal land grants during the colonial period but before the legal founding of the city in the 19th century (Haynie and Peponis, 2009). After the adoption of the 1785 Land Ordinance, land division and urban development followed its conceptual order in giving rise to the large-scale orthogonal grids surrounding these urban centers (Kostof, 1991). This is not dissimilar to the planning principles at work in Ildefons Cerdá's *Barcelona Eixample*. In the American context, the spectrum between regularity and deformity – and scale of land areas in relative terms – in the urban pattern is not as extreme as that found between the deformed grid of *Ciutat Vella* (Old City) in Barcelona and the orthogonal grid of the *Eixample*. Atlanta and Baltimore also demonstrate the effect of the 1785 Land Ordinance for intensifying the American preference to regularity not only occurred in gross terms (i.e. number of town plans based on the regular grid before and after adoption, see Chapter 4). It also found expression in individual cities, being literally 'written' into their urban pattern, even those that predate the Land Ordinance.

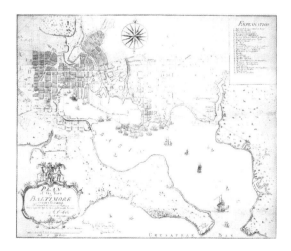

Figure 8.7 – *Baltimore 1792–1836*: (top) 1792 plan of Town of Baltimore and its Environs; and, (bottom) 1836 plan of the City of Baltimore.

Seattle offers a more acute example of local topographical conditions profoundly shaping an urban pattern based on offset grids in a settlement over time. According to archaeological excavations, humans inhabited the Seattle area around Elliot Bay at least 4,000 years before the arrival of Europeans (Source: Burke Museum, College of Arts and Sciences, University of Washington). The founding of Seattle occurred in 1853 on Elliot Bay, a part of Puget Sound. Puget Sound is an inlet of the Pacific Ocean and west of Lake Washington, which is a large freshwater lake with a catchment area of 315,000 acres or 1,275 square kilometers. *A priori* conditions of local topography in Seattle lends the area to human settlement primarily for two reasons: as a natural port for water transportation of trade to Pacific markets and local markets further inland in the continental United States and Canada; and, a readily available source of freshwater in nearby Lake Washington. This location is also eminently defensible. However, this criteria was probably of less importance at the time in comparison to colonial settlements founded during the 16th and 17th centuries such as St. Augustine and Charleston. A history of boom-and-bust cycles characterizes the urban growth of Seattle due to its dependence as a port for the transport of extensive natural and mineral resources in the area, first for the lumber industry and later during the Klondike Gold Rush (Shear, 2002). Seattle is the 8th largest port, 15th largest metropolitan area with approximately 3.6 million inhabitants, and the fastest growing major city in the United States today (Source: Port of Seattle and U.S. Census Bureau).

The earliest plan for Seattle in 1853 was an orthogonal grid oriented to the cardinal directions (**Figure 8.8**, left). Based on the dating of the town plans, Reps (1979) discusses the Seattle town plans out of chronological sequence by first describing the 1856 plan. He then focuses on how the 1853 plan for the "design of the enlarged community" was "dignified with a public square at the north end of Sixth Street whose boundaries splayed outward at its intersection with Washington Street to create a triangular open space in front of its square" (Reps, 1979; 364). Thomas Phelps' 1855–56 surveys of the town during the Battle of Seattle (a minor skirmish during the Puget Sound War with local native Americans) represent a settlement that has yet to grow into its initial plan but

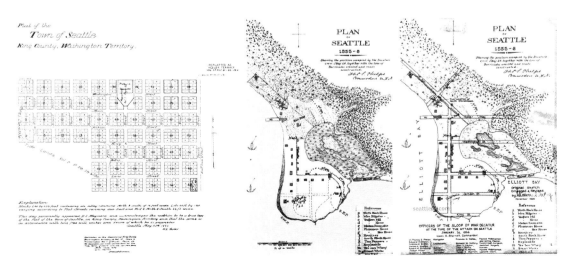

Figure 8.8 – Early historical growth of Seattle, Washington: (left) original 1853 plat for the city; and, (right) two 1855–56 maps of Seattle. The central east–west road (Jackson Street) in the 1855–56 surveys is also the most central and longest east–west road in the 1853 plan.

had already begun deviating from the conceptual order of that plan. Phelps' surveys show small-scale regular grids offsetting to one another to maximize the number of buildable lots in relation to shorelines, principally Elliot Bay (**Figure 8.8**, right). Like many American settlements, Seattle experienced a period of rapid growth in the period after the Civil War; in particular, from 1870 to 1890 (Shear, 2002). "With a population of just over 1,100 in 1870, it increased to 3,500 by the end of the decade" and "by 1890 its population reached 43,000, more than twelve times the number of inhabitants only ten years earlier" (Reps, 1979; 381). An 1891 bird's eye view of Seattle clearly demonstrates how the settlement pattern of offset grids orients to acute topographical conditions in the area (**Figure 8.9**, left). By 1891, it is clear the topography of the land to the north of the earliest areas in the settlement represents a somewhat larger stretch of uninterrupted land. Subsequently, a large-scale orthogonal grid logic oriented to the cardinal directions began to emerge in this area, which would later become the Northwest Seattle area including the University District around the University of Washington.

Figure 8.9 (right) shows a diagram of the original orthogonal grid layout for Seattle (shaded in dark gray), the sequence of grids offsetting to this orthogonal grid (in black) in relation to the Elliot Bay shoreline, and all non-rectangular blocks (in light gray) coalesced along the seam streets between these offset grids and the shoreline itself. The lightest shaded blocks (in off white) are non-rectangular due to block manipulation (subdivision in this case) within the bounds of the original settlement layout. The 1940 opening of the Lacey V. Murrow Bridge (now Interstate 90) – the second longest permanent floating or pontoon bridge on Earth at 2,020 meters (6,620 feet) – immediately south of the CBD/historical area opened Mercer Island and the lands east of Lake Washington to development in the post-war period. Later, the 1963 opening of the Evergreen Point Floating Bridge (also Highway 520) – longest permanent floating bridge on Earth at 2,310 meters (7,580 feet) – north of the CBD/historical area and south of Northwest Seattle/Union Bay in 1963 further facilitated such development east of Lake Washington (Source: Washington State Department of Transportation).

 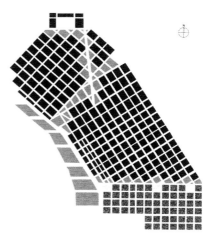

Figure 8.9 – *Early historical growth of Seattle, Washington: (left) bird's eye view of Seattle, Washington and environs in 1891; and, (right) diagram showing the original orthogonal grid (shaded bottom), offset grids (in black) and non-rectangular blocks (in dark gray) generated by deformation in relation to local topographical conditions in Seattle, 1856.*

Emergence–convergence in Baltimore and Seattle

The historical plans of Baltimore effectively demonstrate the formal-spatial processes of grid deformation, in response to local topographical conditions, and grid expansion, in response to the pattern of land division imposed by the 1785 Land Ordinance, at work in shaping its early urban pattern. If we examine the contemporary space syntax model of metropolitan Baltimore, we can see how street extension and discrete separation came into play to consolidate the emergent spatial structure of that city.

Figure 8.10 shows the pattern of global integration in metropolitan Baltimore within Interstate 695/895 (Shah, 1996b). The author double-checked, updated, and revised this model (originally constructed by Shazia Shah in 1996). The parameters for construction are the same, but without any constraints on axial size as outlined in Chapter 5 (Major, 2015a and c). The axial size is 11,637 lines, which is over nine times larger than the space syntax model of Baltimore used in Chapter 5. We can see offset grids strongly characterize the urban center of Baltimore including two oriented

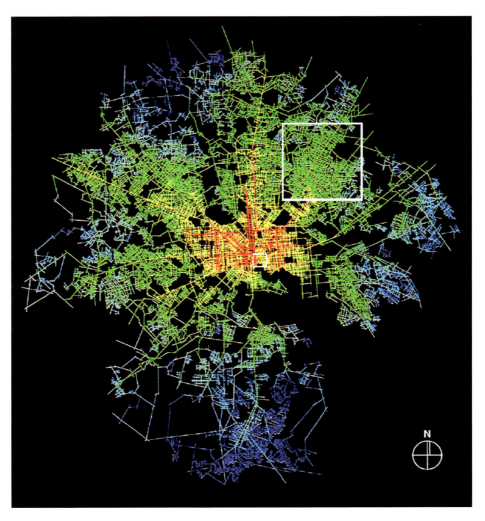

Figure 8.10 – *Pattern of global integration in metropolitan Baltimore. An area measuring one square kilometer (outlined in white) is located in the CBD/historical area (Scale=1:350,000). Box outlined in white serves as orientation for Figure 8.12.*

to highly integrated diagonal streets, which connect from the city center to the northeast and northwest periphery. The most integrated north–south streets (St. Paul Street and Calvert Street) more or less define the western edge of the CBD and historical area. The role of diagonal streets in patterning the urban grid in the periphery and connecting that periphery back into the city center is striking, as is the segregated nature of suburban developments (e.g. discrete separation) within the interstitial areas defined by these diagonals.

Figure 8.11 (left) shows a close-up of the pattern of local integration along Route 147 in northeast Baltimore. It demonstrates the degree to which local development is aggregated to and dependent upon these diagonal routes to integrate into the urban grid from center-to-edge. The closer (in terms of Cartesian distance) these suburban developments are located to these diagonal routes and the city center, then the more globally integrated they are; the further away, the more segregated. The close-up of Route 147 also demonstrates the degree to which the alignment of local streets is formally composed by these diagonal routes since most connect to the diagonals at or near a right angle. **Figure 8.11** (right) shows a diagram of Route 147 and all streets connecting to it, most of which do so at or near a right angle. It effectively demonstrates how the alignment of Route 147 serves as a formal organizing mechanism in this peripheral area of Baltimore in a similar manner previously seen in the historical growth of New Haven. An extensive system of parks in Baltimore also generates several 'holes' in the urban fabric, whereas the large-scale effect of topography in defining the framework of the urban grid is more apparent to the south of the city center where the Inner Harbor is located.

Emergent spatial structure in metropolitan Baltimore has a well-defined ortho-radial pattern, which directly arises from these processes of grid deformation and expansion, street extension, and discrete separation (as well as block manipulation). In fact, we can detect examples for all of these formal-spatial processes at work in the spatial configuration of Baltimore. It provides a good example of how "differences in local texture and invariants in global patterning" characterize cities

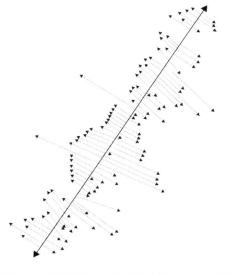

Figure 8.11 – *(left) The pattern of local integration along Route 147 in northeast Baltimore; and, (right) the longest and straightest segment of Route 147 and the length of all streets intersecting with it showing how it serves as an organizing mechanism in northeast Baltimore.*

based on laws of spatial convergence (Hillier, 2002; 155). Laws of spatial convergence are "processes whose rules… converge on particular global types which may vary in detail but at least some of whose most general properties will be invariant," usually ortho-radial grids such as that found in the emergent spatial structure of Baltimore (Hillier, 1996b; 245).

We also saw an example of grid deformation at work in the early historical plans of Seattle, and initial evidence for grid expansion to the north of the oldest areas in the settlement. We can again see the results of street extension and discrete separation of suburban layouts in the contemporary space syntax model of metropolitan Seattle. However, the results on emergent spatial structure in the city appear extreme due to local topographical conditions (in particular, Lake Washington) and street extension principally occurring via the Interstate Highway System. **Figure 8.12** shows the pattern of (log) global integration in the space syntax model of contemporary Seattle without (left) and with limited access highways (right). The author double-checked, updated, and revised this 2002 model of metropolitan Seattle (originally constructed by Paul Bottege in 1994). Again, the parameters for construction are the same but without any constraints on axial size as outlined in Chapter 5 (Major, 2015a and c). The methodology for inclusion of highways and interstates was a simplified vehicular-only network that only takes into account changes in cardinal directions as long as all access points (on- and off-ramps) in that network are included. There are 20,213 axial lines, which is over ten times larger than the space syntax model of Seattle used in Chapter 5. Over more than 150 years of growth, the Seattle urban fabric 'wrapped' around Lake Washington so there is a 'doughnut' shape

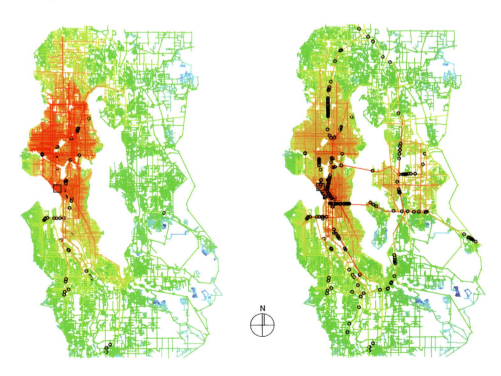

Figure 8.12 – *Space syntax models of contemporary Seattle, Washington without cul-de-sacs showing the pattern of (log) global integration: (left) without; and, (right) with limited access highways and interstates. The CBD/historical area is outlined in black (1 sq/km) with Lake Union/Union Bay located immediately northeast of the CBD/historical area (Scale=1:375,000).*

to the urban fabric with a large hole at the center. Local topographical conditions in Seattle strongly governed the configurational possibilities for urban growth in that city over time.

The modeling of the Seattle urban grid without the highways reveals a highly integrated 'dual core' structure focused on the CBD/historical area and the orthogonal grid section in Northwest Seattle. Over time, the integration core in Seattle has shifted northwards away from its earliest layout; at least, in terms of the metric scale of that core if not the actual integration levels since the spread of highly integrated streets in Northwest Seattle is much larger than in the CBD/historical area, which is more compact. However, in order to identify the configurational relationship of these two cores, we can measure step-depth up to one step away (the street and all streets immediately accessible from it) from the two most integrated streets in each area. In this way, we can see how the Northwest Seattle integration core 'reaches' back to incorporate the CBD/historical area, independently of the highway system in the city. This is the basis of describing Seattle as a 'dual core' system. However, measuring step-depth in this manner is not really necessary. The 'dual core' system seems readily apparent in the normal distribution of global integration in the space syntax model of metropolitan Seattle (**Figure 8.13**). However, step-depth does help to better define the nature of these 'dual cores' as distinct but related spatial systems. Over time, this dual core structure has evolved to strongly link these two areas together in a north–south direction despite the topographical barriers of Lake Union and Union Bay separating them. It is also worth noting the manner in which the integration core of the Seattle urban grid begins to partially wrap around the

 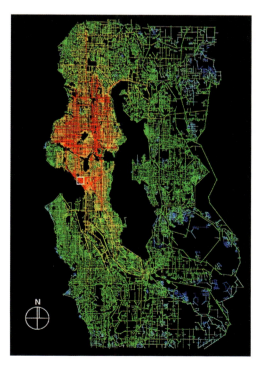

Figure 8.13 – *Space syntax models of contemporary Seattle without cul-de-sacs and limited access highways showing: (left) step-depth one step away from the most integrated streets in Northwest Seattle and CBD/historical area (in red); and, (right) normal distribution of global integration (Scale=1: 375,000).*

western banks of Lake Washington to the north and south independently of the highway system. Finally, exclusion of the highways also eliminates Mercer Island altogether from the model since its layout is entirely dependent upon the connection provided by Interstate 90/Murrow Bridge to access the rest of metropolitan Seattle. The effect of modeling the Murrow Bridge/Interstate 90, Evergreen Point Bridge/Highway 520, and other limited access highways in metropolitan Seattle is dramatic, especially for the layouts east of Lake Washington (compare models in Figure 8.12). The effect on the historical CBD and Northwest Seattle integration cores is less dramatic, but still important. A trio of integration cores now characterizes emergent spatial structure in metropolitan Seattle: CBD/historical area, Northwest Seattle, and the Bellevue area east of Lake Washington between Interstate 90 and Highway 520. The layout on Mercer Island is now also included in the model with the inclusion of Interstate 90. The 'wrap-around effect' of the integration core in relation to the western shoreline of Lake Washington is now principally characterized by the alignment of Interstates 5 and 405 to the north and south, shifting away from streets running immediately parallel to the shoreline to these highways located further inland. The most integrated sequence of lines in Seattle is now segments of Interstate 5 from Northwest Seattle to the immediate east of the CBD/historical area intersecting with Highway 520 and Interstate 90. The effect on spatial structure is to shift the highest levels of integration to the interstate highways. As a gross level, integration appears to have dropped in the CBD/historical area and Northwest Seattle. However, this is an artifact of the color scale. Both of these areas are still highly integrated, even more so than before with the inclusion of the highways. In fact, segments of Interstate 5 between the CBD/historical area and Northwest Seattle replicate the north–south connections between these two areas at the street-level of the urban grid.

These space syntax models of metropolitan Seattle (with and without highways) identify a couple of things. First, the importance of the highways and bridges for integrating Mercer Island and lands east of Lake Washington into the urban spatial network and, second, street-level connections of the urban grid are more important than the highways for integrating the historical CBD and Northwest Seattle cores together in the emergent spatial structure of the city. In this sense, the highways and bridges supplement – not determine – the configurational importance of the historical CBD and Northwest Seattle areas. The configurational inequalities differentiating and privileging the historical CBD and Northwest Seattle derive principally from the street-level connections between them in privileging these areas for spatial configuration in the composition of the urban grid. This provides a sharp contrast to the Bellevue area east of Lake Washington, which derives its configurational importance within the emergent spatial structure of Seattle solely from the Interstate Highway System. This suggests Bellevue and the surrounding areas tend to be much more automobile-dependent than the older areas of Seattle (**Figure 8.14**). This is not surprising. Much of the urban layout east of Lake Washington appears characteristic of post-war 20th century suburban sprawl (i.e. discrete separation) found in many American cities today.

Figure 8.14 – *Bellevue, Washington against the backdrop of Seattle and Lake Washington in 2011.*

Metric Parameters	AREA	K/SQKM	MAX LENGTH (m)	MEAN LENGTH (m)	MEAN SEG (m)
Seattle	49.4	39.1	7390.2	639.4	113.1
Denver	102.2	20	17823.2	1121.4	154.7

Spatial Parameters	K-LINES	MAX GLOBAL	MEAN GLOBAL	MAX CN	MEAN CN	MAX LOCAL	MEAN LOCAL	MAX DEPTH	MEAN DEPTH	INTELL.	SYNERGY
Seattle	1929	2.6	1.5	61	5.6	7.2	2.9	11	5.2	0.28	0.53
Denver	2046	4.1	2.2	128	7.6	8.7	3.5	10	4.1	0.38	0.79

Table 8.1 – *Comparison of metric and configurational parameters of Seattle and Denver in sample of 20 American urban grids from Chapter 5.*

Table 8.1 shows the metric and spatial parameters in the Seattle and Denver space syntax models of Chapter 5, which were paired together based on similar axial size. In this comparison, the urban grid of Denver covers twice as much metric area, mean street length is nearly twice as long, and the maximum street length is over two and half times longer than in Seattle, despite both urban grids being of similar axial size. Average block size in Denver (5.9 acres) is also nearly twice as large in metric area compared to Seattle (3.2 acres) (see Table 5.5). This has a significant effect on the spatial parameters for both urban grids. The Denver urban grid is nearly 50% more globally integrated and over 35% more connected than Seattle. The difference is similar for synergy and intelligibility, respectively. This is due to local topographical conditions allowing for the possibility to more pervasively realize a large-scale orthogonal logic in the Denver urban grid, both in terms of street length and block sizes, than in Seattle. Land speculators capitalized on the economic potential for larger block sizes and longer streets in grid expansion offered by the local topographical conditions in Denver (Reps, 1965). In Seattle, this potential only exists in Northwest Seattle since the lands east of Lake Washington were not opened for development until the post-war period, by which time the regulatory regime of Euclidean zoning and roadway classifications of modern transportation planning affected the pattern of urban growth in this part of the city. However, land speculators did capitalize on the possibilities for grid expansion offered by local topological conditions in Northwest Seattle, if only on a smaller scale in comparison to Denver, to give rise to the distinctive, historical dual core spatial structure of Seattle. It was later transformed into a trio of integration cores by the impact of the Interstate Highway System in overcoming the acute topographical conditions of Lake Washington in that city.

Despite their obvious differences, emergent spatial structure in metropolitan Baltimore and Seattle tends to conserve the primacy of the center in the form of the CBD and/or historical area by resolving the tension between centrality and linearity during the evolution of the urban pattern. In doing so, we can clearly see how the local design methods of grid expansion and deformation, street extension, and discrete separation (as well as block manipulation) played a crucial role in shaping the emergent spatial structure of these cities based on an inter-dependent family of relations, not discrete, independent locations.

9 Learning from the Grid

"Orthogonal features, when combined, can explode into complexity."
- Yukihiro Matsumoto

This chapter further investigates emergence–convergence in American cities. The focus of this analysis is two contemporary American cities primarily characterized by large-scale orthogonal super grids: metropolitan Chicago, Illinois and Las Vegas, Nevada. It identifies a 'strip effect' along the prime activity axes or capital routes of these two American cities (Major, 1997a; Karimi et al., 2005). This phenomenon of *strip intensification* is a variation on grid intensification discussed in the previous chapter whereby a long street and its immediate connections – instead of an area or neighborhood – patterns pervasive centrality into the urban grid. It then argues there are subtle differences between emergent spatial structure in Chicago and in Las Vegas, despite both possessing a large-scale orthogonal super grid, which is the material manifestation of the national grid system imposed by the 1785 Land Ordinance. Both cities demonstrate particular approaches to conserving the primacy of the center in the form of the CBD/historical area by varying street length and connections in a manner consistent with regular grid planning principles. However, emergent spatial structure in Chicago is symptomatic of the 19th century land speculation process described by Reps and others (Reps, 1965 and 1979; Kunstler, 1993). In contrast, emergent spatial structure in Las Vegas is more indicative of the segregation of land uses and modes of movement associated with Euclidean zoning and modern transportation planning in the United States during the post-war period. In many ways, Chicago and Las Vegas represent quintessential examples of American town planning during the 19th and 20th century, respectively.

Chicago and Las Vegas: a brief overview
Chicago is the 3rd largest urban area in the United States today with a population of over 8.5 million people and the 3rd largest in land area covering nearly 6,400 square kilometers (km^2) or over 2,400 square miles. The source for population, population density, and land area data in this chapter is the 2010 census of the U.S. Census Bureau, using their definition of urban area and U.S. Office of Management and Budget definition of metropolitan

Combined Statistical Area. Chicago only ranks 36th for population density with over 1,500 people/km^2 or nearly 4,000 people per square mile. Las Vegas is the 23rd largest urban area with a population of nearly 2 million people and its land area is ranked 48th, covering nearly 1,100 km^2 or over 400 square miles. Las Vegas is ranked 10th for population density with nearly 1,800 people/km^2 or 4,600 people per square mile. Based on these statistics, metropolitan Chicago is over four times larger than Las Vegas for population and nearly six times larger in land area, but population density in Las Vegas is 20% greater compared to Chicago. However, this is merely an artifact of the U.S. Census Bureau definition of metropolitan size (see the definitions previously outlined at the beginning of Chapter 4). The population density in the City of Chicago proper is nearly 4,500 people/km^2 or 12,000 people per square mile, which is two and a half times greater than Las Vegas. There is hardly any difference for population density in the City of Las Vegas compared to its metropolitan region. Population density is marginally denser (+5%) at the metropolitan level than in the city itself. This is probably reflective of the segregation of land uses in Euclidean zoning with a greater intensity of non-residential land uses in the city and more residential land uses located outside of its political jurisdiction.

According to a local journalist, "Chicago is a city of contradictions, of private visions haphazardly overlaid and linked together" (Colander, 1985) whereas English poet Rudyard Kipling (1899) more acidly described Chicago as "inhabited by savages".[1] To American writer Abbott Joseph Liebling (1952), who coined a popular moniker for the city (e.g. "Second City"), "Chicago seems a big city instead of merely a large place" and American architect Frank Lloyd Wright (1994), who lived and worked in Chicago for more than a decade, said in 1939, "eventually, I think Chicago will be the most beautiful great city left in the world."[2 & 3] Chicago was founded in 1833 on the shores of Lake Michigan near a portage of the Mississippi River watershed allowing navigation via a constructed canal to that river. Because of this, river navigation is possible from Chicago to St. Louis and New Orleans in the south. Its location on Lake Michigan also allows for easterly water navigation via the St. Lawrence Seaway to the Atlantic Ocean. According to Reps (1965), "Chicago owes its origins, its growth, and its future prospects to transportation" (300). Initially, this meant water

Figure 9.1 – *The Rapid Growth of Chicago:* (left) 1834 plan of Chicago; (middle) 1892 bird's eye view from Lake Michigan; and, (right) 1901 U.S. Geological Survey topographic map.

navigation, but later the railroad. He points out the original plan for Chicago was "so that a few lots might be sold in order to meet current expenses. Chicago thus had its origins in a speculative real estate transaction, an event endlessly repeated" in the early years of the city (300). 'Current expenses' means those associated with construction of the canal through the Mississippi River watershed. A visitor described this speculative real estate process in 1840 as follows: "in the mania for planning cities, and buying and selling house-lots, which then prevailed all over the United States, Chicago held a distinguished place" (Buckingham quoted in Reps, 1979; 25). **Figure 9.1** demonstrates the growth of Chicago beginning with a 1834 plan. The original 6 x 10 block alignment of the 1830 town plat is located along and interrupted by the canal that runs east-to-west to the fork in the Chicago River (running basically north-to-south at this location). "The beginnings of the vast gridiron that is modern Chicago are clearly to be seen… with each succeeding addition to the town, new streets were laid out connecting with or parallel to… (the) original grid system" (Reps, 1965; 300). Reps (1979) judges the plan of Chicago to be an "unimaginative design that established the beginning of Chicago's almost unending and relentless gridiron pattern" (22–23). Soon, the railroad was the impetus for accelerated growth in Chicago. "The first rail line opened in 1848, and by the end of the next decade the basic fabric of Chicago's existing railroad network had been woven… thus a few years before the Civil War the city was the focal point of ten rail lines, its population was approaching 100,000 and its rate of growth was steadily increasing" (Reps, 1965; 302). The most rapid population increase in any American city ever took place in Chicago after the Civil War. About 180,000 people lived there in 1865, which doubled by 1872, and then quadrupled by 1885 so the "land boom continued, broken only by short periods of depression" (Reps, 1979; 25). Reps (1965) points out "in the vast extensions required to accommodate this remarkable increase the gridiron plan predominated. A few of the old trails and rural roads leading into the city on radial lines did manage to survive and are important and useful elements of the modern street system" in the "relentless pattern of Chicago's oppressive grid, magnificent only because of its scale and… the tenacity with which… (it was) extended" (302).

Urban growth in Chicago "demonstrated the potential financial rewards that successful town promotion and real estate development could bring" (Reps, 1979; 25). Hoyt (1933) demonstrates this by examining land valuations for the 211 square mile area (or 135,040 acres) of the city in his 1933 University of Chicago study, *One Hundred Years of Land Values in Chicago* (data reprinted in Gallion and Eisner, 1963) (**Table 9.1**). Based on the Hoyt (1933) study, average annual land appreciation in Chicago over 100 years was over 32%, beginning with a land value of only $1.25 per acre in 1833 and rising to $14,810 per acre a century later, despite the Great Depression, U.S. Civil War, and financial panics in 1837 and 1857. The 1932 values are also 150% below the 1926 high

LAND VALUE IN CHICAGO, ILLINOIS FROM 1833–1932

Year	Total Value	Per Acre	Annual Appreciation (per acre)
1833	$ 168,000	$ 1.25	-
1836	$ 10,500,000	$ 77.75	+730%
1842	$ 1,400,000	$ 10.40	-27.2%
1856	$ 125,000,000	$ 925.65	+66.5%
1861	$ 60,000,000	$ 444.30	-15.9%
1897	$ 1,000,000,000	$ 7,405.20	+6.9%
1926	$ 5,000,000,000	$ 37,026.05	+5.4%
1932	$ 2,000,000,000	$ 14,810.40	-14.1%

Table 9.1 – *Land value in Chicago, 1833–1932 (after Hoyt, 1933).*

point of the Chicago real estate market boom. Hoyt's valuations for Chicago are Total Land Value in this table. The author calculated Per Acre value (which is rounded off to the nearest 0 or 5 for simplicity's sake) and Annual Appreciation percentage based on Hoyt's raw data. Annual appreciation is based on an average monetary increase or decrease from year-to-year between each date. This does not take into account any costs associated with owning/developing the land. The decrease in land values from 1836 to 1842 is due to a financial crisis during the Panic of 1837. The decrease from 1856 to 1861 is due to another financial crisis during the Panic of 1857 and the start of the U.S. Civil War. The decrease from 1926 to 1932 is due to the Great Depression. In examples of rapid growth such as Chicago, where land appreciation tends to drive profit margins in real estate, the more land value increases then the smaller the profit margin becomes, statistically, on an annual percentage basis over time. Reducing cost is a common manner to alleviate for this statistical artifact over the long term in real estate development. As discussed in Chapter 6, the average price of land for sale in Chicago today is more than $3 million per acre according to a contemporary source.

American satirical novelist Chuck Palahniuk (1999) writes in *Invisible Monsters*, "Las Vegas looks the way you'd imagine heaven must look at night." American writer Norman Mailer (1999), in *An American Dream*, describes the city like this, "the night before I left Las Vegas I walked out in the desert to look at the moon. There was a jeweled city on the horizon, spires rising in the night, but the jewels were diadems of electric and the spires were the neon of signs ten stories high." English journalist and naturalized American citizen Alistair Cooke (1973) in *Alistair Cooke's America* observes, "Las Vegas is Everyman's cut-rate Babylon… not far away there is, or was, a roadside lunch counter and over it a sign proclaiming in three words that a Roman emperor's orgy is now a democratic institution: Topless Pizza Lunch."[4] Las Vegas received its name from the Spanish. They used artesian wells for water in the area, supporting green meadows (*vegas* in Spanish), on journeys along the Old Spanish Trail from Texas during the 19th century. Mormons were the first to settle in the area in 1855 when Brigham Young assigned 30 missionaries from Salt Lake City to convert the local Paiute Indian population to Mormonism (Reps, 1979). These missionaries constructed a fort

 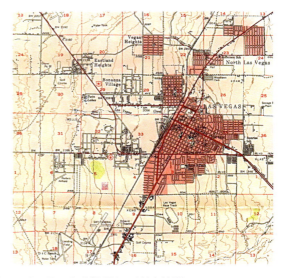

Figure 9.2 – *U.S. Geological Survey topographical maps of Las Vegas in: (left) 1908; and, (right) 1952.*

near to the current downtown area, which served as a stopover for travelers between Salt Lake City and Los Angeles. However, the missionaries abandoned the settlement a couple of years later. Las Vegas became a railroad town in 1905 when it was still a crossroads hamlet. The settlement briefly prospered in the early 20th century due to mining activities in the area and as a rail stopover between Denver/Salt Lake City and Los Angeles (**Figure 9.2**). Official incorporation of the city occurred in 1911 and the State of Nevada legalized gambling in 1931. This led to the construction of the first casino-hotels in Las Vegas, which gained notoriety and success due to organized crime figures such as Bugsy Siegel and Meyer Lansky. Siegel and Lansky were associated with the Genovese crime family (one of New York City's Five Families of the *Cosa Nostra*, i.e. American mafia). However, Mormon-owned banks fronted Siegel and Lansky, which provided legitimacy for their activities. Siegel was a driving force behind large-scale development of Las Vegas until his murder in 1947. The casino-hotels led to an explosion of urban growth that eventually made Las Vegas one of the top entertainment and tourist destinations in the world (Wilkerson III, 2000; Moehring and Green, 2005; Chung, 2005; City of Las Vegas).

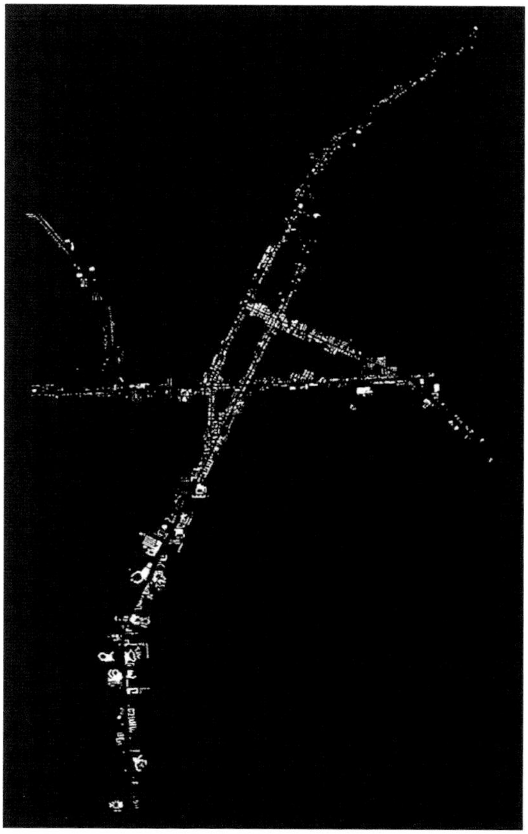

In 1972, the city was the focus of a seminal study in *Learning from Las Vegas* by Robert Venturi, Denise Scott Brown and Steven Izenour. The subject was the Las Vegas Strip "as a phenomenon of architectural communication" where the "symbol in space (comes) before form in space" (Venturi et al., 1972; 3–8). The book identifies three streets as forming the famous Las Vegas Strip (Las Vegas Boulevard, Fremont Street, and Charleston Boulevard). However, the term usually refers to only the southern segments of Las Vegas Boulevard, which is not in the political jurisdiction of the City of Las Vegas but the unincorporated townships of Paradise and Winchester. Venturi et al. (1972) were interested in the semantic nature of sign culture in Las Vegas and its impact on the articulation and scale of architectural form, or as they refer to it "architectural symbolism" (xvii). This book attempts to expand Venturi's theories outlined 6 years earlier in *Complexity and Contradiction in Architecture* to the urban level (Venturi, 1966; Wolfe, 1982). These two books narrow the debate against the architectural precepts of Modernism in favor of a new theoretical approach, which marked the beginnings of Post-Modernism in the United States. In this, it is also a good example of an almost zealous regard for the formal articulation of the architectural object arising from an a-spatial perspective of the city (Boyer, 1983; Hillier

Figure 9.3 – Figure-ground representation of building footprints along the Las Vegas Strip during the late 1960s. The casino-hotels are the large building footprints along the southern segments of Las Vegas Boulevard (Image: Venturi, Scott Brown and Associates, Inc.).

and Hanson, 1984). However, in taking this approach, Venturi et al. (1972) still utilize plan representations such as figure-ground drawings and the 'Nolli map' to reveal information about the functional structure of urban space in Las Vegas during the late 1960s. The Nolli map is a common representational technique based on a mid-18th century drawing by Italian architect Giambattista Nolli. It is a figure-ground representation distinguishing between public and private space in Rome to clearly reveal the structure of civic space (i.e. streets and squares).[5] Though not the explicit focus of their study, Venturi et al. (1972) appear to acknowledge a spatial dimension to the pattern of urban functions in the city. In Las Vegas, there "is a set of intertwined activities that form a pattern on the land… the Las Vegas Strip is not a chaotic sprawl but a set of activities whose pattern, as with other cities, depends on the technology of movement and communication and the economic value of land" (ibid.; 76). Pope (1996) reiterates this point, arguing the "urbanism of the Strip was itself structured on a relentless linear armature… in contrast to the original Las Vegas gridiron and the pedestrian 'strip' of Fremont Street, the organization of the upper strip was a discrete and reductive axis of development – a complete linear city" (197). This 'pattern on the land' is apparent in the Venturi et al. (1972) figure-ground drawing of building footprints along Las Vegas Boulevard, Fremont Street, and Charleston Boulevard (**Figure 9.3**, previous page). By investigating this pattern on the land, we can better understand Chicago and Las Vegas, in particular, and the American city, in general, as an urban network in terms of spatial configuration.

The author constructed space syntax models of metropolitan Chicago and Las Vegas for this purpose using U.S. Geological Survey topographical maps dated 1993 (Las Vegas) and 1987 (Chicago) (and later updated in 2002). The parameters for construction of these models in terms of boundaries, cul-de-sacs, highways, and parks are the same as those outlined in Chapter 5 but without any constraint on size (Major, 2015a and c). The inclusion of interstate highways tends to reinforce the pattern of global integration of the urban grid itself at the macro-scale of both cities, so highways are not included in these models. The boundaries of the Chicago model are, more or less, defined by Lake Michigan to the east, Route 53/Interstate 355 to the west (running north–south), Interstate 80 to the south (running east–west from Gary, Indiana to Joliet, Illinois), and Route 22 to the north (running east-to-west from north of Highland Park through north of Buffalo Grove to east of Lake Zurich). **Figure 9.4** is a diagrammatic map of key features in Chicago for orientation purposes. The axial size is 30,469 lines. The land area is approximately 5,700 square kilometers or 2,220 square miles. This model is nearly the size of the Chicago urban area (-11%). It is only 20% of the

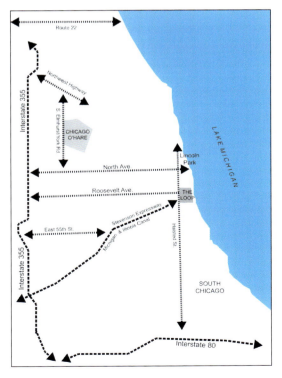

Figure 9.4 – *Diagrammatic map of key features in metropolitan Chicago.*

metropolitan Combined Statistical Area but over nine times larger than the City of Chicago proper. **Figure 9.5** shows the pattern of global and local integration in the city. It is impossible to discern finer details about the urban grid at this scale. In this format, it is also difficult to appreciate the scale of the metropolitan Chicago model. Laid out, the scaled map sections used to construct the model would completely cover the floor of a room measuring 88 square feet or 8 square meters. The land area covered is more than twice the size of the country of Luxembourg. The distance from the northwest to southeast corners of this model (or vice versa) is equivalent to the distance from central London to Portsmouth in England. However, what is apparent is the extent of the orthogonal logic in the metropolitan region as a whole. The most integrated streets form a super grid in the city reaching across a large portion of the urban fabric from north-to-south and completely from east-to-west including North Avenue from Lincoln Park in the east to Glendale Heights in the west and Roosevelt Road from just south of The Loop in the east to Lombard/Wheaton in the west. In some places, streets composing the super grid in Chicago are actually two extremely long axial lines overlapping for some distance due to minor deviations in street alignment and building footprints.

The eastern and southern portions of the metropolitan region most pervasively realize the orthogonal grid logic. There are more interruptions to this logic in the west and north. For example, in the southwest there is a super grid 'remnant' formed by East 55th Street and a series of perpendicular streets running north-to-south. This is due to large-scale interruptions to the urban fabric east of this location, which are the Chicago River/Illinois and Michigan Canal, railroad lines, and portions of the Stevenson Expressway/Interstate 55 running parallel to the canal. We describe this as a super grid 'remnant' because it is more locally than globally integrated and tenuously connects into the super grid via a series of less integrated north–south streets. In the northwest, there are more extensive super grid remnants bisected by the diagonal of U.S. Route 14/Northwest Highway, which is a street level highway

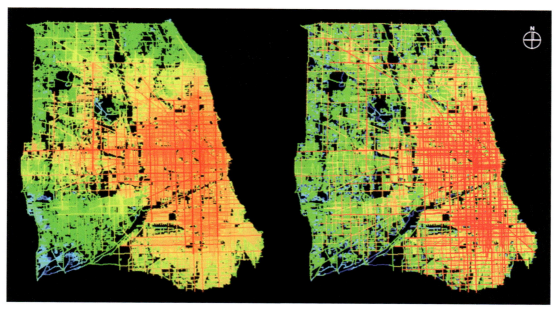

Figure 9.5 – Metropolitan Chicago: (left) pattern of global integration; and, (right) pattern of local integration (Scale=1:1,350,000).

– not a limited access one – and one of the surviving old trail/rural roads cited by Reps (1965). This is more apparent in the pattern of local integration. The overall effect of this diagonal and the South Elmhurst/York Road (running north–south immediately west to O'Hare International Airport) is to connect the northwest remnants into the super grid since York Road intersects with both North Avenue and the Northwest Highway, which is more apparent in the pattern of global integration. The most globally integrated streets in metropolitan Chicago are Western Avenue (north–south) and North Avenue (east–west). Western Avenue runs north-to-south west of The Loop/Interstate 94 from Evanston in the north to Blue Island/Little Calumet River in the south. North Avenue is the longest east–west street. These streets intersect about 15–20 blocks north of The Loop west of Lincoln Park in the trendy Wicker Park/Bucktown neighborhood. At this scale, there is a clear center-to-edge pattern of global integration more or less radiating outward from the oldest parts of the city towards the west, north, and south. This pattern skews southward since South Chicago most pervasively maintains the orthogonal logic of the grid south of the river/canal, railroads, and interstate highway previously mentioned. It serves to overcome the effect of these interruptions to the urban fabric and highly integrate South Chicago within the overall network. This is probably reflective of the historical location for manufacturing and industry in South Chicago (and Gary, Indiana just over the state border) in the manner previously described by Hoyt (1939). Expansion of the orthogonal grid logic to this area facilitated access for residents to those industries and jobs via the street network. The periphery areas to the north, west, and southwest edges more weakly integrate into the metropolitan region than the south. Generally, these areas are suburban residential areas.

The boundaries of the Las Vegas model are more or less defined by mountains to the east and south, Craig Road to the north (running east–west), Interstate 215 and Route 160/Blue Diamond Road to the south, and Rainbow Road/Route 595 and Highway 95 to the west (running north–south). **Figure 9.6** is a diagrammatic map of the key features in Las Vegas for orientation purposes. The axial size is 8,371 lines so it is about 27% the size of the metropolitan Chicago model. The land area is approximately 412 square kilometers or 160 square miles, which is only about 7% of the metric area for the metropolitan Chicago model. The Las Vegas model is 21% larger than the City of Las Vegas proper. The Las Vegas metropolitan Combined Statistical Area encompasses all of Clark County, which covers approximately 7% of the total land area in the State of Nevada. This model encompasses only 2% of Clark County itself. **Figure 9.7** shows the pattern of global and local integration. At this scale, it is more possible to discern finer details of the urban grid though it is still difficult in some areas.

The super grid in Las Vegas is more apparent in the pattern of local integration. However, we can also

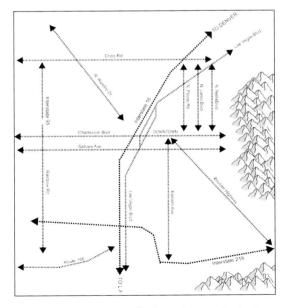

Figure 9.6 – Diagrammatic map of key features in metropolitan Las Vegas.

see it includes the most globally integrated streets of Charleston Boulevard and Sahara Avenue (east–west), and Eastern Avenue, Lamb Boulevard, Pecos Road, and Nellis Boulevard (north–south), all aligned to the cardinal directions. There are also highly integrated routes running diagonal to the orthogonal grid logic forming part of this super grid. This includes Las Vegas Boulevard, North Rancho Drive/U.S. 95 Business, and the Fremont Street/Boulder Highway. Las Vegas Boulevard runs southwest to northeast along two different alignments, one from the downtown area to the southeast where it changes direction into a north–south street and the other from the edge of downtown beginning as Main Street and merging into Las Vegas Boulevard to the northeast. North Rancho Drive/U.S. 95 Business is the principal diagonal in the northwest of the urban grid. Fremont Street/Boulder Highway begins at the edge of downtown and bisects the urban grid to the southeast. All of these diagonal streets are old trails/rural roads, the origins of which we can detect in the 1908 topographical map of Las Vegas (see Figure 9.2). The center-to-edge integration pattern in Las Vegas is less apparent than in Chicago but the pattern of global integration in Las Vegas does appear to privilege the downtown area. The offset grid in downtown – running parallel/perpendicular to Las Vegas Boulevard/Main Street at this location – is the most integrated area in the city. Instead of a clear center-to-edge integration pattern, segregation appears embedded within the interstitial areas defined by the orthogonal streets of the Las Vegas super grid.

This also occurs at the small-scale in Chicago but not to the extent seen in Las Vegas. A notable example in Chicago is the Riverside suburb designed by Frederick Law Olmsted in 1869. In Riverside, the curvilinear street network of Olmsted's plan discretely separates the suburb in spatial terms from the large-scale grid logic in Chicago by making the most direct paths for movement around – rather than through – the residential area. Streets were "laid out as to afford moderately direct routes of communications between different parts of the neighborhood (but) they would be inconvenient to be followed for any purpose of

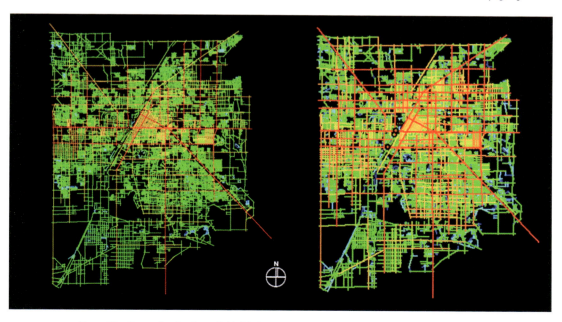

Figure 9.7 – *Metropolitan Las Vegas: (left) global integration; and, (right) local integration (Scale=1:550,000).*

business beyond the mere supplying of the wants of the neighborhood itself. That is to say, it would be easier for any man wishing to convey merchandise from any point a short distance on one side of the neighborhood to a point a short distance on the other side to *go around it* (our emphasis) rather than through it" (Olmsted quoted in Reps, 1979; 179). This Olmsted quote is 3 years before the planning of Riverside about the curvilinear street plan designed for a residential community on the University of California, Berkeley campus (Olmsted, Vaux and Company, 1866; 23–24). However, the principle for the street plan in Riverside is the same. In Hillier's (1996b) terms, the curvilinear street plan is designed to privilege centrality amongst locations internal to the suburb whilst retarding linearity to the outside world, i.e. the rest of the Chicago.

The effect is to shift non-residential land uses to Harlem Avenue, Ogden Avenue, and Burlington and Quincy Streets. Harlem Avenue is the eastern perimeter street running north-to-south in a manner consistent with the large-scale grid logic of Chicago. Ogden Avenue is another perimeter street to the south, which is a diagonal route running more or less parallel to the railroad lines bisecting the suburb itself. Burlington and Quincy are diagonal streets Olmsted designed to run through the center of Riverside (**Figure 9.8**). He designed the suburb around a pre-existing railroad line (i.e. the diagonal running through the center of the 1869 plan) so Burlington and Quincy Streets run parallel to the railroad. These streets later became extensions of the suburb's central business district, indicated in red in the contemporary zoning map. Olmsted's 1869 plan only cites this as "Land Not Belonging to the Company." In any case, it is the perimeter and diagonal streets that most relate to the Chicago urban grid rather than the curvilinear street network in the rest of the plan. Despite this example of Riverside, the Chicago grid more pervasively realizes the orthogonal logic of streets at the large- and small-scale of the urban fabric than Las Vegas. Streets are longer, more highly connected, and more interconnected from area-to-area. This is why there are fewer clear-cut examples of segregated areas embedded within interstitial areas formed by the Chicago super grid except nearer to the more segregated southwest, northern, and western periphery of the metropolitan region.

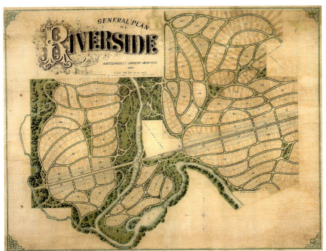

Figure 9.8 – Riverside, Illinois: (left) Olmsted's 1869 plan; and, (right) satellite view from 5 km indicating there are 18 historical access points to the east/south towards Chicago and only 7 access points to the north/west towards the residential suburbs.

The morphology of the American street

According to Hillier (2002), grid intensification is a micro-economic process whereby "in its loci of most concentrated activity it will generate not a linear system that minimizes universal distance in the system as a whole, but a locally intensified grid that minimizes movement from all origins to all destinations in the local region" (172). In the American urban object, the need to generate linearity to minimize universal distance in the spatial network as a whole is much less urgent since it is an inherent attribute of the regular grid itself. We have already seen in the preceding chapter some examples of a locally intensified grid emerging from the uniqueness of street connections in a local area or neighborhood of an American city. This generates an intelligible pattern to the neighborhood, which makes it easy to read and understand at the global and local scale of space. However, there appears to be an element of chance in these examples since the uniqueness of connections would appears to be sensitive to configurational changes that are not exclusively internal to the neighborhood itself. This might also implicate the role of space in how the 'attractiveness' of some local areas/neighborhoods appears to wax and wane over time. There may be a configurational component altering movement levels through such neighborhoods due to interventions outside of the neighborhood.

It is reasonable to speculate there must be another, more stable manner that loci of concentrated activity is built into and detectable within the American regular grid. It turns out this is the case, which produces a different – though still related – kind of grid intensification in the American city. This occurs by building loci of activity on and near to major gridlines already privileged for linearity in the regular grid. This phenomenon is a local subsystem formed by a street and all those immediately connected to it. Linearity at the global scale of space strongly characterizes this type of intensification whilst still patterning centrality into the urban grid at the local scale of space. In this, a commonly accepted boundary – for example, as prescribed by Lynch (1960) – to distinguish between inside or outside of an area or neighborhood does not define it. Rather, it is the prime activity axis or capital route itself that provides this definition (Karimi et al., 2005). We can describe this as *strip intensification* (or a 'strip effect'). This terminology is meant to distinguish the phenomena from that of 'strip development' in cities, which is a term loaded with (mostly negative) connotations in the American planning tradition. However, the patterning of strip intensification into the urban grid appears fundamentally related to the phenomenon of strip development. By its very nature, strip intensification emphasizes linearity at the global scale of space but also has a local dimension in that areas of micro-economic activity emerge by means of intensifying the immediacy of local connections. This is a defining characteristic of grid intensification. It is about making intelligible where one is in the urban grid as a whole and what one has immediate access to locally.

There is evidence that strip intensification is a generic attribute of all urban grids since it is detectable in cities with different types of layout. The key to this phenomenon appears to be highly integrated streets of long length and high connectivity, in relative terms for any particular layout. Research has identified strip intensifications in a European context in a periphery area of Amsterdam characterized by 'ribbon' or strip development (Hillier, 1999b; Major, 2000b). Hillier (1999c) detected a similar phenomenon in the deformed grid layout of European cities based on the series of axial lines forming high (or retail) streets and their immediate connections. The spatial effect is a tendency to intensify the degree of local circulation or griddiness in the urban layout. This is an example of what Hillier (2009) describes as *pervasive centrality*. However, it was the extreme length of streets in the American urban object that initially made the spatial pattern of this subsystem more apparent (Major, 1997a). The result is certain segments along a long gridline are spatially shallower via connection to a larger number of streets than other segments of that gridline. Certain segments are also spatially shallower to longer and more highly connected streets than are others via proximity to the most globally integrated areas of the urban spatial network or some variation thereof. This serves to privilege some segments of the gridline over others for different scales of movement. Land uses locate to capitalize on these movement potentials, or perhaps are responsible for the early privileging of these gridline segments in the first place by means of strip development, which today is a dominant characteristic of commercial development patterns in the American urban periphery. The block and lot sizes, building footprints and floor areas, and even the street widths appropriate to these land uses are then adjusted to accommodate them. Of course, this is not the only factor as evidenced by the larger blocks, lot sizes, and building footprints associated with industrial and manufacturing land uses adjacent to canals and railroad lines in Chicago, but it is an important part of the total picture.

Figure 9.9 (top) shows the spatial pattern formed by Halsted Street and all of its immediate connections in the Chicago urban grid (and their level of integration within the urban whole). We can discern several characteristics about this sub-system. First, there is a broad range of integration values for all streets immediately connected to Halsted Street. Second, there is a clear pattern along the length of Halsted Street with the most integrated streets tending to be centrally located near and just north of The Loop. Third, the intensity of connections to Halsted Street varies along its length with more connections near The Loop and in the north and sparser connections to the south. Fourth, there is an effect from diagonal routes. Diagonal streets generate an intensity of connections that form local

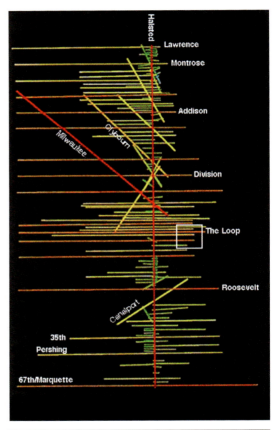

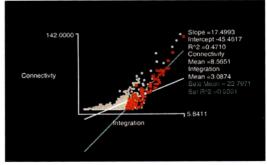

Figure 9.9 – *Strip Intensification*: (top) Halsted Street and all streets immediately connected showing the length and global integration for each; and, (bottom) intelligibility of Halsted Street and all streets immediately connected (in red) within Chicago (in gray).

areas of circulation in the grid to make the immediate context even more accessible. This occurs more so for the northern segments than those in the south along Halsted Street. Finally, there is a striking amount of variation in the length of streets (and, by implication, their integration value) immediately connected to Halsted Street and, as a consequence, the availability of the potential connections via those streets. In this way, it can be seen in spatial terms how variations in movement levels, street widths, land uses, lot sizes, and floor areas might arise along the length of Halsted Street within the large-scale orthogonal logic of the Chicago gridiron. However, Halsted Street is more than just a long gridline. It is also the focus of a well-structured intensification in the Chicago urban grid. **Figure 9.9** (bottom) shows the intelligibility scattergram for the subsystem of Halsted Street and all its immediate connections (red dots) within the Chicago axial map as a whole (gray dots). It forms a highly intelligible subsystem ($R^2=0.9091$, $p<0.001$) that steeply crosses over the regression line for the whole into the higher ranges of connectivity.

Strip intensification is not limited to large-scale orthogonal streets in the American urban object. It also occurs in the subsystem formed by the southeasterly segment of Las Vegas Boulevard (more commonly referred as "The Strip" where the greatest intensity of large casino-hotels are located) and all its immediate connections in Las Vegas (**Figure 9.10**, left). Venturi et al. (1972) imply and Pope (1996) explicitly argues there is a spatial dimension to the famous Las Vegas Strip, perhaps one of the most famous attractors in the world, and even the name itself ("The Strip") derives from its physical characteristics as realized in space. In the case of the Las Vegas Strip, there is an intelligible subsystem along a historical diagonal bisecting across the large-scale orthogonal logic of the urban grid. It is not as extensive as Halsted Street in Chicago. The most intense area of grid circulation occurs in the CBD/historical area of Las Vegas, principally defined by the intersection of Charleston Boulevard and Fremont Street. **Figure 9.10** (right) also shows the spatial pattern of Las Vegas Boulevard and all of its immediate connections (red dots) form a highly intelligible subsystem ($R^2=0.8034$, $p<0.001$) that steeply crosses over the correlation line for the spatial network as a whole (gray dots) into the higher ranges of connectivity. Strip intensifications are detectable along streets and their immediate set of connections in numerous American cities. This includes cities such as Chicago or Las Vegas, where movement at the global scale can occur along streets

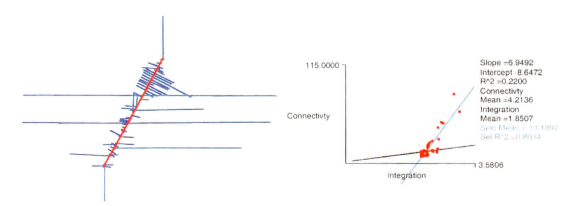

Figure 9.10 – *The Strip Effect in Las Vegas:* (left) southeasterly segment of Las Vegas Boulevard (in red) and all immediate connections (in blue); and, (right) intelligibility showing this subsystem (in red) steeply crossing over the regression line for the whole (in gray).

nearly connecting from edge-to-edge. It also occurs along diagonal routes that connect from center-to-edge in cities such as Baltimore and Washington, D.C. This suggests Duany and Talen (2002) may have created an idealized model of this phenomenon in their article "Transect Planning" in an effort to better classify streetscape design for application in form-based zoning regulations at the most local level of the street (**Figure 9.11**). Strip intensification is one manner in which cities exploit "movement constructively to create dense, but variable, encounter zones" as "mechanisms for generating contact" (Hillier, 1996b; 130). What varies from one type of layout to another is the scale at which it occurs, relative to street lengths in the layout as a whole. Peponis describes this as designing cities as "interfaces between scales of movement" (Peponis quoted in Hillier, 1996b; 131).

Conserving the center

Hillier (1996b) argues there is a tendency for cities to conserve their existing spatial structure during urban growth by gearing new development to preserve that structure. We saw several examples in the previous chapters. At first glance, there is also evidence for this tendency in the spatial structure of metropolitan Chicago and Las Vegas shown in Figures 9.5 and 9.7. However, the manner in which American urban form evolves over time to conserve the historical area – in both cities, the CBD – is actually subtler and richer than perceivable at this gross level. In Chicago, the core in terms of its most integrated streets is located at the intersection of Western Avenue/North Avenue about 15–20 blocks north of The Loop. The integration core in Chicago has shifted northwest from The Loop during urban growth, which is a common characteristic of many cities previously identified by Hillier (1996b). Variations of street length and connectivity in the Chicago urban grid enable The Loop to remain highly privileged within the spatial structure even as the integration core has shifted. **Figure 9.12** (top) demonstrates this in the spatial pattern formed by the intersection of Western Avenue/North Avenue (in red) and all of their immediate connections (in blue) within metropolitan Chicago. We can easily discern the intensity of connections along the length of these streets. We can also see the intensity of circulation routes forming local grids, especially in the areas to the northwest and southwest near the intersection of Western Avenue/North Avenue. However, the area of the urban grid with the most intense collection of circulation routes forming a local grid – that is also importantly the *most distant* from the intersection of Western Avenue and North Avenue – is The Loop itself (outlined in black). At first glance, we might think The Loop represents a perfect candidate for grid intensification. However, this is not the case.

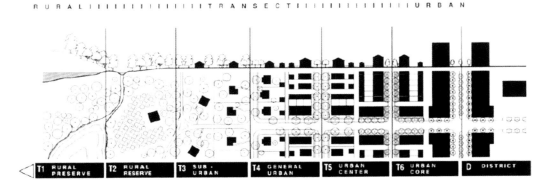

Figure 9.11 – *Duany and Talen's (2002) model of the Urban Transect (Image: DPZ).*

Figure 9.12 (bottom) shows the streets of The Loop (red dots) as a subsystem in the urban grid as a whole (gray dots), which mostly hovers above the correlation line in the higher ranges of connectivity. The reason is quite simple. All streets passing through The Loop remain highly connected and related to the urban grid as a whole. This is appropriate for its role as the historical area/CBD of a major metropolitan center in the United States and even the world. The effect of the Chicago "L" rail transit system has been to accentuate the importance of The Loop by speeding up movement and compressing space to and within the CBD since its fixed infrastructure has been mostly located in place since the beginning of the 20th century, or nearly 64% of the city's existence as of 2017 (Source: Chicago"L". org). The cumulative effect has maintained The Loop and its importance as the epicenter of Chicago during urban growth over time even as the city has greatly expanded in area.

The evolution of urban form in Las Vegas has also privileged the CBD over time. However, it occurs in a much different manner. In Las Vegas, there are two congruent spatial structures at work in the urban grid. By congruent, we mean coinciding at all points in terms of location since one is super-imposed over the other. First, there is a structure based on the macro-scale orthogonal grid logic arising from the pattern of land division imposed by the national grid system. Second, there is a structure based on the micro-scale urban fabric including the historical diagonal routes from the CBD to the edges of the city. The first structures the city from edge-to-edge and the second structures it from center-to-edge. We can demonstrate this by identifying all of the orthogonal routes aligned to the cardinal directions in Las Vegas arising from the pattern of land division (**Figure 9.13**, top on next page). Some of these streets are long and highly connected. Others are not but all are evenly spaced apart in terms of metric distance arising from the historical process described by Reps (1965 and 1979). These streets represent the "strong prescriptive order" of the national grid system as realized on the ground over time in the urban object (Pope, 1996). We can also compare this drawing to the topographical maps of Las Vegas in 1908 and 1952 in Figure 9.2. This shows none of these streets existed in 1908, though the section lines along which several would later emerge are evident. By 1952, this large-scale orthogonal grid logic was beginning to take shape in Las Vegas. Some of the Las Vegas super grid is composed of these large-scale orthogonal streets. This includes highly integrated routes such

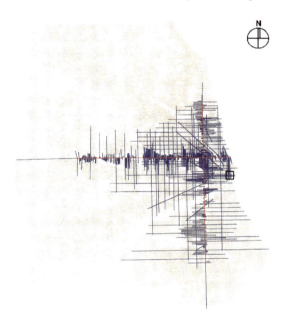

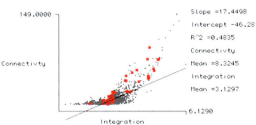

Figure 9.12 – *Conserving the Center: (top) Western Avenue/North Avenue (in red) and all immediate connections (in blue) of The Loop (outlined in black); and, (bottom) intelligibility of The Loop (in red) within Chicago as a whole (in gray).*

as Charleston Boulevard and Sahara Avenue (running east–west), Eastern Avenue, Pecos Road, Lamb Boulevard, and Nellis Boulevard (running north–south), and the southern segment of Las Vegas Boulevard (running north–south). However, the urban grid does not perfectly realize the orthogonal logic. There are two reasons. First, the national grid system is a conceptual division of the land. The process Reps (1965 and 1979) describes of section lines becoming main roads and so forth did not always occur for every tract of land. Second, the national grid lays over the circumstance of the Earth. Bryson (1994) succinctly summarizes the problem this causes for surveyors. "One problem with such a set-up is that a spherical planet does not lend itself to square corners. As you move near the poles, the closer the lines of longitude grow… (so) to get around this problem, longitudinal lines were adjusted every twenty-four miles… (which) explains why north–south streets… so often taken a mysterious jag" (136). This appears evident in diversions along the length of several north–south streets connecting to Charleston Boulevard in Las Vegas.

In any case, we can literally 'peel' off this large-scale orthogonal street network in the Las Vegas model, similar to Gandelsonas et al. (1991) peeling off streets inconsistent with the orthogonal grid logic in Chicago to reveal the underlying degree of

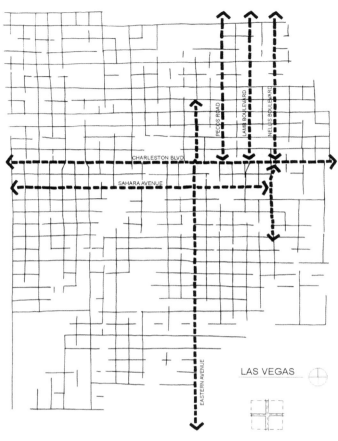

Figure 9.13 – Orthogonal streets in Las Vegas arising from pattern of land division imposed by national grid system including Charleston Boulevard and Sahara Avenue (east–west) and Eastern Avenue, Pecos Road, Lamb Boulevard, Nellis Boulevard, and southern segment of Las Vegas Boulevard (north–south) (Scale 1"=10,000").

Figure 9.14 – (opposite page, top) Spatial structure of Las Vegas without large-scale orthogonal streets arising from the national grid system. The CBD/historical area is outlined in white (Scale=1:1,400,000).

Figure 9.15 – (opposite page, bottom) Drawing showing the center-to-edge pattern of the micro-scale street network in conserving the center and discrete separation in spatial terms of suburban-type layouts in metropolitan Las Vegas (Scale: 1"=10,00").

	National Grid Orthogonal	Urban Fabric Underlying	Las Vegas Whole
Global	2.3	0.73	1.8
CN	17.7	3.1	3.7
Local	4.8	1.9	2.4
Depth	3.0	9.8	4.9
Intell	0.44	0.05	0.17
Synergy	0.66	0.13	0.60

Table 9.2 – Configurational parameters for large-scale orthogonal streets arising from the national grid system, underlying urban fabric without these streets, and urban grid as a whole in metropolitan Las Vegas.

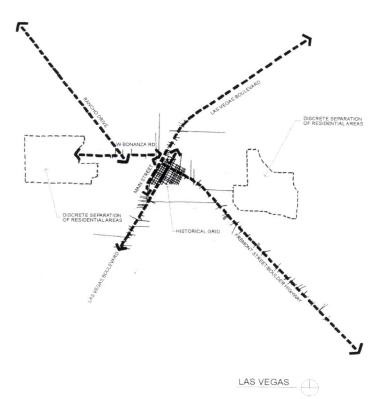

variation in the urban layout. We can then reprocess the space syntax model of Las Vegas (**Figure 9.14**). It reveals a striking center-to-edge pattern for global integration formed by the historical diagonal routes and micro-scale street network. This shows how movement might utilize the urban grid in Las Vegas independently of the large-scale orthogonal streets. The effect of this micro-scale street network is clear. The CBD/historical area (outlined in white) is highly privileged in Las Vegas. **Table 9.2** shows the mean values for the spatial parameters of only the large-scale orthogonal streets within the Las Vegas model (first column), the same for the underlying urban fabric without these streets (second column), and the entire Las Vegas urban grid as a whole (third column). It demonstrates the mean values for the micro-scale street network more closely relate to the Las Vegas urban grid as a cohesive whole.

However, spatial parameters intensify along the large-scale orthogonal streets so these routes operate as 'super integrators' in Las Vegas. This is especially true for connectivity, which on average is about six times greater in comparison to the rest of the urban fabric. This macro-scale spatial structure in Las Vegas is reminiscent of the kinds of hierarchy imposed on the urban fabric by large-scale interventions throughout history. For example, Haussmann's boulevards for Paris in the 19th century, modernization in Iranian cities during the late 20th century (Karimi, 1997 and 1998), and, to a certain degree, the construction of the Federal Interstate Highway System in the United States during the 1960s and 1970s (Major, 1993). However, there are three key differences. First, the national grid system is a conceptual order imposed for the basis of land division. Development patterns allow this spatial hierarchy to emerge during the evolution of urban form in American cities instead of being a later imposition as a kind of a remedial correction to the urban fabric. Second, this large-scale orthogonal street network is distinct from the Las Vegas super grid though some north–south and east–west streets compose both. However, some of the most important streets in the Las Vegas super grid are the diagonal routes of Las Vegas Boulevard, Main Street, Fremont Street, and Rancho Drive. For example, if we removed the Las Vegas super grid (i.e. its most integrated streets regardless of formal composition) from the model in a similar experiment, then the entire urban spatial network would fall apart into discrete elements due to the absence of these diagonals. The computer would not be able to process the model. Finally, there is the highly segregated nature of some interstitial areas of the urban grid (dark blues to the east and west in Figure 9.14). These are suburban developments poorly connected into the urban grid except via the large-scale orthogonal routes defining their perimeter. **Figure 9.15** (previous page) shows a drawing of this micro-scale spatial structure. It shows the center-to-edge pattern formed by the diagonal routes in conserving existing spatial structure. It also shows discrete separation by linear segregation in the suburban developments to the east and west. Often, the only connection from neighborhood-to-neighborhood in these suburbs is via a line of sight available due to parallel curb cuts of entry roads. This has nothing to do with inter-connectivity from neighborhood-to-neighborhood and everything to do with the traffic management of vehicular turning actions. It means these suburban developments are entirely dependent on the large-scale orthogonal streets of the super grid to access the larger urban network.

This is unlike those historical types of spatial hierarchy imposed by large-scale interventions as remedial corrections in other cities. The hierarchy in the emergent spatial structure of Las Vegas at the macro- and micro-scale of the urban object is instead reflective of the separation of land uses and modes of movement associated with Euclidean zoning and modern transportation planning. Federal, State, and local regulatory requirements mandate the design of roads based on traffic speeds and volumes projected to utilize the street network using gravity or origin and destination models (**Figure 9.16**, next page) (Southworth and Ben-Joseph, 2003; Garrison and Levinson, 2005; Marshall, 2005). The American Association of State Highway and Transportation Officials (AASHTO) has established these road design guidelines and construction standards, which include street width, stopping distance, frequency of curb cuts, turning radius, and so on. These standards are also largely driven by the demands of local fire departments for the turning movements of their large vehicles (Duany et al., 2000; Speck, 2013).

Local governments in the United States have almost universally adopted these standards into their development review regulations (Duany et al., 2000). The types of roads typically utilized in the modern development process are highways, arterials, collector roads, local roads, and cul-de-sacs. The standards for these road types have had a profound impact on the evolution of American urban form since the mid-20th century. The developer follows the standard business practice of reducing costs by severely limiting the number of street connections from a new development to its surrounding urban context as a means to increase profit within the constraints imposed by this regulatory regime. The effect is to shift traffic volumes, and the subsequent long-term costs of road maintenance associated with that traffic, to the periphery. These are usually public roads. It also helps to explain why traffic in these types of settlements seems so much worse than in traditional cities since one or two simultaneous traffic accidents can disrupt vehicular flows across the entire system due to the absence of plentiful alternative routes via surface streets in the urban grid. This type of 'minimum requirements' planning gives rise to a clear-cut spatial hierarchy of streets from the local to the global scale of space, which becomes embedded in the configurational pattern of the urban grid itself.

This also helps to reduce the costs to the developer of any traffic impact fees required by regulatory agencies. An impact fee is a fee implemented by local governments on a new development to help assist or pay for a portion of the costs of that development on public services (Juergensmeyer and Roberts, 2003). However, there are also socioeconomic reasons for the design and construction of suburbs, i.e. improve curbside appeal by creating the perception of community exclusivity/security for the benefit of potential buyers and residents by reducing through traffic. This is the type of planning that Alexander (1965) argues against in his famous article, "A City is not a Tree." Based on the example of Las Vegas, it appears readily apparent that a city can, in fact, be a tree, but it is a different question whether it makes good urban form. Many urban theorists, planners, and commentators today condemn this type of planning as one of the worst symptoms of suburban sprawl in American cities (Garreau, 1991; Fishman, 1987 and 1994; Katz, 1993; Kunstler, 1993; Talen, 1999; Duany et al., 2000; Speck, 2013). However, there are now several generations of Americans who have grown up in the suburbs during the post-war period. These suburbs have defined their experiences of city life. Their opinions might differ from the experts because Americans have continued to build and move to the suburbs for nearly a century. However, this might be starting to change. According to a 2012 Associated Press article in *Time Magazine*, American cities are now growing faster than suburbs for the first time in a century.[6]

Emergence–convergence in orthogonal grids

In the case of both metropolitan Chicago and Las Vegas, we saw evidence of the tendency for emergent spatial structure to converge on the near invariant of the

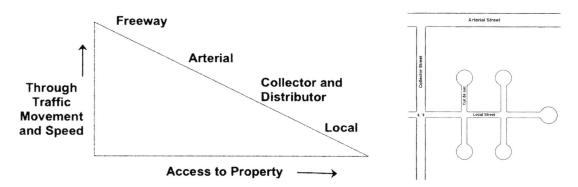

Figure 9.16 – *Road Hierarchy: (left) Diagram of the relationship between traffic speed and access in modern transportation planning; and, (right) drawing demonstrating the hierarchy that typically arises due to modern transportation planning, zoning regulations, and cost-cutting business practices of developers.*

ortho-radial grid (Hillier, 1996b). In Las Vegas, there is a well-defined ortho-radial grid structure partially arising from the national grid system and historical pattern of growth (historical area and incorporation of old trail roads). However, the imposition of Euclidean zoning and modern transportation planning methods during the 20th century obscures it in giving rise to a rigid spatial hierarchy. The spatial parameters of this ortho-radial structure are more in tune with the cohesive spatial pattern of the city as a whole.

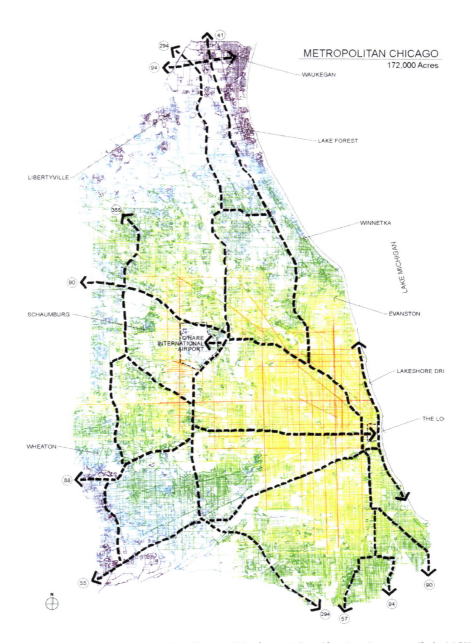

Figure 9.17 – *Pattern of global integration in metropolitan Chicago with key features indicated for orientation purposes (Scale=1:1,500,000)*.

In comparison, the orthogonal streets of Las Vegas represent an extreme example of long street lengths and intensification of connectivity along their length to form an edge-to-edge super grid.

In Chicago, we already saw evidence that, despite the scale of its orthogonal pattern (the largest and most pervasive in the world), eventually the emergent spatial structure of that city also converges on the near invariant of the ortho-radial grid. This is due to modeling more of the peripheral growth in the city and the inability to consistently maintain the orthogonal logic in that periphery. We can further demonstrate this by modeling an even larger area of the Combined Statistical Area of Chicago (**Figure 9.17**). The methodology for construction of this model is the same as before with the elimination of interstate highways and cul-de-sacs (Major, 2015a and c). The alignment of the Interstate Highway System, O'Hare International Airport, and some named areas are indicated for orientation purposes. This model of metropolitan Chicago is about 25% larger in metric area and nearly 55% larger in axial size (number of axial lines is 47,074) than the Chicago model previously examined in this chapter. However, it still only covers about 30% of the metropolitan Combined Statistical Area for Chicago as defined by the U.S. Office of Management and Budget. This model of metropolitan Chicago is twice as large as Greater London within the M25 and six times larger than the entirety of Athens, Greece urban area for metric area. The metropolitan population for Greater London is approximately 12.3 million people whereas it is a little over 4 million in Athens and nearly 9.5 million for Chicago. This suggests at least twice the amount of land is used to accommodate nearly 30% fewer people in Chicago compared to London and six times the amount of land for more than twice as many people in comparison to Athens. As Reps (1965) observes, Chicago probably represents the most pervasive example of regular grid town planning in the United States. This disparity between land area used to accommodate populations would probably be starker still if we constructed a model of the entire Combined Statistical Area of metropolitan Chicago. In fact, we can now say that Americans were not only predisposed to regularity in town planning from the very beginning of colonization but they needed – and still do – the regular grid to overcome building their cities on such a massive scale in the horizontal dimension. However, emergent spatial structure still eventually converges, in one form or another, on the near invariant of the ortho-radial grid in the American city even within the strong prescriptive order of its formal composition (Hillier, 1996b; Pope, 1996).

Chapter 9 Notes

[1] Abbott Joseph Liebling. *Chicago Tribune*, 2012. http://articles.chicagotribune.com/1996-08-25/features/9608260001_1_water-tower-chicago-aaron-montgomery-ward, accessed August 3, 2012.

[2] From Lindberg, Richard C. 1996. *Quotable Chicago*. Wild Onion Books, an imprint of Loyola Press.

[3] Frank Lloyd Wright. BrainyQuote.com, Xplore Inc, 2012. http://www.brainyquote.com/quotes/quotes/f/franklloyd127743.html, accessed August 30, 2012.

[4] Chuck Palahniuk, Norman Mailer Alistair Cooke. QuoteGarden.com. http://www.quotegarden.com/las-vegas.html, accessed August 30, 2012.

[5] See http://upload.wikimedia.org/wikipedia/commons/2/29/Nolli_map1.jpg.

[6] Associated Press. 2012. "Big U.S. Cities Growing Faster than Suburbs", *Time Magazine*, June 28, 2012; available at http://www.time.com/time/nation/article/0,8599,2118256,00.html

CONCLUSION
The Tapestry Being Woven

"Space is what prevents everything from being in the same place."
- Jean Baudrillard

Martindale (1958) argues a fundamental tenet of sociology is that "society eventually reduces to social interaction and meaningful inter-human behavior" (52). He also recognizes that "stabilized patterns persistent through time" also characterize society (52). The city is always changing, even seemingly unstable, so how can the urban object also be a social thing? How can such patterns characterize the city? People are slow to change. The city is not. According to Rossi (1982), "the most recognizable signs of urban dynamics" are "destruction and demolition, expropriation and rapid changes in use... as a result of speculation and obsolescence" (22), but he argues these forces also have a "universal and permanent character" (27). This dual nature can sometimes make the city a difficult subject. The urban object is simultaneously permanent and changing, constant and unstable, and a physical as well as a social thing.

This book has been about the urban morphology of American cities. This is an admittedly broad subject. In the past, there has been a great deal written about regular grids, in general, and American cities, in particular. There are many ideas stretching across a number of fields including archaeology, architecture, history, human ecology, geography, philosophy, sociology, and urban planning. We have seen that some of these ideas are correct while others are misguided. However, no one has ever filtered through these ideas, and the theoretic assumptions underlying them, to produce a comprehensive and cohesive story about the urban morphology of American cities founded on objective description and quantifiable analysis of the thing itself, i.e. the American urban object. However, even in accomplishing this, the book still only tells a small but important part of the story about American cities using space syntax; namely about the generation of the American urban object itself and its possible implications in the socio-functioning of the city. In addition to several new, original discoveries as well as confirmation of some very old ideas about American urban form – many applicable to the study of cities elsewhere in the world – a distinctive and significant contribution of this book to our knowledge has been lifting the 'theoretical fog' that has developed around American cities over the last century or so in telling a simple but powerful story. At the heart of this book has been a narrow question: how and why did the regular grid come to pervasively characterize American urbanism? To provide an answer, the book specifically focused on the relationship between formal composition and spatial configuration during the evolution of American urban form over 400 years from initial colonization of the New World to the post-war period. In doing so, we used space syntax to answer a subset question to the first, which was: is the spatial pattern underlying the apparent strong prescriptive order of American cities really so different compared to other models of urbanism in the world?

The findings of Hillier, Hanson, and many others using space syntax indicate the spatial structure of cities may be one of the most persistent, stabilized patterns of human society over time. These research findings formed the background against which we researched the answer to this subset question. This first comprehensive study of configuration in American cities – that is, the American city as a spatial object – reveals that the American urban object is, indeed, distinctive but still subject to the same spatio-functional processes previously found in other types of cities around the world, i.e. principles of centrality and linearity, laws of spatial emergence and convergence, and so forth. This establishes the foundation to answer the main question of the book: namely, how and why the American regular grid?

Urban theorists commonly see the American city as a radical departure from other forms of urbanism precisely because of its planned nature based on the regular grid, principally arising from the geometric division of the land for economic purposes. However, a brief review about the history of regular grid town planning demonstrated that many other cities of the world including Greek, Roman, Oriental, medieval European, and Pre-Columbian ones began as planned towns using the regular grid. Regular grid planning principles have been a standard part of the town planning vocabulary for over 4,500 years of human settlement. Review of the literature also demonstrated that urban theorists offer multiple rationales – sometimes competing, often contradictory – for widespread use of the regular grid throughout the history of town planning. Despite this, independent critical analysis of the literature suggested the reasons for its widespread use are relatively simple. First, there are its generic qualities as a simple artifact of physical arrangement, meaning as a general consequence to the act of humans placing dwellings in a settlement. Second, there are its utilitarian qualities as a practical planning tool, which are ideally suited not only for the colonization of people or place but also of the land itself. The generic qualities are evident by virtue of regular grid town planning traditions arising separately in Ancient India and Pre-Columbian Mesoamerica, and perhaps elsewhere. The utilitarian qualities are evident by the transmission of regular grid town planning principles from one generation and society to another over time. Widespread use of the regular grid in American urbanism represents the culmination of both its generic and utilitarian attributes in the history of town planning.

We narrowly and precisely defined a typology of urban layouts – linear, cross-axis, deformed, and regular, the last being inclusive of orthogonal, offset, and radial grids – based on the formal composition of their geometric logic. This provided the basis for reviewing a qualitative survey of more than 700 American historical town plans (Major, 2015a), which demonstrated that Americans were predisposed to regularity in the planning of their cities from the very beginning of colonization in the New World. This was due to the influence of the medieval European bastide model for early colonial towns and colonization of the New World occurring during the European Renaissance and Age of Enlightenment. American cities are the epitome of the Renaissance city, initially given expression in the town planning guidelines of the Spanish Laws of the Indies, and town plans of New Haven and Philadelphia. However, William Penn's 1682 plan for Philadelphia was truly visionary not for its formal design but for its size. The scale of Penn's plan was at least four times larger in the horizontal dimension that any colonial predecessor and demonstrated the realm of the possible for city building in the vast lands of the New World. Later, Thomas Jefferson's 1785 Land Ordinance transformed these Renaissance principles into a legal institution by establishing a national grid system for dividing and distributing land over the majority of the continental United States. However, the effect of the 1785 Land Ordinance was to only *intensify* the American predisposition towards regularity in town planning, especially in land speculation activities. Boyer (1983) argues these origins of American city building are deeply rooted in the European Renaissance, which she characterizes as the dream of a rational city.

We then turned to analyzing the metric and spatial parameters of the contemporary American urban grid. This confirmed previous findings that due to larger block sizes, the formal composition of American urban grids is much more expansive and sparse in the horizontal dimension of the plan than found in other models of urbanism, especially in Europe (Major, 2015c). However, the spatial configuration of American urban grids overcomes building on such a massive scale in the horizontal dimension – where, by definition, everything has to be further away from everything else – by means of longer street lengths, which leads to a more integrated and shallower urban spatial network than found in earlier models of urbanism (Major, 2015c). These distinctive characteristics of scale and accessibility in American urban grids are a direct consequence of widespread use of the regular grid in the American town planning tradition. Block sizes and street lengths also distinguish American urban grids from each other in tending to either: distribute connections across the entire spatial network in generating an ortho-radial, center-to-edge pattern; or, intensify connections along fewer streets forming a super grid oriented to the cardinal directions in generating an orthogonal, edge-to-edge pattern. The latter is the material manifestation of the 1785 Land Ordinance in the spatial pattern of the American urban object itself.

During this analysis, we identified three basic types of suburban development during the post-war period in the United States:

- *Repetitive deformity*, whereby a formal element (such as a cul-de-sac or residential pod) is replicated over and over again in generating the plan;

- *Asymmetrical regularity*, whereby a readily apparent geometric logic (such as parallel/perpendicular streets) is used in generating the plan but it is unrelated to the scale of the grid logic in the larger urban context; and,

- *Geomorphic* variations of each, borrowing from Moholy-Nagy's (1968) terminology.

However, what is common to all types of modern suburban development is not their formal composition. It is their process effect on spatial configuration. Suburbs tend to intensify segregation by minimizing connections at their periphery to the surrounding urban context and, often, internally within the suburb itself. We described this as *discrete separation by linear segregation* in that two locations in a suburb may be relatively close in terms of Cartesian distance but there is a tortuous, prohibitive journey between these locations via the street network itself. Using theoretical models, the book then examined the resolution of Hillier's (1996b) principles of centrality and linearity in the formal composition of the American urban grid. The book demonstrated the process effect on spatial configuration in accordance with these principles in obeying laws of spatial emergence and convergence. It was argued emergent spatial structure in American settlements arises from well-defined, local design methods with eminently predictable process effects on spatial configuration in resolving the tension between centrality and linearity during the evolution of urban form, as previously found in other cities of the world. These local design methods are: grid expansion and deformation, street extension, block manipulation (upsizing and subdividing), and discrete separation.

The book concluded with a series of representative case studies to demonstrate the laws of spatial emergence in the design of the American urban grid; that is, predictable "global spatial effects" arising from purely "local physical moves" (Hillier, 1996b; 5). It was argued American cities are also subject to laws of spatial convergence; that is, "processes whose rules... converge on particular global type which may vary in detail but at least some of whose most general properties will be invariant" (Hillier, 1996; 245). These case studies were the historic growth of New Haven from 1638 to 1862 and Savannah from 1733 to 1856, and contemporary spatial structure in metropolitan Baltimore, Seattle, Chicago, and Las Vegas. Large-scale orthogonal super grids characterized the latter two but not the former two cities. Along the way, we made some discoveries about formal composition and spatial configuration in these individual settlements with important lessons about the American urban object, in general. Two basic plan concepts appear to reside at the heart of the American town planning tradition: the Roman *plan castrum* model of Vitruvius and the Spanish Laws of the Indies model derived from Alberti's treatise on architecture and town planning bearing the same name as Vitruvius' own 1st century BC text, *The Ten Books on Architecture*. In New Haven, we saw an example of grid deformation, street extension, and block manipulation in conserving and reinforcing the micro-scale spatial structure based on visual integration and universal distance in the original Nine Square Plan during the process of growth. It was then argued that Oglethorpe's ward plan model in Savannah was an innovative synthesis of the Roman *plan castrum* and Spanish model outlined in the Laws of the Indies in combination with the American tendency for elongated, rectangular blocks (nominally to increase the number of lots, though this was not the case in Savannah). This innovation intensified the loading of dwelling entrances onto east–west streets in Savannah's wards. The effect was to establish and reinforce a distinctive spatial hierarchy in Savannah's ward plan between visitors initially using north–south streets and residents principally using the east–west streets. In the case of Savannah, we saw how other urban functions such as constitution, i.e. location of dwelling entrances, can come into play to either reinforce (or potentially retard) emergent spatial structure during grid expansion of highly ordered, strongly geometric settlements.

In Seattle, we saw an example of acute local topographical conditions allowing, limiting, and/or denying certain possibilities for the growth of the urban pattern over time. We also saw the effect of interstate highways in overcoming these topographical conditions (specifically, Lake Washington) to open new lands for development. This gave rise to a trio of cores (two urban, one suburban) with the CBD/

historical area, a large-scale orthogonal grid centered around the University of Washington to the north of downtown, and contemporary suburban development to the west of Lake Washington in the emergent spatial structure of metropolitan Seattle. In Baltimore, we saw a prototypical example of emergent spatial structure converging on the near invariant of the ortho-radial grid (Hillier, 1996b; Shah, 1996b). We also saw how radial routes connecting from center to edge in the periphery areas of large urban areas serve as the formal organizing mechanism for development to link back into the urban spatial network, which was also seen at a smaller scale in the historic growth of New Haven. The book briefly demonstrated that global and local spatial parameters also differentiate well-defined named areas and neighborhoods in American cities in a manner consistent with that previously found in other cities of the world (i.e. *grid intensification*). This occurs despite most, if not all, streets continuing for some distance due to the uniqueness of connections in an area or neighborhood. This suggested that configurational changes in the urban spatial network of American cities could have profound effects (more so than in other models of urbanism) in disrupting the distinctiveness of local areas even when those changes might occur some distance away (in terms of Cartesian distance) from the area or neighborhood itself. This warrants caution on behalf of architects and planners when evaluating potential design interventions in American urban space as well as for future research into American cities founded on network analysis.

In Chicago and Las Vegas, we also saw how distinctive loci of activity can form based on long streets varied in terms of connectivity along their length in the emergent spatial structure of the American city. This 'strip effect' or *strip intensification* occurred along the length of a street and all of its immediate connections in generating a strong relation between different scales of movement at the global and local pattern of space (Major, 1997a). In Chicago, this occurred along the length of Halsted Street, whereas in Las Vegas it occurred along a segment of Las Vegas Boulevard, e.g. the Las Vegas Strip. Finally, even though a large-scale orthogonal super grid characterizes the formal composition of both Chicago and Las Vegas, the book demonstrated these cities pattern urban growth to conserve the center in the form of the CBD and/or historical area in distinctively different ways. The urban spatial network of Chicago consists of many, extremely long streets that are highly connected to each other as well as other moderately connected streets. This makes emergent spatial structure in Chicago extremely shallow from every location to all others despite the enormous metric scale of that city in the horizontal dimension. The urban spatial network of Las Vegas consists of fewer, extremely long streets that are highly connected in themselves but not necessarily those streets connecting to them. This establishes a clear spatial hierarchy in the emergent spatial structure of Las Vegas at the global scale; one that conserves the center in connecting from center to edge; and the other an extremely integrated, highly connected super grid that introduces shallowness by connecting from edge to edge of the urban fabric. The Chicago urban pattern is symptomatic of the land speculation process in American settlements during the 19th century whereas the Las Vegas urban pattern is more indicative of Euclidean zoning and modern transportation planning in the United States during the 20th century.

Collectively, these findings answer the 'how' of our main question. So, this leaves us with 'why?' The answer intimately ties together physical design with cultural, practical, and socioeconomic factors in the American urban object. Colonization of the New World was predisposed to regularity in town planning from the very beginning since it occurred during the

Space syntax in America

Space syntax has made remarkable progress over the last four decades. It went mainstream in Europe in a relatively short time, only two decades, during the late 1980s/early 1990s. It brings 'added value' to design solutions for the built environment. During the previous 30 years, numerous successful projects (both small and large) in Europe and around the world attest to this fact. The other Americas began extensively using space syntax around the same time, especially in Brazil. By comparison, its impact in the United States over the same time has been minimal at best. Despite this, there have been over two-dozen notable studies of American cities using space syntax; even more about American architecture. There is a well-established program of space syntax research at a leading American university, Georgia Tech. There are natural allies advocating for many of the same principles about cities such as the Congress for New Urbanism. A cursory read of this book should indicate space syntax has something valuable to tell us about cities in the United States. However, space syntax remains only a subject of intellectual curiosity in America... if it is even thought of at all. It is odd. The reason is financial, institutional, and legal barriers retard widespread acceptance of the space syntax approach in the United States. In the main, these barriers derive from 'monetization' of the design, planning, and development evaluation process at every level of American society, i.e. private sector, Wall Street, banking and insurance, Federal, state and local governments, and so on. In other words, it is about money. The status quo has made many people comfortably employed and/or wealthy. The excuse 'but we've always done it that way' is only its most convenient and recognizable symptom. Of course, it is not true. The way Americans designed their cities after World War II is starkly different to the way we did before. Rapid, even greedy real estate speculation in American planning and development before 1926–1945 gave rise to many of its greatest cities, e.g. Boston, Chicago, Los Angeles, New York, New Orleans, Philadelphia, San Francisco, and Savannah (Reps, 1965). At heart, most Americans are capitalists; or at least, we were before the unprecedented growth in the scale and reach of government since the Progressive Era began during the early 20th century. Since then, Federal, State, and local governments have erected a massive regulatory regime around planning and development in the United States. Today, it is more accurate to say we are 'crony capitalists.' What you know (e.g. merit) is far less important than who you know (e.g. favoritism) or how much money you have (e.g. 'pay-to-play') (Story, 2012; Kristof, 2014; Major, 2015b). Given these circumstances, it is imperative for researchers and practitioners to explicitly speak the 'language of money' by quantifying the real value of space syntax in monetary terms for Americans. For example, if space syntax adds only 1% value to a large-scale urban development, this can translate into a great deal of additional income for the project; in the order of more than $700 of profit for every dollar of cost (Major, 2015b). It is likely much more. This also means additional revenues for governments over the long term.

This represents a lot of money to leave on the table for the sake of protecting the status quo. A 'money talks' rationale for space syntax can begin to more effectively cultivate allies and spread its use in the United States. It represents a challenge for the space syntax community and an opportunity for Americans with enormous potential for increasing profits and revenues with minimal cost. Simply put, space syntax is a smart investment.

cultural milieu of the European Renaissance and Age of Enlightenment. The generic and utilitarian qualities of the regular grid made it the most practical tool to initially facilitate certain social outcomes; namely, colonization in the broadest sense of the word as evidenced by widespread use of the bastide model and implementation of the plan model in the Spanish Laws of the Indies in the earliest settlements. This grounding in the order concepts of the European Renaissance became a permanent feature of American urbanism with the adoption of the 1785 Land Ordinance by the newly independent United States, which established a national grid system for the geometric division of land. The 1785 Land Ordinance indoctrinated into legislative action the strategy of dividing and allotting land from a distance, which was a practical concept underlying use of the regular grid in the earliest colonial settlements. The short-term effect of the 1785 Land Ordinance was to *intensify* Americans' predisposition towards regularity in settlement form. During the 19th century, Americans were quick to exploit the opportunities inherent in this national grid system for the rapid, geometric subdivision and sale of property in land speculation activities as the nation expanded westward, especially after the U.S. Civil War. The long-term effects of the 1785 Land Ordinance continue to weave themselves into the tapestry of the American urban object to this day. This is because Americans were not only pre-disposed towards regularity in town planning but *required* regularity in order for spatial configuration to compensate for the formal composition of building their cities on such a massive scale in the horizontal dimension of the plan. Even in American cities where suburban models (repetitive deformity, asymmetrical regularity, and/or geomorphic variations of each) strongly characterize the design of post-war development and growth, the regular grid still tends to emerge as a direct consequence of the 1785 Land Ordinance. We saw examples of this in several American urban grids such as Atlanta, Orlando, and Las Vegas. Objective description and quantitative analysis of the American urban object using space syntax established a foundation from which we can better – and more comprehensively – understand the American city as a physical and social thing in order to advance our knowledge of American urbanism in general.

Ebenezer Howard (1898) argues in his polemical text, *Garden Cities of To-morrow*, that, "it is commonly thought that the cities of the United States are planned. This is only true in a most inadequate sense. American towns certainly do not consist of intricate mazes of streets, the lines of which would appear to have been sketched out by cows; and a few days' residence in any American city except a few of the oldest, will ordinarily enable one to find his way about it; but there is, notwithstanding, little real design, and that of the crudest character. Certain streets are laid out, and as the city grows, these are extended and repeated in rarely broken monotony" (77). We can now see this assessment of Howard, commonly echoed by others such as Reps (1965), is profoundly mistaken. In fact, the design of American cities appears incredibly sophisticated in that they follow clear spatial rules founded on regular grid town planning principles, which simultaneously distinguishes them as both similar and different to other models of urbanism and each other, in giving rise to a distinctive spatial culture. They are similar in that the application of regular grid planning principles still converges on the "near-invariant" of the ortho-radial grid during the process of urban growth in the same manner as other cities (Hillier, 1996b; 174). However, they are also different in that they represent a different scale of metric and spatial possibilities compared to earlier models of urbanism; that is, the invention of a new scale borrowing from Gandelsonas et al.'s (1991) terminology. The source of this distinction lies in the regular grid itself as implemented in real world conditions. Americans required regularity to compensate for the effects of building on such an expansive scale in the horizontal dimension whereby spatial configuration is the key to unlocking how American cities really develop, grow, and function in *overcoming metric separation by linear integration*. This pre-disposition (initially and then permanently) in settlement form and the requirement for regularity due to its remarkable built scale in the horizontal dimension, makes the American urban object unique in the annals of town planning.

This is because the American urban object tends to simultaneously *amalgamate towards* and *fragment from* preconceived formal order. In a sense, all cities do this but few so clearly as the regular grid cities of the United States. This dual process of amalgamation, meaning the act and process of mixing different elements together within a preordained plan, and fragmentation, meaning the act and process of breaking or detaching different elements from that preordained plan, plays a fundamental role in producing the spatial logic of the American city. Perhaps there cannot be any better illustration of this dual process of amalgamation and fragmentation at work than to compare the pattern of urban space yesterday and today in the American city that first demonstrated the full extent of the possible for town planning in the New World: Philadelphia, Pennsylvania. **Figure 10.1** shows a figure-ground representation of the pattern of urban space (blocks in white and space in black) in William Penn's original 1682 plan for Philadelphia compared to that pattern in the city today within the same bounds. There are two remarkable yet seemingly contradictory things about this comparison. First, the remarkable degree to which the original plan has changed over time, principally through the manipulation of block sizes. Second, the remarkable degree to which the integrity of Penn's original plan concept has endured literally thousands of small-scale interventions over 330 years of development. Over time, Philadelphia has amalgamated towards and fragmented from the preconceived order of William Penn's original 1682 plan. For other American settlements, this may mean the plan of the town or the geometric logic of the national grid system itself.

The implications for future research, scholarly inquiry, and policy and practice are profound and numerous; in fact, too many to completely summarize here. Several have been implicitly implied or explicitly stated throughout the course of the book. However, we can touch on a few more of them now. First, in terms of scholarly inquiry, we should never see the regular grid as a deterministic mechanism for creating a certain political, social, or economic order. This includes the fallacy of the regular grid creating an undifferentiated

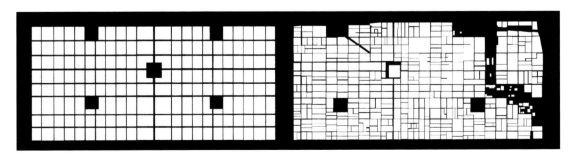

Figure 10.1 – *Figure-ground representation with blocks in white and space in black comparing: (left) William Penn's 1682 plan of Philadelphia; and, (right) today.*

matrix in the American urban object based on block and lot sizes, and street length and widths, sharing some characteristic of sameness. Instead, we should see the regular grid as a probabilistic mechanism that may *facilitate* a social outcome given certain conditions and context. However, the outcome is always and ultimately dependent on human action. Second, the English-type deformed grid layouts in New England towns are of more regional interest than national importance in the American planning tradition. It appears the importance of the English town planning tradition – what Hillier and Hanson (1984) characterize as a restricted random process of aggregating dwellings – in the American urban experience has been somewhat overstated in the literature, which appears mostly due to Boston, Massachusetts. There are almost two–dozen 17th and 18th century plans of Boston available in the historical record, more so than any American settlement during the colonial period. This tends to skew the perspective of historians and urban theorists about the importance of Boston in the American planning tradition. Efforts to elevate Boston in the nation's planning history to a level equal to that city's undoubted importance in American political history as the birthplace of the American Revolution – while certainly understandable – may have also played a role in skewing this historical perspective. The fact is the medieval European bastide model and the town planning guidelines of the Spanish Laws of the Indies had a much more profound influence on early colonial settlements in America and, subsequently in combination with the 1785 Land Ordinance, the American planning tradition over time. Our evaluation of these New England towns does not necessarily have to change so much as become much more nuanced in future scholarly inquiries about the broader American planning tradition.

For future research, the discoveries in this book suggest the space syntax approach is a valid one for American cities. More than this, the findings indicate space syntax has something fundamentally profound to contribute for better understanding the American urban object as a spatial and social thing. As Hillier (1999a) argues, the structure of the line graphs – the foundation for the topological measurements of configuration used in space syntax theory – internalizes the geometric and metric properties of urban space within it. "In doing so (this) allows the graph analysis to pick up the nonlocal, or extrinsic, properties of spaces that are critical to movement dynamics through which the city evolves its essential structures" (169). By 'essential structures,' he is generally referring to spatial structure. By nonlocal properties of space, he means those "defined by the relation of elements to all others in the system, rather than those which are intrinsic to the element itself" (169). In effect, the geometry of the regular grid finds its way into the topological graph through the axial line or, more simply, through the city's streets. This book demonstrates that a configurational approach is able to accurately identify those characteristics of urban space, which are unique to particular American cities. The expansive nature of the American city in the horizontal dimension is not just a function of the regular grid, though it is a contributory factor. In general, it is a function of the way that Americans build their cities. In particular, American consumption of the land.

Figure 10.2 (next page) shows a graphic created by urban designer and journalist Tim De Chant for the *Per Square Mile* blog. This representation shows the amount of land area required in the United States to house the world's entire population in 2011 (6.9 billion people) at the average population density per square mile in Paris, Houston, London, New York, San Francisco, and Singapore, respectively. It is best to be cautious about drawing too many conclusions about this graphic since De Chant does not specify the data sources (most likely, U.S. Census Bureau for the

American cities and individual political jurisdictions for Paris, London, and Singapore). More importantly, it is unclear if the sources compiled population data in a consistent manner, especially with reference to the definition of boundary for these urban populations. However, despite this, the truth inherent in this diagram is the greater amount of land consumed in Houston based on average population density compared to these other cities. Of the three American cities portrayed in this graphic, Houston is the only city principally characterized by 20th century development. Between the city's founding in 1850 and 1900, Houston grew from nearly 2,500 to almost 45,000 people, or 18 times in size (850 people per year on average). Between 1900 and 2011, Houston grew from nearly 45,000 to more than 2.1 million people, or nearly 50 times in size (18,681 people per year on average). Nineteenth century growth more so characterizes New York and San Francisco. New York had a population of nearly 7.3 million people in 1900. San Francisco had a population of nearly 350,000 people in 1900 (Source: U.S. Census Bureau). The differences in population size for New York and San Francisco are due to political boundaries.

The metropolitan population of San Francisco in 1900 was almost 700,000 people and today it is over 7.1 million people (or ten times in size since 1900), which ably illustrates why caution is necessary in discussing this diagram.

Twentieth century suburbs consume as much – if not more – land than the regular grid. However, suburban sprawl does nothing in terms of spatial configuration to help compensate for the expansive nature of the American urban object in the horizontal dimension. Americans have designed suburbia to intensify *discrete separation by linear segregation*. The more American cities suburbanize, then the more difficult it becomes for the American urban grid to overcome its expansive scale in the horizontal dimension. The amount of land Americans consume in building their cities remains consistently and remarkably excessive, but the formal principles and their spatial effect in the 20th century are radically different compared to what came before. In fact, they are diametric opposites, i.e. overcoming metric separation by linear integration (regular grid) in the 18th and 19th centuries and discrete separation by

Figure 10.2 – *The world's population in 2011 concentrated in the United States based on average population density in six world cities.*

linear segregation (suburbia) in the 20th century. For nearly a century, the regular grid as an instrumental tool of pre-20th century American town planning has been able to bear the weight of introducing ever more spatial segregation into the urban fabric. However, it appears we are approaching a breaking point when we will no longer be able to abuse the instrumental power of the regular grid by flooding ever more traffic volumes onto fewer and fewer roadways as done during the 20th century. This is what lies behind the public acknowledgment of some American transportation planners that enough lanes cannot ever be practically built for interstate highways and arterial roads to carry the increasing flows of traffic projected by gravity or origin and destination modeling (Tocknell, 2007). It has even contributed to examples of 'road dieting,' whereby regulatory agencies eliminate lanes from arterial roads in order to redistribute traffic over the larger urban spatial network, if feasible (Federal Highway Administration, 2004). However, this is not an option for many American cities – especially those experiencing rapid growth in the post-war period – because they long ago abandoned the regular grid as a design tool in local neighborhoods. These cities lack the alternative routes necessary to support a road diet strategy.

However, consuming the land is not unique to suburban sprawl. It is also common to regular grid town planning in American history. Consumption of the land has been a feature of American town planning since William Penn's 1682 plan for Philadelphia. In this sense, the United States has always been a country founded on consumption. In terms of the land, environmental groups in the United States have a right to be concerned. However, the manner in which these groups have sought to protect the environment through Federal government legislation such as the 1969 National Environmental Quality Act and 1972 Clean Water Act appears to have actually accelerated – instead of retarded – Americans' consumption of the land. Federal environmental mandates led to blanket 'one-size-fits-all' protections at the local level where elected officials do not have the experts to design a humanistic-based sustainable model tailored to every development, which carefully balances environmental protection while accommodating urban growth in their community. **Figure 10.3** shows an example of one Florida county where widespread, blanket environmental protection regulations, in effect, limit urban growth to suburban

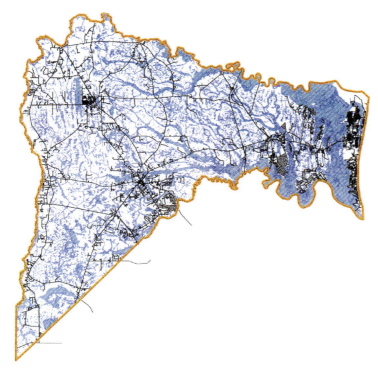

Figure 10.3 – *Protected water bodies and wetlands (in blue) in one Florida county.*

sprawl due to development constraints in protecting wetlands. Regulatory agencies do not have the desire to alter these conditions because of political opposition from local environmental groups, which tend to adopt extremist perspectives to almost any form of development. More often than not, this is really homeowner NIMBYism ("Not in My Backyard") masquerading in the name of a higher cause. The result is the topography of protected environmental areas tends to define and embed within suburban layouts. This does not penalize developers or home builders. Quite the opposite; they design suburban layouts to minimize their environment impact (the costs of which are prohibitive) to within the letter of the law. They enjoy a financial windfall due to reducing construction costs for roads and charging premium prices for lots adjacent to protected areas. They also charge a premium for lots adjacent to stormwater management facilities (i.e. retention ponds), advertising them as 'waterfront properties' to potential buyers. Because these suburban layouts are low density in nature, they consume more land to accommodate their residential populations and protected environments. **Figure 10.4** shows a simple diagram demonstrating the benefits of higher residential densities in conserving the land and reducing the demand for roads, stormwater management, and impervious surfaces. This simple example of the benefits of density for conserving the land and reducing demand on public services does not take into account the effect of environmental protection regulations on development patterns. However, the key for environmental protection in this example is the drastic reduction in impervious surfaces, which reduces non-point pollution sources associated with rainwater runoff from asphalt shingle roofs. This can be further reduced using alternative pervious surfaces for low-traffic roads to assist with the absorption of water into the soil.

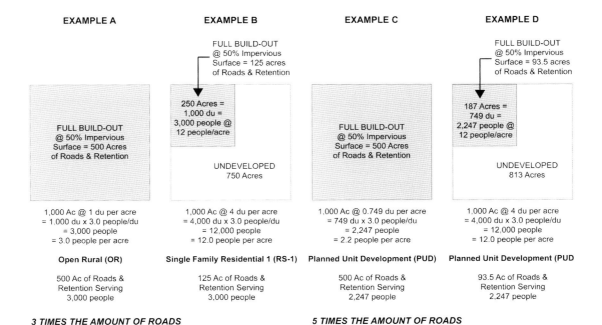

Figure 10.4 – Diagram illustrating the benefits of higher residential densities in urban development for reducing land consumption, demand on public services such as roads and stormwater management, and impervious surfaces. Key: OR=Open Rural zoning district; RS-1=Residential, Single Family 1 zoning district; PUD=Planned Unit Development.

In part, this also helps to explain why public transportation such as rail transit is a difficult proposition for so many American cities. Because of the expansive nature of the American city in the horizontal dimension, public transportation corridors need to extend further in terms of Cartesian distance to reach residential populations that could potentially use such facilities. In order for public transportation to be self-sustaining in economic terms, there have to be frequent stops in order to cater to the largest constituency of potential users. This increases the cost for constructing, operating, and maintaining the infrastructure associated with public transportation in the American context. It also retards the effectiveness of public transportation as an alternative to automobile travel in American cities because trips via public transport are just as long but also more time-consuming due to frequent stops. It is common in proposals for public transportation in the United States to reduce the number of stops in order to make the system more efficient in terms of costs and journey times. The result is public transportation does not provide services to a large enough population to be economically self-sustaining over the long-term. Thus, the 'public purse' has to subsidize the system. This appears to make cost-effective public transportation a self-defeating proposition in the here and now for all but a few American cities. Twentieth century, post-war suburbanization in America has only exacerbated the situation since housing densities are too low to adequately support public transportation. These segregated, poorly connected layouts also purposefully deter pedestrian movement flows needed to feed the use of such facilities by resident populations. The result is that the application of regular grid planning principles in American urbanism is extremely resilient for personal, private transport like the automobile but inefficient for public mass-transit. Inexpensive private transportation in the form of the automobile affords more opportunities for developers to exploit cheap land for quick profit. Cheap agricultural land on the urban periphery remains the driving force for building American cities (as discussed with reference to leapfrog development in Chapter 6).

In the last decade, advocates of alternative transportation planning solutions have shifted their focus to high-speed rail proposals, which combine mechanical enhancements and a much larger inter-city corridor network with fewer stops between to increase the speed of moving people as well as reduce the financial costs of such projects, especially with regards to regulatory takings. The goal is to overcome the inherent problems presented by the expansive nature of the American urban landscape. However, it is debatable whether high-speed rail adequately addresses the inherent problems of American urban form, even caters to those populations most in need of alternative transit options, and actually accentuates rather than solves the inherent problems with rail transit in American cities. To many people, the similarities between high-speed rail projects and the limited highway access solutions of modern transportation planning are a little too close for comfort. Interstate highways have been the public transportation projects of America during the post-war period. However, many highways have already reached – and many more are approaching – the limits of road capacity in terms of lane widening to accommodate increasing traffic and efficiently move Americans in the urban landscape (Tocknell, 2007). Many public agencies are beginning to realize this stark truth and there are no easy solutions. Public transportation alternatives will never become feasible in most American cities until the urban object itself becomes more compact and resident populations more dense, which can only mean a radical change in the American lifestyle. Americans have built this lifestyle on the demand for more space, bigger homes, and feeding a ravenous appetite for land consumption more than four centuries old. Recent public policy efforts to support research into the production of alternative fuels represent attempts to kill several – rather than just the proverbial two – birds with one stone. There are several explicit and implicit objectives in the promotion of alternative fuels. First, to reduce American dependence on foreign oil but maintain Americans' dependence on the automobile for access to jobs, goods, and services. Second, to maintain the degree of spatial mobility and freedom that the automobile provides for the American lifestyle. Third, to forgo the radical change to that lifestyle necessary to effectively construct, operate, and support viable public transportation alternatives. Lastly, to maintain the flow of jobs and profits for industries and professional services associated with road construction in America. Steve Mouzon (2010) describes this approach as the promise of 'Gizmo Green.' However, too often, this comes across to many people as a vague promise of a technological solution in the future while avoiding the real problem all together in the present. There is a fatal flaw with this approach. It does not address the fundamental problem, which is the capacity of our roads and highways to effective and efficiently accommodate the volumes of traffic generated by the American lifestyle. Vehicular trips continue to become longer and slower. Literally, millions of Americans find themselves imprisoned within their automobiles for several hours each day. This should bring into question the real cost and value of that lifestyle.

American cities are at a crossroads. However, there is a simple question at the heart of this problem. What do we want our cities to be? American cities began to undergo a radical change beginning with the U.S. Supreme Court ruling that Euclidean zoning was a constitutional exercise of police power in 1926. This led to the implementation of a slew of new government planning regulations and policies first instituted during the earliest days of the New Deal under the Roosevelt administration in the 1930s (Boyer, 1983). This radical change continued with the 1949 National Housing Act under the Truman administration, construction of the Interstate Highway System beginning in the 1950s during the Eisenhower administration, and adoption of modern roadway classifications/standards during the 1960s. Finally, it reached an apex with the adoption of restrictive environmental protections in the National Environmental Quality Act and the Clean Water Act during the Nixon administration in the late 1960s/early 1970s.

Figure 10.5 – *Suburban sprawl: (left) along the urban growth boundary of Portland, Oregon; and, (right) in Scottsdale, Arizona.*

Today, because of the cumulative effect of these government policies and their associated regulations, Americans appear to consistently answer the question 'what do we want our cities to be' in an unequivocal manner. We want our cities to be suburbs (Fishman, 1987). The business practices of our real estate developers and home builders only provide what our public policies and development regulations have consistently told them time and time again: Americans really want suburbs, which Reps (1965) aptly describes as "cemeteries for the living" (325) (**Figure 10.5**). Oddly, whether it is true or not that Americans really want suburbs is beside the point.

The real estate industry continues to take the path of least resistance to the most profits. Public policy efforts in support of alternative fuels provide the same answer to the question given over the last century. Public policy efforts in support of rail transportation alternatives typically avoid answering the question altogether because the truth is akin to political suicide. However, if Americans truly want to develop sound public policy for the sustainable planning and development of our cities into the near and distant future, the question 'what do we want our cities to be' demands a different answer than the same one given over and over again during the last century. If Americans do not want suburbia, then we as architects, planners, and policy makers have a responsibility to our fellow citizens to offer a different answer. If Americans want a different outcome, then it is time to start doing something different. Albert Einstein famously said the definition of insanity is doing the same thing over and over and expecting different results. Never was this truer than when it comes to the planning and development process in America's cities today where we build the same suburbs over and over again and call it a city. It is only after we recognize this truth that we can begin to plan accordingly for the future of our cities.

For a century, Americans have vastly undervalued the instrumental power of the regular grid. Or, perhaps, it is more accurate to say Americans have understood all-too-well the instrumental power of the regular grid to overcome metric separation by linear integration by abusing and exploiting it in the single-minded pursuit of its diametrical opposite over the last century, i.e. suburban sprawl. Americans have a choice. We can continue down the unsustainable path we have been traveling for the last century or we can embrace a radical return to a more traditional and truly sustainable model of urbanism (Mouzon, 2010). To do this, we need the regular grid in order to compensate for the already expansive nature of the American city in the horizontal dimension. The choice is ours but we must choose wisely. Reps (1965 and 1979) characterizes the American city as relentless and oppressive in its addiction to the regular grid. However, as the epitome of the Renaissance ideal – Boyer's (1983) dream of a rational city – American cities are nothing if not resilient and relentless in their magnificence as urban objects. We need to seek to better understand this magnificent and intricate tapestry that is constant – and constantly being woven in the American urban object – before it is too late.

Acknowledgments

It took more than 20 years to complete the research for this book. It is impossible to thank every person who offered support along the way. However, several people merit a special mention.

I cannot put into words the gratitude and respect I have for my University College London Ph.D. supervisors and mentors, Professor Bill Hillier and Professor Alan Penn. Their constructive criticism and sheer determination in pushing me towards completion of this research is discernible on every page. By its very nature, research does not stand alone but on the broad shoulders of those who preceded you. I have no hesitation in acknowledging Dr. Julienne Hanson, who helped to originally lay the foundations of this research. Thank you, Julienne, for your encouragement and feedback over the years.

A special thank you to: Dr. John Peponis at the Georgia Institute of Technology, whose encouragement never ceased to raise my fallen spirits during this long trek; Nick "Sheep" Dalton, who originally wrote the brilliant user-friendly, Apple-based space syntax software used in this research; and his wife, Dr. Ruth Conroy Dalton. As a fellow member of the 'next generation' of space syntax practitioners and researchers emerging during the 1990s from London and elsewhere, Ruth was kind enough to write the Foreword to this book. I have shared numerous conversations with Nick and Ruth about the subject matter of this book over the years. I am pleased to count them among my friends. I would also like to convey my sincerest thanks and deepest love for my friend and colleague Tim Stonor, his wife Anna, and their family. There are several past and current members of the Unit for Architectural Studies/Space Syntax Limited and The Bartlett School of Graduate Studies to thank as well. There are too many to list here but it certainly includes Dr. Beatriz de Campos and her family (Victor, Anita, and Julia), Dr. Kayvan Karimi, Dr. Jake Desyllas, Georgia Spiliopoulou, Professor Young Ook Kim, Professor Api Kasemsook, and Dr. Laura Vaughan. Other colleagues who deserve thanks for discussing and reflecting on the substance of this research include Professor Philip Steadman, Professor Stephen Marshall, Professor Tom Markus, Professor Michael Batty, Dr. Stephen Read, and Margarita Greene. Special thanks to my former colleagues at or associated with Pulte Homes/Del Webb in Jacksonville, Florida including David Smith, Rick Covell, David Kalosis, N. Hugh Mathews, and Juanitta Clem. I learned about the business and logistics of real estate development from them and I am grateful for their insight. I would also like to thank the students whom I taught on the M.Sc. in Architecture: Advanced Architectural Studies program from 1994 to 2000 at University College London. They were always a joy to interact with on a daily basis. They taught me that my first love is – and always will be – teaching. I would especially like to cite by name Shazia Shah, Ginette Bone, Ros Diamond, Stefania Maniati, Maria Doxa, Stephanie Rees, Nicholas Sarris, and Polly s.p. Fong.

I would also like to thank my friends, Dr. Lilian Leung and Eva Culleton-Oltay, who helped to keep me sane when I wrote the first draft of this research in 1999–2000. They went beyond the call of friendship in the process. I would also like to convey thanks to Julia Starr Sanford for her encouragement to return to this research and finally see it through to a successful conclusion. I owe additional gratitude to Eva and Reem Zako, who were kind enough to read and edit the first draft of this research. Thanks are also due to my mother, Mary E. Skrha, who read and edited almost every draft of this book to help ensure 'even my mother could understand it.' Other members of my family to provide unwavering support over the years include my aunt and uncle, Kathy and Lee Francies, who originally sent me on a London adventure with their jaw-dropping Christmas gift in 1991, and my stepfather Frank Skrha. I would like to pay tribute to my grandfather, Jesse Francies, Sr., who unfortunately passed away during the course of this research while I was still living in London. He never failed to support me in any endeavor, which is only one reason why I love and miss him so much. I would also like to thank and convey my love to friends and classmates on the 1992–93 M.Sc. Course at University College London – Katerina Danadiadis, Bess Tremonto, Ralf Walter, and especially Jerry Yao – whose friendship convinced me to stay in London a little longer, which eventually turned into nearly a decade.

Thank you to Kathryn Schell, Nicole Solano, Krystal LaDuc, Elizabeth Spicer, and Louise Baird-Smith at the Routledge/Taylor & Francis Group. Finally, I would also like to thank my ex-wife, Jane Penney, who I courted, married, and separated from during the course of this research while I was living in London. Despite this, we took away the best part of the marriage, which was the friendship. We remain friends to this day despite living on opposite sides of the world. Jane made me a better person and I am eternally grateful. She is the rock upon which this research was built. This book is dedicated to her.

Dr. Mark David Major, AICP, CNU-A

Bibliography

Adams, J.T. 1931. *The Epic of America*. Boston: Little, Brown and Company.

Alberti, L.B. 1452. *De re Aedificatoria. On the Art of Building in Ten Books* (Trans. J. Rykwert, R. Tavernor and N. Leach). Cambridge, Massachusetts: MIT Press, 1988.

Alexander, C. 1965. "A City is not a Tree," *Architectural Forum*, 122(1): 58–61.

Allen, D., J. Peponis, R. Dalton. 2001. *Subdivision and Zoning, Crabapple, Georgia. Urban Design Case Study*. Atlanta, Georgia: Georgia Institute of Technology.

Al Sayed, K., A. Turner, S. Hanna. 2009. "Cities as Emergent Models: The Morphological Logic of Manhattan and Barcelona," *Seventh International Space Syntax Symposium Proceedings* (Eds. D. Koch, L. Marcus and J. Steen), Stockholm: KTH, 2009: 001.1–001.12.

Anderson, S. 1993. "Savannah and the Issue of Precedent: City Plan as Resource," *Settlements in the Americas: Cross-Cultural Perspectives* (Ed. Ralph Bennett). Newark: University of Delaware Press, 110–144.

Anderson, S. (Ed.). 1986. *On Streets*. Cambridge, Massachusetts: MIT Press.

Attoe, W., D. Logan. 1989. *American Urban Architecture: Catalysts in the Design of Cities*. Berkeley, CA: University of California Press.

Bacon, E.N. 1976. *Design of Cities* (Revised Edition). New York: Penguin Books.

Badawy, A. 1966. *A History of Egyptian Architecture: The First Intermediate Period, the Middle Kingdom, and the Second Intermediate Period*. Berkeley: University of California Press.

Banham, R. 1971. *Los Angeles: The Architecture of Four Ecologies*. Harmondsworth, Middlesex, England: Penguin Books.

Bannister, T.B. 1961. "Oglethorpe's Sources of the Savannah Plan," *Journal of the Society of Architectural Historians*, (20)2: 47–62.

Barth, G. 1975. *Instant Cities: Urbanization and the Rise of San Francisco and Denver*. New York: Oxford University Press.

Batty, M. 2008. "The Size, Scale, and Shape of Cities," *Science*, 8 February 2008, 319: 769–771.

Batty, M., S. Rana. 2004. "The Automatic Definition and Generation of Axial Lines and Axial Maps," *Environment and Planning B: Planning and Design*, 31: 615–640.

Batty, M., P. Longley. 1994. *Fractal Cities: A Geometry of Form and Function*. London: Academic Press, Harcourt Brace and Company.

Baudrillard, J. 1988. *America* (Trans. C. Turner). London: Verso.

Benedikt, M.L. 1979. "To Take Hold of Space: Isovists and Isovists Fields," *Environment and Planning B: Planning and Design*, 6: 47–66.

Beresford, M. 1967. *New Towns of the Middle Ages: Town Plantation in England, Wales and Gascony*. London: Lutterworth Press.

Bermejo Tirado, J. 2015: "Aplicaciones de Sintaxis Espacial en Arqueología: Una Revisión de Algunas Tendencias Actuales," *Arqueología de la Arquitectura*, 12: e031.

Blumenfeld, H. 1982. "The Modern Metropolis," *American Urban History: An Interpretive Reader with Commentaries*. New York: Oxford University Press, 480–491.

Bone, G. 1996. *New Orleans – The Grid: Symbol or Instrument?* M.Sc. Thesis, M.Sc. Architecture: Advanced Architectural Studies. Copies available from the Environmental Science Library, University College London.

Botero, G. 1606. *The Reason of State* (Trans. R. Peterson). London: Routledge. Originally written in 1588, republished by Routledge in 1956.

Boyer, M.C. 1983. *Dreaming the Rational City: The Myth of American City Planning*. Cambridge, MA: MIT Press.

Bryson, B. 1994. *Made in America*. London: Black Swan Books.

Bustard, W. 1997. "Space, Evolution and Function in the Houses of Chaco Canyon," *First International Space Syntax Symposium Proceedings* (Eds. M.D. Major, L. Amorim, F. Dufaux), 2: 23.01–23.21.

Callow, Jr., A.B. 1982. *American Urban History: An Interpretive Reader with Commentaries*. New York: Oxford University Press.

Campos, M.B. 1999. "All that Meets the Eye: Overlapping Isovists as a Tool for Understanding Preferable Location of Static People in Public Squares," *Second International Space Syntax Symposium Proceedings* (Eds. F. de Holanda, L. Amorim, F. Dufaux), 1: 20.01–20.10.

Campos, M.B. 1997. "Strategic Space: Patterns of Use in Public Square of the City of London," *First International Space Syntax Symposium Proceedings* (Eds. M.D. Major, L. Amorim, F. Dufaux), 2: 26.1–26.11.

Carlson, L.A. 1981. *Indians, Bureaucrats, and Land*. Westport: Connecticut.

Carstensen, V. 1988. "Patterns on the American Land," *Journal of Federalism*, 18(4): 31–39.

Carter, H. 1983. *An Introduction to Urban Historical Geography*. London: Edward Arnold.

Carvalho, R., A. Penn. 2004. "Scaling and Universality in the Micro-structure of Urban Space," *Physica A*, 32: 539–547.

Chung, S.K. 2005. *Las Vegas: Then and Now*. San Diego, California: Thunder Bay Press.

Clay, G. 1973. *Close-up: How to Read the American City*. London: Pall Mass Press.

Colander, P. 1985. "A Metropolis of No Little Plans," *New York Times*, 5 May 1985.

Conroy Dalton, Ruth, S. Bafna. 2003. "The Syntactical Image of the City: A Reciprocal Definition of Spatial Elements and Spatial Syntaxes," *Fourth International Space Syntax Symposium Proceedings*, London, 2003: 59.1–59.22.

Conroy Dalton, R.A., N. Dalton. 2001. "OmniVista: An Application for Isovist Field and Path Analysis," *Third International Space Syntax Symposium Proceedings* (Eds. J. Peponis, J. Wineman, S. Bafna), Atlanta, 2003: 25.1–25.10.

Conroy, R.A. 2001. *Spatial Navigation in Immersive Virtual Envrionments*. Ph.D. Thesis. Copies available from Senate House, University of London.

Cooke, A. 1973. *Alistair Cooke's America*. New York: Basic Books.

Cooley, C.H. 1894. "The Theory of Transportation," *Publications of the American Economic Association*, Volume 9, Issue 3 (May, 1894), 13–148.

Copjec, J. 1991. "The Democracy of the Grid," *The Urban Text* (M. Gandelsonas, J. Copjec, C. Ingraham, and J. Whiteman). Cambridge: MIT Press. 12–19.

Davis, M. 1990. *City of Quartz: Excavating the Future in Los Angles*. London: Vintage Books.

Dawson, M. 1996. "The Best Laid Plans: The Rise and Fall of Growth Management in Florida," *Journal of Land Use and Environmental Law*, Tallahassee, Florida: Florida State University, 11(2): 325-374.

Dawson, P.C. 2006. "Seeing Like an Inuit Family: The Relationship between House Form and Culture in Northern Canada," *Études/Inuit/Studies*, 30(2): 113–135.

Desyllas, J. 1999. "Why Pay to be There? Office Rent and the Location Variable," *Second International Space Syntax Symposium Proceedings* (Eds. F. de Holanda, L. Amorim, F. Dufaux), 1: 26.01–26.17.

Desyllas, J. 1997. "Berlin in Transition: Analysing the Relationship Between Land Use, Land Value, and Urban Morphology," *First International Space Syntax Symposium Proceedings* (Eds. M.D. Major, L. Amorim, F. Dufaux), 1: 04.1–04.15.

Duany, A., E. Talen. 2002. "Transect Planning," *APA Journal*, 68(3): 245–266.

Duany, A., E. Plater-Zyberk, J. Speck. 2000. *Suburban Nation: The Rise of Sprawl and the Decline of the American Dream*. New York: North Point Press.

Easterling, K. 1993. *American Town Plans: A Comparative Time Line*. New York: Princeton Architectural Press.

Elson, H.. 1904. *History of the United States of America*. New York: The MacMillan Company.

Eltis, D., S.D. Behrendt, D. Richardson, and H.S. Klein. 1999. *The Trans-Atlantic Slave Trade: A Database on CD-ROM*. Cambridge: Cambridge University Press.

Fairman, H.W. 1949. "Town Planning in Pharaonic Egypt," *Town Planning Review*, 20: 31–51.

Federal Highway Administration. 2004. *Summary Report: Evaluation of Lane Reduction 'Road Diet' Measures and Their Effects on Crashes and Injuries*. U.S. Department of Transportation Publication Number: FHWA-HRT-04-082, March 2004.

Fishman, R. 1994. "Space, Time and Sprawl," Special Issue on The Periphery, *Architectural Design*, 108: 44–47.

Fishman, R. 1987. *Bourgeois Utopias: The Rise and Fall of Suburbia*. New York: Basic Books.

Flink, J.J. 1988. *The Automobile Age*. Cambridge: The MIT Press.

Fortes de Sousa, R. 1985. *The Grid In Two American Towns: New York and Washington*. M.Sc. Thesis, M.Sc. Architecture: Advanced Architectural Studies. Copies available from the Environmental Science Library, University College London.

Foster, N. 1999. "Opening Address," *First International Space Syntax Symposium Proceedings* (Eds. M.D. Major, L. Amorim), 3: xvii–xxi.

Fyfe, N., J. Kenny, Eds. 2005. "Introduction to Part One," *The Urban Geography Reader*. New York: Routledge.

Gallion, A.B., S. Eisner. 1963. *The Urban Pattern: City Planning and Design*, Second Edition. Princeton: D. Van Nostrand Company, Inc.

Gandelsonas, M. 1999. *X-Urbanism: Architecture and the American City*. New York: Princeton Architectural Press.

Gandelsonas, M., J. Copjec, C. Ingraham, J. Whiteman. 1991. *The Urban Text*. Cambridge: MIT Press.

Garreau, J. 1991. *Edge City: Life on the New Frontier*. New York: Anchor Books.

Garrison, W.L., D.M. Levinson. 2005. *The Transportation Experience: Policy, Planning, and Deployment*. New York: Oxford University Press.

Gasparini, G. 1993. "The Pre-Hispanic Grid System: The Urban Shape of Conquest and Territorial Organization," *Settlements in the Americas: Cross-Cultural Perspectives* (Ed. R. Bennett). Newark: University of Delaware Press, 78–109.

Goldfield, D.R., B.A. Brownell. 1979. *Urban America: From Downtown to No Town*. Boston: Houghton Mifflin.

Green, E.B., V.D. Harrington. 1932. *American Population before the Federal Census of 1790*. New York: Columbia University Press.

Gropius, W. 1965. *The New Architecture and the Bauhaus*. Cambridge, Massachusetts: MIT Press.

Hacking, I. 1983. *Representing and Intervening: Introductory Topics in the Philosophy of Science*. Cambridge: Cambridge University Press.

Hanson, J. 2009. "The Economic 'Health' of Market Towns: A Configurational Approach to Accessibility," *Seventh International Space Syntax Symposium Proceedings* (Eds. D. Koch, L. Marcus, J. Steen), Stockholm: KTH, 2009: 014.1–014.28.

Hanson, J. 1998. *Decoding Homes and Houses*. Cambridge: Cambridge University Press.

Hanson, J. 1989. "Order and Structure in Urban Design," *Ekistics*, 334/335: 22–42.

Hanson, J, B. Hillier. 1987. "The Architecture of Community: Some New Proposals on the Social Consequences of Architectural and Planning Decisions," *Architecture and Comportement, Architecture and Behaviour*, 3(3): 251–273.

Harris, C., E. Ullman. 1945. "The Nature of Cities," *Annals of the American Academy of Political and Social Science*, 242: 7–17.

Haynie, S.D., J. Peponis. 2009. "Atlanta: A Morphological History," *Seventh International Space Syntax Symposium Proceedings* (Eds. D. Koch, L. Marcus, J. Steen), Stockholm: KTH, 2009: 87.1–87.13.

Hillier, B., A. Turner, T. Yang, H. Park. 2010. "Metric And Topo-Geometric Properties Of Urban Street Networks: Some Convergences, Divergences and New Results," *Journal of Space Syntax*, 17 December 2010, 1(2): 258–279.

Hillier, B.. 2009c. "Spatial Sustainability in Cities Organic Patterns and Sustainable Forms," *Seventh International Space Syntax Symposium Proceedings* (Eds. D. Koch, L. Marcus, J. Steen), Stockholm: KTH, 2009: Keynote Address, K01:1–K01:20.

Hillier, B. 2009b. "The Genetic Code for Cities – Is it Simpler than We Think?" Keynote Paper, *Complexity Theories of Cities Have Come of Age: An International Conference*. TU Delft, Department of Urbanism, September 2009.

Hillier, B. 2009a. "The City as a Socio-Technical System: A Spatial Reformulation in the Light of the Levels Problem and the Parallel Problem," Keynote Paper, *Conference on Spatial Information Theory*, September 2009.

Hillier, B., L. Vaughan. 2007. "The City as One Thing," *Progress in Planning*, 67(3): 205–230.

Hillier, B. 2005b. "The Art of Place and the Science of Space," *World Architecture*: *Special Issue on Space Syntax*. Beijing: 11(185): 24-34 (in Chinese); 96–102 (in English).

Hillier, B. 2005a. "Between Social Physics and Phenomenology: Explorations Towards an Urban Synthesis?," *Fifth International Space Syntax Symposium Proceedings* (Ed. A. Van Nes), Delft 2005: 3–23.

Hillier, B., S. Iida. 2005. "Network Effects and Psychological Effects: A Theory of Urban Movement," *Fifth International Space Syntax Symposium Proceedings* (Ed. A. Van Nes), Delft 2005: 553–564.

Hillier, B., C. Stutz. 2005. "New Methods in Space Syntax," *Urban Design Quarterly: Urban Morphology*, Winter 2005, 93: 33–34.

Hillier, B. 2003. "The Knowledge that Shapes the City: The Human City Beneath the Social City," *Fourth International Space Syntax Symposium Proceedings*, London 2003: 01.1–01.20.

Hillier, B. 2002. "A Theory of the City as Object: or, How Spatial Laws Mediate the Social Construction of Urban Space," *Urban Design International*, 7: 153–179.

Hillier, B., V. Netto. 2001. "Society Seen through the Prism of Space: Outline of a Theory of Society and Space," *Third International Space Syntax Symposium Proceedings* (Eds. J. Peponis, J. Wineman, S. Bafna), Atlanta 2003: 13.1–13.27.

Hillier, B. 1999c. "Space as a Paradigm for Understanding Strongly Relational Systems," *Second International Space Syntax Symposium Proceedings* (Eds. F. de Holanda, L. Amorim, F. Dufaux), 2: 52.01–52.16.

Hillier, B. 1999b. "Centrality as a Process: Accounting for Attraction Inequalities in Deformed Grids," *Urban Design International*, 4: 107–127.

Hillier, B. 1999a. "The Hidden Geometry of Deformed Grids: or, Why Space Syntax Works When It Looks As Though It Shouldn't," *Environment and Planning B: Planning and Design*, 26(2): 169–191.

Hillier, B. 1996b. *Space is the Machine: A Configurational Theory of Architecture*. Cambridge: Cambridge University Press.

Hillier, B. 1996a. "Cities As Movement Economies," *Urban Design International*, 1(1): 41–60.

Hillier, B., M.D. Major, J. Desyllas, K. Karimi, B. Campos, T. Stonor. 1996. *Tate Gallery, Millbank: A Study of the Existing Layout and New Masterplan Proposal. Technical Report*, Unit For Architectural Studies, Bartlett School of Graduate Studies, University College London.

Hillier, B. 1993. "Specifically Architectural Knowledge: A Partial Account of the Ascent from Building to Cultural Transmission to Architecture as Theoretical Concretion," *Harvard Architectural Review*, 9: 9–27.

Hillier, B., A. Penn, J. Hanson, T. Grajewski, J. Xu. 1993. "Natural Movement: or, Configuration and Attraction in Urban Pedestrian Movement," *Environment and Planning B: Planning and Design*, 20: 29–66.

Hillier, B. 1989. "The Architecture of the Urban Object," *Ekistics*, 334/335: 5–20.

Hiller, B., J. Hanson, H. Graham. 1987. "Ideas are in Things: An Application of Space Syntax Method to Discovering Housing Genotypes," *Environment and Planning D: Planning and Design*, 14: 363–385.

Hillier, B. 1986. "City of Alice's Dreams," *Architects Journal*, London: Royal Institute of British Architects, 9th July 1986: 39–41.

Hillier, B., J. Hanson. 1986. *Spatial Configuration and Use Density at the Urban Level: Towards a Predictive Model*. Final Report to the Science and Engineering Research Council, SERC GR/D/13337.

Hillier, B., J. Hanson. 1984. *The Social Logic of Space*. Cambridge: Cambridge University Press.

Hoch, C. 2000. *The Practice of Local Government Planning*, 3rd Edition (Municipal Management Series). International City/County Management Associates: Washington, D.C.

Howard, E. 1898. *To-morrow: A Peaceful Path to Real Reform*. Republished in 1985 as *Garden Cities of To-morrow*. Powys, Wales: Attic Books.

Howsley, K. 2003. "Uncovering the Spatial Patterns of Portland's Gentrification," *Seventh International Space Syntax Symposium Proceedings* (Eds. D. Koch, L. Marcus, J. Steen), Stockholm: KTH, 2009: 76.1–76.16.

Hoyt, H. 1939. *The Structure and Growth of Residential Neighbourhoods in American Cities*. Washington: Federal Housing Administration.

Hoyt, H. 1933. *One Hundred Years of Land Values in Chicago*. Chicago: University of Chicago Press.

Jacobs, J. 1961. *The Death and Life of Great American Cities*. Harmondsworth, Middlesex, England: Penguin Books.

Jiang, Peng, J. Peponis. 2009. "Tower Place Drive: A Private Road," *Seventh International Space Syntax Symposium Proceedings* (Eds. D. Koch, L. Marcus, J. Steen), KTH, Stockholm, 47.41–47.11.

Jiang, P., J. Peponis. 2005. "Historic and Emerging Urban Centers in the Metropolitan Atlanta Region: Spatial Dynamics and Morphogenesis," *Fifth International Space Syntax Symposium Proceedings* (Ed. A. Van Nes), Delft, 2005: 283–294.

Juergensmeyer, J.C., T.E. Roberts. 2003. *Land Use Planning and Development Regulatory Law*. St. Paul, MN: West Group.

Karimi, K., M. Mavridou, M. Armstrong. 2005. "Understanding Cities Through the Analysis of their Prime Activity Axes: The Capital Routes," *Fifth International Space Syntax Symposium Proceedings* (Ed. A. Van Nes), Delft, 2005: 507–525.

Karimi, K. 1998. *Continuity and Change in Old Cities: An Analytical Investigation of the Spatial Structure in Iranian and English Historic Cities Before and After Modernisation*. Ph.D. Thesis. Copies available from Senate House, University of London.

Karimi, K. 1997. "The Spatial Logic of Organic Cities in Iran and the United Kingdom," *First International Space Syntax Symposium Proceedings* (Eds. M.D. Major, L. Amorim, F. Dufaux), 1: 06.–06.17.

Katz, P. 1993. *The New Urbanism: Toward an Architecture of Community*. New York: McGraw-Hill Education.

Kemp, B. 1989. *Ancient Egypt: Anatomy of a Civilization*. London and New York: Routledge.

Kenoyer, J.M. 1998. "Indus Cities, Towns, and Villages," *Ancient Cities of the Indus Valley Civilization*. Islamabad: American Institute of Pakistan Studies.

Kim, J. 2007. "Testing the Street Connectivity of New Urbanism Projects and Their Surroundings in Metro Atlanta Region," *Sixth International Space Syntax Symposium Proceedings*, İstanbul, 2007: 092.1–092.12.

Kipling, R. 1899. *American Notes*. Boston: Brown and Company.

Kostof, S. 1992. *The City Assembled: The Elements of Urban Form Through History*. London: Thames and Hudson, Ltd.

Kostof, S. 1991. *The City Shaped: Urban Patterns and Meaning Through History*. London: Thames and Hudson, Ltd.

Kristof, N. 2014. "A Nation of Takers?" *New York Times*, March 27, 2014, A31, retrieved at http://www.nytimes.com/2014/03/27/opinion/kristof-a-nation-of-takers.html?

Krugler, J.D. 2004. *English and Catholic: The Lords Baltimore in the Seventeenth Century*. Baltimore: Johns Hopkins University Press.

Kubler, G. 1993. "Cities of Latin America since Discovery," *Settlements in the Americas: Cross-Cultural Perspectives* (Ed. R. Bennett). Newark: University of Delaware Press, 17–22.

Kunstler, J.H. 1993. *The Geography of Nowhere: The Rise and Decline of America's Man-Made Landscape*. New York: Simon and Schuster.

Kupperman, K.O. 1984. *Roanoke: The Abandoned Colony*. Rowman & Littlefield.

Lamar, H.R. 1977. *The Trader On The American Frontier: Myth's Victim*. College Station: Texas A & M University Press.

Le Corbusier. 1925. *The City of To-morrow and Its Planning* (1987 Trans. F. Etchells). New York: Dover Publications.

Liebling, A.J. 1952. *Chicago: The Second City*. New York: Knopf.

Lilly, K.D. 1998. "Taking Measures Across the Medieval Landscape: Aspects of Urban Design before the Renaissance," *Urban Morphology*, 2(2): 82–92.

Lynch, K. 1960. *The Image of the City*. Cambridge: MIT Press.

Mailer, N. 1999. *An American Dream*. London: Vintage Books.

Major, M.D. 2015c. "The Invention of a New Scale: The Paradox of Size and Configuration in American Cities," *Journal of Space Syntax*, University College London, Autumn 2015, 170–191.

Major, M.D. 2015b. "The Hidden Corruption of American Regular Grids: Why Space Syntax Doesn't Work in the United States, When It Looks Like It Should," *Tenth International Space Syntax Symposium Proceedings*, 13–17 July 2015, University College London, 75:1–75:12.

Major, M.D. 2015a. *Relentless Magnificence: The American Urban Grid*. Ph.D. Thesis, University College London, Copies available from the Environmental Science Library, University College London including in Appendix: Major, M.D. 2015b.

Major, M.D. 2013. "The City's Essential DNA: Formal Design and Spatial Processes in the Urban Pattern," *Journal of Space Syntax*, University College London, 4(1): 160–164.

Major, M.D. 2001. "When is a Door More Than a Door? The Role of Constitution in Strongly Geometric Configurations," *Third International Space Syntax Symposium Proceedings* (Eds. J. Peponis, J. Wineman, S. Bafna), 37.1–37.14.

Major, M.D., Sarris N. 2001, "Cloak-and-Dagger Theory: Manifestations of the Mundane in the Space of Eight Peter Eisenman Houses," *Environment and Planning B: Planning and Design*, Pion Press Limited, 28(1): 73–88.

Major, M.D. 2000b. "Designing for Context: The Use of Space Syntax as an Interactive Design Tool in Urban Development," *Planning Forum*, University of Texas, 6: 40–56.

Major, M.D. 2000a. *Cities of Infinite Space: An Analytical Approach to American Urban Space and Culture*. Ph.D. Thesis (draft), University of London, copies available from the author.

Major, M.D., Sarris N. 1999, "Cloak and Dagger Theory: Manifestations of the Mundane in Eight Peter Eisenman Houses," *Second International Space Syntax Symposium Proceedings* (Eds. L Amorim, F Dufaux), 1: 17.01–17.14.

Major, M.D., A. Penn, B. Hillier. 1999. "The Urban Village and City of Tomorrow Revisited," *Second International Space Syntax Symposium Proceedings* (Eds. F. de Holanda, L. Amorim, F. Dufaux), 2: 48.01–48.18.

Major, M.D. 1997b. "Are American Cities Different: If So, How Do They Differ?," *First International Space Syntax Symposium Proceedings* (Eds. M.D. Major, L. Amorim, F. Dufaux), 3:09.01–09.14.

Major, M.D. 1997a. "Building the American City," Presentation at the *First International Space Syntax Symposium*, London, 15–18 April 1997. Copies available from the author.

Major, M.D. 1993. *Space and Racial Re-segregation in the American City*. M.Sc. Thesis, M.Sc. Architecture: Advanced Architectural Studies, Copies available from the Environmental Science Library, University College London.

Marshall, S. 2005. *Streets and Patterns*. London: Spon Press.

Martin, L. 1972. "The Grid as Generator," *Urban Space and Structures* (Eds. L. Martin, L. March). Cambridge: Cambridge University Press, 6–27.

Martindale, D. 1958. "Prefatory Remarks: The Theory of the City" in Weber M, 1958, *The City* (Trans. D. Martindale, G. Neuwirth). New York: The Free Press, 9–62.

Middlekauff, R. 2005. *The Glorious Clause: The American Revolution, 1763–1789*. New York: Oxford University Press.

Moehring, E.P., M.S. Green. 2005. *Las Vegas: A Centennial History*. Reno, Nevada: University of Nevada Press.

Moholy-Nagy, S. 1968. *Matrix of Man: An Illustrated History of Urban Environment*. New York: Frederick A Praeger Publishers.

Morton, S.G., M.M. Peuramaki-Brown, P.C. Dawson, J.D. Seibert. 2012. "Civic and Household Community Relationships at Teotihuacan, Mexico: A Space Syntax Approach," *Cambridge Archaeological Journal,* 22:3; 387–400

Mountford, K. 2003. "History Behind Sugar Trade, Chesapeake Not Always Sweet," *Bay Journal*, July 1, 2003, retrieved at http://www.bayjournal.com/article/history_behind_sugar_trade_chesapeake_not_always_sweet.

Mouzon, S. 2010. *The Original Green: Unlocking the Mystery of True Sustainability*. Miami Beach: The New Urban Guild Foundation.

Mumford, L. 1961. *The City in History: Its Origins, Its Transformations and its Prospects*. London: Penguin Books.

Norberg-Schulz, C. 1985. *The Concept of Dwelling: On the Way to Figurative Architecture*. New York: Electa/Rizzoli International Publications.

Olmsted, Vaux and Company. 1866. *Report upon a Projected improvement of the Estate of the College of California, at Berkeley, near Oakland*, New York: William C. Bryant & Co.

Olson, S. 1979. "Baltimore Imitates the Spider," *Annals of the Association of American Geographers*, 64(4): 557–74.

Owens, E.J. 1991. *The City in the Greek and Roman World*. London: Routledge.

Özbil, A., J. Peponis, B. Stone. 2011. "Understanding the Link between Street Connectivity, Land Use and Pedestrian Flows," *Urban Design International*, 16: 125–141.

Özbil, A., J. Peponis, S. Bafna. 2009. "The Effects of Street Configuration on Transit Ridership," *Seventh International Space Syntax Symposium Proceedings* (Eds. D. Koch, L. Marcus, J. Steen), KTH, Stockholm 84.81–84.88.

Palahniuk, C. 1999. *Invisible Monsters*. New York: W. W. Norton & Company.

Park, R.E., E.W. Burgess. 1925. *The City: Suggestions for the Investigation of Human Behavior in the Urban Environment*. Chicago: University of Chicago Press.

Penn, A. 2005. "The Complexity of the Elementary Interface: Shopping Space," *Fifth International Space Syntax Symposium Proceedings* (Ed. A. Van Nes), Delft, 2005: 25–42.

Penn, A. 2001. "Space Syntax and Spatial Cognition: Or, Why the Axial Line?" *Third International Space Syntax Symposium Proceedings* (Eds. J. Peponis, J. Wineman, S. Bafna), Atlanta, 2003: 11.1–11.17.

Penn, A., B. Hillier, D. Banister, Xu, J. 1998. "Configurational Modeling of Urban Movement Networks," *Environment and Planning B: Planning and Design*, 25: 59–84.

Penn, A., B. Hillier. 1992. "The Social Potential of Buildings: Spatial Structure and the Innovation Milieu in Scientific Research Laboratories," *Corporate Space and Architecture International Symposium*, Paris, France, 1–3 July 1992: 39–45.

Peponis, J., D. Allen, S. French, M. Scoppa, J. Brown. 2007b. "Street Connectivity and Urban Density: Spatial Measures and Their Correlation," *Sixth International Space Syntax Symposium Proceedings*, İstanbul, 2007: 004.1–004.12.

Peponis, J., D. Allen, D. Haynie, M. Scoppa, Z. Zhang. 2007a. "Measuring the Configuration of Street Networks: The Spatial Profiles of 118 Urban Areas in the 12 Most Populated Metropolitan Regions in the U.S.," *Sixth International Space Syntax Symposium Proceedings*, İstanbul, 2007: 002.1–002.16.

Peponis, J. 2004. "Space Syntax," *Implications*. University of Minnesota: InformeDesign, 4:2, retrieved at http://www.informedesign.org/_news/dec_v04r-p.pdf.

Peponis, J. 1997. "Geometries of Architectural Description: Shape and Spatial Configuration," *First International Space Syntax Symposium Proceedings* (Eds. M.D. Major, L. Amorim, F. Dufaux), 2:34.01–34.08.

Peponis, J. 1989. "Space, Culture and Urban Design in Late Modernism and After," *Ekistics*, 334/335: 93–107.

Peponis, J., E. Hadjinikolaou, C. Liveratos, D.A. Fatouros. 1989c. "The Spatial Core of Urban Culture," *Ekistics*, 376/377/378: 43–55.

Peponis, J., C. Ross, M. Rashid. 1989b. "The Structure of Urban Space, Movement, and Co-presence: The Case of Atlanta," *Geoforum*, 28(3–4): 341–358.

Peponis, J., C. Ross, M. Rashid, S.H. Kim, G. Varela, L. Sentosa. 1989a. "Regularity and Change in Urban Space: A Syntactic Analysis of Movement and Co-presence in Atlanta, *Ekistics*, 376/377/378: 4–15.

Pierce, N. 1998. "Smart Growth: Thinking about Limits," *UrbanAge*. Spring: 28–29.

Pinelo, J., A. Turner. 2010. *Introduction to UCL Depthmap 10*. University College London.

Pope, A. 1996. *Ladders*, Architecture at Rice 34. New York: Princeton Architectural Press.

Popper, K.R. 1972. *Objective Knowledge: An Evolutionary Approach*. New York: Oxford University Press

Psarra, S., C. Kickert and A. Pluviano. 2013. "Paradigm Lost: Industrial and Post-industrial Detroit – An Analysis of the Street Network and its Social and Economic Dimensions from 1796 to the Present," *Urban Design International*, 24 December 2013, 18(4): 257–281.

Rachlis, K. 2001. "The Golden Age," Special Issue on Everything You Know About Traffic is Wrong: How Come We're Not Moving?, *Los Angeles Magazine*, April 2001: 6.

Raford, N., B. Hillier. 2005. "Correlation Landscapes: A New Approach to Sub-area Definition in Low Intelligibility Spatial Systems," *Fifth International Space Syntax Symposium Proceedings* (Ed. A. Van Nes), Delft, 2005: 573–585.

Raford, N. 2004. *Movement Economies in Fractured Urban Systems: The Case of Boston, Massachusetts*. M.Sc. Thesis, M.Sc. Built Environment: Advanced Architectural Studies, Built Environment Report, Copies available from the Environmental Science Library, University College London.

Raford, N. 2003. "Looking Both Ways: Space Syntax for Pedestrian Exposure Forecasting and Collision Risk Analysis," *Fourth International Space Syntax Symposium Proceedings*, London, 2003: 51.1–51.16.

Reps, J.W. 1979. *Cities of the American West: A History of Frontier Urban Planning*. Princeton, NJ: Princeton University Press.

Reps, J.W. 1965. *The Making of Urban America: A History of City Planning in the United States*. Princeton, NJ: Princeton University Press.

Rockman, J.S.M. 2003. *The Colonization of Unfamiliar Landscapes*. London: Routledge.

Rossi, C. 2004. *Architecture and Mathematics in Ancient Egypt*. Cambridge University Press.

Rossi, A. 1982. *The Architecture of the City* (Trans. D. Ghirardo, J. Okman). Cambridge, MA: MIT Press.

Rybczynski, W. 1996. *City Life*. New York: Charles Scribner's Sons.

Rykwert, J. 1988. *The Idea of a Town: The Anthropology of Urban Form in Rome, Italy and the Ancient World*: Second Edition. Cambridge, Massachusetts: MIT Press.

Salah-Salah, F. 1987. *Cities in the Sahara, Spatial Structures and Generative Processes*. Ph.D. Thesis. Copies available from Senate House, University of London.

Schwartz, J. 1982. "Evolution of the Suburbs," *American Urban History: An Interpretive Reader with Commentaries*. New York: Oxford University Press, 492–514.

Schweitzer, F., J. Steinbrink. 1998. "Estimation of Megacity Growth," *Applied Geography*, 18(1): 69–81.

Scoppa, M., S. French, J. Peponis. 2009. "The Effects of Street Connectivity Upon the Distribution of Local Vehicular Traffic in Metropolitan Atlanta," *Seventh International Space Syntax Symposium Proceedings* (Eds. D. Koch, L. Marcus, J. Steen), Stockholm: KTH, 2009: 98.1–98.9.

Seamon, D. 2007. "A Lived Hermetic of People and Place: Phenomenology and Space Syntax," *Sixth International Space Syntax Symposium Proceedings*, İstanbul, 2007: iii01–iii16.

Shah, S. 1996b. *The Grid As Generator*. M.Sc. Thesis, M.Sc. Built Environment: Advanced Architectural Studies, Copies available from the Environmental Science Library, University College London.

Shah, S. 1996a. *Spatial Morphology and Growth Patterns: American Historical Towns*. Case Study Paper, M.Sc. Built Environment: Advanced Architectural Studies, University College London.

Shapiro, J.S. 2005. "A Space Syntax Analysis of Arroyo Hondo Pueblo, New Mexico," *School of American Research Press*, Santa Fe, New Mexico, Arroyo Hondo Archeological Series, 9, retrieved at http://www.arroyohondo.org/publications/monographs/space-syntax-analysis-arroyo-hondo-pueblo-new-mexico.

Shapiro, J.S. 1997. "Fingerprints on the Landscape: Cultural Evolution in the North Rio Grande," *First International Space Syntax Symposium Proceedings* (Eds. M.D. Major, L. Amorim, F. Dufaux), 2:21.01–21.21.

Shaw, J. 2003. "Who Built the Great Pyramids?," *Harvard Magazine*, July/August, 2003: 40–49, 99.

Shear, E. 2002. *Seattle: Booms and Busts*. New Haven. Conneticut: Yale University.

Shin, H.W., Y.O. Kim, A.H. Kim. 2007. "A Study on the Correlation between Pedestrian Network and Pedestrian Volume According to Land Use Pattern," *Sixth International Space Syntax Symposium Proceedings*, İstanbul, 2007: 116.01–116.08.

Shpuza E. 2014. "Allometry in the Syntax of Street Networks: Evolution of Adriatic and Ionian Coastal Cities 1800-2010," *Environment and Planning B: Planning & Design*, 41: 450–471.

Shu, S., B. Hillier. 1999. "Housing Layout and Crime Vulnerability," *Second International Space Syntax Symposium Proceedings* (Eds. F. de Holanda, L. Amorim, F. Dufaux), 1:25.01–25.12.

Siksna, A. 1997. "The Effects of Block Size and Form in North American and Australian City Centres," *Urban Morphology*, 1: 19–33.

Smith, P.J. 1962. "Calgary: A Study in Urban Pattern," *Economic Geography*, 38(4): 315–329.

Soja, E. 1989. *Postmodern Geographies: The Reassertion of Space in Critical Social Theory*. London: Verso.

Southworth, M., E. Ben-Joseph. 2003. *Streets and the Shaping of Towns and Cities*. Washington, D.C.: Island Press.

Speck, J. 2013. *Walkable City: How Downtown Can Save America, One Step at a Time*. New York: North Point Press.

Stanislawski, D. 1946. "The Origin and Spread of the Grid-Pattern Town," *The Geographic Review*, 36: 105–120.

Stewart, I., M. Golubitsky. 1992. *Fearful Symmetry: A God A Geometer?* London: Penguin Books.

Stewart, I. 1989. *Does God Play Dice: The New Mathematics of Chaos*. London: Penguin Books.

Stonor, T. 1991. *Manhattan: A Study of its Public Spaces and Patterns of Movement*. M.Sc. Thesis, M.Sc. Architecture: Advanced Architectural Studies, Copies available from the Environmental Science Library, University College London.

Story, L. 2012. "As Companies Seek Tax Deals, Governments Pay High Price," *New York Times*, retrieved December 1, 2012 at http://www.nytimes.com/2012/12/02/us/how-local-taxpayers-bankroll-corporations.html.

Talen, E. (Ed.) 1999. *Charter of the New Urbanism*. New York: McGraw Hill Education.

Tocknell, S. 2007. "Transportation Planning Overview," *Presentation at the 2007 AICP Examination Preparation Course*. Jacksonville, Florida: First Coast Section, Florida Chapter of the American Planning Association.

Treat, P.J. 1910. *The National Land System, 1785-1820*. New York: EB Treat and Company.

Tremonto, B. 1993. *Inner City Island*. M.Sc. Thesis, M.Sc. Architecture: Advanced Architectural Studies, Copies available from the Environmental Science Library, University College London.

Turner, A. 2009. "Stitching Together the Fabric of Space and Society: An Investigation into the Linkage of the Local to Regional Continuum," *Seventh International Space Syntax Symposium Proceedings* (Eds. D. Koch, L. Marcus, J. Steen), Stockholm: KTH, 2009: 116.1–116.12

Turner, A. 2008. *Introduction to UCL Depthmap 7*. Bartlett School of Graduate Studies, University College London.

Turner, A. 2007b. "From Axial to Road-centre Lines: A New Representation for Space Syntax and a New Model of Route Choice for Transport Network Analysis," *Environment and Planning B: Planning and Design*, 34(3), 539–555.

Turner, A. 2007a. "To Move Through Space: Lines of Vision and Movement," *Sixth International Space Syntax Symposium Proceedings*, İstanbul, 2007:037.01–037.12.

Turner, A., A. Penn, B. Hillier. 2005. "An Algorithmic Definition of the Axial Map," *Environment and Planning B: Planning and Design*, 32(3): 425–444.

Turner, A. 2004. *Depthmap 4: A Researcher's Handbook*. Bartlett School of Graduate Studies, University College London.

Turner, A. 2003b. "Analysing the Visual Dynamics of Spatial Morphology," *Environment and Planning B: Planning and Design*, 30(5): 657–676.

Turner, A. 2003a. "Reversing the Process of Living: Generating Ecomorphic Environments," *Fourth International Space Syntax Symposium Proceedings*, London 2003: 15.1–15.12.

Turner, A. 2001b. "Angular Analysis," *Third International Space Syntax Symposium Proceedings* (Eds. J. Peponis, J. Wineman, S. Bafna), Atlanta, 2003: 30.1–30.11.

Turner, A. 2001a. "Depthmap: A Program to Perform Visibility Graph Analysis," *Third International Space Syntax Symposium Proceedings* (Eds. J. Peponis, J. Wineman, S. Bafna), Atlanta, 2003: 31.1–31.9.

Turner, A., M. Doxa, D. O'Sullivan, A. Penn. 2001. "From Isovists to Visibility Graphs: A Methodology for the Analysis of Architectural Space," *Environment and Planning B: Planning and Design*, 28(1): 103–121.

Turner, A., A. Penn. 1999. "Making Isovists Syntactic: Isovist Integration Analysis," *Second International Space Syntax Symposium Proceedings* (Eds. F. de Holanda, L. Amorim, F. Dufaux), 1:11.01–11.14.

Venturi, R., D. Scott Brown, S. Izenour. 1972. *Learning from Las Vegas*. Cambridge, Massachusetts: MIT Press.

Venturi, R. 1966. *Complexity and Contradiction in Architecture*. New York: The Museum of Modern Art.

Vitruvius. 1960. *The Ten Books on Architecture (Bks. I-X)* (Trans. M.H. Morgan). New York: Dover Publications, Inc.

Wacher, J. 1974. *Towns of Roman Britain*. Berkeley and Los Angeles: University of California Press.

Warner, Jr, S.B. 1972. *The Urban Wilderness: A History of the American City*. New York: Harper and Row Publishers.

Whyte, W.H. 1988. *City: Rediscovering the Center*. University of Pennsylvania Press: Philadelphia.

Wilkerson III, W.R. 2000. *The Man Who Invented Las Vegas*. Bellingham, Washington: Ciro's Books.

Wilson, T.D., P. O. Shay. 2014. "Oglethorpe and Savannah: A Historical Plan has Modern Applications," *Planning Magazine*, March 2014, 30–35.

Wineman, J. D., R.W. Marans, A.J. Schulz, D.L. Westhuizen, G.B. Mentz, P. Max. 2014. "Designing Healthy Neighborhoods: Contributions of the Built Environment to Physical Activity in Detroit," *Journal of Planning Education and Research*, 34: 180–189.

Wolfe, T. 1982. *From Bauhaus to Our House*. London: Jonathon Cape Limited.

Woodroffe, J., D. Papa, I. MacBurnie. 1994. "An Introduction," Special Issue on The Periphery, *Architectural Design*, 108: 6–7.

Wright, F.L. 1994. *Frank Lloyd Wright Collected Writings, 1939-1949* (Ed. B.B. Pfeiffer). New York: Rizzoli International Publications.

Yang, T., B. Hillier. 2007. "The Fuzzy Boundary: The Spatial Definition of Urban Areas," *Sixth International Space Syntax Symposium Proceedings*, İstanbul, 2007: 091.1–091.16.

Yang, T. 2006. "The Role of Space in the Emergence of Conceived Urban Areas." Presented at S*patial Cognition '06: Space Syntax and Spatial Cognition Workshop*, Bremen, Germany.

Zook, J. B., Y. Lu, K. Glanz, C. Zimring. 2012. "Design and Pedestrianism in a Smart Growth Development," *Environment and Behavior*, 44, 216–234.

Illustration Credits

ALL ILLUSTRATIONS BY THE AUTHOR UNLESS OTHERWISE NOTED.

Introduction: 0.1 – (left) Courtesy of Duany Plater-Zyberk & Company, Image: Alex MacLean/Landslides; (right) Racial Dot Maps created by Dustin A. Cable, Weldon Cooper Center for Public Service, University of Virginia, Reference Data by Stamen Design: Map data by OpenStreetMap, under CC-BY-SA, http://demographics.coopercenter.org/DotMap/. **0.2** – (right) Google Earth © 2011. **0.3** – Las Vegas, Nevada (Major, 1997). **A.1** – Foster, N. 1999. "Opening Address," *First International Space Syntax Symposium Proceedings* (Eds. M.D. Major, L. Amorim), 3, xviii. Photograph by Richard Davies. **A.2** – (left) Wikipedia, https://upload.wikimedia.org/wikipedia/commons/thumb/a/a0/Tate_Modern_et_Millennium_Bridge.jpg/1024px-Tate_Modern_et_Millennium_Bridge.jpg; (right) City of Linz, Austria, http://www.linz.at/images/solarcity1_druck.jpg. Photograph by Luftbild Pertlwieser/PTU.

Chapter One: 1.1 – (left) Smith, M.E. 2007. "Form and Meaning in the Earliest Cities: A New Approach to Ancient Urban Planning," *Journal of Planning History*, 6:1, http://works.bepress.com/michael_e_smith/1/, modified after Jansen, M.R.N. 1993. "Mohenjo-Daro: Type Site of the Earliest Urbanization Process in South Asia," *Urban Form and Meaning in South Asia: The Shaping of Cities from Prehistoric to Precolonial Times* (Ed. H. Spodek and D.M. Srinivasan), Vol. 31, Studies in the History of Art, Center for Advanced Study in the Visual Arts, Symposium Papers XV (Washington, D.C.: National Gallery of Art, 1993), 42, Image: © 2017, Trustees of the British Museum; (right) Wikipedia, https://upload.wikimedia.org/wikipedia/commons/6/65/Panoramic_view_of_the_stupa_mound_and_great_bath_in_Mohenjodaro.JPG. **1.2** – (left) Thornbury. 1897. "Old and New London. A Narrative of Its History, Its People, And Its Places," *The City: Ancient And Modern, Volume I*, MAPCO: Map and Plan Collections Online, http://archivemaps.com/mapco/preview/index.htm; (right) John Norden's Map of London, 1593, engraved by Pieter Van den Keere and published in Norden's "Middlesex" dated 1593 from *Maps of Old London*, London: Adam and Charles Black, 1908, Wikipedia, http://upload.wikimedia.org/wikipedia/commons/thumb/5/5a/. **1.3** – (left) From a plan made and published by Professor Flinders Petrie, Illahun, Kahun and Gurob, published in Maspero, G. 1903. *History of Egypt, Chaldæa, Syria, Babylonia, and Assyria*, Volume 2 (of 12), London: Grolier Society, pl. xi, available from Project Gutenberg at http://www.gutenberg.org/ebooks/17322; (right) Metropolitan Museum of Art, http://www.metmuseum.org/toah/works-of-art/48.11.5a,b. **1.4** – (left) Haverfield, F. 2004. *Ancient Town Planning*, Project Gutenberg, http://www.gutenberg.org/files/14189/14189-h/images/fig2.jpg, plan of Piraeus originally from Hirschfeld, G. 1878. *Berichte der sächs. Ges. der Wissenschaften*, xxx. I. Haverfield questions the accuracy of the drawing; (middle) Plan of Miletus from Gerkan A. 1924, *Griechische Stadteanlagen*. Berlin and Leipzig. Wellcome Library, London, https://wellcomeimages.org/indexplus/obf_images/b0/24/891b9939b376d8efc5c4864543c0.jpg; and (right) Plan of Priene from Gerkan A. 1924, *Griechische Stadteanlagen*. Berlin and Leipzig. Wellcome Library, London, https://wellcomeimages.org/indexplus/obf_images/24/06/86bc5d41413aee1452f303d0df20.jpg. **1.5** – (left) Owens, E.J. 1991. *The City in the Greek and Roman World*. London: Routledge, 104; (right) CAD Drawing by Frederik Pöll based on an image from Benevolo, L. 1981. *L'arte e la città antica*, Laterza: Editori Laterza, available from Wikipedia Commons, https://upload.wikimedia.org/wikipedia/commons/8/87/Timgad_-_Expansion_in_2nd_and_3rd_Century.jpg. **1.6** – Beresford. M. 1967. *New Towns of the Middle Ages: Town Plantation in England, Wales and Gascony*. London: Lutterworth Press: (far left) 17; (middle left) 32; (center) 148; (middle right) 146; (far right) 145. **1.7** – (left) Kostof, S. 1991. *The City Shaped: Urban Patterns and Meaning Through History*. London: Thames and Hudson, Ltd, 140, http://classconnection.s3.amazonaws.com/382/flashcards/676284/jpg/7.jpg; (middle) Moholy-Nagy, S. 1968. *Matrix of Man: An Illustrated History of Urban Environment*. New York: Frederick A Praeger Publishers, 162–63, 18th century European plan, Wikipedia, https://upload.wikimedia.org/wikipedia/commons/2/2a/John_Gaspar_Scheuchzer_-_Ichnographia_urbis_Miaco_-_Historical_map_of_Kyoto_-_18th_century.jpg; (right) Moholy-Nagy. 1968. 162–63, redrawn plan from Kiang, Heng Chye. 1999.

Cities of Aristocrats and Bureaucrats: The Development of Medieval Chinese Cityscapes. Honolulu: University of Hawai'i Press, http://www.civilization.org.uk/wp-content/uploads/ChangAn-plan.jpg. **1.8** – (left) Reps, 1965, 121. Manuscript redrawing by John Gibson in 1962 of a map of Wethersfield, Connecticut in 1640 from Andrews, C.M. 1889. *The River Towns of Connecticut*. Baltimore; (middle) Wikipedia Commons, https://upload.wikimedia.org/wikipedia/commons/b/b9/New_Orleans_de_la_Tour_map_1720_1759.jpg; (right) Reps, 1965, 72. Originally from Belin, 1764, *Le Petit Atlas Maritime*. **1.9** – (left) Kostof, 1991, 113, also at http://www.britishempire.co.uk/images4/santodomingolarge.jpg; (middle) Drawn by D. Joseph de Villaseñor based on the original in the Archivo General y Público, Mexico, Provincias Internas, from Bolton, H.E. 1915. *Texas in the Middle Eighteenth Century*. Berkeley: University of California Press; (right) Satellite image, © 2015, Terra Metrics and Google Earth. **1.10** – (left) Bureau of Land Management, U.S. Department of the Interior, Wikipedia, http://en.wikipedia.org/wiki/File:Theoreticaltownshipmap.gif; (right) Drawing by author based on Easterling, K. 1993. *American Town Plans: A Comparative Time Line*. New York: Princeton Architectural Press, 17. **1.11** – Atwater, E.E. 1887. *History of New Haven to the Present Time*. New York: W.W. Munsell & Co., Gilbert Genealogy, http://gilbert-genealogy.info/foanh/ui33.html. A similar 1748 plan of New Haven is available in Reps, 1965, 129. **1.12** – (right) Reps, 1965, 162. Originally drawn by Thomas Holme, sold by Andrew Sowle, London, 1683. From a restrike in Lowber, JC. 1812. Ordinances of the City of Philadelphia. Philadelphia, Olin Library. Haverford College Library, http://www.haverford.edu/library/special/images/philadelphiamap_large.jpg. **1.13** – Google Earth © 2017. **A.3** – (left) Le Corbusier. 1925. *The City of To-morrow and Its Planning* (1987 Trans. F. Etchells). New York: Dover Publications, https://rosswolfe.files.wordpress.com/2010/09/01_18_le_corbusier_la_ville_radieuse_1930-31.jpg; (right) Photograph by Skot Weidemann, © 2017 Frank Lloyd Wright Foundation, Scotsdale, AZ and The Frank Lloyd Wright Foundation Archives, The Museum of Modern Art | Avery Architectural & Fine Arts Library, Columbia University, New York.

Chapter Two: 2.1 – (far left) and (middle right) Google Earth © 2016; (middle left) Wikipedia, https://upload.wikimedia.org/wikipedia/commons/thumb/b/b6/California_Street_in_San_Francisco_(02).jpg/682px-California_Street_in_San_Francisco_(02).jpg; (far right) Wikipedia, https://upload.wikimedia.org/wikipedia/commons/8/8f/View_of_Ragusa_Ibla_from_Ragusa_Superiore_-_Sicily,_Italy_-_14_Oct._2014.jpg. **2.2** – (left) The original map is available in the Stokes Collection, New York Public Library, New York, New York, Wikipedia, http://upload.wikimedia.org/wikipedia/commons/e/e7/CastelloPlanOriginal.jpg. A redraft of the Castello Plan drawn in 1916 is also available in Reps, 1965, 151; (right) Reps, 1965, 176. Originally drawn by Edward Crisp, from Ramsey. 1809. *The History of South Carolina*, Volume 2. Charleston, South Carolina Historic Society, http://www.pressomatic.com/schistoricalsociety/upload/gs_1704CrispMap.jpg. **2.3** – Ludlow's War of American Independence, University of Texas at Austin, from Colbeck, C. Eds. 1905. *The Public Schools Historical Atlas*, http://www.emersonkent.com/map_archive/north_america_1775.htm. **2.4** – (left) Reps, 1965, 142. Originally drawn by John Bonner, printed by Fra. Dewing, Boston, 1722, Stokes Collection, New York Public Library, New York, New York, http://www.doak.ws/1722MapOfBostonJohnBonner.jpg; (right) See Figure 1.12. **2.5** – (left) Google Earth, Image NOAA, TerraMetrics © 2017; (right) Google Earth © 2017, Image Landstat and Copernicus. **A.5** – (left) Gropius, W. 1965. *The New Architecture and the Bauhaus*. Cambridge, Massachusetts: MIT Press, 104, © 1965 Massachusetts Institute of Technology, by permission of The MIT Press; (right) Map Data ©2017 GeoBasis-DE/BKG (©2009), Google; available as an Interactive Map, http://www.telegraph.co.uk/news/earth/greenpolitics/planning/9708387/Interactive-map-Englands-green-belt.html.

Chapter Three: 3.1 – Google Earth © 2017. **3.3** – (right) Reps, 1965, 48. Manuscript copy of a plan of the Presidio of San Francisco, California, made in 1905 from the original copy drawn in 1880, Bancroft Collection, University of California, Berkeley Library. **3.4** – (left) Reprinted in *The Journal of San Diego History* (Winter, 1991), Wikipedia, http://upload.wikimedia.org/wikipedia/commons/e/e0/Presidio_of_San_Diego_1820_map.jpg; (center) Reps, 1965, 442. (untitled, unsigned and undated manuscript), Virginia State Library, Richmond, Virginia. **3.6** – (left) Reps, 1965; 140. Manuscript redrawing by John Gibson in 1962 of a reconstruction of street and property lines in Boston, Massachusetts, in 1640, prepared by Samuel C. Clough in 1927 and reproduced in Whitehill, W.M. 1959. *Boston: A Topographical History*. Cambridge, available from Cornell University, Department of City and Regional Planning, Ithaca, New York with insert drawings by the author; (right) Google Maps Street View © 2010, http://maps.google.com/. **3.11** – (left) Reps, 1965, 307. Originally drawn by William M. Eddy, New York, 1849, from Map Division, Library of Congress, Washington, D.C., Stanford University, http://www.stanford.edu/class/history104/coursework/maps/San_Francisco/1849_plan_of_SF.jpg. **3.13** – (left) Pierre Charles L'Enfant, 1792, Plan of the City of Washington, March 1792, Philadelphia: Thackara & Vallance sc., Engraving on paper, The Library of Congress American Memory Collection, http://memory.loc.gov/cgi-bin/query/h?ammem/gmd:@field%28NUMBER+@band%28g3850+ct000509%29%29. **A.06** – Major, M.D. 2000b. "Designing for Context: The Use of Space Syntax as an Interactive Design Tool in Urban Development," *Planning Forum*, The University of Texas, 6: 40–56. **A.07** – Major M.D., Sarris N. 2001, "Cloak-and-Dagger Theory: Manifestations of the Mundane in the Space of Eight Peter Eisenman Houses," *Environment and Planning B: Planning and Design*, Pion Press Limited, 28(1): 73–88.

Chapter Four: 4.1 – U.S. Census Bureau, U.S. Department of Commerce, Wikipedia, http://upload.wikimedia.org/wikipedia/commons/thumb/c/c1/USA-Urban-Areas.svg/2000px-USA-Urban-Areas.svg.png. **4.2** – (top) Reps, 1965, 35. Unsigned, undated plan of St. Augustine, Florida based on a survey by Don John de Solis drawn circa 1770. Details of publication are unknown, Library of Congress, Map Division, Washington, D.C.; (bottom) see note for Figure 1.8. **4.3** – (top) Reps, 1965, 76. Manuscript copy made in 1846 of the plan of St. Louis, Missouri in 1764, drawn by Auguste Chouteau, Missouri Historical Society, St. Louis, Missouri; (middle) Reps, 1965, 107. Manuscript copy made in 1748 of a manuscript plan of Annapolis, Maryland, drawn by James Stoddert in 1718, Maryland Hall of Records, Annapolis, Maryland; (bottom) Reps, 1965, 85. Drawn by I. Tanesse, published by Charles Del Vecchio and P. Maspero, New York, 1817, Library of Congress, Map Division, Washington, D.C. World Maps Online, http://www.worldmapsonline.com/images/1whistoricmaps/1w-la-no-1815.jpg. **4.4** – Reps, 1965, 298. Map of New York City and the Island of Manhattan. Commissioners' Plan of New York, from William Bridges, *Map of New York City and the Island of Manhattan; with Explanatory Remarks and References*. New York, 1811, New York Historical Society, http://www.codex99.com/cartography/images/nyc/bridges_1811_lg.jpg. **4.5** – Reps, 1965, 295. A New & Accurate Plan of the City of New York in the State of New York in North America. Plan of New York City drawn by B. Taylor. New York, 1797, State of New York, http://www.raremaps.com/maps/medium/29050.jpg. **4.6** – The Charlotte-Mecklenburg Historic Landmarks Commission, http://www.cmhpf.org/radburn2.gif. **4.8** – Online Levittown Museum, http://www.levittowners.com/images/PLANNING/PLAN%20FHILLS%20MAP%20DUCKETT%201952.JPG. **A.08** – Permission granted by Space Syntax Limited, Map of Tokyo, Japan by Shinichi Iida in 1999. **A.09** – (left) Permission granted by Space Syntax Limited, Map of Greater London within the North and South Circular Roads constructed by Hua Yoo in 1991 with updates and revisions by various researchers including the author. The grayscale version of this space syntax model for Greater London appears in Major, M.D., 2000b, 43–44; (right) Wikipedia, https://upload.wikimedia.org/wikipedia/commons/4/49/Oxford_Street_December_2006.jpeg.

Chapter Five: 5.1 – "Los Angeles By Night" Photograph by ©André M. Hünseler, Courtesy of André M. Hünseler. **5.2** – (left) Originally appeared in the June 1947 issue of *Life Magazine*, Image: © Christopher Dean/Photo: Loomis Dean, and Courtesy of Getty Images and Christopher Dean; (middle) Photo by Remi Jouan, Wikipedia, https://en.wikipedia.org/wiki/Judge_Harry_Pregerson_Interchange#/media/File:Los_Angeles_-_Echangeur_autoroute_110_105.JPG; (right) Wikipedia, https://upload.wikimedia.org/wikipedia/commons/e/e2/I-5_north_approaching_I-10_east_split-_long_view.jpg. **5.3** – Library of Congress Prints and Photographic Online Catalog, http://www.loc.gov/pictures/item/2011661021/. **5.4** – Miami, Balitimore, Washington, D.C., Minneapolis, Philadelphia, Salt Lake City, Seattle, Denver, Orlando, Las Vegas, Detroit, Phoenix, Atlanta, Dallas, Los Angeles, Houston, St. Louis, and New Orleans © 2017 Google Earth; San Francisco © 2017 Google Earth and TerraMetrics, Data CSUMB SFML, CA OPC; Chicago © 2017 Google Earth and TerraMetrics, Image: NOAA. **5.5** – The references for the axial maps of the 20 American urban grids are: (in chronological order based on author and date of construction) St. Louis, Missouri (Major, 1993); Seattle, Washington (Bottege, 1994); Atlanta, Georgia (Major, 1994); Miami, Florida (Major, 1994); San Francisco, California (Major, 1994); Washington, D.C. (Major, 1994); Las Vegas, Nevada (Major, 1995); Baltimore, Maryland (Shah, 1996); New Orleans, Louisiana (Bone, 1996); Chicago, Illinois (Major, 1998); Minneapolis, Minnesota (Major, 2002); Philadelphia, Pennsylvania (Major, 2002); Salt Lake City, Utah (Major, 2002); Denver, Colorado (Major, 2002); Orlando, Florida (Major, 2002); Detroit, Michigan (Major, 2002); Phoenix, Arizona (Major, 2002); Dallas, Texas (Major, 2002); Houston, Texas (Major, 2002); and Los Angeles, California (Major, 2002). **5.9** – National Wetlands Inventory, U.S. Fish and Wildlife Service, http://www.fws.gov/wetlands/Data/Mapper.html. **5.10** – Development kept anonymous by the author, available in the public records of Duval County, Florida. **A.10** – San Francisco ca. 1926. Market Street from Ferry Building, public domain photograph, http://www.shorpy.com/files/images/SHORPY-755.jpg. **A.11** – Courtesy of Space Syntax Limited © 2011, https://timstonor.files.wordpress.com/2011/10/greater_washington_choice_rn.png. **A.12** – Photograph by David Iliff, Wikipedia, https://upload.wikimedia.org/wikipedia/commons/f/fa/Trafalgar_Square_360_Panorama_Cropped_Sky%2C_London_-_Jun_2009.jpg.

Chapter Six: 6.1 – Gandelsonas, M., J. Copjec, C. Ingraham, J. Whiteman. 1991. *The Urban Text*. Cambridge: MIT Press, © 1991 Massachusetts Institute of Technology, by permission of The MIT Press. **6.2** – (left) Gallion and Eisner, 1963, 359; (middle) Gallion and Eisner, 1963, 234, Permission to reprint granted by John Wiley & Sons, Inc.; (right) Permission to reprint granted by Sherry Olson from Kostof, 1992, 297. **6.6** – (right) Drawn by the author based on Figure 6.7 and 3.11. **6.3** – Drawing by the author based on: (left) Park, R.E., E.W. Burgess. 1925. *The City: Suggestions for the Investigation of Human Behavior in the Urban Environment*. Chicago: University of Chicago Press; (middle) Hoyt, H. 1939. *The Structure and Growth of Residential Neighbourhoods in American Cities*. Washington: Federal Housing Administration; (right) Harris, C., E. Ullman. 1945. "The Nature of Cities," *Annals of the American Academy of Political and Social Science*, 242: 7–17. **6.7** – (left) Reps, 1965, 305. San Francisco, unsigned plan of San Francisco, California, drawn in September 1848, Stokes Collection, New York Public Library, New York, New York; (right) Reps, 1979, 158. A Map of the Town of San Francisco, photocopy made in 1867 of an unsigned manuscript plan of San Francisco, California, in 1847, from the transcript of appeal, 1860, case 2703, *Lestrade v. Barth*, 12th Judicial District Court of California, Supreme Court Record Group, *Paul Lestrade v. Frederick Barth*, File 6431, 35, California State Archives, Sacramento, California. **6.15** – (right) Riverside in Chicago © 2015 Google Earth. **A.13** – (left) Hillier, B., M.D. Major, J. Desyllas, K. Karimi, B. Campos, T. Stonor. 1996. *Tate Gallery, Millbank: A Study of the Existing Layout and New Masterplan Proposal. Technical Report*, Unit For Architectural Studies, Bartlett School of Graduate Studies, University College London; (right) Permission to reprint granted by Space Syntax Laboratory, University College London, Visibility Graph Analysis model of Tate Gallery, Millbank originally by Maria Doxia and Alasdair Turner, 1999. **A.14** – *Leixcons of Urbanism* by Duany Plater-Zyberk & Company Architects & Town Planners (DPZ), Miami, FL, 62, http://www.dpz.com/uploads/Books/Lexicon-2014.pdf.

Chapter Seven: 7.4 – Line drawings by author based on original plans available: (top left) Easterling, 1993, 18; (top middle) Reps, 1965, 12. Originally drawn by W. Lyon, published by T. Kensett in 1806 from the New York Historical Society, New York, New York; (bottom left) Original survey by D.W. Buckingham, Yale University Map Collection, http://www.library.yale.edu/MaqColl/amcity.htm; (right) Original survey by R. Whiteford from Yale University Map Collection, http://www.library.yale.edu/MaqColl/amcity.htm. **7.8** – Drawing by the author based on Reps, 1965, 201. Savannah, Georgia: 1733–1856. Manuscript plans of Savannah, Georgia, drawn by John W. Reps in 1959. **7.15** – Reps, 1965, 200. Map of the City of Savannah, unsigned plan of Savannah, Georgia, published by John M. Cooper & Co. New York, 1856, available in Library of Congress, Maps Divisions, Washington, D.C., Courtesy of Hargrett Rare Book and Manuscript Library/University of Georgia Libraries, http://www.libs.uga.edu/darchive/hargrett/maps/1856c6.jpg. **7.16** and **7.19** – Photographs by the author, June 27, 2014. **7.18** Figure 7.18 – *The City and Harbor of Savannah, Georgia*, a wood engraving drawn by J. O. Davidson and published by *Harper's Weekly*, November 1883. **A.16** – (left) Drawing by M. Ritchie and K. Sugiyama after Millon, R. 1973. *Urbanization at Teotihuacan, Mexico*. Austin: University of Texas Press and Millon, Drewitt and Cowgill. 1973. *The Teotihuacan Map. Part Two: Maps*. Austin: University of Texas Press, Vanderbilt University, http://www.vanderbilt.edu/AnS/Anthro/Anth210/mesoamerica.htm; (right) Bermejo Tirado, J. 2015: "Aplicaciones de sintaxis espacial en Arqueología: una revisión de algunas tendencias actuales," *Arqueología de la Arquitectura*, 12: e031, http://arqarqt.revistas.csic.es/index.php/arqarqt/article/viewFile/184/246/1648. Originally in Morton, S.G., M.M. Peuramaki-Brown, P.C. Dawson, J.D. Seibert. 2012. "Civic and Household Community Relationships at Teotihuacan, Mexico: A Space Syntax Approach," *Cambridge Archaeological Journal*, 22:3; 387–400. **A.17** – Least line axial analysis of Teotihuacan, Mexico by Guillermo Sanchez in 1998.

Chapter Eight: 8.1 – Hillier, B. 1996b. *Space is the Machine: A Configurational Theory of Architecture*. Cambridge: Cambridge University Press, 128. Originally prepared by M.D. Major. **8.2** – Lynch, K. 1960. *The Image of the City*. Cambridge: MIT Press. © 1960 Massachusetts Institute of Technology, by permission of The MIT Press. **8.4** – (left) Stonor, T. 1991. *Manhattan: A Study of its Public Spaces and Patterns of Movement*. M.Sc. Thesis, M.Sc. Architecture: Advanced Architectural Studies, Copies available from the Environmental Science Library, University College London; (right) Raford, Noah. 2004. *Movement Economies in Fractured Urban Systems: The Case of Boston, Massachusetts*. M.Sc. Thesis, M.Sc. Built Environment: Advanced Architectural Studies, Built Environment Report, Copies available from the Environmental Science Library, University College London. **8.5** – Google Earth © 2017. **8.6** – (top) Planning Department, City of Baltimore, Wikipedia, http://upload.wikimedia.org/wikipedia/commons/thumb/5/57/Baltimore_neighborhoods_map.png/1280px-Baltimore_neighborhoods_map.png; (bottom) Plan of Baltimore in 1729 containing 600 acres divided into 60 lots. Hambleton Print Collection, Maryland Historical Society, http://www.mdhs.org/sites/default/files/imagecache/digitalimage/h10_plan%20of%20baltimore_1729.jpg. **8.7** – (top) Folie's Plan of the Town of Baltimore and its Environs, 1792, Library of Congress, Map Dvision, Washington, D.C., http://www.bigmapblog.com/maps/map03/IBAOhszbCABWizza.jpg; (bottom) The city plan of Baltimore, 1852 by Fielding Lucas, Jr. of Baltimore (after last Annexation of 1818 and before future Annexations of 1888 and 1918–1919), Wikipedia, http://upload.wikimedia.org/wikipedia/commons/b/b4/Lucas_Baltimore_1852_Cityplan.png. **8.8** – (left) Reps, 1979, 365. Originally unsigned manuscript plan of Seattle, Washington in 1853, redrawn in 1875 by S.C. Harris, Office of Recorder, King County, Seattle, Washington; (center) Plan of Seattle 1855–6, A map of Seattle, drawn at the time of the Battle of Seattle, part of the Puget Sound War, University of Washington Libraries. Special Collections Division. Seattle Photograph Collection, Wikipedia, http://upload.wikimedia.org/wikipedia/commons/1/11/Plan_of_Seattle_1855-6.jpg; (right) Reps, 1979, 364. Plan of Seattle 1855–6. Plan of Seattle, Washington in 1856, drawn by Thomas Phelps, as copied and revised in 1930, Seattle Historical Society, Seattle, Washington. **8.9** – (left) Birds Eye View of Seattle And Environs. King County, Washington, 1891. Eighteen Months after the Great Fire by August Koch, Library of Congress; (right) Drawn by author based on 1856 plan of Seattle, *Seattle Times*, http://seattletimes.com/art/news/local/seattle_history/maps_sept16/covermap02.gif. **8.10** – Original axial map of Baltimore, Maryland constructed by by Shazia Shah in 1996, updated, revised, and double-checked by author in 2002. **8.11** – (left) See Figure 8.10. **8.12 and 8.13** – Original axial map of Seattle, Washington constructed by Paul Bottege in 1994, updated, revised, and double-checked by author in 2002. **8.14** – Aerial view of Bellevue, Washington, Wikipedia, http://upload.wikimedia.org/wikipedia/commons/thumb/2/21/Aerial_Bellevue_Washington_November_2011.jpg/1280px-Aerial_Bellevue_Washington_November_2011.jpg. **A.18** – (right) Wikipedia, https://upload.wikimedia.org/wikipedia/commons/9/9c/St_Pauls_and_Millennium_Bridge_at_night.jpg.

Chapter Nine: **9.1** – (left) Reps, 1965, 301. Originally drawn by Joshua Hathway, Jr. in 1934, Chicago Historical Society, Illinois, Wikipedia, https://upload.wikimedia.org/wikipedia/commons/2/23/1834_Map_of_Chicago_by_Hathaway.jpg; (center) Reps, 1965, 303. Originally published by Currier and Ives, New York in 1892, New York Historical Society, American Architecture, http://www.american-architecture.info/USA/CHICAGO/140y.JPG; (right) U.S. Geological Survey, 1901, University of Texas Perry-Castañeda Library Map Collection, http://www.lib.utexas.edu/maps/historical/chicago_1901.jpg. **9.2**– U.S. Geological Survey topographical maps, University of Texas Perry-Castañeda Library Map Collection: (left) http://www.lib.utexas.edu/maps/historical/las_vegas_nv_1908.jpg; (right) http://www.lib.utexas.edu/maps/historical/las_vegas_1952.jpg. **9.3** – Venturi, R., D. Scott Brown, S. Izenour. 1972. *Learning from Las Vegas*. Cambridge, Massachusetts: MIT Press, 31, original image by D. Southworth, Image: Venturi, Scott Brown and Associates, Inc. **9.8** – (left) Reps, 1965, 345. Original drawing by Olmsted, Vaux & Co., printed by Chicago Lithographing Co., Chicago, 1869, Map Division, New York Public Library, New York, New York, The Olmsted Society, http://www.olmstedsociety.org/wp-content/uploads/2008/11/general-plan-of-riverside.jpg; (right) Access drawing by the author on a base satellite image Landstat/Copernicus, Google Earth © 2017. **9.11** – Duany, A., E. Talen. 2002. "Transect Planning," *APA Journal*, Summer 2002, 68(3): 245–266, *Planetizen*, http://www.planetizen.com/files/oped/20040817-transect-urban.jpg, Image: DPZ. **9.16** – (left) Levinson, D.M. 2004. University of Minnesota, Wikipedia, http://en.wikipedia.org/wiki/File:HierarchyOfRoads.png.

Conclusion: **10.2** – Per Square Mile by Tim de Chant, January 18, 2011, http://persquaremile.com/2011/01/18/if-the-worlds-population-lived-in-one-city. **10.3** – Protected wetlands map of Nassau County, Florida in 2003, GIS Department, Nassau County, Florida. **10.4** – Redrawn image with corrections based on a PowerPoint Presentation prepared by the author for a 2003 Growth Management Workshop with the Nassau County Board of County Commissioners/Planning and Zoning Board, October 14, 2003. **10.5** – (left) July 12, 2007, Suburban Development at the Edge of Portland, Oregon Urban Growth Boundary, Image © 2009, Metro, Portland, Oregon and © Google, 2008, http://freeassociationdesign.files.wordpress.com/2009/12/edge-4.jpg; (right) View of suburban development in the Phoenix metropolitan area, Wikipedia, https://upload.wikimedia.org/wikipedia/commons/f/f2/Scottsdale_cityscape4.jpg.

Index

A

Abercrombie, Patrick 43
absolute monarchy 25
accessibility 85–86, 105, 121–122, 125
adjacency 60, 120–121
adverse possession 46
Africa 24
Age of Enlightenment 16, 67, 77, 201, 205
Alberti, Leon Battista 129–130, 136, 143, 202
Alexander, Christopher 195
Alexander the Great 24
Algeria 25
algorithms 61
alternative fuels 211
AASHTO 194
American
    Dream 48
    Independence 39, 71, 137, 143, 166–167, 207
    lifestyle 211–212
    Native 40, 44, 54, 71, 169
    self-identity 35, 48–49
    Southwest 135
Amsterdam, The Netherlands 188
Ancient Egypt 14, 21, 23, 35, 37
Ancient India 14, 21–23, 26, 37, 200
Anderson, Stanford 148
Annapolis, Maryland 76, 109, 166
anthropology 134–135
Appalachian Mountains 31, 71
archaeology 13, 134, 199
architecture 5–6, 13, 181, 199
aristocratic paternalism 143
Aristotle 24
Asia Minor 39, 46
a-spatial 5, 11, 115, 164
Assyria 22–23

Asylum, Pennsylvania 70
Athens, Greece 197
Atlanta, Georgia 10, 70, 93, 127, 167, 205
Atlantic Ocean 41, 44, 58, 75
attraction 73, 156
Augustus, Emperor 130
Aurora, Nevada 70
automobile 85–87, 113, 115, 153
Aztecs 26–27, 56

B

Babylon 24
Baltimore, Maryland 10, 17–18, 93, 109–110, 126, 155, 165–167, 170–171, 202–203
Banham, Reyner 85
banking 204
Bannister, Turpin B. 143
Barcelona, Spain 167
bastides 14–15, 21, 25, 27, 30, 45–46, 67, 70, 74–76, 78, 201, 205
Batty, Michael 3, 7, 19, 27
Baudrillard, Jean 84, 99
beachfront 58
Beaumont de Périgord, Gascony, France 25
beingness 90
Belize 26
Beresford, Maurice 25, 39
blocks
    American and European 131–132
    elongated 132, 153
    manipulation 16–17, 107, 116, 119–120, 129, 171
    size 88, 98, 113, 157, 175
    structure 130
    subdivision 119–120, 124, 137
    upsizing 119, 124
Board of County Commissioners of Brevard County v. Snyder 102
boomtown 47, 63, 118

Boston, Massachusetts 10, 41, 44–45, 57, 70–71, 75–77, 133, 161, 164, 166
Botero, Giovanni 5
Boyer, M. Christine 5
Brazil 204
British occupation 44, 46
Broadacre City 28
Brockett, John 133
Brunswick, Georgia 141
Burnham, Daniel 65

C

California 47, 63, 70, 78
Canada 135, 168
capital routes 18, 97
Cardiff, Wales 25
Caribbean 41, 166
Cartesian distance 88, 91, 39, 203
Cataneo, Pietro di Giacomo 143
Central Business District (CBD) 18, 111, 115–116, 122, 138, 155, 169, 171, 173–175
centralized power 25–26, 46
Centre for Transport Studies 43
Cerdá, Ildefons 167
Ch'ang-an, China 26
Charleston (or Charles Towne), South Carolina 40, 41, 44, 68, 71, 143, 166, 168
Charlotte, North Carolina 69
Chicago, Illinois 10, 17–18, 47, 65, 68, 72, 78, 86, 93, 96–97, 99–100, 102, 104–105, 108–111, 121, 123, 126–127, 157, 159–162, 177–180, 182–184, 186–191, 202–203
Chicago Tribune 48
Cholula and Chucuito 26, 27
cities as movement economies 18, 155
City Beautiful Movement 65, 127
Clean Water Act (CWA) 101–103, 209
colonization 15, 26–27, 37–39, 40, 41, 44–46, 49, 67, 69, 74, 76, 81, 130, 200, 203, 205
    Asia Minor 39
Colorado River 41
Columbus 27
Combined Statistical Area 183–184, 197
commercial development 40, 45, 46, 47, 54, 188
composition 4, 13–17, 51–52, 58, 62, 67, 69, 107, 109, 130, 139, 142, 148, 200–203, 205
compromise 163
configuration 4, 8, 13, 15, 17, 51, 52, 60, 62, 107, 116, 117, 122, 126, 127, 131, 148, 200, 201, 202, 205, 207, 208
connectivity 6, 88–89, 104, 125, 138, 190, 194, 197
constitution 142, 149, 152–153, 202
context 112, 114
Cook County, Illinois 121
Cooke, Alistair 180, 197
Cooley, Charles 110
Cooper, Anthony Ashley 143
correlation contour mapping 161, 164
Cosa Nostra 181
Costa Rica 26
covenant restrictions 46
crony capitalists 204

D

Dali, Salvador 112

Dallas, Texas 70, 87, 93, 104
Davis, Michael 86
Dawes Act 71
De Chant, Tim 207
deep structures 162–163
deep-water port 44, 49
democracy 4
density 207, 210–211
Denver, Colorado 93, 97, 98, 100, 132, 174–175
design 6–7, 16–17, 41–42, 107, 112, 116–117, 123, 135, 146
determinism 42–43
Detroit, Michigan 10–11, 27, 93
development 114, 163–164, 195, 204, 213
diagnostic tool 135
dichotomy 3
discrete locations 175
Disney, Walt 101
Dommen, Gascony, France 26
Duany, Andres 190

E

ecology 199
economic 46–47, 115–116
egalitarianism 4, 35, 39, 48
Einstein, Albert 213
Eisenhower, Dwight D. 87
Eisenman, Peter 61
Ellicott, Andrew 65
El Salvador 26
embeddedness 156
emergent spatial structure 116–117, 123, 155, 170
Emperor Kammu 26
engineering 5
England 25, 39, 166
English
    language 90, 92
    planning 76, 133, 143
environmental protection 209
Etruscans 25
Euclidean zoning 18, 115, 175, 177, 203, 212
Europe 4, 16, 22, 25, 45, 84

F

Federal Highway Administration 209
Fernandina Beach, Florida 30–31
fire department 194
Florida 58, 47, 102–103
Ford, Henry 87
form and process 52
form-based zoning 190
fortified towns 40, 46, 70
Fort Leavenworth, Kansas 78
Fort Lincoln, Nebraska 78
Fort Worth, Texas 68
France 25, 30, 39
Fredericksburg, Virginia 70
free market capitalism 38, 46
French Huguenots 54, 55

G

gambling 181
Gandelsonas, Mario 87, 99, 108, 115

Garden City Movement 110, 127
Garven, Anthony 136
Gascony, France 25
General Land Office 31
Genovese crime family 181
Geographical Information Systems 5–7
geography 13, 110, 117, 199
George II 143
Georgia Colony 143
ghost town 70
Gizmo Green 212
Great Depression 69, 179
Great Fire of London 143
Great Lakes 41
Greco-Roman tradition 26
Greece 3, 4, 14, 21, 22–24, 38, 39, 45–46, 80, 200
green belt or sprawl 43
grid
  block manipulation 202
  deformation 16–17, 107, 116, 123–125, 129, 171–172, 175, 202
  deformed 15, 51–52, 56–57, 70, 74–75, 79, 200
  edge definition 62
  erosion 103
  expansion 16–17, 107, 116, 129, 170–171, 175, 202
  intensification 18, 155–156, 159–160, 203
  offset 75, 78, 107, 123–124, 129, 164, 167, 200
  orthogonal 74, 78, 116, 200
  radial 51–52, 78
Gropius, Walter 43
Guatemala 26

H

Han Dynasty 26
Hanson, Julienne 4–8, 10, 19, 200, 207
Harris and Ullman 115
Hatunqolla 27
Haussmann, Baron Georges-Eugène 65, 165
Heijokyo, Japan 26
highways 18, 111, 155, 172, 174–175, 182, 184, 209, 211–212
Hillier, Bill 4–6, 7–8, 10–11, 16–17, 19, 41, 47, 105, 200, 207
  deformed wheel structure 96–97
  Type 1, 2 and 3 laws 10, 13
Hippodamus 23
history 13, 21, 37, 134, 199
homebuilding industry 81
homesteaders 71
Honduras 26
Houston, Texas 70, 87, 93, 105, 126, 207
Howard, Ebenezer 110, 205
Hoyt, Homer 111, 115, 120, 179
humanities 134–135

I

Imhotep 23
impact fees 195
Inca settlements 27
information theoretic redundancy 131
insider vs. outsider 45, 152
insurance 204
internal movement capture 165
Ireland 30
Italy 14, 21, 24–25, 37–39
Izenour, Steven 181

J

Jacobs, Jane 7, 107
jargon 90, 92
Jefferson, Thomas 14, 21, 31, 35, 48, 64, 143, 201

K

King's Highway 166
Kingsport, Tennessee 80
Kipling, Rudyard 178
Klee, Paul 92
Klondike Gold Rush 168
Kostof, Spiro 22, 148
Kyoto, Japan 26

L

La Ciudad Linear 110
Land Ordinance 14–15, 18–19, 21, 31, 35, 46, 67, 69–71, 75, 77, 80, 162, 167, 170, 201, 205, 207
land 46, 88, 115, 120–121, 180, 197, 207, 209
  speculation 18, 15, 47, 122, 179, 201, 203, 205
  use 18, 111, 152, 153, 156, 161, 165, 186
language of money 204
Lansky, Meyer 181
Las Vegas, Nevada 10–11, 17–18, 47, 69–70, 79, 93, 96, 98, 100–105, 109, 123, 126, 136, 157, 160, 162, 165, 177–178, 180–182, 184–185, 189, 192–194, 197, 202–203, 205
laws of spatial emergence and convergence 17, 116–117, 155, 200, 202
leapfrog development 115–116, 121–122
Le Corbusier 157
L'Enfant, Pierre Charles 64–65, 77
Levittowns 80–81
Liebling, Abbott Joseph 178, 197
linearity (or axiality) 108, 187
Liverpool, England 25
Llewellyn Park, Trenton, New Jersey 78
locality 159, 187
local topographical conditions 46, 58, 76, 123, 126, 136, 155, 168–170, 172–173, 175
London, United Kingdom 22–23, 43, 58, 72–73, 75, 92, 112–113, 127, 133, 143, 156–157, 163, 197, 207
Longley, Paul 3, 27
Los Angeles, California 52, 84–85, 93, 97, 100–101, 105, 160
Lost Colony of Roanoke, Virginia 74
Louisiana Purchase 31, 35
Luxembourg 183
Lynch, Kevin 85, 157–159

M

Madison, James 48
Mafia 181
Magganuba 23
Mailer, Norman 180, 197
Maine 71
Manakin, Virginia 54–55, 75
Manhattan effect 164
manufacturing 11, 111, 184, 188
market perversion 101
Marzabotto, Italy 24
Massachusetts Bay Colony 133
mass production 39, 80
Mata, Soria y 109, 110

medieval period 25, 38, 47, 75, 200
Mediterranean Basin 23, 25, 38, 45
mercantile capitalism 38
Mesoamerica 26
Mexico City, Mexico 26, 134–135
Miami, Florida 69, 93, 160–161
Middle Eastern settlements 4, 57, 160, 194
Mies van der Rohe 42
migration 73
military 25–26, 40, 46, 143
minimum requirements 195
mining 181
Minneapolis-St Paul, Minnesota 69, 93
Mississippi River 31, 41, 46, 76, 179
Missouri River 41
models of city growth 16, 107, 110–111, 115
Modernism 42, 181
Mojave Desert 101
money 204
Mormonism 70, 181
Mountgomery, Sir Robert 143
Mouzon, Steve 212
movement 10, 14, 29, 41–42, 73, 156, 158, 161, 164, 165
multiplier effect 156

N

National
  Environmental Quality Act 101, 102–103, 209, 212
  Housing Act 212
  Interstate and Defense Highways Act 87
  Wetlands Inventory 101
neighborhood 124, 157, 162–163, 187, 194
Newcourt, Richard 143
New Deal 212
New England 27, 74, 76, 133, 136
New Haven, Connecticut 17, 32, 34–35, 39, 57, 62, 71, 129, 132–133, 136–139, 143, 171, 201–202
Newark, New Jersey 79–80
New Orleans, Louisiana 10, 27, 39, 68, 70, 75–78, 93, 204
New Salisbury, Wiltshire, England 25
New Urbanism 5–7, 10, 127
New Winchelsea, Sussex, England 25
New World 14, 21–22, 26–27, 34, 38, 41, 45, 67, 77, 130, 200, 203, 206
New York (or New Amsterdam), New York 10, 39–41, 40, 44, 52, 68, 71, 74–78, 133, 141, 161, 164, 166, 181, 207–208
New York Times 48
Nicaragua 26
Nicholson, Francis 166
NIMBYism 210
Nolli, Giambattista 182, 197
non-discursive 92
non-point pollution 210
Norberg-Schulz, Christian 90
Normandy 25
North America 54
North Carolina 74
Northern Ireland 143

O

Oakland, California 10
Occam's Razor 42, 88
occupation 41
office buildings 54

Oglethorpe, James 17, 129, 139, 141, 143, 202
Ohio River 41
Oklahoma Land Rush 71
Old Spanish Trail 180
oligarchic structure 45
Olmecs 26–27
Olmsted, Frederick Law 127, 185–186
Olson, Sherry H. 166
order concepts 52
organized complexity 13, 17
Orient 14, 21, 26, 37, 200
Orlando, Florida 93, 96, 100–104, 165, 205
orthogonal grid 51–52, 56, 57–59, 62, 65
ortho-radial grid 19, 172, 203, 205

P

Pacific Ocean 31, 41, 168
Paiute Indians 181
Palahniuk, Chuck 180, 197
panoramic or bird's eye view 69
paradigm 7
Paradise, Nevada 181
parent tract 63, 120
Paris, France 84, 65, 165, 194, 207
Park and Burgess 110, 115, 117, 120
park and landscape design 134
pay-to-play 204
pedestrian sheds 113, 114
Penn, Alan 7
Penn, William 14, 21, 32–33, 44, 133, 143, 201, 206, 209
Peponis, John 9, 156, 190
Peru 27
pervasive centrality 156
Phelps, Thomas 168
phenomenology 131
Philadelphia, Pennsylvania 14, 21, 32–34, 41, 44, 68, 71, 97, 133, 141, 143, 201, 204, 206, 209
Phoenix, Arizona 70, 93, 100–103, 165
Planning Magazine 146
plan symmetry 57–58
Pope, Albert 108
Portland, Oregon 10
Portsmouth, England 183
Post-Modernism 181
Po Valley, Italy 24
Pre-Columbian Mesoamerica 14, 21, 25–26, 37, 56, 200
preconceptions 162
Pre-Hispanic Grid 26
presidio 54–55, 63, 70, 75–78
prime activity axes 18
principle of centrality and linearity 16–18, 107–111, 115–116, 155, 175, 200, 202
probability 42–43
profit 180, 195, 211
Progressive Era 204
protected wetlands 101, 102, 103
Psarra, Sophia 11–12
public
  housing 157
  policy 213
  transportation 210
Puget Sound War 168
Puritans 133

Q

quasi-judicial 102

R

Radburn, New Jersey 78–80, 146, 149
Raford, Noah 161
Ragusa, Sicily, Italy 38
railroad 178–179, 183–184, 188
rainwater runoff 210
Raleigh, Sir Walter 74
Reagan, Ronald 65
real estate 46, 116, 121, 179–180
record keeping 71, 74
regional centers 115
regular grid 67, 200
  adaptive 38–40, 47, 109
  efficiency 38–40, 47, 109, 124
  egalitarian qualities 48
  generic qualities 37, 40, 45, 49, 200, 205
  instrumental power 213
  offset 15, 51–52, 62, 64
  overcoming metric separation by linear integration 105, 127, 206, 208, 213
  process of amalgamation and fragmentation 206
  standardization 39–40, 48, 109
  utilitarian qualities 37–38, 49, 200, 205
regulatory takings 211
Renaissance 15, 27, 30, 32, 38, 67, 77, 129, 143, 201, 205, 213
Reps, John 18, 22, 27, 34, 39, 67, 71
residential exclusivity 127
restricted random process 38, 207
Richmond, Virginia 70
right angle 15, 53–54, 56
Riverside, Illinois 68, 127, 185–186
Riverside-San Bernardino, California 69
road 194
  arterial 122, 195, 209
  classifications 162, 175
  collector 122, 195
  cul-de-sac 80, 195
  curb cuts 194
  diet 209
  local 195
  maintenance 195
Rome 22–22, 38, 45, 80
  military 49
  plan castrum 17, 129–131, 141–143, 202
  planning 3–4, 17, 23, 25, 40, 143, 200
Rossi, Aldo 52, 199

S

Safire, William 48
Salem, Massachusetts 133
Salt Lake City, Utah 93, 181
San Antonio, Texas 30
San Diego, California 54–55, 75
San Francisco, California 38, 54, 63–65, 75, 89, 93, 103, 118–119, 125, 132, 159, 207–208
Santo Domingo, Dominican Republic 30, 39
Savannah, Georgia 17–18, 57, 68, 129, 132, 139–146, 148–152, 162, 202
science, 90, 156
Scott Brown, Denise 181
Seattle, Washington 17, 18, 93, 155, 168–169, 172–175, 202
settlements
  crossroads (or cross-axis) 15, 51–53, 75–76, 79, 120, 181, 200
  dispersed 75, 76, 78
  generic function 14, 41, 46, 49, 117, 124
  linear 51–52, 74–76, 78, 120, 200
  self-similarity 16, 99
Sicily 38
Siegel, Bugsy 181
Singapore 207
slavery 44, 143
small town America 34
Smart Growth 114
social 47–49, 134–135, 163, 199
sociology 13, 110, 199
Sonoran Desert 101
South America 26
space syntax 7–8, 10, 13, 16, 19, 28, 42, 51, 62, 107, 116–118, 131, 137, 158, 161, 164, 174, 199, 205, 207
  'all lines' axial analysis 117, 131, 147
  betweenness 89
  choice 89
  connection 53–56, 62
  design 163
  edge effect 91
  explained 72, 112, 134, 135, 162
  intelligibility 88–89, 104, 109, 125, 139, 159–161, 191
  in the United States 204
  King's Cross, London 8
  Linz Solar City, Austria 9
  mean depth 88, 104, 159
  measurement 88, 162, 164
  metric parameters 88, 97–98
  Millennium Bridge, London 9
  modeling technique 113, 158, 162, 164
  representations 28–29, 61, 162
    axial line 29, 91
    axial map 117, 127
    axial size 87–88, 159
    convex space 29, 91
    isovist or visual field 29, 91, 117, 130
  software 61, 72
  step-depth 164, 173
  synergy 88–89, 104, 159, 160, 162
  Tate Gallery, Millbank, London 9, 112
  theory of natural movement 72–73, 155, 163, 165
  value 204
  visibility graph analysis 112
  visual integration 117, 121, 124, 130, 132, 137–139
Spain 30, 39
Spanish Laws of the Indies 14, 17, 21, 27, 30, 32, 34, 62, 76, 129–132, 133, 141–143, 201–202, 205, 207
spatial
  emergence-convergence 196
  consolidation 117, 126, 170
  hierarchy 194, 197
  parameters 98, 102, 104
  'ping pong' 117
  redundancy 131
Stanislawski, Dan 21–22, 38
status quo 204
St. Augustine, Florida 39, 70–71, 75, 81, 168
St. Denis, Aude, Gascony, France 25
Ste. Foy la Grande, Gironde, Gascony, France 25

St. Lawrence River and Seaway 41
St. Louis, Missouri 10, 76, 93, 96, 99, 102, 104–105, 114, 159–160, 163
Stonor, Tim 161
stormwater management 101–103, 210
strategic locations 40, 45, 156
street 88, 89, 163
   cross-axis 119–121, 129–130
   diagonal or radial 52, 62, 64, 76, 109, 123, 125–126, 171
   extension 16–17, 107, 116, 121, 125, 129, 136, 171, 175, 202
   hierarchy 146, 152–153
   intersection 53–56, 62, 69, 74–75, 87
   seam 123, 157, 167
   shopping or high 73, 156, 188
strip development 187
strip effect or strip intensification 18, 162, 177, 187–189, 203
strong prescriptive order 191
Sub-Saharan Africa 134
suburbs 17–18, 69, 78, 80, 100–101, 105, 123, 125–127, 149, 155, 165, 171, 175, 208, 211–213
   layouts 52, 107, 116, 122, 126
     asymmetrical regularity 16, 103, 116, 122–123, 126, 205
     discrete separation by linear segregation 16–17, 107, 116, 122, 125, 126, 171, 175, 202, 208
     geomorphic 16, 126, 205
     repetitive deformity 16, 79, 116, 126–127, 201, 205
   pods 80
surveying 23, 39, 47, 71
sustainable urbanism 114, 213

T

Tacoma, Washington 68
tactical locations 40, 45
Talen, Emily 190
Tampa-St Petersburg, Florida 69
Tenochtitlán 26–27, 56, 134, 135
Texas State Library and Archives Commission 67
theme park 134
The Netherlands 39
Time Magazine 195
Timgad 25
Tokyo, Japan 26, 72
topography 32, 38, 40–41, 58–59, 63, 67, 69, 75, 77, 117, 122, 125, 167, 169, 171, 202
topology 8, 10, 131, 149, 207
Tories 44
trading posts 78
traffic 194, 195, 210
   management 146
   models 155, 165, 194, 209
   parking 153
   stopping distance 194
   turning radius 194
   volumes 209
Trajan, Emperor 25
transportation 111, 116, 122, 178, 210–211
   planning 18, 175, 177, 194–195, 203, 211
Treaty of Paris 31, 71
Turkey 24

U

United States of America 35, 41, 49, 51, 69, 71
   Bill of Rights 48
   Bureau of Land Management 31

Census Bureau 68, 178
   urban area, defined 68
   urban cluster, defined 68
Civil War 65, 70–71, 148, 205
Congress 31, 70
Constitution 48
Declaration of Independence 35, 48
Department of the Interior 67
Federal Interstate Highway System 194
Geological Survey 67, 71
land area 49, 71, 86
population 49, 68
Revolutionary War 31, 41, 44, 46, 71, 76
street life 84
Supreme Court 69, 115, 212
universal distance 117, 121, 124, 131, 137, 139, 158
University of California, Berkeley 186
University of Chicago 110
University of Georgia Hargrett Library Rare Map Collection 67
University of Texas Perry-Castañeda Library Map Collection 67
University of Washington 168, 203
unrealized historical plan 70
Unwin, Raymond 110
urban
   design 89, 91, 135
   growth 110, 108
   legend 84
   transect 190
utopian vision 143

V

Venturi, Robert 69, 181
Vermont 71
vertical construction 38, 39, 52, 120
Village of Euclid, Ohio v. Ambler Realty Co. 69, 71
Ville Radieuse 28
Virginia Beach, Virginia 69
Vitruvius 17, 30, 129, 131, 136, 143, 202

W

Wales 25, 30
Wall Street 204
Washington, D.C. 10, 52, 64–65, 64, 77, 93, 109, 159–161, 166
Washington, George 64
water navigation 178
wayfinding maps 70
Western Roman Empire 25
West Virginia 71
westward expansion 67, 69, 71
Wethersfield, Connecticut 27
wetlands 101, 209
Winchester, Nevada 181
World War I 70
World War II 42, 69, 70, 78, 80
Wright, Frank Lloyd 178, 197

Y

Young, Brigham 180

Z

zoology 134

About the Author

Dr. Mark David Major, AICP, CNU-A is an Assistant Professor of Architecture and Urban Design in the Department of Architecture and Urban Planning, College of Engineering, at Qatar University in Doha. He is the author of the *Poor Richard* series of almanacs for architects and planners.

Mark is an architect and urban planner with more than two decades of experience, a certified planner of the American Institute of Certified Planners, accredited member of the Congress for New Urbanism, and member of the American Planning Association. He is a former Professor of Urban Design at the Savannah College of Art and Design. Previously, Mark was a Director of Space Syntax Limited, an urban design and planning consulting firm in London, United Kingdom where he was a consultant to Foster & Partners, Richard Rogers Partnership, Zaha M. Hadid Architects, the British Government, and London Metropolitan Police among many others. While living in London, he was a Lecturer/Course Director in the Bartlett School of Architecture and Planning at University College London where he founded the International Space Syntax Symposia.

Mark has been a visiting lecturer at the Savannah College of Art and Design, University of Florida, Florida State University, Florida Atlantic University, University of Texas, Georgia Institute of Technology, University of Illinois at Chicago, the Architectural Association, University of Westminster and University of Greenwich in London, University of São Paulo in Brazil, Politecnico di Milano in Italy, and Pontificia Universidad Catolica de Chile. Born and raised in St. Louis, Missouri, he has a Doctorate of Philosophy in Architecture from University College London, Masters of Science in Architecture from the University of London, and Bachelors of Arts in History and Design (Architecture) from Clemson University in South Carolina. *The Syntax of City Space: American Urban Grids* is his thirteenth book.